# Call Center
# People Management
# Handbook and Study Guide
## Version 2.1

**Brad Cleveland and Debbie Harne**
**Editors**

*Part of ICMI's Handbook/Study Guide Series*

Published by:
Call Center Press
A Division of ICMI, Inc.
Post Office Box 6177
Annapolis, Maryland 21401 USA

# Call Center
# People Management
# Handbook and Study Guide
## Version 2.1

**Brad Cleveland and Debbie Harne**
**Editors**

*Part of ICMI's Handbook/Study Guide Series*

Call Center Press™
*A Division of ICMI, Inc.*

# Acknowledgements

The publications in this series are the result of a lot of hard work on the part of many people. We would like to thank the following individuals for their contributions:

Gerry Barber
Jean Bave-Kerwin
Michael Blair
Lori Bocklund
Henry Dortmans
Mike Dunne
Rebecca Gibson
John Goodman
Cindy Grimm
Linda Harden
Susan Hash
Cheryl Helm
Ellen Herndon
Ted Hopton
Betty Layfield
Jill Leigh
Greg Levin
Don McCain
Teresa Metzler
Jay Minnucci
Tim Montgomery
Rose Polchin
Paul Pope
Laurie Solomon
Wanda Sitzer

Without their hard work, dedication and talents, this project would not have been possible!

Brad Cleveland and Debbie Harne
Editors

To Sophia, may the little things in life continue to bring you joy.

Debbie Harne




To Kirsten, thank you for your unfailing love and support.
And to Grace Elizabeth Cleveland (born August 2002); Grace means God's love, and you truly are!

Brad Cleveland

# Call Center
# People Management
# Handbook and Study Guide
## Version 2.1

**Brad Cleveland and Debbie Harne**
**Editors**

*Part of ICMI's Handbook/Study Guide Series*

# Contents

# Introduction

**People Management**

Thank you for purchasing this publication – we hope it provides you with solid information that helps you advance your organization and your career! Although designed to stand alone, it is one of an integrated, four-part series, which includes:

- Call Center People Management Handbook and Study Guide
- Call Center Operations Management Handbook and Study Guide
- Call Center Customer Relationship Management Handbook and Study Guide
- Call Center Leadership and Business Management Handbook and Study Guide

The series was originally developed to prepare call center professionals for CIAC Certification assessments (and it follows the CIAC competency model and format, providing 100 percent coverage of CIAC competencies for both strategic and operational levels). However, many people have told us they are using the guides for internal training programs, team meetings and general reference. Content is sliced into digestible servings of information that lend themselves to these uses.

If you have received training from ICMI in the past, you will see some familiar diagrams and explanations. We have compiled information from ICMI courses, books and *Call Center Management Review* to develop an effective resource. We encourage you to be creative so you get the most out of this material.

However you plan to use the series, we hope it will also serve as an introduction (or re-introduction) to Incoming Calls Management Institute (ICMI) and the many content areas in which we can provide training and consulting services. We've included a summary of ICMI's products and services, but be sure to visit www.icmi.com for the latest offerings.

If we can assist you in any way, please let us know. We welcome your comments, feedback and questions, so let us know how we can help you.

Best wishes,

*Brad Cleveland*
Brad Cleveland
President and CEO
ICMI, Inc.
bradc@icmi.com

*Debbie Harne*
Debbie Harne
Director, Educational Services
ICMI, Inc.
debbieh@icmi.com

# If You Are Pursuing Certification

**People Management**

If you are pursuing CIAC certification, congratulations on your decision to increase your skills and knowledge in the area of People Management. As you prepare for CIAC assessments, you will learn valuable information to help you succeed in your profession.

We have worked hard to provide you with a handbook/study guide that is clear, concise and complete. Since each of us has a different set of past experiences and training, there will be some topics that you know well and others with which you may be unfamiliar. This guide is intended to meet a variety of needs by providing summary review information, as well as reference lists for further study. We encourage you to use it in whatever way works best for you. (Please remember that all material is either owned and copyrighted to ICMI or has been used with permission and noted as such; any reproduction of this material by any means is strictly prohibited.)

The remainder of this section includes the following:

## ICMI's Role with the Call Center Industry Advisory Council (CIAC)

Incoming Calls Management Institute (ICMI) is an independent think tank and membership organization that specializes in call center management research, education, publications and consulting. While ICMI co-founded the CIAC in 1997, the CIAC is now a nonprofit organization consisting of an elected body to represent the industry in certification matters. ICMI is independent of the CIAC and does not control the quality or administration of the CIAC certification process.

## CIAC Certification Options – Strategic vs. Operational

The CIAC certification assessments are delivered at both the operational and strategic levels:

- Managers with tactical, day-to-day operational responsibilities will generally choose to take the operational level exams, and are certified with the CIAC Certified Operations Manager (CCOM) designation. The operational role competencies are also applicable to individuals pursuing certification as a CIAC Certified Management Apprentice (CCMA).

- Managers with higher-level, strategic responsibilities will generally choose to take the strategic level exams, and are certified with the CIAC Certified Strategic Leader (CCSL) designation. The strategic role competencies are also applicable to individuals pursuing certification as a CIAC Certified Management Consultant (CCMC).

This handbook/study guide is designed to prepare you for either the operational (CCOM or CCMA) or strategic (CCSL or CCMC) level of certification. If you are pursuing operational level certification, you can skip over the topics labeled strategic. If you are pursuing strategic level certification, you will need to be knowledgeable in all areas of the study guide. For each certification level, we have included an outline of the competencies and the contents of this guide. The strategic outline begins on page 5; the operational outline begins on page 9.

Note: In many call centers, the line between what is strategic and what is operational is becoming increasingly blurry as distinctions between job roles fade. In short, we encourage managers in operational roles to also acquire an understanding of strategic issues.

## How to Get the Most From Your Handbook/Study Guide

To get the most out of this guide, we'd like to explain how it works. In the pages that follow, you will find the CIAC People Management competency outlines, as well as information on ICMI services. We hope these assist you in understanding CIAC certification and the ways in which ICMI can support you in achieving your certification goals.

The CIAC People Management competency outlines provide the competencies and where they are covered in this study guide. We have carefully structured each section to cover the required material in the most logical manner. The material is presented in a building-block fashion for review purposes, and does not always flow in the same order as the competency model.

Sections three through seven include the content for the assessment. Each section is divided into topics that are organized as follows:

- Subject
- Key Points
- Explanation
- Exercise (in the back of each section)
- References for further study (in the back of each section)

This structure is designed to give you the flexibility to spend as much or as little time studying each topic as you require. The boxes on the top right of each topic are available for you to perform a self-assessment. Read through the key points to determine if your understanding of the material is:

1 unfamiliar territory, more time is needed here
2 pretty good, but worth reviewing
3 excellent

You can then review your self-assessment to focus your study time in the areas that need it the most. To complete a self-assessment of all topics at once, see page 13 of this introduction.

We've provided article reprints and other materials including a comprehensive glossary in sections eight and nine. Each section provides references for further study. These are intended to give you more detailed information on areas that you may have limited knowledge. We hope you'll continue to use this material for ongoing self-development.

The goals of the *Call Center People Management Handbook and Study Guide* are:

- Increase learners' knowledge and skills regarding people management in call centers

- Prepare candidates to pass the CIAC certification knowledge assessment for Module One, People Management

The learning objectives of the *Call Center People Management Handbook and Study Guide* include the ability of the learner to:

1. Recognize, identify, discuss, and/or list key people management concepts, principles, and processes related to:
   - Organizational design and strategic staffing
   - Hiring and retention
   - Training and development
   - Measuring and improving performance
   - Maximizing human resources

2. Apply key people management concepts, principles, and processes to call center situations

## Assessment Information

CIAC certification exams assess knowledge, skills and abilities in each competency domain. Candidates demonstrate role-specific knowledge and skills, and the application of these on the job through an objective assessment and work products.

This guide is intended to prepare you for the objective assessment. The objective assessment is composed entirely of multiple-choice questions. Some questions simply involve selecting from a list of possibilities to determine the correct answer, to the stated question. Other questions may require you to select the choice that is not true or the exception, select the choice that is the best or least correct answer, or select all of the correct answers from a list of choices. Multiple-choice questions also are included that require the interpretation of tables, charts or scenarios to determine the correct answer.

Your handbook/study guide includes exercises in many different formats, such as fill in the blank, multiple choice, and matching, with the answers to the exercises included in Section 10. These exercises are intended to help you determine your readiness to take the CIAC exam.

The specific questions on the CIAC assessments have been developed and validated by a diverse team of industry professionals. As an independent organization, ICMI provides educational services for the assessments, but is not responsible for the quality of the test questions.

For more information:

- See the CIAC Certification Overview in Section 11
- See www.ciac-cert.org
- See www.icmi.com

Section 2

## The CIAC People Management Competency Outline – Strategic Level

This document maps the content of this study guide with CIAC people management competencies. In order to produce a study guide that is easy to use and understand, we have presented the contents of each section in building-block fashion. Therefore, contents may be presented in a different order than in the competency list. We have taken care to ensure that all content is covered in each section, so that you can be confident in your preparation for the test at the strategic level.

This guide covers requirements for certification at both the strategic and operational levels. If you are studying for certification at the strategic level, you will need to be knowledgeable in all areas of the guide. The "Strategic" designation of some topics within each content section of the guide indicates that managers pursuing certification at the operational level do not need to be familiar with this material.

| Study Guide Contents | People Management Competencies – Strategic Level |
|---|---|
| | **A. Determine Resource Requirements and Implement Staffing Plan** |
| Organizational Design and Strategic Staffing Section 3 | 1. Develop and execute a staffing strategy that aligns with the organization's business objectives <br> • Define a structure, roles, and responsibilities that support the center's staffing strategy <br> 2. Create, implement, and manage a strategic staffing plan to support the organization's business objectives <br> • Analyze workforce composition for required knowledge, skills, and abilities <br> • Develop, implement, and manage a short-term (3-12 months) staffing plan with an appropriate workforce mix <br> • Develop, implement, and manage a long-term (12-60 months) staffing plan |
| Maximizing Human Resources Section 7 | • Develop and execute a succession strategy <br> • Create, implement, and manage a succession plan |
| Hiring and Retention Section 4 | 3. Apply the principles and best practices for recruiting, interviewing and hiring <br> • Create and implement a recruiting plan <br> • Recruit a diverse workforce <br> • Conduct an interview <br> • Select required personnel <br> 4. Develop and execute a retention strategy <br> • Identify factors that contribute to and distract from staff retention |

| Study Guide Contents | People Management Competencies – Strategic Level |
|---|---|
| | **B. Determine Professional Development and Learning Needs; Develop and Execute a Professional Development and Training Strategy** |
| Training and Development Section 5 | 1. Create and sustain a work environment and culture that enables professional development and continuous learning<br>• Provide opportunities for ongoing professional development and continual learning<br>• Provide access to appropriate tools and resources for professional development and learning<br>• Establish and apply principles of mentoring and coaching<br>2. Determine knowledge and skill requirements for all job roles in the center<br>3. Determine present and future professional development and learning needs of center staff<br>4. Identify the strengths and development needs of direct reports<br>5. Develop, execute, and support a training strategy<br>• Create and implement a professional development and training plan based on established strategy<br>• Create and implement a plan to evaluate the effectiveness of training<br>6. Align the center's training initiatives with the organization's business objectives<br>7. Implement and support an orientation program (to the organization; center; job role; and team)<br>8. Identify areas for self-improvement; create and implement a plan for ongoing self-improvement |
| | **C. Manage Individual and Team Performance** |
| Measuring and Improving Performance Section 6 | 1. Establish objectives for individual and team performance<br>2. Develop a methodology to monitor and improve performance<br>3. Implement a monitoring and coaching program<br>4. Address poor performance constructively and within applicable guidelines<br>5. Conduct a performance review<br>• Identify different behavioral styles of staff<br>• Collaborate with staff to establish performance objectives and work standards<br>• Discuss strengths and weaknesses of staff<br>• Document a performance review |

| Study Guide Contents | People Management Competencies – Strategic Level |
|---|---|
| Maximizing Human Resources Section 7 | 6. Develop, implement, and administer a compensation plan to recognize and reward performance excellence |
| Measuring and Improving Performance Section 6 | 7. Cultivate and sustain a work environment that motivates high performance, recognizes and rewards individual and team excellence; and instills employee loyalty<br>• Implement and administer an incentive plan |
| | **D. Manage Human Resources** |
| Maximizing Human Resources Section 7 | 1. Build, manage, and leverage a diverse workforce |
| Hiring and Retention Section 4 | 2. Manage contract and temporary staff in accordance with applicable organizational policy and regulations |
| Maximizing Human Resources Section 7 | 3. Align employee related decisions with applicable organizational policy and regulations |
| Hiring and Retention Section 4 | 4. Manage remote staff in accordance with applicable organizational policy and regulations |
| Maximizing Human Resources Section 7 | 5. Address privacy issues in accordance with applicable organizational policy, regulations, and moral/ethical considerations<br>6. Design and establish a career path model<br>7. Create and administer an employee satisfaction survey<br>• Identify and implement appropriate actions based on survey results<br>• Track and use organization-wide satisfaction data to enhance the center's image and resolve issues<br>8. Apply principles of conflict resolution<br>9. Identify and enable empowerment opportunities<br>• Provide the tools, authority, and support to enable employee decision-making (including decisions formerly dictated by management)<br>• Identify and address obstacles to empowerment<br>• Develop the trust and support of center staff and other personnel |

| Study Guide Contents | People Management Competencies – Strategic Level |
|---|---|
| | **E. Create and Lead Teams** |
| Maximizing Human Resources<br>Section 7 | 1. Establish and sustain a culture that enables a high-performance team<br>2. Create and sponsor a cross-functional team through shared vision, goals, and planning<br>  • Develop and align team goals with organizational objectives<br>  • Access the organization's resources to support shared initiatives and objectives<br>  • Lead a cross-functional team<br>3. Identify and execute a strategy for building team effectiveness<br>  • Determine and establish a team structure<br>  • Model and instill team building skills (e.g., conflict resolution; role clarification; effective communications; goal setting)<br>4. Leverage expertise and build collaborative relationships |

Section 2

## The CIAC People Management Competency Outline – Operational Level

This document maps the content of this study guide with CIAC people management competencies at the operational level. In order to produce a study guide that is easy to use and understand, we have presented the contents of each section in building-block fashion. Therefore, contents may be presented in a different order than in the competency list. We have taken care to ensure that all content is covered in each section, so that you can be confident in your preparation for the test.

This guide covers requirements for certification at both the strategic and operational levels. If you are studying for certification at the operational level, you will need to be knowledgeable in the areas of the guide that are NOT designated as "Strategic."

| Study Guide Contents | People Management Competencies – Operational Level |
|---|---|
| | **A. Determine Resource Requirements and Implement Staffing Plan** |
| Organizational Design and Strategic Staffing<br>Section 3 | 1. Define a structure, roles, and responsibilities to support the center's staffing strategy<br>2. Develop, implement, and manage a short-term (3-12 months) staffing plan with an appropriate workforce mix |
| Maximizing Human Resources<br>Section 7 | 3. Implement and manage a succession plan |
| Hiring and Retention<br>Section 4 | 4. Apply the principles and best practices for recruiting, interviewing, and hiring<br>• Create and implement a recruiting plan<br>• Recruit a diverse workforce<br>• Conduct an interview<br>• Select personnel<br>5. Identify factors that contribute to and distract from staff retention<br>• Execute and manage a retention strategy |
| | **B. Determine Professional Development and Learning Needs; Develop and Execute a Professional Development and Training Strategy** |
| Training and Development<br>Section 5 | 1. Provide opportunities for ongoing professional development and continual learning<br>• Provide access to appropriate tools and resources for professional development and learning<br>• Establish and apply principles for mentoring and coaching |

| Study Guide Contents | People Management Competencies – Operational Level |
|---|---|
| Training and Development<br>Section 5<br>*(continued)* | 2. Determine present and future professional development and learning needs of center staff<br>3. Identify the strengths and development needs of direct reports<br>4. Create and implement a professional development and training plan based on established strategy<br>  • Create and implement a plan to evaluate the effectiveness of training<br>5. Implement and support an orientation program (to the organization; center; job role; and team)<br>6. Identify areas for self-improvement; create and implement a plan for ongoing self-improvement |
| | **C. Manage Individual and Team Performance** |
| Measuring and Improving Performance<br>Section 6 | 1. Implement a monitoring and coaching program<br>2. Address poor performance constructively and within applicable guidelines<br>3. Conduct a performance review<br>  • Identify different behavioral styles of staff<br>  • Collaborate with staff to establish performance objectives and work standards<br>  • Discuss strengths and weaknesses of staff<br>  • Document a performance review |
| Maximizing Human Resources<br>Section 7 | 4. Develop, implement, and administer a compensation plan to recognize and reward performance excellence |
| Measuring and Improving Performance<br>Section 6 | 5. Cultivate and sustain a work environment that motivates high performance; recognizes and rewards individual and team excellence; and instills employee loyalty<br>  • Implement and administer an incentive plan |
| | **D. Manage Human Resources** |
| Maximizing Human Resources<br>Section 7 | 1. Build, manage, and leverage a diverse workforce |
| Hiring and Retention<br>Section 4 | 2. Manage contract and temporary staff in accordance with applicable organizational policy and regulations |

| Study Guide Contents | People Management Competencies – Operational Level |
|---|---|
| Maximizing Human Resources<br>Section 7 | 3. Align employee related decisions with applicable organizational policy and regulations |
| Hiring and Retention<br>Section 4 | 4. Manage remote staff in accordance with applicable organizational policy and regulations |
| Maximizing Human Resources<br>Section 7 | 5. Address privacy issues in accordance with applicable organizational policy, regulations, and moral/ethical considerations<br>6. Establish a career path model<br>7. Create and administer an employee satisfaction survey<br>  • Identify and implement appropriate actions based on survey results<br>  • Track and use organization-wide satisfaction data to enhance the center's image and resolve issues<br>8. Apply principles of conflict resolution<br>9. Identify and enable empowerment opportunities<br>  • Provide the tools, authority, and support to enable employee decision-making (including decisions formerly dictated by management)<br>  • Identify and address obstacles to empowerment<br>  • Develop the trust and support of center staff and other personnel |
| | **E. Create and Lead Teams** |
| Maximizing Human Resources<br>Section 7 | 1. Develop and align team goals with organizational objectives<br>2. Lead a cross-functional team<br>3. Identify and execute a strategy for building team effectiveness<br>  • Model and instill team building skills (e.g., conflict resolution, role clarification, effective communications, goal setting)<br>4. Leverage expertise and build collaborative relationships |

## Pre/Post Self-Assessment for Call Center People Management Study Guide

The purpose of this self-assessment tool is to provide you with an opportunity to identify areas where you are confident in your knowledge and experience, and areas where you may need to do some additional study or receive additional training.

First, go through the pre-assessment and circle your perceived level of knowledge for each area designated. As you study the guide, focus on the areas where you are not satisfied with your current knowledge level.

Following your study, conduct a post-assessment. For each area, note the shift in your ratings. Place a check (√) by the content areas you in which want to pursue more in-depth training. (ICMI offers training and further resources on most of these topics. For further information, see About ICMI, section 12.)

Use the following scale to indicate your level of knowledge in the areas described.

1 = Unfamiliar territory, more time is needed here

2 = Pretty good, but worth reviewing

3 = Excellent

| | Pre-Assessment | | | | Post Assessment | | | | √ Training |
|---|---|---|---|---|---|---|---|---|---|
| **Organizational Design and Strategic Staffing, Section 3** | | | | | | | | | |
| **Organizational Structure and Strategy** | | | | | | | | | |
| 1. Principles of Call Center Organizational Design [Strategic] | 1 | 2 | 3 | | 1 | 2 | 3 | | |
| 2. Forms of Organizational Structure [Strategic] | 1 | 2 | 3 | | 1 | 2 | 3 | | |
| 3. Aligning Structure and Strategy [Strategic] | 1 | 2 | 3 | | 1 | 2 | 3 | | |
| 4. Call Center Roles and Responsibilities | 1 | 2 | 3 | | 1 | 2 | 3 | | |
| 5. Building Effective Agent Groups | 1 | 2 | 3 | | 1 | 2 | 3 | | |
| 6. Management Ratios (Span of Control) [Strategic] | 1 | 2 | 3 | | 1 | 2 | 3 | | |
| **Job Evaluation and Staffing Plans** | | | | | | | | | |
| 7. The Job Evaluation Process | 1 | 2 | 3 | | 1 | 2 | 3 | | |
| 8. Components of a Strategic Staffing Plan [Strategic] | 1 | 2 | 3 | | 1 | 2 | 3 | | |
| 9. Strategic Staffing: Predicting FTEs | 1 | 2 | 3 | | 1 | 2 | 3 | | |
| 10. Strategic Staffing: Required Qualifications and Development Plans [Strategic] | 1 | 2 | 3 | | 1 | 2 | 3 | | |
| 11. Strategic Staffing: Workforce Mix and Scheduling Alternatives | 1 | 2 | 3 | | 1 | 2 | 3 | | |

| | Pre-Assessment | | | | Post Assessment | | | | √ Training |
|---|---|---|---|---|---|---|---|---|---|
| **Hiring and Retention, Section 4** | | | | | | | | | |
| **Recruiting, Interviewing and Hiring** | | | | | | | | | |
| 1. Creating and Implementing a Recruiting Plan | 1 | 2 | 3 | | 1 | 2 | 3 | | |
| 2. Sources and Methods for Recruiting | 1 | 2 | 3 | | 1 | 2 | 3 | | |
| 3. Internal vs. External Hiring | 1 | 2 | 3 | | 1 | 2 | 3 | | |
| 4. Conducting Effective Interviews | 1 | 2 | 3 | | 1 | 2 | 3 | | |
| 5. Selecting Required Employees | 1 | 2 | 3 | | 1 | 2 | 3 | | |
| 6. Ensuring Legally Sound Employee Selection | 1 | 2 | 3 | | 1 | 2 | 3 | | |
| **Staffing Alternatives** | | | | | | | | | |
| 7. Temporary, Contracted and Managed Staff | 1 | 2 | 3 | | 1 | 2 | 3 | | |
| 8. Telecommuters | 1 | 2 | 3 | | 1 | 2 | 3 | | |
| 9. Staff-Sharing Arrangements | 1 | 2 | 3 | | 1 | 2 | 3 | | |
| 10. Service Bureaus | 1 | 2 | 3 | | 1 | 2 | 3 | | |
| **Managing Turnover** | | | | | | | | | |
| 11. Types and Causes of Turnover | 1 | 2 | 3 | | 1 | 2 | 3 | | |
| 12. Calculating and Tracking Turnover Rate | 1 | 2 | 3 | | 1 | 2 | 3 | | |
| 13. Positive and Negative Aspects of Turnover | 1 | 2 | 3 | | 1 | 2 | 3 | | |
| 14. Effective Agent Retention Strategies | 1 | 2 | 3 | | 1 | 2 | 3 | | |
| **Training and Development, Section 5** | | | | | | | | | |
| **Creating a Learning Environment** | | | | | | | | | |
| 1. Definitions and Purpose of Training and Development | 1 | 2 | 3 | | 1 | 2 | 3 | | |
| 2. Cultivating a Learning Organization | 1 | 2 | 3 | | 1 | 2 | 3 | | |
| 3. Knowledge Management Issues [Strategic] | 1 | 2 | 3 | | 1 | 2 | 3 | | |
| 4. Principles of Effective Mentoring | 1 | 2 | 3 | | 1 | 2 | 3 | | |
| 5. Self-Development | 1 | 2 | 3 | | 1 | 2 | 3 | | |
| 6. Sources of Industry Information | 1 | 2 | 3 | | 1 | 2 | 3 | | |
| **Developing and Implementing Effective Training** | | | | | | | | | |
| 7. Developing a Call Center Training Strategy | 1 | 2 | 3 | | 1 | 2 | 3 | | |
| 8. Drivers of Call Center Training Requirements [Strategic] | 1 | 2 | 3 | | 1 | 2 | 3 | | |
| 9. Identifying Training Needs | 1 | 2 | 3 | | 1 | 2 | 3 | | |
| 10. Barriers to Successful Training | 1 | 2 | 3 | | 1 | 2 | 3 | | |
| 11. Adult Learning Principles | 1 | 2 | 3 | | 1 | 2 | 3 | | |

| | Pre-Assessment | | | | Post Assessment | | | √ Training | |
|---|---|---|---|---|---|---|---|---|---|
| 12. Instructional Design/Development | 1 | 2 | 3 | | 1 | 2 | 3 | | |
| 13. Training Courseware | 1 | 2 | 3 | | 1 | 2 | 3 | | |
| 14. Training Delivery Methods | 1 | 2 | 3 | | 1 | 2 | 3 | | |
| 15. Training Facilitators | 1 | 2 | 3 | | 1 | 2 | 3 | | |
| **Evaluating and Leveraging Training Opportunities** | | | | | | | | | |
| 16. Evaluating Training Effectiveness [Strategic] | 1 | 2 | 3 | | 1 | 2 | 3 | | |
| 17. Aligning Call Center Training with Organizationwide Initiatives [Strategic] | 1 | 2 | 3 | | 1 | 2 | 3 | | |
| 18. Creating and Implementing an Orientation Program | 1 | 2 | 3 | | 1 | 2 | 3 | | |
| **Measuring and Improving Performance, Section 6** | | | | | | | | | |
| **Establishing Objectives and Tracking Performance** | | | | | | | | | |
| 1. Measuring and Tracking Performance Objectives | 1 | 2 | 3 | | 1 | 2 | 3 | | |
| 2. The Contribution of Roles/Responsibilities to Objectives [Strategic] | 1 | 2 | 3 | | 1 | 2 | 3 | | |
| 3. Setting Performance Objectives | 1 | 2 | 3 | | 1 | 2 | 3 | | |
| 4. Key Objectives for Agents | 1 | 2 | 3 | | 1 | 2 | 3 | | |
| 5. Avoiding Conflicting Objectives | 1 | 2 | 3 | | 1 | 2 | 3 | | |
| 6. Improving Call Center Processes | 1 | 2 | 3 | | 1 | 2 | 3 | | |
| **Effective Monitoring and Coaching** | | | | | | | | | |
| 7. Developing a Monitoring and Coaching Program | 1 | 2 | 3 | | 1 | 2 | 3 | | |
| 8. Types of Monitoring | 1 | 2 | 3 | | 1 | 2 | 3 | | |
| 9. Scoring and Calibration | 1 | 2 | 3 | | 1 | 2 | 3 | | |
| 10. Monitoring Technologies | 1 | 2 | 3 | | 1 | 2 | 3 | | |
| 11. Legal Considerations of Monitoring | 1 | 2 | 3 | | 1 | 2 | 3 | | |
| 12. Principles of Effective Coaching and Feedback | 1 | 2 | 3 | | 1 | 2 | 3 | | |
| 13. Steps to Effective Coaching and Feedback | 1 | 2 | 3 | | 1 | 2 | 3 | | |
| **Performance Reviews and Motivation** | | | | | | | | | |
| 14. Purposes and Benefits of Performance Reviews | 1 | 2 | 3 | | 1 | 2 | 3 | | |
| 15. Conducting Performance Reviews | 1 | 2 | 3 | | 1 | 2 | 3 | | |
| 16. Motivation Theory and Principles | 1 | 2 | 3 | | 1 | 2 | 3 | | |
| 17. Enabling a Highly Motivated Environment | 1 | 2 | 3 | | 1 | 2 | 3 | | |

**Section 2**

| | Pre-Assessment | | | | Post Assessment | | | | √ Training |
|---|---|---|---|---|---|---|---|---|---|
| 18. Types of Incentives | 1 | 2 | 3 | | 1 | 2 | 3 | | |
| 19. Pros and Cons of Incentives | 1 | 2 | 3 | | 1 | 2 | 3 | | |
| 20. Addressing Poor Performance | 1 | 2 | 3 | | 1 | 2 | 3 | | |
| 21. Disciplinary Principles and Practices | 1 | 2 | 3 | | 1 | 2 | 3 | | |
| **Maximizing Human Resources, Section 7** | | | | | | | | | |
| **Employee Career Development and Satisfaction** | | | | | | | | | |
| 1. Differentiating Career and Skill Path Models | 1 | 2 | 3 | | 1 | 2 | 3 | | |
| 2. Creating and Communicating Career and Skill Paths | 1 | 2 | 3 | | 1 | 2 | 3 | | |
| 3. Succession Planning [Strategic] | 1 | 2 | 3 | | 1 | 2 | 3 | | |
| 4. Types of Compensation | 1 | 2 | 3 | | 1 | 2 | 3 | | |
| 5. Compensation-Related Factors | 1 | 2 | 3 | | 1 | 2 | 3 | | |
| 6. Implementing Compensation Plans | 1 | 2 | 3 | | 1 | 2 | 3 | | |
| **Building a High-Performance Culture** | | | | | | | | | |
| 7. Contributors to Employee Satisfaction | 1 | 2 | 3 | | 1 | 2 | 3 | | |
| 8. Employee Satisfaction Surveys | 1 | 2 | 3 | | 1 | 2 | 3 | | |
| 9. Cultivating Empowerment | 1 | 2 | 3 | | 1 | 2 | 3 | | |
| 10. Building Trust | 1 | 2 | 3 | | 1 | 2 | 3 | | |
| 11. Conflict Resolution | 1 | 2 | 3 | | 1 | 2 | 3 | | |
| 12. Diversity in the Workforce | 1 | 2 | 3 | | 1 | 2 | 3 | | |
| **Creating and Leading Teams** | | | | | | | | | |
| 13. Implementing Teams | 1 | 2 | 3 | | 1 | 2 | 3 | | |
| 14. Team Roles and Responsibilities | 1 | 2 | 3 | | 1 | 2 | 3 | | |
| 15. Building Team Effectiveness | 1 | 2 | 3 | | 1 | 2 | 3 | | |
| 16. Leading Crossfunctional and Distributed Teams | 1 | 2 | 3 | | 1 | 2 | 3 | | |
| **Legal Requirements and Privacy** | | | | | | | | | |
| 17. Managing Within Legal Requirements – U.S. | 1 | 2 | 3 | | 1 | 2 | 3 | | |
| 18. Managing Within Legal Requirements – Canada | 1 | 2 | 3 | | 1 | 2 | 3 | | |
| 19. Privacy-Related Issues | 1 | 2 | 3 | | 1 | 2 | 3 | | |

## Frequently Asked Questions

**What is CIAC certification?**

The Call Center Industry Advisory Council (CIAC) is a nonprofit and independent organization established and funded to develop competencies and provide industry-standard certification for call center managers. Successful completion of CIAC certification means formal recognition of the individual's mastery of specified competencies and commitment to staying abreast of new developments in the profession.

CIAC Certification requires successful completion of the CIAC certification assessment process. There are four modules; each has its own test:
• People Management
• Operations Management
• Customer Relationship Management
• Leadership and Business Management

Tests are provided at regularly scheduled times and locations. See www.ciac-cert.org for a complete listing.

**Why does ICMI support CIAC certification?**

In recent years, a number of call center vendors have promoted their own versions of certification programs. Some of these programs have since come and gone, but ICMI has maintained from the beginning that there can be no valid certification program without a broadly-representative and recognized body overseeing the process. The CIAC is a nonprofit organization established by the industry to develop, administer and govern professional certification for the call center profession. It has broad support from end-users, consultants and suppliers, and will likely remain in favor with the industry as long as it remains unbiased, representative, open and tuned in to industry needs.

**Are certain training classes required?**

No. The CIAC does not provide educational services, but is instead committed to an "open-systems" approach whereby managers can acquire required competence through the combination of on-the-job experience, training courses and published materials they choose. This ensures that call center professionals are free to choose the best training programs and publications available as they build their knowledge and skills. And it enables experienced managers to avoid the expense and time involved in the prescribed training classes that are often necessary in other programs.

**Do these handbooks/study guides replace ICMI seminars?**

That depends on your objectives. The handbook/study guide series is designed to cover CIAC certification competencies. Each guide covers a significant range of material in a review fashion but does not replace the need for job experiences nor the formal training other ICMI courses provide. However, through a step-by-step review process, the guides enable managers with sufficient experiences or management training to identify areas that require further study, and they provide the essential information needed to fill in any gaps.

**How else can ICMI help?**

ICMI has developed innovative review courses and self-study resources for those who want an efficient review of the content areas addressed by CIAC competencies. In addition, ICMI's full range of call center management training and publications support specific content areas included in the CIAC competencies. See information on additional ICMI services, next page.

**Where can I find more information?**

- See the CIAC Certification Overview in Section 11
- See www.ciac-cert.org
- See www.icmi.com

## Additional ICMI Services

If you have chosen to pursue certification through the CIAC, ICMI is the authoritative source for the information and training you need for success. The CIAC is a nonprofit organization that administers certification but, by design, does not provide certification training. That enables you to choose the training alternatives you need and prefer.

That's where ICMI comes in. ICMI offers many choices, including:

### Handbook/Study Guide Series

The ICMI handbook/study guide series, which this book is part of, includes four publications:

- *Call Center People Management Handbook and Study Guide*
- *Call Center Operations Management Handbook and Study Guide*
- *Call Center Customer Relationship Management Handbook and Study Guide*
- *Call Center Leadership and Business Management Handbook and Study Guide*

These guides provide a 100 percent comprehensive review of each module along with self-study tools to ensure you are prepared.

### Foundational Seminars

ICMI's powerful instructor-led seminars are designed to provide a practical working knowledge of core call center management disciplines. As over 50,000 ICMI alumni from around the world will attest, these two-day courses offer an unmatched combination of content, support materials, expert facilitation and interaction. Current offerings include:

- *Essential Skills and Knowledge for Effective Call Center Management*
- *Monitoring and Coaching for Improved Call Center Performance*
- *Contact Center Technology: What Works, What's New, What Drives Results*
- *Effective Leadership and Strategy for Senior Call Center Managers*
- *Workforce Management: The Basics and Beyond*

### Study Courses

Perhaps you'd like to combine the power of self-study with personal guidance from call center experts. ICMI's CIAC study courses enable your entire management team to successfully prepare for certification. Through expert facilitation and focused study, your team will prepare for the assessment, and acquire the skills and knowledge you need to advance your call center's services. These courses can be delivered in traditional classroom style or, for organizations with geographically dispersed centers, over the Internet. Public seminars (Web-based and in-person) are also available. ICMI's handbook/study guide series is included with these courses.

### Combination

Those who need preparation only in specific content areas can choose from ICMI's full range of Web seminars, books, papers, studies and other services. Consistency, quality and usability are trademarks of these services.

For more information, or help with planning your approach, contact us at icmi@icmi.com or 410-267-0700.

# Organizational Design and Strategic Staffing

# Section 3: Organizational Design and Strategic Staffing

## Contents

# 1. Principles of Call Center Organizational Design [Strategic]

Ready? | 1 | 2 | 3 |

## Key Points

- Organizational design refers to the structure of jobs, positions and reporting relationships that are used to construct the organization.

- The forces of organizational design are constantly at work; organizational design defines issues such as job roles and responsibilities, lines of communication and authority, analyst and support positions, manager-to-agent ratios, and others.

- Although structure can differ significantly from one organization to the next, there are dependable, consistent principles behind any effective design.

## Explanation

*Every organized human activity – from the making of pots to the placing of a man on the moon – gives rise to two fundamental and opposing requirements: the division of labor into various tasks to be performed, and the coordination of those tasks to accomplish the activity.*– Henry Mintzberg (*Structure,* p. 2)

Like the road network in a community or the design of the hull on a boat, the forces of organizational design (also called "organizational structure") are constantly at work. A well-designed organization will enable the call center to be flexible, fast and efficient. When structured poorly, it will hamper communication, create barriers to performance and lead to unpredictable and inefficient workarounds.

A well-structured organization is particularly important to call centers, given that the "powerful pooling principle" – the immutable law that says consolidation of resources will result in improved efficiencies – lies at the heart of call center effectiveness. In fact, when call centers began catching on several decades ago, the big challenge was to get callers to abandon the need to reach specific individuals. Today, as building customer relationships and loyalty have reached the forefront of strategy, the need to develop effective, collaborative organizations is more important than ever.

**Definitions of Organizational Design**

An organizational structure provides the alignment of roles and responsibilities for business units, departments and individuals. There are many reasonable definitions of organizational structure, but almost all refer to both the division of labor, and the coordination of responsibilities and tasks. For example:

- "Organization design refers to the framework of jobs, positions, clusters of positions and reporting relationships among positions that are used to construct the organization." (Mintzberg, *Structure*, p. 2)

- "The structure of an organization is the sum total of the ways in which its labor is divided into distinct tasks and then its coordination is achieved among these tasks." (Mintzberg, *Structure*, p. 2)

A generic but typical example of a call center organization is illustrated in the figure below.

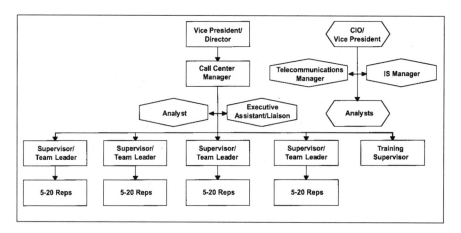

Organizational design is constantly exerting its forces as it channels communications, shapes protocol and establishes lines of authority. Major issues defined or impacted by organizational design include:

- The call center's position in the larger organization

- The call center's significance to the organization; e.g., vs. other channels of service delivery (retail locations or direct sales/service)

- The call center's overall mission and responsibilities

- Specific job roles and responsibilities

- Lines of communication and authority

- Political protocol

- Agent group structure

- Analyst and support positions

- Ratios (e.g., staff to supervisor)

- Number of sites and level of integration

- Process, technology and facility requirements

- Budgetary apportionment

**Principles of Effective Design**

To design an effective call center structure, you must consider:

1. The strategic purpose of the organization

2. The mission, vision and values of the organization

3. Customer characterization and requirements

4. The culture and environment of the organization

Although the knowledge, skills and abilities of existing workers are obviously important for the implementation of a structure, they should not dictate the ideal design. Rather, the vision of where the organization is going should be the primary driver of structure.

While some aspects of organizational design are similar from one call center to the next – e.g., the basic components illustrated in the figure are present in most organizations – there are about as many unique organizational structures as there are organizations. Even so, there are solid, consistent principles behind any effective design. These include the following.

**The organization's mission and strategy drive the structure:** Organizational design is a strategy to help the enterprise reach its objectives; design helps translate strategy into operations. Answers to major questions such as the call center's role, to whom the call center reports and how the call center will be positioned vis-à-vis other service delivery methods (e.g., the sales force, retail operations and online services) must flow from the highest levels of strategy. Structure follows strategy. (See Aligning Structure and Strategy, this section.)

The culture and environment of the organization tend to play a large role in determining structure. For example, more formal, bureaucratic organizations tend to have formal structures, while less formal organizations often choose flatter structures with dispersed responsibilities.

(For a complete discussion of mission and strategy, see ICMI's *Call Center Leadership and Business Management Handbook and Study Guide*.)

**Informal and formal structures are well-aligned:** The formal structure is the one defined by organization charts and in position and process descriptions. The informal structure consists of the unofficial relationships among individuals and work groups. For example, informal structures dominate in situations where call centers must grow ad hoc training and technology support functions because the formal structure can't support the center in a timely fashion.

Organizations are complex, and there will always be some degree of informal communication and workflow. But if an informal structure grows topsy-turvy, it's time for management to address the root causes of these developments. Just as great sports teams define positions around natural talent and abilities (e.g., quarterback), formal structures should reflect efficient flows, natural lines of authority and earned responsibilities. (See Forms of Organizational Structures, this section.)

**Current agent groups form the foundation of call center structure:** Once the call center's place in the larger organization is defined, the call center should be built from agent groups upward. (Definition: Agent groups share a common set of skills and knowledge, handle a specified mix of contacts and can be comprised of hundreds of agents across multiple sites. Supervisory groups and teams are often subsets of agent groups.) Agent groups should be designed to serve customer characterization (segmentation) and requirements.

The ideal agent group is one in which each person is proficient at handling every type of contact, through any channel, speaks all required languages, and can maintain the company's branding and image for every customer segment. That, of course, is not realistic in most environments — thus, building and supporting agent groups often involves such approaches as tiered groups, network configurations, overflow parameters, skills-based routing and other methods to get the right contact to the right place at the right time.

Everything – e.g., hiring, training programs, supervisory and management responsibilities, analyst activities, quality standards and workforce planning – becomes based on agent group structure. But as agent group requirements evolve, the larger organization built on those groups can become obsolete.

This is an issue that requires constant review. If the superstructure become obsolete even as agent group requirements have moved on, managers must

rethink design, e.g., by redefining responsibilities, adjusting ratios and revamping training programs. (See Building Effective Agent Groups, this section.)

**Divisions and ratios are supported by the highest priorities:** Any defined team, agent group, functional area or location (unless networked seamlessly to other sites) is defined by dividing lines, and divisions should be justified by the highest priorities. It's important to constantly review any divisions.

For example, a governmental organization combined dozens of local call centers into a few consolidated regional call centers. They decided that consistent overall service to clients was a higher priority than satisfying the interests pushing to keep the jobs in each local community.

In another case, a computer company with 24x7 technical support combines several daytime groups into a pooled group at night equipped to handle a broad range of transactions; although handling time is higher, quality remains consistent with daytime service. The organization decided that the ability to reach an agent – albeit one who may need a bit more time to handle the contact – wisely wins out over maintaining small, specialized groups in early morning hours. (See Management Ratios, this section.)

**Reporting arrangements assign appropriate accountabilities:** There are situations in which the call center is dependent on people who report to other areas that have different or even competing interests. Everybody is ultimately on the same team; however, when different areas have different priorities, problems can emerge.

The solution is to communicate with colleagues across divisions and identify objectives and accountabilities that may be in conflict. Perhaps training should report to the same area as the call center, or even to the call center director. Perhaps some expenditures spread across IT, marketing and customer service budgets should be combined. Perhaps some support functions ought to be brought under the call center umbrella.

**Support positions are enablers:** Roles geared around ensuring compliance, establishing rules and creating exception reports are often counterproductive. Alternatively, creating better processes, facilitating collaboration and, in general, supporting and enabling the call center's highest values are support responsibilities that will contribute to overall success. Those in support roles must find a good balance between burdensome control and an organization so loosely managed that it loses effectiveness. (See Call Center Roles and Responsibilities, this section.)

**The structure facilitates branding:** The organization's desired image, how it wishes to define and serve customer segments, and the specific requirements of individual customers should comprise objectives that span the organization's marketing efforts, the products and services it provides, and the contributions of the call center. While that doesn't necessarily mean that separate divisions or agent groups within the call center are required to serve different customer segments, it does mean that divisions, groups and responsibilities should further rather than hinder branding requirements.

### Ensuring Buy-in When Changing Structure

Organization structure should evolve as the needs of the organization and the customers it serves evolve. However, since structure impacts job roles and responsibilities as well as lines of communication and authority, it is usually best to get input (what's working, what isn't and recommended changes) from call center personnel and internal business units before looking to outside sources (e.g., consultants or benchmarking efforts) for help.

Many managers have also discovered that an effective way to facilitate the transition to a new structure is to establish the performance criteria for new jobs and enable employees to express a choice (e.g., 1st, 2nd, 3rd) in roles they would prefer. Final job role decisions must also, of course, consider past and current performance. But often, there's a good fit between an employee's proficiencies and jobs they would prefer.

These steps maximize the chance for buy-in from individuals within the organization, and often help identify specific problems and corresponding solutions that can be addressed by structural changes. Designing the right organization conceptually is just the first step; to be effective, the organizational structure must also have the support of those who are part of it.

## 2. Forms of Organizational Structures [Strategic]

Ready? | 1 | 2 | 3 |

**Section 3**

### Key Points

- At a general level, organizationwide structures can be classified as:
  - Bureaucratic: Traditional, hierarchical structures
  - Flat: Structures with few layers of management
  - Team-oriented: Built around small groups of people working toward common objectives
  - Matrix: Structures with a combination of vertical and horizontal lines of authority
  - Product- or service-oriented: Structures built around the organization's products and services
  - Geographic-oriented: Structures dictated by geographical areas that the organization serves
  - Customer-oriented: Structures built around customer segments

- Each major form has distinct advantages and disadvantages that must be considered in the design process. Many combinations and iterations of these structures are possible.

### Explanation

In the proceeding section, Principles of Call Center Organizational Design, key principles of effective call center design were identified and summarized. However, the call center is, of course, part of a larger organization.

*(continued, next page)*

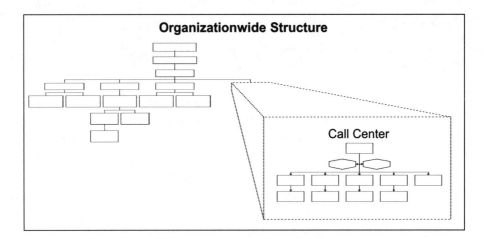

It is not necessary that call center structure reflect organizationwide structure. However, an understanding of general organizational structures will enable call center managers to better understand associated strategic and cultural implications, and the call center's role in supporting the organization's mission.

At a general level, organizational structures can be classified as:

- Bureaucratic structures

- Flat structures

- Team-oriented structures

- Matrix structures

- Product- or service-oriented structures

- Geographic-oriented structures

- Customer-oriented structures

Other classification systems exist, and many iterations and combinations are possible. But these descriptions are fairly common in traditional management literature, and enable managers to recognize characteristics and consider tradeoffs and implications when designing a structure. Characteristics, advantages, disadvantages and implications for each type of structure are summarized in the following sections.

**Bureaucratic Structures**

This is the traditional pyramid structure, or hierarchy, typically with many layers of management and based on functional divisions of labor. It is generally

characterized by a top-down management approach. Jobs are narrowly defined and highly specialized, and there are rigid boundaries between jobs and business units. Career paths are oriented toward working up the hierarchy, usually within a department or specific functional area.

Advantages that have been traditionally associated with bureaucratic structures include:

- Increased productivity at the task level, due to specialties within the division of labor

- Greater control by upper-level management

- Policies and procedures that guide work processes

- Expertise concentrated around specialized tasks/functions

- Consistent rules across the organization

- Job procedures that result in less dependency on specific individuals

Disadvantages of bureaucratic structures include:

- At odds with a culture of empowerment and participative management

- Inconsistent with many employees' values and participative spirit

- Requires significant coordination between business units; "silos" often become barriers

- Many decisions are made by executives who are distant from the front lines

- Divisions of labor can lead to overly routinized jobs that people find boring

- Is increasingly cumbersome and unwieldy in the information-based economy

In many organizations, there has been a movement away from bureaucratic structures over the past two decades; that is true both for organizationwide structures as well as for call centers. Some call centers are still justifiably criticized for operating modern "sweat shops," and continue to focus on unit output and command-and-control style production. But overwhelmingly, evolving management trends coupled with new capabilities in call center technologies have enabled a shift from bureaucratic to flatter structures, driven by multiskilled teams and empowered agents.

**Flat Structures**

Flat organizations have very few levels of management. Most individuals in a flat organization have broadly defined jobs and tend to wear many hats. Decision making is decentralized, and the organization tends to encourage (and depend on) employee involvement in decisions. Flat organizations are usually divided into work units by customer, product or service, or geography, and generally have a strong focus on customers. There are few boundaries between jobs and business units; where they exist, they are often flexible. Individuals often work in teams or crossfunctional work groups, and career paths are oriented toward horizontal opportunities (across functions).

Advantages of flat structures include:

- Generally, less administrative overhead costs due to the need for relatively fewer supervisors, managers and analysts

- Higher degree of self-management, empowerment, trust and participation

- Collaborative decision making which encourages buy-in

- A high degree of initiative and innovation (the result of collaboration and input)

- Individuals with a broad base of skills and knowledge

Disadvantages of flat structures include:

- Requires better-educated individuals

- Generally requires more training

- Traditional career paths (moving up layers) are limited

- Often provides less formal feedback to individuals

- Coordination and communication require constant effort

- Less rigid boundaries between jobs and units can result in unclear policies and procedures

As positive as the move to flatter structures has been, it has created a significant challenge: there are fewer formal layers with which to structure traditional career paths. This has been particularly challenging in call centers. Consequently, managers have had to redefine the meaning of career path – no, it doesn't have to involve moving up a traditional ladder – and build opportunities that are increasingly focused on skill development and lateral moves. (See Creating and Communicating Career and Skill Paths, Section 7.)

**Section 3**

**Team-Oriented Structures**

A team can be defined as "a small number of people with complementary skills who work toward common goals for which they hold themselves mutually accountable" (Katzenback and Smith, p. 45). A team-oriented structure is built on a shared purpose and commitment to common objectives. Individuals bring high-level, mixed skills to the team, and performance goals are shared, resulting in interdependency among members and mutual accountability for results. Trust among members is essential, as is a climate of commitment, collaboration and open communication. Strategies are often collectively developed and implemented, and team goals take precedence over personal goals.

Advantages of team structures include:

- The pooling of knowledge and skills can result in a higher quality output

- The diversity of teams encourages innovation

- Generally, there is a high level of trust and buy-in to projects and direction

- Individuals build a broad base of skills and knowledge

- Teams often cultivate and encourage natural leaders within the group

- Encourages empowerment and a participative environment

Disadvantages of team structures include:

- Striving for consensus can increase the time to bring a project or task to completion

- Difficult to reward individual contribution

- In some cases, individual accountability may decrease

- Team members must be trained in team process skills

- There may be a tendency not to end a project and dissolve the team

- Overbearing or dominating participants can lead to "group think"

Many organizations – including many call centers – have been successful in moving toward more team-based structures. However, it's important to note that few call centers have bonafide "self-managed" teams (a management trend that gained much popularity in the 1990s); instead most opt for hybrid structures that fall somewhere between autonomous groups and traditional reporting structures. Teams are covered in Section 7.

### Matrix Structures

In a matrix structure, there are both vertical and horizontal lines of authority. While traditional vertical lines of authority are present and ongoing, people are frequently assigned to crossfunctional projects with horizontal responsibilities and accountabilities. In other words, people from different parts of the organization work on common long-term projects but remain part of their line management. Project managers have a diverse pool of expertise – whatever the organization can offer – with which to accomplish goals. For each project, the manager must build a business case for the specialists they need. These managers have limited, short-term authority over the team members, and relinquish them to their normal duties when projects are finished.

Advantages of a matrix structure include:

- Project managers have access to a diverse pool of resources

- Managers have greater control over projects

- Specialists are brought in on a project-by-project basis, providing flexibility

- Individuals develop a broad base of skills and experiences

Disadvantages of a matrix structure include:

- Internal competition for specialists

- Difficulties in rewarding specialists due to multiple "bosses"

- Competition to secure specialists may lead to exaggerated business cases

- Can create counter-productive politics (e.g., persuasion, negotiation, exchange of favors, etc.) among project managers

Matrix structures that involve agents are rare in call centers. However, call centers depend on and impact many parts of the organization; consequently, individuals with analyst and management responsibilities are frequently involved in cross-functional projects and processes, such as forecasting, analysis of customer trends and feedback, technology applications, etc. Although these individuals are part of horizontal lines of authority, they also answer to project managers from other parts of the organization who are not part of the typical reporting structure. Consequently, hybrid forms of matrix structures that include call center personnel are common and often necessary.

**Product- or Service-Oriented Structures**

With this type of organization, products or services define the organization's structure. The product or service group often has its own research and development (R&D), production, marketing, sales and customer service functions, and is usually responsible for its own financial results.

Advantages of product- or service-oriented structures include:

- High degree of focus and expertise on specific products and services

- Individuals and/or units are accountable for profits

- Increased control over an entire operation (the result of all critical functions being under the same umbrella)

- Can lead to increased product development

- Often results in quick responses to rapidly changing market demands

Disadvantages of product- or service-oriented structures include:

- Can create internal competition between the organization's divisions

- Can result in higher overall costs due to duplication of critical functions in each area

- Narrow focus can lead to organizational myopia

- Specific groups may resist necessary change, the eliminating obsolete product lines

Call center structure doesn't always match the organization's structure; e.g., some bureaucratic organizations have flat or team-oriented call centers and vice versa. However, in this case, call centers usually follow the lead of the organization at large; e.g., if the organization is structured around products and services, unique call center services generally exist for each unit. While the call center may operate under one roof, agent groups are likely focused on specific product lines.

**Geographic-Oriented Structures**

With this type of organization, geography dictates the structure. Structure can be built to serve specific counties, states, regions of the country or regions/countries of the world.

Advantages of geographic-oriented structures include:

- The organization is close (in orientation) to the customer
- May result in faster response times to serve customer needs
- Can result in more efficient distribution of products and services
- Leverages localized knowledge and/or languages
- Enables efficient service when laws or customs vary

Disadvantages of geographic-oriented structures include:

- Can create inefficiencies and duplication of services
- Associated costs may be higher than a pooled approach
- Finding required skills and knowledge for each division can be challenging
- Internal communications and coordination across divisions can be challenging
- Can encourage funding imbalances among divisions

As with product-focused organizations, call centers usually follow the lead of the organization; e.g., if the organization is structured to serve geographic divisions, unique call center services generally exist for each division. While the call center may operate under one roof, agent groups are usually assigned to specific geographic markets.

**Customer-Oriented Structures**

With a customer-oriented design, the organization is structured around customer segments. One alternative is to create a structure that enables focus on key accounts that offer high current or future profit potential. Another is to focus on general customer groups; e.g., consumer, industrial, government, small business, large business, etc.

Advantages of customer-oriented structures include:

- Places the customer at the center of organizational efforts
- May enable an increase in market penetration
- May increase cross-sell and upsell opportunities
- Can enable ongoing input and feedback from customers
- Can facilitate improved market and competitive research

Disadvantages of customer-oriented structures include:

- May create internal competition for product development, executive time and other enterprise resources

- May result in redundancy in product development or other functions due to specialized needs or poor communication

- Customized products for specific segments can be costly

- Policies and procedures are often less consistent (the result of specific services developed for unique customer segments)

In a sense, the trend toward customer relationship management (CRM) is superimposing a customer-oriented focus on organizations in general – and call centers specifically – regardless of the underlying structures. CRM essentially consists of tools, processes, technologies and strategies that enable the organization to focus on specific customer segments, and even individual customers.

This trend underscores a key point: There is an infinite number of iterations and combinations of organizational structures that are possible. These classifications exist to help managers describe and define organizational structures and identify the general advantages and disadvantages of each.

## 3. Aligning Structure and Strategy [Strategic]

Ready? | 1 | 2 | 3 |

### Key Points

- As with definitions of organizational structure, there are many ways to identify and define corporate strategies. One common framework classifies strategies into these categories:
  - Cost leadership
  - Differentiation
  - Focus
  - Defender
  - Prospector

- Each strategy has specific implications for organizational structure and for the call center's role in furthering the organization's mission.

- A customer access strategy provides a link between corporate strategy and call center strategy.

### Explanation

The organization has corporate and business unit objectives that impact the call center. Put another way, the call center can and should help the business unit and enterprise achieve primary strategic objectives. Common objectives include:

- Increase sales or margins on sales

- Increase profitability

- Introduce new products

- Increase customer retention

- Improve customer satisfaction

- Advance into new customer markets or geographic areas

- Reduce costs

- Increase productivity (output per person)

Having an effective strategy is a prerequisite to meeting these objectives. But strategy can be difficult to define, let alone to create and implement. To some, strategy consists of a position or perspective. To others, it is a ploy or specific maneuver to outwit a competitor or create an advantage in the market. Here,

we refer to strategy generally as the creation of an overall approach to accomplish the organization's objectives.

## Major Strategies

Major corporate strategies include cost leadership, differentiation, focus, defender and prospector. As with organizational structures, in practice, there is much interplay and overlap between these general classifications.

Further, a wide variety of analysts and scholars have presented alternative frameworks. For example, Michael Treacy and Fred Wiersema, in *The Discipline of Market Leaders*, cite only three corporate operating models: operation excellence, product leadership and customer intimacy. In *Strategy Safari*, Bruce Ahlstrand, Joseph Lampel and Henry Mintzberg group strategy formation into 10 overall schools of thought, ranging from a visionary process to a process of transformation – each with different frameworks and outcomes.

Even so, the framework presented here offers a common and useful perspective for recognizing and assessing general corporate strategies. Each is summarized, along with typical implications for organizational structure. The link is then established between organizational strategy and call center strategy.

**Cost leadership:** With this strategy, the intent is to achieve a cost leadership position through policies, practices, procedures and actions that enable the organization to be the low-cost provider. Management is focused on cost control in areas such as scale, overhead control, avoidance of marginal customer accounts, etc. The intent is that low-cost production will result in an above-average return on the organization's investments.

Generally, a more bureaucratic form of organizational structure best supports this strategy. Organization design requirements include:

- Tight cost control and efficient production
- Frequent and detailed cost reports
- Highly structured job roles and responsibilities
- Incentives based on meeting strict targets
- Explicit job descriptions
- Job-specific training
- Performance appraisals focused on productivity and cost control

It's important to note that a cost leadership strategy at the organizational level

may result in higher call center operating costs. For example, comprehensive (and higher cost) call center services may reduce the need to maintain a direct sales force or minimize the inventory that would otherwise be necessary in retail outlets.

**Differentiation:** This strategy involves differentiating the organization by creating product and service offerings that are perceived by the market as unique. Differentiation can take the form of design or brand image, technology, features, customer service and quality. Effective differentiation can create brand loyalty and provide a safety net against price sensitivity. Because it increases margins, it can reduce the need to be a low-cost provider.

Flat or team organizations often best fit a differentiation strategy. Design requirements include:

- Strong coordination among functions of R&D, marketing, and product development

- Amenities to attract a highly skilled labor pool

- Emphasis on innovation and flexibility

- Broad job classes with flexible work planning

- Team-based training

- Emphasis on individual pay

- Performance appraisals focused on individual development and innovation

The call center can be a powerful factor in supporting a differentiation strategy by providing superior service or customized support solutions geared around specific products or customer segments.

**Focus:** This strategy involves targeting defined customer groups, product lines or geographic markets in order to serve those segments better than competitors. Functional policies are developed with this intent in mind. A combination of organizational requirements focused at strategic markets or customer segments is required.

Product- or service-oriented, geographic-oriented or customer-oriented structures are required to support a focus strategy. Design requirements usually include:

- Teams and services focused on the customer group, product line or geographic market

- Hiring, orientation and training processes geared toward the area of focus

- Strong leadership and cultural orientation to the area of focus

- Employee understanding of the area of focus as the organization's competitive advantage

- Budgeting and resource allocation that supports the area of focus

- Sufficient flexibility to respond to changes in the customer group, product line or geographic market

The call center often represents an ideal strategic tool for supporting and furthering the organization's area of focus. The call center's operations, technologies, processes and other components must be closely aligned with this focus.

**Defender:** This strategy is often pursued by organizations with a significant market share and with a stable market, customer base, and line of products and services. Defenders do not generally seek new markets, but instead are focused on protecting the market share they have (e.g., developing brand loyalty). There is usually much emphasis placed on management control, policies, effective processes and procedures, and detailed planning.

A bureaucratic leaning organization often best suits the defender strategy. Design requirements usually include:

- Management control, reliability and employee retention

- Explicit job descriptions and detailed work planning

- Internal recruitment

- Formal hiring and orientation processes

- Uniform appraisal procedures

- Job-specific and individual training

- Emphasis on job security through fixed, job-based and seniority pay

The call center can facilitate consistent implementation of policies and reliable performance to meet customer expectations and help maintain market share.

**Prospector:** This strategy is pursued by organizations that move aggressively in the market. They are generally highly competitive, innovative and focused on speed to market. They generally operate in markets that are rapidly changing.

To support this strategy, the organizational structure must be flexible. Flat,

decentralized and team-based organizations are typical. Design requirements include:

- Emphasis on speed, innovation, flexibility and creativity
- Broad job classes with flexible work planning
- A high degree of external recruitment
- Customized appraisals with a focus on change and contribution
- Team-based and cross-functional training
- Decentralized pay that rewards risk-taking

To effectively support this strategy, the call center must be flexible and agile, and able to quickly respond to enterprise and market changes. It can enable the organization to aggressively pursue customer and market opportunities, and to better position products and services.

---

**Align the Organization to the Strategy**

Synergy is the overarching goal of organizational design. Organizations consist of numerous sectors, business units and specialized departments, each with its own strategy. For organizational performance to become more than the sum of its parts, individual strategies must be linked and integrated. The corporation defines the linkages expected to create synergy and ensures that those linkages actually occur – a task, however, that is easier said that done.

Organizations are traditionally designed around functional specialties such as finance, manufacturing, marketing, sales, engineering and purchasing. Each function has its own body of knowledge, language and culture. Functional silos arise and become a major barrier to strategy implementation, as most organizations have great difficulty communicating and coordinating across these specialty functions.

Strategy-focused organizations, however, break through this barrier. Executives replace formal reporting structures with strategic themes and priorities that enable a consistent message and consistent set of priorities to be used across diverse and dispersed organizational units. New organization charts are not necessary. Business units and shared service units become linked to the strategy through common themes and objectives....

Excerpt from *The Strategy-Focused Organization*, by Robert S. Kaplan and David P. Norton, Harvard Business School Press, 2001

---

### The Link Between Organizational Strategy and Call Center Strategy

Developing effective strategy is a pervasive characteristic of organizations that create sustainable customer loyalty and marketplace value. In the call center environment, strategy is embodied in what is often termed a "customer access

---

strategy," which is a framework – a set of standards, guidelines and processes – defining the means by which customers are connected with resources capable of delivering the desired information and services.

While corporate strategy must ultimately define the customer access strategy, the customer access strategy can influence broader corporate strategy. For example, 24x7 call center services have enabled some insurance companies to differentiate their services from competitors who only provide in-person service. Similarly, call center and Web-based sales and services have enabled some computer companies to become low-cost providers vs. competitors who sell through distributors.

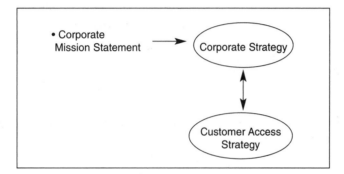

When approached with the right commitment and buy-in, a customer access strategy is a powerful tool for unleashing the potential and value of the call center. As with general corporate strategy, a customer access strategy can take many different forms. However, the most sustainable customer access strategies include the following components:

- **Customer segmentation:** How customers and the market in general will be segmented and served by the organization; reflects the organization's cost leadership, differentiation, focus, defender or prospector direction.

- **Major contact types:** General categories include placing orders, changing orders, checking account status, problem resolution, etc.

- **Access channels:** The organization's communication channels, (e.g., telephone, Web, fax, email, IVR, kiosk, handhelds, face-to-face service, postal mail, etc.) along with corresponding telephone numbers, Web URLs, email addresses, fax numbers and postal addresses.

- **Service level and response time objectives:** How fast the call center intends to respond to customer contacts.

- **Hours of operation:** The days and hours the call center will be open for business.

- **Routing methodology:** How, by customer, type of contact and access channel, each contact will be routed and distributed.

- **Person/technology resources required:** The resources, including people, technologies and databases, required to provide callers with the information and assistance they need, and the organization with the information it needs to track and manage customers and services.

- **Knowledge bases:** The information systems used to capture, store and process information on customers, products and services.

- **Tracking and integration:** The methods/systems required to capture information on each customer interaction, and how that data will be used to strengthen customer profiles, identify trends and improve products and services.

From a customer's perspective, an effective customer access strategy will enable simplified access, consistent services, ease of use and a high degree of convenience and satisfaction; in short, the organization will be easy to do business with. From the organization's perspective, the customer access strategy translates the organization's overall strategic direction into operational realities in the call center, and includes such benefits as lower overall costs, increased capacity, higher customer retention and a workable framework that guides ongoing developments.

Note: Customer access strategy and supporting operational issues are discussed in ICMI's *Call Center Operations Management Handbook and Study Guide* and *Call Center Leadership and Business Management Handbook and Study Guide.*

## 4. Call Center Roles and Responsibilities

Ready? | 1 | 2 | 3 |

### Key Points

- Today's call centers require increasingly demanding skills sets at every level.

- Reporting structures will vary depending on the mission and job types present in the center.

- Typical components of a job description include the job purpose, definition of responsibilites, and skills and experience.

### Explanation

Today's call centers require increasingly demanding knowledge and skills sets, at every level:

- Agents must serve increasingly well-informed and diverse customers; adjust to rapid changes in products, services and technologies; operate in a time-sensitive, multimedia environment; communicate quickly and accurately in both verbal and written forms; understand Web- and IVR-based applications; and help customers use those alternatives.

- The responsibilities of supervisors/team leaders are also increasing, as they assume roles involving data analysis, process improvements and inter-departmental coordination, all of which shape the overall performance of their teams. The ability to assess and improve performance across proliferating contact channels is a central responsibility – and a significant challenge.

- Call center managers and directors find themselves on a path similar to the one chief information officers (CIOs) traveled some 20 years ago. Just as information technology (IT) became the organization's life-blood, call center directors now answer to higher levels of management and are increasingly involved in shaping strategy.

- The demands on analysts, workforce managers, trainers and others are also increasing, commensurate with those faced by agents, supervisors and managers.

With requirements of all personnel levels within the call center snowballing, recruitment, hiring, and training practices all must be continuously updated.

The table below illustrates how job titles and responsibilities are typically defined in larger call centers. Note, the larger the center, the more specialization around specific responsibilities required. Smaller call centers may combine several areas of responsibility into one job title, or may not have a need for the function at all.

Job roles and responsibilities for a large call center include:

| Job | Responsibilities |
|---|---|
| Agent | • Identify and handle customer inquiries<br>• Apply customer service policies<br>• Perform business retention activities<br>• Resolve customer problems<br>• Educate customers on products and services offered<br>• Match product benefits with customer needs<br>• Enter coding and tracking information completely and accurately |
| Team Leader/ Supervisor | • Resolve agent and customer issues<br>• Participate in new-hire interviews<br>• Conduct performance reviews and team meetings; administer rewards<br>• Perform the work of agents during peak periods (in many organizations)<br>• Conduct monitoring and coaching sessions<br>• Coordinate with training and quality assurance to identify systemic quality-improvement opportunities<br>• Represent the team on special projects/initiatives |
| Technical Support Manager | • Maintain existing software/hardware<br>• Recommend technology solutions<br>• Install technology systems and upgrades<br>• Provide technical assistance to operations<br>• Update call-routing tables and systems<br>• Troubleshoot technical problems<br>• Plan and schedule system backup/outages to minimize customer impact |
| Workforce Manager | • Spearhead the call center planning process<br>• Ensure key planning concepts are understood by the entire organization<br>• Ensure call center and staffing models include accurate, updated information<br>• Conduct meetings with relevant departments regarding forecast and workload requirements<br>• Present key performance results to executive management<br>• Research and recommend vendor and software for forecasting and scheduling activities<br>• Train team leaders, managers and trainers on the use of workforce planning tools (e.g., work modes, schedule adherence, etc.)<br>• Provide executive management with reports on workload trends and staffing requirements |

| Workforce Analyst | • Develop reports on daily workload<br>• Participate in forecasting meetings with relevant departments; develop accurate short- and long-term workload forecasts<br>• Control master systems files with schedule information and shift preferences<br>• Serve as initial point of contact for all issues regarding schedules<br>• Process day-off requests and update systems<br>• Determine workforce requirements to meet service level and response time objectives<br>• Determine agent schedules to meet call center objectives |
|---|---|
| Workforce Real-Time Analyst | • Provide intra-day monitoring and reporting<br>• Recommend real-time schedule changes and identify efficiency opportunities<br>• Adjust schedules based on workload/forecast shifts<br>• Update systems with real-time shift adjustment information<br>• Develop and distribute real-time summary reports to management team |
| Training Manager | • Work with operations to determine new-hire and ongoing training needs<br>• Develop or buy appropriate training courses; implement programs<br>• Determine best methods of delivery<br>• Create effectiveness evaluations and update/improve training accordingly<br>• Partner with operations on new initiatives and determine training resources necessary for support |
| Quality Assurance Manager | • Recommend, implement and direct monitoring program (e.g., side-by-side, silent, remote, mystery shopper, etc.)<br>• Work with managers and supervisors/team leaders to calibrate monitoring processes and results<br>• Research and recommend vendors for automated processes<br>• Gather and distribute results<br>• Align internal monitoring with external customer feedback |
| Call Center Manager | • Implement call center strategies and tactics<br>• Establish agent and team objectives<br>• Work with the workforce management team to ensure accurate staffing and scheduling<br>• Work with supervisors/team leaders, analysts and support positions to establish and manage priorities<br>• Coordinate with VP/director and other managers to monitor budget requirements and compliance<br>• Conduct supervisor/team leader performance reviews and administer rewards<br>• Provide on-the-job training and mentoring<br>• Oversee recruiting, hiring and training processes |

*(continued, next page)*

| Vice President/ Director | • Collaborate with senior-level management to determine the strategic direction of the call center<br>• Align call center objectives with enterprise and customer objectives<br>• Oversee implementations of strategies<br>• Develop and manage budgets; secure required resources<br>• Determine and communicate the call center's return on investment to the organization<br>• Oversee recruiting, hiring and training of managerial staff<br>• Conduct performance reviews of managers and administer rewards<br>• Champion the call center throughout internal and external channels |
|---|---|

### Developing Job Descriptions

Job descriptions should reflect the mission of the center and be reviewed on a regular basis to ensure they reflect the current expectations of positions. At a minimum, job descriptions should include:

- **Job purpose:** Summarizes how the position furthers the mission of the organization; i.e., the benefits to the organization's stakeholders, the issues/opportunities addressed by the position and the position's direct and indirect customers.

- **Definition of responsibilities:** Provides a listing of responsibilities and duties from the most important tasks of the position; i.e., the time generally expected to be allocated between key tasks and how each responsibility supports the department's mission.

- **Skills and experience:** Identifies and documents the education, skills and experiences required. This enables those involved in recruiting and hiring to speed these processes and ensure that only qualified candidates are considered.

### Sample Job Descriptions

The following are abbreviated samples of job descriptions for several call center positions. Note: Job descriptions can vary widely depending on the services being provided; e.g., while many agent positions require only high school diplomas, some (i.e., nurse support lines or licensed financial traders) require advanced or specialized degrees.

### Title: Agent

**Job Purpose:** Handles incoming prospect or customer inquiries or concerns and uses company resources and call center policies and procedures to provide complete, accurate responses. Uses call center technologies and follows

processes in accordance with call center standards to ensure contact handling accuracy and operational effectiveness.

**Definition of Responsibilities:**

- Identify and handle customer inquiries completely and accurately.

- Resolve customer complaints and problems to the satisfaction of the customer.

- Use customer service and sales skills to optimize the opportunity of each customer contact.

- Educate the customer about the organization's products and services and direct them toward available resources for self-help.

- Complete necessary documentation to manage customer complaints, issues and subsequent solutions.

- Alert management of issues or concerns that require escalation for complete resolution or which may indicate a larger, underlying problem.

- Schedule, assign or act on any required customer follow-up in accordance with call center guidelines.

- Maximize opportunities to upsell or cross-sell company products and services.

- Enter customer data and other relevant information into call center database or other data repository, as required.

- Suggest call center process improvements and participate in call center initiatives for increased effectiveness.

- Use technology tools as directed and within established guidelines.

- Maintain confidentiality of the organization's customers and data.

- Participate in individual and team trainings and meetings to ensure knowledge is up-to-date.

- Adhere to work schedule as planned.

**Skills and Experience:**

- High school diploma or equivalent

- Exceptional verbal and/or written communication skills

- Ability to organize and communicate information clearly

- Problem-solving and analytical skills

- Positive, professional, customer-oriented attitude

- Accepts coaching and direction

- Customer contact work or relevant service industry experience

- Computer skills, including accurate keyboarding

- Relevant industry experience

**Title: Team Leader/Supervisor**

**Job Purpose:** Manages and directs the activities of the department's agents who provide customer support. Responsible for ensuring resources are utilized efficiently, in accordance with call center objectives and in ways that consistently promote customer quality and satisfaction.

**Definition of Responsibilities:**

- Responsible for the development and motivation of assigned employees, and ensuring they have the necessary tools and information.

- Monitor and document employee performance results.

- Conduct coaching and performance appraisal sessions to identify opportunities and recognize positive behaviors.

- Identify team and individual training needs and develop plans for immediate and long-term performance improvements.

- Proactively solve problems and provide timely resolution to ensure minimal impact to customer and employee satisfaction. Identify the most appropriate course of action for problem resolution and effectively communicate plans to those impacted.

- Provide management support to frontline agents.

- Promote a supportive environment in which employees are encouraged to solve problems and address customer issues.

- Ensure the organization's core values are continually reinforced.

- Monitor and control expenses in support of department's financial goals.

- Participate in special project activities and support teams by providing ad hoc information and reports.

- Coordinate the distribution of employee bonuses and incentives in

accordance with organization guidelines.

- Interview prospective employees and extend job offers.

### Skills and Experience:

- Bachelor's degree or equivalent combination of education and work experience
- Demonstrated ability to think critically and analytically
- Proven ability to organize and clearly communicate thoughts and ideas
- Strong written and verbal communication skills
- Customer contact work (e.g., as an agent)
- Proven supervisory skills
- Experience conducting performance appraisal and delivering coaching
- Computer skills
- Leadership ability
- Relevant industry experience

### Title: Technical Support Manager

**Job Purpose:** Provides technical support for the call center. Coordinates the installation, relocation, maintenance and upgrades of systems that support the delivery of call center services.

### Definition of Responsibilities:

- Responsible for installation and setup of all call center systems.
- Serve as the primary technical point of contact for vendor interactions related to system/software changes and upgrades.
- Respond to internal trouble tickets, and if necessary, coordinate the involvement of other departments to facilitate problem resolution.
- Produce and/or distribute documents that outline technical specification for call center systems and software applications.
- Coordinate the installation, relocation and maintenance activities for systems and software upgrades.
- Responsible for systems maintenance, performance monitoring and troubleshooting.

- Evaluate and provide technical expertise for new products or equipment to support the mission of the call center.

### Skills and Experience:

- Bachelor's degree or applicable technical certifications

- Previous experience providing systems support and maintenance

- Education or experience with call center technology

- Proven supervisory skills

- Experience with budgeting, purchasing and managing vendors

- Basic understanding of staffing and queuing principles*

- Relevant industry experience

*The relationship between staffing and systems issues are discussed in detail in ICMI's *Call Center Operations Management Handbook and Study Guide.*

### Title: Workforce Manager

**Job Purpose:** Partners with the management team to share responsibility for meeting service level and response time objectives across all contact channels. Ensures effective and efficient utilization of resources. Plans, organizes and manages the workload through accurate forecasts, staff calculations, schedules and management reports.

### Definition of Responsibilities:

- Continually improve the forecasting and scheduling predictions across all contact channels.

- Ensure maximum utilization of existing technologies to support efficient traffic distribution and use of staff.

- Develop special forecasts for all operational areas to assist in developing staffing plans for projects as well as ongoing planning.

- Provide ongoing training to the management team and agents on call center dynamics.

- Plan and distribute daily work schedules for agents and provide historical adherence reports to management.

- Monitor real-time queue and adherence reports to ensure service level and response time objectives are met; oversee real-time escalation plans.

- Develop long-term capacity plans and provide accurate workload predictions for annual budgeting and planning.

**Skills and Experience:**

- Bachelor's degree or equivalent combination of education and work experience

- Analytical and mathematical proficiency

- Detail orientation

- Ability to communicate clearly through verbal and written communication

- Relevant customer contact experience

- Computer skills

- Familiarity with call center technology

- Comfortable using forecasting tools/methods

- Familiarity with budgeting and queuing principles

**Title: Call Center Manager**

**Job Purpose:** Plans and manages the operational activities of the call center. Ensures an efficient workload/workforce balance through the effective utilization of assigned resources and administration of activities, in support of the organization's vision, mission and customer access strategies.

**Definition of Responsibilities:**

- Responsible for developing and maintaining the center's customer access channels.

- Provide feedback to unit and team leaders/managers on productivity and quality results.

- Maintain and improve the center's real-time responsiveness.

- Stay current on available technologies and work processes that have potential to improve customer services.

- Ensure workload planning and work schedules support the organization's financial objectives and customer expectations.

- Oversee the training and development of supporting positions in the call center.

- Provide management information and analysis regarding workload, traffic distribution and service performance.

- Develop and maintain departmental budgets. Ensure departments meet financial goals and objectives as outlined by the organization's operational plans.

  - Plan, organize and control resources for optimal utilization to deliver appropriate customer service.

  - Monitor/control service costs by auditing and analyzing expenses and developing plans for corrective action where appropriate.

  - Ensure all access channels provide adequate support of the organization's mission and coordinate activities with all operational and staff areas.

  - Coordinate the distribution of employee bonuses and incentives in accordance with company employees.

- Create and maintain an environment that encourages input from subordinates.

- Interview prospective employees and extend job offers.

**Skills and Experience:**

- Bachelor's degree or equivalent call center experience

- Demonstrated ability to think critically and analytically

- Proven ability to organize and clearly communicate thoughts and ideas

- Strong written and verbal communication skills

- Previous customer contact work

- Supervisory skills

- Proven ability to lead, coach and mentor staff

- Computer skills

- Familiarity with call center technology

- Budgeting experience

- Relevant industry and organizational leadership experience

## 5. Building Effective Agent Groups

Ready? | 1 | 2 | 3 |

### Key Points

- Agent groups are the building blocks of call center structure.

- The most efficient structures typically cross-train agents in order to create pooled agent groups; however, trends toward serving specific customer needs and the requirements for specific skills and abilities are driving more specialized groups.

- There is no ideal formula for deciding how pooled or how specialized agent groups should be. The symptoms of groups that are too pooled or too specialized are relatively easy to identify.

### Explanation

Once the overall strategy and structure is in place, the call center must design appropriate agent groups. Agent groups share a common set of skills and knowledge, handle a specified mix of contacts and can be comprised of hundreds of agents across multiple sites. (Supervisory groups and teams are often subsets of agent groups.) Agent groups are the building blocks of call center structure and must reflect – as necessary – product and service requirements, customer requirements, existing skill sets, experience levels and languages.

The most efficient structures typically pool agents into cross-trained groups, and some have dubbed the "multimedia queue" – the ability to deliver any combination of contact channels to pooled groups of agents – as the ultimate group design.

As the table on the following page illustrates, mathematically, larger groups of pooled agents are more efficient than smaller groups, at the same service level. All other things equal, if you take several small, specialized agent groups, effectively crosstrain them and put them into a single group, the result will be a more efficient environment.

| Calls in 1/2 Hour | Service Level | Agents Required | Occupancy | Avg. Calls Per Agent |
|---|---|---|---|---|
| 50 | 80/20 | 9 | 65% | 5.6 |
| 100 | 80/20 | 15 | 78% | 6.7 |
| 500 | 80/20 | 65 | 90% | 7.7 |
| 1000 | 80/20 | 124 | 94% | 8.1 |

Assumption: Calls last an average 3.5 minutes.

A clear trend in recent years, though, is the recognition that different types of callers often have different needs and expectations, and that different agents with a mix of aptitudes and skills are required to provide the necessary knowledge base. Capabilities in the intelligent network and in intelligent ACDs give call centers the means to pool resources, as well as segment and prioritize their customer base. Skills-based routing is a notable example.

In short, as real and pervasive as the pooling principle is, it is not an all-or-nothing proposition. There is a continuum between pooling and specialization, and there is no ideal formula for deciding how pooled or specialized agent groups should be.

However, the symptoms of groups that are too pooled or too specialized are usually evident. For example, symptoms of agent groups that are too specialized include:

- Small groups with low occupancy and/or erratic service level/response time results

- A planning process that is overly complicated

- Many calls are not handled by the intended group (due to overflow)

- Agents become frustrated with narrow responsibilities

Conversely, symptoms of agent groups that are too generalized include:

- Calls have a higher average handling time than necessary, as agents grapple with a broad range of issues

- There is a high number of transferred calls

- Training time is long

- Quality often suffers

- Agents are frustrated with too much to know

Finding the right group structure for today's complex and multichannel environment requires being in tune with these issues. Structure must support the customer access strategy, as well as reflect the realities of agent skills and the technologies they have to work with. (See Aligning Structure and Strategy, this section.)

Setting up separate groups to handle email and telephone contacts is not likely to be a sustainable approach as contact channels converge. Many call centers are improvising with various degrees of contingency-based routing and varying levels of specialization, but are moving toward pooled groups with universal queues.

---

### The Universal Agent Evolution: Centers Are Adopting a Hybrid Approach

The complexity of the call center environment continues to intensify with agents responsible for handling multiple products and services, multiple customer segments and multiple contact channels.

Over recent years, the definition of a universal agent has expanded with the environment – initially describing agents who could handle all types of inbound phone calls, then adding outbound calls to the mix and, today, including the skills to handle multimedia contacts (phone, email, text-chat, fax and even video) – thus accounting for the more recent moniker, "super agent."

#### A Few Management Challenges

There are seemingly many potential advantages associated with a super agent environment, including service consistency, highly motivated staff, higher first-contact resolution rates and a more flexible workforce.

However, theories don't always translate effortlessly to the actual working environment. According to Jay Minnucci, ICMI's director of consulting, although many managers expect higher overall productivity from super agents, they may find that it actually declines.

"Generalists often operate at lower production rates than specialists because they don't have the opportunity to concentrate on only one task," he points out. "In addition, some productive time is 'lost' to the transition from one task to another – especially when different manual tasks are required to support each of the different channels."

#### The Hybrid Approach

While each call center environment is unique, Minnucci recommends an approach in which centers start out specialized to ensure agents develop expertise with systems, processes and product knowledge. Managers can then ease into a more universal setup by installing systems that can support any degree of specialization at any level, and gradually move toward growing the majority of call center staff into super agents.

---

*(continued, next page)*

"Develop plans and processes that assume a 'mixed' environment – some super agents and some specialists," Minnucci says. "Scheduling, workflow routing, training and compensation are just a few examples of the issues that need to be reviewed to ensure they will fit this type of environment."

First Citizens Bank, headquartered in Raleigh, N.C., evolved its online banking call center as its products developed from dialup, computer-loaded PC software to Internet-based banking applications for both consumers and business. Senior Vice President Mark Coble, who oversees all voice-based and Internet-based sales and support functions, describes the center's setup as a hybrid approach in which agents are generalists, but specialized by product set. Agents are grouped by business and consumer products.

"We don't subscribe in theory to the universal agent concept," Coble says. "There are diminishing returns at some point with that." The key challenges, he says, are agent turnover and constantly evolving products (for instance, the bank's software products are generally upgraded at least once a year).

"Those two dynamics make things very complicated in terms of trying to have that universal agent," he says. "We have to walk a fine line to ensure we're not expecting people to have an overly extensive base of knowledge. We try to balance the skills we think it's reasonable for someone to have versus product knowledge."

Excerpt from "The Universal Agent Evolution: Centers Are Adopting a Hybrid Approach" by Susan Hash, published in *Call Center Management Review*, July 2002.

## 6. Management Ratios (Span of Control) [Strategic]

Ready? | 1 | 2 | 3 |

### Key Points

- When determining management ratios, there are no easy-to-apply rules of thumb.

- Most call centers have between 10 and 20 staff per supervisor, with 12 to 15 being common range. However, ratios vary widely from one organization to another.

- Factors that tend to increase span of control (increase the number of people a manager must supervise) include growing workloads, budget constraints, the growth of teams and lower turnover. Factors that tend to reduce span of control include the growing complexity of contacts, more extensive monitoring and the proliferation of small call centers.

### Explanation

Span of control refers to the number of individuals a manager supervises. A large span of control means that the manager supervises many people. A small span of control means the manager supervisors fewer people. Span of control decreases as the complexity and variability of the conditions in the environment increase.

**Agent-to-Supervisor Ratios**

In call centers, the agent-to-supervisor ratio is an especially important consideration. Effective ratios are dependent on the tasks, standards and responsibilities of both agents and supervisors. Most call centers have between 10 and 20 staff per supervisor, with 12 to 15 being the most common range.

However, there are notable differences by industry. For example, mutual funds and insurance companies tend to be on the low end of that spectrum (have smaller spans of control), while catalog companies and telecommunications services providers tend to be on the high end. Further, there can be significant exceptions; e.g., some reservations centers have a relatively large span of control, sometimes 40 or more staff per supervisor. And technical support centers and other complex environments can have as few as five staff per supervisor. Even

within an industry, there can be a wide variance (one well-known catalog company has 40 agents per supervisor, while another has 10).

### Trends Influencing Span of Control

Be careful about drawing quick conclusions based on these figures or industry benchmarks. There are no simple answers along the lines of, "If you are a such and such type of call center, you ought to have X staff per supervisor." Some of today's trends are working to drive the span of control up, including:

- **Growing workloads:** In many environments, the call center's workload continues to increase. As call centers struggle to keep up with growth, the span of control tends to increase.

- **Budget constraints:** As organizations have gone through restructurings, budget freezes and, in some cases, cutbacks, they have reduced the relative number of supervisors (increased spans of control). Many managers admit they would ideally adjust span of control downward, but insist that funds simply are not available for more supervisor/manager positions.

- **Growth of teams:** A positive development has been the growth of team-based environments, which has challenged the traditional role of supervisors. Call centers are generally moving away from production-oriented "factories" toward organizations that are flatter and more team-oriented. (See Forms of Organizational Structures, this section.) Teams of agents are assuming functions that traditionally have been in the domain of management and supervision: planning, organizing, coordinating, directing and controlling.

- **Lower turnover:** Another positive development is that a growing number of call centers are directly and successfully reducing turnover. As the average experience level of agents moves upward, less supervision is generally required. (See Effective Agent Retention Strategies, Section 4.)

Other developments in today's environment tend to drive span of control down, including:

- **The growing complexity of contacts:** As better-applied technologies offload routine calls and as new channels of contact proliferate, agents are handling contacts that require more human "know-how." The growing complexity of the workload inherently requires more supervision, coaching and feedback.

- **More monitoring, more extensively:** There are more call centers

monitoring agents today than five or 10 years ago. Monitoring, feedback and coaching take a significant amount of time. (See the discussion on monitoring, Section 6.)

- **More small call centers:** This may be the biggest reason that the average ratio across the industry has moved down – there are simply more small groups in the sample. For example, if a new call center has only seven or eight agents, it will still likely have a supervisor even though that person will be able to supervise more people as the center grows.

There are potentially other factors that can confuse the issue of ratios. For example, the tasks of supervisors vary widely from one organization to the next. Some lean more toward "lead agent" responsibilities, in which they lead a team but also help handle the workload while others are much more involved in management responsibilities. Further, the time that supervisors spend monitoring and coaching (the most time-consuming supervisory responsibilities in most call centers) can vary by many multiples. Some organizations have set up internal help desks to field calls from agents who have trouble handling contacts – a responsibility traditionally handled by supervisors.

Recommendations in general business literature vary from the "train them, empower them and get out of the way" school of thought on one end of the spectrum to a more structured approach on the other. In the respected book, *Executive Leadership*, Elliot Jacques and Stephen D. Clement mince no words: "There is more nonsense centering around the topic of span of control than around nearly any other subject in the whole field of organization and management." They go on to criticize managers who search for "easy-to-apply rules of thumb which need no thought." That is true in the call center environment; while 12 or 14 agents per supervisor makes sense in many call centers, a 5:1 or 25:1 ratio may be equally justifiable.

**Supervisor-to-Manager Ratios**

In terms of supervisor-to-management spans of control, ratios of between 5:1 and 12:1 are typical. Give the higher level and more complex interactions that must take place between managers and supervisors, spans of control are smaller than those for agents/supervisors. That underscores a principle generally true in most organizations: the higher up in the organization, the smaller the spans of control.

## 7. The Job Evaluation Process

Ready?  | 1 | 2 | 3 |

### Key Points

- Job evaluation is the process of identifying and describing jobs, and determining the relative worth or value of a job to the organization.

- The six steps of the job evaluation process include:
    1. Analyze the job
    2. Write the job description
    3. List the job specifications
    4. Rate the job
    5. Develop a job hierarchy
    6. Classify jobs into grades

### Explanation

Jobs and responsibilities are traditionally described and rated through a job evaluation process. Job evaluation is the process of determining the relative worth or value of a job to the organization. The end result is to achieve internal equity of jobs within a pay structure.

*(Note: There are many opponents of this traditional job evaluation approach. Concerns with these systems – common in government, large organizations and union environments – generally fall into two categories: 1) concern that they are overly rigid, and 2) concern that pay grades don't accurately reflect fair market value of positions. While any organization needs a consistent approach for determining pay scales and job worth, a trend in many organizations in recent years has been to move away from the most formal, inflexible types of job grading systems.)*

There are six steps of the traditional job evaluation process:

**1. Analyze the job:** This includes the collection and analysis of information regarding a job's responsibilities, duties, tasks and elements so managers can understand how the jobs are performed. It is a component of human resources (HR) planning, selection, training and development, compensation, and performance reviews. Call center managers have the responsibility of working with the HR department to accurately define what the job responsibilities, duties and tasks are, as well as the desired outcomes/results of the job.

**2. Write the job description:** The results of the job analysis are synthesized into a job description. The job description contains a summary statement of the intent of the job, a listing of responsibilities and job duties. Call center managers have the responsibility to ensure that all job responsibilities accurately reflect the purpose and objectives of the organization.

**3. List the job specifications:** This is a list of job requirements, such as years of experience, years of education and area of study, certificates, skills, etc. This information is used to determine the value of the job, which impacts pay and qualifications for hiring.

**4. Rate the job:** This step determines the relative value of the job (not an individual) to the organization. Common compensable factors include knowledge (e.g., of the market, organization, systems/processes, etc.), educational level, skills, financial responsibilities, span of control, working conditions, customer service and influence.

Different job classifications (e.g., technical, managerial, sales) have different compensable factors. Compensable factors are usually weighted by assigning a number and degree. This provides a figure that represents the relative value of jobs within the same job classification. Then, the job is given a value and degree.

A formal system, called points by degree, is usually found in larger, more hierarchical organizations. While many organizations use a less formal approach to value jobs, the intent is the same: determine the relative value of the job to the organization.

**5. Develop a job hierarchy:** This is a listing of jobs in order of their importance, based on their total number of points, from the highest to lowest.

**6. Classify jobs into grades:** Based on the number of points, jobs are grouped into grades. Jobs within the same grade are judged to be of the same relative value to the organization. Once you have the grades established, the worth of each grade is determined.

Each grade is given a minimum, midpoint and maximum dollar value. There is no standard spread between the minimum and maximum. It is based on the organization's overall compensation philosophy and strategy, and on the nature of the jobs.

Where such grading systems exist, when a person reaches the top of a grade, they must either settle for cost-of-living adjustments, have the job re-evaluated based on additional responsibilities or look for a promotion.

Many managers wanting to retain agents who have reached the top of pay grades are working to reclassify jobs.

When comparing jobs with those of other organizations for external equity, the sequence of steps generally includes:

- Compare job responsibilities to be sure the jobs are the same.

- Determine the difference in compensation.

- Present findings to managers involved in establishing compensation; make a decision about whether or not to adjust compensation.

- If the decision is made to raise wages, adjust accordingly.

## 8. Components of a Strategic Staffing Plan [Strategic]

Ready? | 1 | 2 | 3

### Key Points

- A strategic staffing plan is a forecast of future staffing requirements – which includes quantity and qualifications – generally over a one- to three-year timeframe.

- The plan focuses on three major issues:
    1. The number of staff required
    2. Required staff qualifications and associated development plans
    3. Feasible workforce mix and scheduling alternatives

- Because of the importance of the strategic staffing plan – as well as the significant level of funding generally required – it is necessary to garner support for staffing plans from top-level management.

### Explanation

Anywhere from 60 percent to 70 percent of the costs required to operate a call center are related to staffing expenses. The development of an effective staffing plan is therefore a significant part of the organization's success.

A strategic staffing plan is a forecast of future staffing requirements – which includes quantity and qualifications – generally over a one- to three-year timeframe. The plan focuses on three major issues: 1) the number of staff required, 2) required staff qualifications and associated development plans, and 3) feasible workforce mix and scheduling alternatives.

The first major focus is to forecast the number of full-time equivalents (FTEs) required to handle the expected workload. (See Strategic Staffing: Predicting FTEs, this section.) This is then compared to the amount of expected staff on board – current staff minus existing staff based on the historical turnover factor. (See Calculating and Tracking Turnover Rate, Section 4.) The difference will determine the timing of new-hires and associated training classes. Key steps include:

- Establishing service level and response time objectives

- Forecasting the workload, which includes historical information on call volume and average handling time as well as changing factors that will affect the workload (e.g., marketing, new products and services)

- Calculating base staff and trunk requirements

- Determining rostered staff factors (shrinkage)

- Assessing support staff requirements

- Reviewing scalability alternatives

The second area of focus in strategic staff planning is to assess required staff qualifications and associated development plans (See Strategic Staffing: Required Qualification and Development Plans, this section). Key considerations include:

- Call center roles and responsibilities

- Job descriptions

- Recruitment and hiring strategies

- Training and development requirements

- Retention strategies

The third area of the staffing plan focuses on the workforce mix and scheduling alternatives (See Strategic Staffing: Workforce Mix and Scheduling Alternatives, this section). Major steps involve:

- Developing an appropriate workforce mix

- Identifying feasible scheduling alternatives

- Scheduling parameters

**Creating a Base of Support**

Because of the importance of the strategic staffing plan – as well as the significant level of funding generally required – it is necessary to garner support for staffing plans from top-level management. Helpful steps include:

- Get a senior management sponsor to support the plan. Then broaden that support to include others in senior management.

- Determine who needs to be involved in the development of the plan. This may include managers from marketing, customer service, sales, product development, human resources and elsewhere. Input from frontline agents should also be sought, particularly in areas of scheduling and retention.

- To implement the staffing plan, develop strategies and tactics with timelines and designated responsibilities.

- Determine how you will measure the progress and success of the staffing plan, and identify actions to take if you get off course.

- Develop methods to adjust the plan as circumstances evolve.

It is important that budget not be a major consideration in the initial stages of developing a strategic staffing plan. The plan is a baseline that should be built on expected workload and staff requirements. The budget is a resource plan that includes the business case to secure the resources required to implement the staffing plan. Developing the staffing plan comes first, then the budget. The budget should not, at this point, dictate the staffing plan.

**Section 3**

## 9. Strategic Staffing: Predicting FTEs

Ready? | 1 | 2 | 3 |

### Key Points

- Determining full-time equivalent (FTE) requirements is a process built on a combination of scientific calculations, business decisions and sound judgment. It depends on good communication and a solid understanding of resource tradeoffs.

- The process inherently involves virtually every aspect of operating a call center, including setting service level objectives, forecasting, scheduling and budgeting.

- Effective staffing and planning require that decision-makers have a good understanding of the unique call center environment.

### Explanation

Predicting short- and long-term staffing requirements is an important part of developing a strategic staffing plan – and is a management responsibility that is fundamental to operating an effective call center. The process involves establishing the call center's mission, predicting the workload, defining agent groups, identifying required skills, determining staff and schedule requirements, and anticipating costs. In short, it spans virtually every aspect of operating a call center.

Determining quantitative staffing requirements – typically represented as full time equivalents (FTEs) – is a multifaceted process laden with both science and judgment. The steps based firmly on science (formulas, principles or immutable laws that yield predictable results) tend to be the most straightforward. Those that require decisions around tradeoffs and unknowns tend to be more difficult and time-consuming. Knowing where judgment comes in vs. the analysis best left to science is a challenge, but it's an important prerequisite to developing an appropriate budget. The following summarizes this process.

Section 3

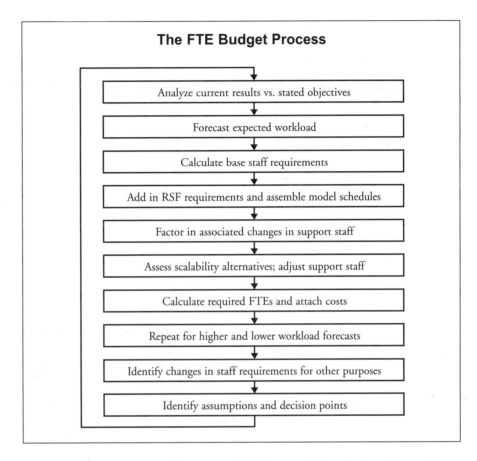

1. **Analyze current results vs. stated objectives:** What is the call center's mission? What are the supporting objectives for service level, response time and quality? Are you meeting them? Why or why not? Was the budget from the last cycle appropriate? Did you forecast requirements accurately? What adjustments to the budget would you have made? Could you have better predicted outcomes? What can you learn this time around? What is the nature of new marketing campaigns? This important first step includes some scientific analysis, but is largely based on business decisions.

2. **Forecast expected workload:** The principles of time-series forecasting (based on historical data), regression analysis (e.g., contacts vs. new customers) and other types of quantitative forecasts are grounded in science. However, virtually all forecasts also require some judgment. For example, how will the call mix change as Web traffic grows? How should you structure agent groups, (one crosstrained group requires one forecast while many specialized groups require many specific forecasts)? What

impact will changes in marketing, competitor activities, laws, consumer behavior and other developments have on the workload? Also remember, forecasting involves more than simply predicting the number of contacts; the process must also anticipate the expected handling time of those contacts.

**3. Calculate base staff requirements:** Staff calculations are relatively straightforward and firmly based on science. Granted, all mathematical formulas or simulation models contain assumptions (e.g., for busy signals and abandoned calls). But the resources it will take to consistently achieve service level and response time objectives is a matter of mathematics.

Note: Staff calculations must be based on the Erlang C formula, some derivative of that formula or on a simulation model. Calculating staff using simple arithmetic will not work because of the complexity involved in random call arrival and the consideration of occupancy rates. For a complete discussion of calculating staff, see ICMI's *Call Center Operations Management Handbook and Study Guide.*

**4. Add in rostered staff factor (RSF) requirements and assemble model schedules:** RSF (also called an "overlay" or "shrink factor") leads to the minimum staff needed on schedule over and above base staff required. Although planning around issues such as schedule adherence and nonphone activities requires judgment, the RSF calculations themselves are straightforward and reliable. Defining schedule alternatives and coverage rules, on the other hand, tends to be more of an iterative, creative process.

**5. Factor in associated changes in support staff:** What should your staff-to-supervisor ratio be? How should the call center be organized? What analyst roles are necessary? This step depends more on observation, experience and good business sense than on science.

**6. Assess scalability alternatives; adjust support staff:** Scalability refers to the call center's ability to expand or contract without making changes in FTEs. For example, can other departments help handle the load when the call center is busy? What other staffing contingencies are available? How committed is the organization to consistently meeting service level and quality objectives? These are business decisions.

**7. Calculate required FTEs and attach costs:** At this point, FTE and cost calculations are relatively straightforward. They are, of course, built on all of the assumptions that have come before.

**8. Repeat for higher and lower workload forecasts:** This step acknowledges any uncertainties in forecasts and is geared around different assumptions for workload.

**9. Identify changes in staff requirements for other purposes:** As in step five, identifying the needs for staff not directly associated with handling the workload is largely a matter of experience and observation.

**10. Identify assumptions and decision points:** In this final, critical step, you do an inventory of the assumptions made along the way. Not only will this be useful for those involved in financial decisions, it will create an efficient basis for discussing key issues and coming to agreements. Most importantly, it will increase everybody's understanding of key tradeoffs and improve the overall quality of the final budget.

Note: Resource planning subjects, such as forecasting, staffing and scheduling are covered extensively in ICMI's *Call Center Operations Management Handbook and Study Guide*. For more information on budgeting, see ICMI's *Call Center Leadership and Business Management Handbook and Study Guide*.

**No Magic Formula**

New managers often ask for "the formula" to calculate future staff requirements. Unfortunately, there's no such thing. Instead, this is a process built on a combination of scientific calculations, business decisions and sound judgment. It depends on good communication and a solid understanding of the tradeoffs. And it requires that every decision-maker have a good understanding of what makes call centers operate effectively.

A particularly effective approach to explaining staffing requirements to decision-makers is to begin by illustrating today's baseline. In other words, if you don't get one single additional contact – if everything remains as is – what would the ideal staffing plan look like? You can then discuss anticipated efficiency gains for upcoming timeframes included in the forecasts, and illustrate the additional contacts to be handled and associated resource requirements. The baseline (what's happening today) establishes a "stake in the ground" for resource discussions, and helps put additional staffing requirements in context.

## 10. Strategic Staffing: Required Qualifications and Development Plans [Strategic]

Ready? | 1 | 2 | 3 |

### Key Points

* The second area of focus in strategic staffing is to determine the qualifications and development plans for staff required.

* This step involves bringing up-to-date and/or developing required roles and responsibilities, job descriptions, recruiting and hiring strategies, training and development requirements, and retention strategies.

### Explanation

The second area of focus in strategic staff planning is to assess required staff qualifications. Key considerations and areas of update/development (as required) include:

* Call center roles and responsibilities (See Aligning Structure and Strategy, this section.)

* Job descriptions (See Call Center Roles and Responsibilities, this section.)

* Recruitment and hiring strategies (See Creating and Implementing a Recruiting Plan, Section 4.)

* Training and development requirements (See discussions on training and performance issues, Sections 5 and 6.)

* Retention strategies (See Effective Agent Retention Strategies, Section 4.)

## 11. Strategic Staffing: Workforce Mix and Scheduling Alternatives

Ready? | 1 | 2 | 3 |

Section 3

### Key Points

- After the quantitative and qualitative staffing requirements are determined, the workforce mix and feasible scheduling alternatives are identified and addressed.

- Creativity is essential; in today's environment, many alternatives are available for meeting the workforce requirements of call centers.

- Important scheduling parameters include the scheduling horizon, agent preferences, union and legal requirements, and the special considerations of 24x7 operations.

### Explanation

After the quantitative and qualitative staffing requirements are determined, the workforce mix and feasible scheduling alternatives are identified and addressed. In today's environment, there are – with some creativity and effort – many alternatives available to managers of call centers.

#### Developing an Appropriate Workforce Mix

The type of workforce can be divided into core or full-time employees, and contingent workers (part-time, temporary, contractors, on-call workers, etc.). Primary alternatives include:

- **Full-time or core employees:** Generally, these workers put in 40 hours per week and enjoy the full benefits of the organization. They provide stability to meet ongoing workload demands.

- **Temporary staff:** These agents are usually assigned to short-term projects or seasonal workloads. In most cases, they are employees of a staffing agency, but may become a source for employee recruitment. (See Temporary, Contracted and Managed Staff, Section 4.)

- **Part-time employees:** These employees work fewer hours than full-time employees and may receive fewer benefits.

- **Contract workers:** These workers contract with the organization for specific projects or predefined periods of time. They are self-employed,

often have special knowledge and skills, and may have other clients. (See Temporary, Contracted and Managed Staff, Section 4.)

- **College interns:** Interns generally require more initial supervision but can be an excellent source of support. They also may become a source for recruitment.

- **Service bureaus:** Today, service bureaus of all types and capabilities are available. Some can handle contacts of virtually any type or degree of complexity (See Service Bureaus, Section 4.)

- **On-call workers:** These are individuals who are ready to respond to high call demand. They may be former agents who are now in other departments.

### Identifying Feasible Scheduling Alternatives

In addition to the workforce mix, available work schedules must also be developed. Requirements are dictated by the center's hours of operation and workload patterns, but the needs of the staff must also be considered when creating schedules. Quite a few alternatives exist, though not all are feasible in every case. This aspect of planning involves identifying the scheduling approaches that are feasible in your environment. Alternatives include:

- **Conventional shifts:** Most call centers have a core group of agents who work traditional five-day-a-week shifts during "normal hours" (e.g., 9 a.m. to 5 p.m.).

- **Staggered shifts:** For example, one shift begins at 7 a.m., the next at 7:30 a.m., the next at 8 a.m., until the center is fully staffed for the busy mid-morning traffic. This is a common and effective approach. These shifts should be periodically adjusted as workload patterns change.

- **Flex-time scheduling:** This alternative is most often used when workload patterns change significantly from week to week. Several weeks in advance, agents are promised schedules within a window of time (e.g., only Tuesdays through Saturdays or from 8 a.m. to 8 p.m. any day of the week), according to their personal availability. Then, specific work hours, and in some cases, days worked, are determined from week to week as forecasted staff requirements are refined. This approach may involve the entire staff, but usually includes only a subset of employees.

- **"Internal" part-timers:** This approach is sometimes called the "reinforcement method." When contact-handling duties are combined with other types of tasks, such as correspondence, outbound calling or data-entry, the agents assigned to these collateral duties can act as

reinforcements when the calling load gets heavy. This is like being able to bring in part-timers on an hourly, half-hourly or even five-minute basis.

- **"Swat Team":** This approach takes the reinforcement method one step further. For example, some financial organizations keep service levels high by calling in "reservists," non-call center employees from other departments to help when significant changes in stock markets cause call volumes to soar.

- **Concentrated shifts:** Given the choice, some agents prefer to work fewer days, with more hours per day. Others prefer to work fewer hours in a day, even if that means a six- or seven-day work week. "Four-by-10" shifts (four days on for 10 hours each, with three days off) are particularly popular with many agents. (An important consideration is whether they can handle the longer hours without losing effectiveness.)

- **Overtime:** No additional training is required and many agents will volunteer for the extra work. (However, overtime can be expensive as an ongoing strategy. Further, as with concentrated shifts, an important consideration is whether agents can remain effective in extended hours.)

- **Option to go home, without pay:** This is a popular strategy on slower days, and there are usually enough agents willing to take you up on it. It's something referred to as LWOP (leave without pay, pronounced "el-wop").

- **Split shifts:** Split shifts, in which agents work a partial shift, take part of the day off, then return later to finish their shift, are not common. But don't count this alternative out all together; it works well in some situations. If you hire college students, for example, they may prefer to work in the mornings and evenings, leaving afternoons free for classes.

- **Telecommuting program:** This is not a scheduling alternative, per se, but it can provide an environment in which unpopular shifts can be more palatable and enable agents to begin handling the workload on short notice.

- **Service bureau:** Arrangements can be made to send all or some call center traffic to a service bureau, either on a scheduled basis or as circumstances dictate. Coordination and capacity capabilities must be determined in advance.

**Scheduling Parameters**

As you identify scheduling alternatives, there are a number of other parameters to consider:

- **Scheduling horizon:** How far in advance you determine schedules is the schedule horizon. If you schedule further out, say for six month blocks of time, schedules will be less efficient; they will be locked in place, even if call load deviates from the forecast. But a big plus is that they will be more agreeable to your staff, who prefer to know their work schedules well in advance. On the other hand, if you use a shorter timeframe, the scheduling process will be less popular with some agents, but schedules will likely be more accurate. So, this issue is a balancing act.

- **Agent preferences:** Obviously, schedules have to work for both the call center and individuals. Generally, the greater the degree of staff input when establishing schedules, the greater the buy-in.

- **Union and legal requirements:** Any union or legal restrictions on part-time staff, hours worked and overtime pay will impact the alternatives you can use. If you are in a union environment, union representatives should be involved in scheduling decisions upfront.

- **24x7 operations:** There are special considerations for 24x7 operations. Key considerations include:

  - Employee safety

  - Variations in daily call arrival patterns (e.g., is the volume at night low enough that agent groups should be combined?)

  - Agent productivity by shift (e.g., productivity standards and staffing calculations must account for workload variations)

  - Night coverage for meals/breaks

  - Night coverage for absenteeism

Other scheduling alternatives/considerations are of a more tactical nature; e.g. adjusting breaks, lunch, meeting and training schedules, forecasting and planning for regular collateral work, etc.

(Staffing and scheduling are covered in detail in ICMI's *Call Center Operations Management Handbook and Study Guide*.)

# Organizational Design and Strategic Staffing

### Exercises

**Principles of Call Center Organizational Design [Strategic]**

1. True or false

_____Once the call center's place in the larger organization is defined, the call center's organizational structure should be built beginning with the agent groups and moving upward.

**Forms of Organizational Structures [Strategic]**

2. Select the most appropriate answer to each question.

One disadvantage of the following structure is that it can be at odds with a culture of empowerment and participative management:

    a. Bureaucratic

    b. Flat

    c. Matrix

    d. Team-oriented

The following structure generally results in less administrative overhead costs, but usually requires more training:

    a. Bureaucratic

    b. Flat

    c. Matrix

    d. Team-oriented

It can be especially difficult to reward individual contributions in which of the following two structures:

    a. Geographic-oriented and flat

    b. Matrix and bureaucratic

    c. Team-oriented and flat

    d. Team-oriented and bureaucratic

**Aligning Structure and Strategy [Strategic]**

3. Match the following types of strategy with the recommended structure to achieve that strategy. You will use some structures more than once.

_____Cost leadership      a. Bureaucratic

_____Defender      b. Flat or team-oriented

_____Differentiation      c. Product- or service-oriented, geographic-oriented or customer-oriented

_____Focus

_____Prospector

**Building Effective Agent Groups**

4. True or false

_____Mathematically, smaller groups of specialized agents are more efficient than larger groups of pooled agents, at the same service level.

5. Beside each statement below, indicate whether it is a symptom of agent groups that are too specialized (with an "s") or too generalized (with a "g").

_____A planning process that is overly complicated

_____Agents are frustrated with too much to know

_____Agents become frustrated with narrow responsibilities

_____Calls have a higher average handling time than necessary, as agents grapple with a broad range of issues

_____Many calls are not handled by the intended group (due to overflow)

_____Quality often suffers

_____Small groups with low occupancy and/or erratic service level/response time results

_____There is a high number of transferred calls

_____Training time is long

**Management Ratios (Span of Control) [Strategic]**

6.  Select the most appropriate answer to each question.

Although effective ratios are dependent on the tasks, standards and responsibilities of both agents and supervisors, most call centers have between:

  a. 5 and 10 staff per supervisor

  b. 10 and 20 staff per supervisor

  c. 12 and 25 staff per supervisor

The following is a trend that drives the span of control down (fewer staff per supervisor):

  a. Budget constraints

  b. Lower turnover

  c. More monitoring, more extensively

**The Job Evaluation Process**

7. Put the six steps of the job evaluation process in order by placing a number (1-6) in the blank beside each one.

_____Analyze the job

_____Classify jobs into grades

_____Develop a job hierarchy

_____List the job specifications

_____Rate the job

_____Write the job description

**Components of a Strategic Staffing Plan [Strategic]**

8. True or false

_____An effective staffing plan should begin with the budget allocated for the business unit and then adjust as needed.

**Answers to these exercises are in Section 10.**

Note: These exercises are intended to help you retain the material learned. While not the exact questions as on the CIAC Certification assessment, the material in this handbook/study guide fully addresses the content on which you will be assessed. For a formal practice test, please contact the CIAC directly by visiting www.ciac-cert.org.

## Organizational Design and Strategic Staffing
## Reference Bibliography

Related Articles from *Call Center Management Review*
(See Section 9)

Maximizing the Value of Your Workforce Management Team

## For Further Study

### Books/Studies

Cleveland, Brad and Julia Mayben. *Call Center Management on Fast Forward: Succeeding in Today's Dynamic Inbound Environment.* Call Center Press, 1999.

DeNisi, Angelo, and Ricky Griffin. *Human Resource Management.* Houghton Mifflin Company, 2001.

Jacques, Elliot and Stephen D. Clement. *Executive Leadership: A Practical Guide to Managing Complexity.* Cason Hall & Co. Publishers, 1991.

Kaplan, Robert S. and David P. Norton. *The Strategy Focused Organization.* Harvard Business School Press, 2000.

Mintzberg, Henry, Bruce Ahlstrand and Joseph Lampel. *Strategy Safari: A Guided Tour Through the Wilds of Strategic Management.* Simon & Schuster, 1998.

Mintzberg, Henry. *Structure in Fives: Designing Effective Organizations.* Prentice Hall, 1992.

Treacy, Michael and Fred Wiersema. *The Discipline of Market Leaders.* Perseus Press, 1997.

### Articles

Hash, Susan. "The Universal Agent Evolution: Centers Are Adopting a Hybrid Approach." *Call Center Management Review*, July 2002.

Katzenbach, Jon R. and Smith, Douglas K. "The Discipline of Teams." *Harvard Business Review*, March/April 1993.

**Section 3**

### Seminars

*Effective Leadership and Strategy for Senior Call Center Managers* public seminar, presented by Incoming Calls Management Institute.

# Hiring and Retention

## Section 4: Hiring and Retention

## Contents

## 1. Creating and Implementing a Recruiting Plan     Ready? | 1 | 2 | 3 |

### Key Points

- Recruiting is the process of developing a pool of qualified candidates who are interested in working for your call center.

- There are six fundamental steps in a sound recruitment and selection process:
    1. Analyze job tasks
    2. Identify specific skills and competencies required
    3. Describe the performance required by the job
    4. Develop a job description
    5. Identify source pools and create a recruitment plan
    6. Define and implement the selection process

### Explanation

Recruiting is the process of developing a pool of qualified candidates who are interested in working for your call center. Recruiting is a two-way street; just as you are looking for qualified candidates, those individuals are also looking for the right employer. Consequently, the two primary goals of recruiting include:

1. Develop a pool of qualified candidates for the organization

2. Provide realistic job previews to candidates – honest and candid assessments of what kinds of jobs and opportunities are potentially available

As with many other aspects of call center management, recruiting is most effective when it is driven by a practical, proven process. The following process is drawn from "How to Develop a Retention-Oriented Agent Recruiting and Selection Process" by Anita O'Hara, published in *Call Center Management Review.*

*(continued, next page)*

## A Six-Step Recruiting and Selection Process

**1. Analyze job tasks:** Begin by taking a detailed look at your top-performing agents. Consider both the efficiency and effectiveness with which they perform their tasks. It may also be useful to re-review your star agents' resumes. Also, take the time to observe and conduct follow-up interviews with a group of "experts" performing their jobs. Try to identify common tasks they perform well.

**2. Identify specific skills and competencies required:** Use this analysis to create a list of skills that are critical, such as communication and articulation, analytical skills, organizational skills, call center or customer service experience, listening skills and computer skills. If you are creating a customer service organization from the ground up and have no stars from whom to create a standard, try benchmarking with a similar type of company. Generally, you'll find that, regardless of industry, call center managers are looking for agents with similar skills.

**3. Describe the performance required by the job:** Next, consider which competencies or behaviors you want your prospective employees to demonstrate. A few common competencies include: positive attitude, flexibility, teamwork and cooperation, customer orientation, self-reliance and stamina. There are a variety of companies that can help you to identify these and which can even create a hiring instrument that will improve your retention rates.

**4. Develop a job description:** Once you know what type of agent you're looking for, you can identify the type of performance required and write your job description. At this stage, you're prioritizing your desired and required skills and competencies, describing the work environment in which employees will coexist, identifying the scope and breadth of the job (e.g., what kinds of decisions will prospective agents make).

In addition, this is the point at which you should identify the agents' pay structure. It's best to include two key groups in this process – HR and senior leadership. Human resources can help to assess compensation in the external market. They can also help to price your jobs comparable to other jobs within the organization. The senior leadership team can help you to identify your pay strategy. That is, do you want to be the employer of choice or simply pay the market average? (See Compensation-Related Factors, Section 7.)

**5. Identify source pools and a recruitment plan:** Every staff selection strategy should include recruitment sources as well as a selection plan. It's important to track your sources and analyze their success over time. For each candidate hired, be sure to track and record the following: 1) source; 2) performance; 3) attendance record; and 4) tenure.

In this manner, you can determine the success of each source. If one source yields consistently high-performing agents who stay, keep using it. If, on the other hand, a source results in an agent pool that regularly turns over, it's time to stop recruiting through that source. (See Sources and Methods for Recruiting, this section.)

**6. Define and implement your selection process:** The most common pitfall managers make during the final selection is to put too much weight on a single facet of the screening/interview process. For instance, a candidate may be terrified by the job interview, yet have an excellent background, great references, score well on the behavioral screen, and may have presented himself in an excellent fashion during the phone screen. Consider all parts of the process, as well as the weight you will attach to each, before making your final selection. (See Conduting Effective Interviews, this section.)

Excerpts from "How to Develop a Retention-Oriented Agent Recruiting and Selection Process" by Anita O'Hara, *Call Center Management Review*, April 2001.

**Determining the Required Number of New-Hires**

Part of any effective recruiting strategy is an accurate forecast of the number of new-hires required and when they will need to be hired. This forecast should be based on the expected turnover rate and growth rate (positive or negative) of required full-time equivalents (FTEs). (See Strategic Staffing: Predicting FTEs, Section 3.)

The following considerations should also be a part of determining the new-hire requirements:

- Seasonality of turnover

- Scheduling considerations (e.g., number of part-timers for flexibility, shift requirements or the use of temporary staff)

- Length of new-hire training

- Percentage of new-hires that do not successfully complete new-hire training

For example, Call Center A currently has 100 agents with a past turnover rate of 15% for the month of April. The call center will begin to support two new product lines in June and, based on the increased workload, expects a need of 20 additional full-time equivalents (FTEs) based on a 40 hour work week. Since the new-hire training period lasts 6 weeks, these new employees need to be hired in April. Past experience has shown that scheduling is most effective if about 10% of the FTE requirement is made up of agents who work 20 hours each.

This scenario would result in the need of a total of 37 new-hires – 15 agents because of attrition, and 18 full-time agents (40 hours per week) and 4 part-time agents (20 hours per week) because of the new product lines.

The timeframe for setting goals for number of new-hires should be calculated on a monthly, quarterly or yearly basis depending on the size of the call center and seasonal considerations.

**Site Selection Considerations**

The ability to recruit the required workforce is heavily influenced by the location of the call center. If recruiting sources are chronically unable to produce the necessary number of appropriately skilled staff, moving the call center to another location may make sense.

Some site selection considerations that impact recruiting include:

- Labor pool

- Unemployment and underemployment rates

- Population growth (number of new residents versus residents that are leaving)

- Compensation rates for the area

- Educational level of labor pool

- Languages spoken by labor pool (if multiple languages are a requirement)

- The labor pool's perceived prestige of the organization or desirability of the position

(For more information on site selection, see ICMI's *Call Center Operations Management Handbook and Study Guide.*)

## 2. Sources and Methods for Recruiting

### Key Points

- There are many sources of candidates and many possible methods of recruiting. Organizations with the most successful recruiting programs track and assess the success rates of each method, and correlate the performance of new-hires to recruiting sources.

- Recruiting for diversity may require targeted recruiting campaigns.

### Explanation

To support the recruiting process, there are a number of sources you can use to develop a pool of candidates, including:

- **Current employees:** The organization's current employees usually hear about job openings from an internal job posting system.

- **Referrals from current employees:** Generally, new-hires who result from referrals of current employees have greater loyalty, tenure and job satisfaction than those from other recruiting sources. (Key reason: current employees provide the most realistic job preview.)

- **Former employees:** These could be temporaries, those who were laid off, those who quit but wish to return, or contractors.

- **Customers:** Customers are familiar with products and services and often have insights into how you can improve customer service.

- **Competitors:** New-hires from competitors can provide valuable experience to the organization.

- **Schools/local colleges:** Many schools have intern programs that enable interns to gain experience, organizations to benefit from their contribution and the potential for future recruitment and full employment. A growing number of local colleges also have call center or customer service programs.

- **Staff-sharing:** Staff-sharing is when call centers with complementary busy seasons form a staffing alliance to help each center cost-effectively handle the workload. (See Staff-Sharing Arrangements, this section.)

- **Disabled candidates:** Physically disabled candidates represent an

excellent and largely untapped pool of candidates for many call centers.

- **Employment agencies:** Many call centers use external resources for recruitment especially those specializing in call centers.

### Methods of Recruiting

Just as there are many sources of candidates, there are many related methods of recruiting. Examples include:

- Internal job postings; e.g., through an Intranet

- Recommendations by a team leader, supervisor or manager

- The union hall

- The organization's Web site

- Career/job sites on the Internet

- Employment agencies

- Print advertisements; e.g., local and national papers, professional journals, trade magazines, inserts in catalogs and sales flyers

- Job fairs

- Mall handouts

How do you know which method is most effective? What criteria should be used to evaluate the sources and methods? Some factors to consider when determining the most effective methods include:

- Average cost per hire

- Tenure

- Job performance issues:
  - The time it takes for a new-hire to become fully productive
  - The candidate's previous job performance
  - The candidate's current job performance

- Ability to match candidates to position requirements (e.g., willingness to work certain shifts or locations)

- Applicant-to-hire ratio

Organizations with the most successful recruiting programs track and assess the success rates of the methods they use to find job candidates. They correlate the performance of new-hires to recruiting sources, both to improve the recruiting process and to focus training and retention programs.

**Section 4**

### Using Employment Specialists

Leading staffing companies, including Kelly Services, Manpower, Olsten Staffing and Remedy Intelligent Staffing, offer a wide range of options to meet call center staffing needs. Managers can use one or a combination of the following staffing approaches:

**Temporary:** Temporary agents may be used to fill staffing gaps during peaks in the call center on a regular basis, or to handle special projects (such as a new product introduction). Seasonal assignments (i.e., handling heavy volume during the holiday season) may have a firm beginning and end. Other more long-term assignments may be open-ended, with temporary workers supplementing a core group of permanent agents on the call center's staff.

**Temporary to permanent:** This increasingly popular approach has two key benefits: First, the call center can try out a potential employee on the job before making the decision to hire. Second, since the likelihood of turnover is generally highest during an agent's first three or four months on the job, the temp-to-perm approach helps companies minimize their investment in agents who wind up leaving. (See Temporary, Contracted and Managed Staff, this section.)

**Permanent:** Sometimes called "direct placement," this is the more traditional approach to staffing, wherein the staffing agency identifies candidates, pre-screens them, then presents them to the call center (or the company's human resources department) for selection. These employees immediately go on the call center's payroll.

In addition, some staffing companies offer on-site management to oversee temporary or contingent agents or to manage the entire operation. But companies that have had call centers for years have recruited and hired their own call center agents. Why are they now willing to pay an employment agency to do the job? In part because staffing is the core competence of employment agencies, thus they can afford to make the investment required in such areas as:

- Research that reveals the behavior, skills and attributes of successful call center agents
- Development of specialized testing instruments that identify candidates most likely to perform well in the call center
- A wide range of recruitment approaches that enable them to assemble a large pool of skilled workers
- Training specifically targeted to the call center environment

Excerpts from "Call Center Managers Turn to Employment Specialists for Staffing Solutions" by Leslie Hansen Harps, *Call Center Management Review,* December 1999.

### Recruiting a Diverse Workforce

Recruiting for diversity can be somewhat different then general recruiting. For example, you may need to identify the diverse groups you want to target and develop a recruiting campaign directed toward them. Some of the more prominent sources for recruiting minorities include:

- State employment agencies

- Regional equal employment opportunity offices
- The Small Business Administration
- Community organizations
- City council offices
- County human rights commissions
- State departments of rehabilitation
- Colleges and universities
- Professional, student and alumni associations
- Church organizations

## 3. Internal vs. External Hiring

Ready? | 1 | 2 | 3 |

### Key Points

- Call center management must carefully examine the potential implications of hiring for open positions from within the organization (internally) or outside (externally).

- This internal or external hiring question is important in making certain the right person fills the job, standard and fair hiring practices are followed and larger call center objectives are filled.

- Generally, organizations prefer to fill the majority of open positions internally because it supports knowledge management and career-pathing principles and has a positive effect on employee morale. Hiring externally, however, can bring new life to the call center in the form of fresh perspectives and new ideas.

### Explanation

Call center management must carefully examine the potential implications of hiring for open positions from within (internally) or outside (externally). The decision is usually made on a case-by-case or position-by-position basis although most centers have general rules that guide the hiring process.

The internal or external hiring question is important in making certain the right person fills the job, standard and fair hiring practices are followed, and larger call center objectives are fulfilled. Generally, organizations prefer to fill the majority of open positions internally because it supports knowledge management and career-pathing principles and has a positive affect on employee morale. Hiring externally, however, can bring new life to the call center in the form of fresh perspectives and new ideas.

Your organization may, for instance, hire most agents from the outside. Supervisory and quality positions may normally be filled internally from the ranks of the call center agents, though the call center manager may make exceptions depending on call center conditions and individual position requirements. Positions that support and maintain call center technology may be filled by outside candidates since the required skill sets are typically not present in existing call center staff.

The costs and resource implications of the decision are specific to each situation. For example, it may be more cost-effective to hire an outside candidate who already possesses required skills, than to train an internal employee. However, if recruiting costs are expected to be high and the process of finding the right person long, training an internal hire could be the better solution.

**Advantages and Disadvantages**

Some of the advantages of hiring internally include:

- Demonstrates the organization's intent to develop career growth opportunities for employees

- May uncover and leverage employees' hidden knowledge, skills and abilities

- Has a positive effect on employee morale

- Supports knowledge management initiatives by promoting tenure

- Complies with applicable human resource directives to post all positions internally prior to soliciting candidates outside the organization

- May be less expensive to recruit due to reduced advertising costs

- New-hires may be productive more quickly because of familiarity with the organization's processes, network and culture

- New-hires may be able to create alliances between other departments and the call center based on prior relationships

Disadvantages of hiring internally include:

- New-hires' lack of experiences beyond the boundaries of the organization

- May generate resentment of employees who disagree with hiring selection

- Promoted individuals may have difficulty or meet resistance in managing peers

- In some cases, new-hires may require more training for job-specific skills

Advantages of hiring externally include:

- Influx of new ideas and creativity resulting from experiences outside the organization and ability to see the organization and their responsibilities with new eyes

- Depth and breadth of industry exposure may surpass what internal candidates can offer

- New-hires are not bound by standard practices; i.e., current traditions

- By recruiting for the specific skill sets needed, less job-specific training may be required

- May help the organization create a more diverse workforce

Disadvantages of hiring externally include:

- The new employees' ideas and suggestions may not be readily or immediately accepted by current employees

- Additional time may be required to become familiar with the organization's processes, network and culture

- There may be resentment from current employees who feel the position should have been filled internally

- May send the demotivating message that internal career paths are limited

- External candidates are "unknowns;" it may be difficult to determine if they will fit in with the organization's culture and interaction styles

- May be more expensive if recruiting and screening costs are high

In either case, the leadership of the call center can mitigate many of the downsides associated with new-hires by taking steps to support their assimilation into the organization, call center, team and position, regardless of whether they come from within or outside the organization. (See Creating and Implementing an Orientation Program, Section 5.)

## 4. Conducting Effective Interviews

Ready? | 1 | 2 | 3 |

### Key Points

- Interviews are essentially conversations between you and prospective job candidates. Interviewing provides you with the information to determine those who should continue in the selection process and identify those who are not an appropriate fit.

- Structured interviews produce better results than unstructured interviews, by diminishing bias and increasing consistency.

- Interviews may be conducted by the HR department, call center manager, supervisor, team leader, peer or any combination.

- Initial interviews by telephone and/or text-chat are recommended for call center positions, since they simulate the job's performance requirements.

### Explanation

Interviews are essentially conversations between you and prospective job candidates. Interviewing provides you with the information to determine those who should continue in the selection process and those who are not an appropriate fit. The goal is to identify unsuitable applicants early in the process, to save time and reduce costs for both the organization and applicants.

**Screening Tools**

There are many variations of screening tools, from simple to involved, low-tech to high-tech. Examples include:

- **The application form:** The application form is a tool to determine if the applicant meets minimum job requirements. You will need to establish an application checklist of the important items for the job and determine the selection criteria based on that checklist.

- **Resumes and cover letters:** These may be used as part of the screening process, in addition to or in place of the application form. Resumes and cover letters may be less revealing than an application because the employer does not stipulate the information included.

- **Tests:** Short tests can assess job aptitude and knowledge. The tests must be based on job analysis and be valid predictors of successful performance. Tests may include:

  - **Performance tests:** Assesses the ability to perform a skill, such as data entry

  - **Aptitude or cognitive ability tests:** Measures candidate skill level, in areas such as verbal, math and problem-solving aptitude

  - **Physical tests:** Tests a person's strength and endurance (rarely used in call center settings)

  - **Work samples:** Provides insight into the applicant's quality of work

  - **Personality and psychological tests:** Assesses traits or individual characteristics

  - **Drug tests:** Designed to identify problem employees or comply with company policies

  - **Job-match tests:** Attempts to determine the best job fit among candidates

  *Note: Some tests have been found by courts to unfairly favor some candidates over others who are equally qualified for the position. This may violate equal rights and discrimination laws. Questionable tests should be reviewed by legal council competent in this area of law. (See Ensuring Legally Sound Employee Selection, this section.)*

- **Recommendations:** Verbal or written recommendations can provide insight into the applicant's strengths and provide an opportunity to assess the candidate from another perspective.

- **Reference checks:** Dates of employment, positions held and eligibility for rehire is the limit of the information gathered during most standard reference checks. This information is usually supplied by HR departments, which may be limited in the qualitative information they are permitted to disclose.

**Interview Structure**

The two basic types of interview structures include:

- **Unstructured:** The unstructured interview consists of random questions designed to gain insight into the candidate's suitability for the job. The questions are not documented in a standard interview guide. Instead,

Section 4

they are selected by the interviewer "on the spot." This is a common method for selection, but often has low effectiveness and validity, for a number of reasons:

- Interviewers may not use the same criteria for assessing candidates

- There is the potential for personal bias on the part of the interviewer since formal job-related competencies are not used as the basis for the interview questions

- Interviewers have a tendency to make assessments too quickly

- The interview experience is inconsistent from interview to interview for the same job regarding questions to ask, format, criteria for selection, description of job qualifications and responsibilities

- Difficult to defend against discrimination claims, since same questions are not applied to every candidate

- **Structured:** The structured interview is based on the job description for the position. Consistent questions are developed based on job responsibilities and competencies, and standard criteria are used for ranking or rating candidates.

Structured interviews usually consist of three types of questions:

- **Behavior-based questions:** These questions explore how individuals behave in certain job-related situations by asking the applicant to describe events in his or her work history. To support this type of interviewing, the interviewer has a list of job-related competencies and questions formulated to uncover these competencies.

- **Content questions:** These questions are designed to assess whether the applicant possesses the knowledge required to do the job, such as specific industry terminology.

- **Questions related to working conditions:** These questions check the applicant's willingness to work under certain conditions (e.g., work schedules, adherence and monitoring).

**Interviews**

Interviews may be conducted by the HR department, call center manager, supervisor, team leader, peer or any combination. Many organizations schedule

interviews to involve employees who will supervise or work with the applicant.
Interviews may be conducted by individuals or groups.

- **Individual interviews:** These interviews follow a traditional format in which the applicant is involved in a conversation with one interviewer at a time. The selection process may consist of a series of individual interviews, to factor in several interviewers' impressions of the applicant.

- **Group or team interviews:** These interviews involve a select group of people conducting the interview together. An interview structure and protocol is established to ensure the required qualifications and characteristics are assessed. Ratings and perspectives are discussed after the interview. Team interviews can save time. They allow the candidate to be interviewed by a variety of people, and enable a diverse evaluation of the applicant's suitability for the position.

Team interviews can be structured to allow the candidate's future call center team members to participate in the interview process. New-hires may orient to the team more easily if they were able to interact with their team members during the interview process. In turn, team members may be more accepting of the new member if they had a role in his/her selection.

**Interview Media**

Interviews may be conducted by telephone, text-chat and/or face-to-face. Initial interviews by telephone and/or text-chat are recommended for call center positions, since they simulate the job's performance requirements.

- **Telephone:** Conducting an initial in-depth interview by telephone is recommended for call center positions. This medium allows the interviewer to assess an essential requirement – telephone verbal communication skills – prior to inviting the applicant for a face-to-face interview, making it efficient from both a time and cost perspective.

- **Text-chat:** The text-chat interview allows the applicant to demonstrate his or her typing proficiency, ability to communicate via an electronic medium and knowledge of "netspeak," Internet slang with specialized acronyms, abbreviations and emoticons (keyboard symbols that help convey the intent of the message). This type of interview is appropriate for positions that require handling interactions using text-chat, email or other written forms of communication.

- **Face-to-face:** The most common interview medium, face-to-face conversation provides the opportunity to further assess the pre-screened

applicant's communication skills, knowledge and experience. Face-to-face interviews are recommended as a final interview stage, even if telephone and text-chat interviews are conducted.

### Preparing for the Interview

All effective interviews require thorough planning and preparation by the interviewer(s).

To prepare for an interview, a manager should:

- Review the job description

- Refer to job competencies to determine appropriate qualification criteria and interview questions

- Read the candidate's application materials; e.g., application, resume, test scores

- Schedule the interview (either telephone, chat or face-to-face) in a location where the conversation will not be overheard or interrupted

- Determine who will participate in the interview

- Set applicant's expectations regarding the duration of the interview, who will be present, if testing will be administered and other pertinent information

- During the interview, prompt the applicant for more detailed answers or specifics, if necessary

- At the end of the interview, discuss next steps and a timeframe for the decision

## 5. Selecting Required Employees

Ready? | 1 | 2 | 3 |

### Key Points

- Selection is the process of identifying the best candidate or candidates for jobs from among the pool of qualified applicants generated during the recruiting process.

- A carefully planned approach will help managers avoid the risks inherent in the process of selecting employees. The basic steps in the hiring process include:
  1. Screen applicants
  2. Interview applicants
  3. Expose applicants to the work environment
  4. Evaluate candidates
  5. Make the hiring decision
  6. Extend the offer

- The manager coordinating the offer needs to know the organization's policies on how much room he or she has to negotiate since some candidates may make counter-offers.

### Explanation

Selection is the process of identifying the best candidate or candidates for jobs from among the pool of qualified applicants generated during the recruiting process. It is important to strictly follow the organization's human resources policies throughout the selection process; ill-advised hiring decisions have cost organizations considerably in terms of public perception, recruiting, legal fees and court-awarded payments. More importantly, a poor selection process can leave an organization without the talents, knowledge, skills and abilities required to meet its objectives. (See Ensuring Legally Sound Employee Selection, this section.)

A sensible, systematic hiring process will help managers leverage the opportunities – and avoid the risks – inherent in selecting employees. The basic steps in this process include:

1. **Screen applicants:** Screening tools, such as resumes, applications and tests, filter out candidates who fail to meet the basic requirements of the

job. Information collected during screening is useful in assessing the applicant during the evaluation stage of the selection process.

**2. Interview applicants:** Telephone, text-chat and face-to-face interviews provide in-depth opportunities to learn how well candidates match job-specific criteria. You should be able to tell the candidates about the open position, job responsibilities, work environment, reporting structure and call center goals and objectives. (See Conducting Effective Interviews, this section.)

It's important to make candidates aware of monitoring policies and practices. This should include a summary of the types of monitoring, purpose and objectives of the monitoring program, and how information from monitoring is used.

**3. Expose applicants to the work environment:** Spending time observing the call center's operations, usually while sitting side-by-side with a current agent, will help the applicant understand what the job is actually like. It also helps current staff to participate in the selection process and feel ownership for the success of new-hires.

**4. Evaluate candidates:** During the evaluation phase, it is important to refer only to job-related criteria – the knowledge, skills and abilities that are essential for the job. Established evaluation criteria takes the guesswork out of comparing applicants by using a rating-and-ranking system, or other objective method, to evaluate candidates.

**5. Make the hiring decision:** The hiring decision should be based on who is most qualified for the job and who is the best fit for the job, team and organization. Documentation of the entire selection process should support this decision. A weighted ranking system is useful in ensuring the most qualified candidate receives the offer.

**6. Extend the offer:** Verbally communicate the offer to the candidate. You may ask the candidate if she or he is interested in the position, needs more information or would like to take some time to consider it. If the candidate provides you with a verbal acceptance, follow up immediately with a written offer letter. The offer letter should include a summary of the job title and description, compensation and benefits information, the candidate's start date, and the signature of an authorized representative from the organization.

## Negotiation

The manager coordinating the offer also needs to know the organization's policies on how much room he or she has to negotiate since some candidates may make counter-offers. Some areas for possible negotiation include:

- **Starting salary:** Some organizations have a policy to start new employees at the base of the salary grade, while others allow negotiation to first quartile, the midpoint or other thresholds, depending on the candidate's experience and qualifications.

- **Signing bonus:** In a particularly tight or competitive labor market, you may need to negotiate the amount and terms of a signing bonus. Some organizations withhold payment until the employees achieve a certain tenure (e.g., six months).

- **Starting date:** It is customary for candidates to give at least two weeks notice to their current employer. They may want longer to take advantage of financial incentives from their current employer, to complete a contract or assignment or to have some personal time between jobs.

- **Benefits:** Negotiations usually centers on the number of weeks of vacation, as many other benefits (e.g., 401k policies) are not subject to negotiation due to federal or state regulations.

## 6. Ensuring Legally Sound Employee Selection

Ready? | 1 | 2 | 3 |

### Key Points

- Legally sound selection consists of job-related criteria and steers clear of any perception of bias or illegal discrimination.

- To conduct a legal interview, questions for each position should be standardized, documented and asked of each applicant who is being considered for the position.

- Interviewing, hiring and employment issues represent a continually evolving area of the law, so it is important to seek appropriate legal counsel regarding these issues.

### Explanation

Title VII of the U.S. Civil Rights Act of 1964 prohibits discrimination based on race, color, gender, religion or national origin. Later laws expanded the interpretation of the Act to include discrimination based on age, disability, veteran status and other factors. Canadian federal and provincial governments have likewise enacted legislation that prohibits illegal discrimination against protected groups. (See Managing Within Legal Requirements – U.S., and Managing Within Legal Requirements – Canada, Section 7.)

The appearance of discrimination during the selection process can be prevented by establishing job-related hiring requirements, and creating applicant assessment screening tools and interview questions based on these requirements. It is imperative to consistently apply the same selection criteria to each applicant throughout the selection process.

All hiring requirements (in job descriptions, internal postings, advertisements and other selection documentation), screening tools and interview questions should be reviewed by the organization's HR and/or legal counsel. In addition, all employees involved in interviewing applicants should receive instruction about conducting interviews within legal guidelines.

#### Screening Applicants

When conducting any screening activities, such as resume sorting, application review, initial screens or testing, be certain that all employees involved in these

activities are aware of the job-related criteria and are applying that criteria as they eliminate candidates from the selection process. Employees involved in this process should be aware of legal issues that affect the perception of bias. Some common practices, such as eliminating "over-qualified" resumes for entry-level positions, have led to successful lawsuits citing age discrimination.

### Conducting Legal Interviews

To conduct a legal interview, questions for each position should be standardized, documented and asked of each applicant who is being considered for the position.

When responding to the applicant's answers to standardized questions, you may want to ask non-scripted questions for clarification. Be sure you ask only questions that are directly related to the job and based on job requirements. If you are unsure of a question (you feel it relates to the job requirements and yet it falls within the categories below), check with your HR or legal departments prior to asking it. As a rule, you should not ask questions related to:

- Religion
- Age
- Gender or sexual preference
- Family situation, childcare arrangements, marital status, maiden names
- Citizenship and ethnic background
- Physical conditions/disabilities/health or identifying characteristics as weight, height, smoking habits, etc.
- Military service or record
- Previous arrests (you may ask about convictions, but not arrests)
- Hobbies and organizations
- Credit rating

### Applicant Evaluation and Hiring Decisions

During each step of the selection process, interviewers should make notes and complete standard checklists that rate and rank the applicant's performance. These notes and rankings can serve as a valuable tool in substantiating a hiring decision if they can prove the candidate was or was not hired based on job-related requirements. They can also serve to support a discrimination lawsuit if they are not completed consistently or correctly or point to a discriminatory practice.

Post-interview conversations about applicants' qualifications and interviewers' perspectives should include only job-related criteria and should not include discussion of the applicant's appearance or physical attributes, accent, ethnic heritage or other non-job-related factors.

Although discrimination issues in the call center tend to focus on illegal discrimination, there are some forms of discrimination that, while not illegal, will contribute toward a negative work environment. Nepotism is showing favoritism to relatives when making HR-related decisions. It is rarely considered a favorable practice and many organizations have policies to minimize the chance for conflict of interest. Fairness in the organization's hiring practice is essential if the organization is to be viewed as a fair and equitable place to work.

**Getting Legal Advice**

Interviewing, hiring and employment issues represent a continually evolving area of the law. It is important for managers to confer with competent HR and legal sources when considering significant changes to policies and processes.

## 7. Temporary, Contracted and Managed Staff

Ready? | 1 | 2 | 3 |

### Key Points

- Temporary employees ("temps") are often a good fit for short-term and seasonal staffing requirements.

- Contractors are typically used for a small number of specialized vacancies – often in management or analyst positions.

- In a managed staffing arrangement, the staffing company supplies all or part of the organization's employee needs, according to the organization's business rules and guidelines.

### Explanation

Temporary, contracted and managed staff are alternatives that can provide the call center with the flexibility and skills it needs to meet changing workload requirements.

#### Temporary Employees

Temporary employees are often a good fit for short-term assignments; e.g., six to nine months or less. These positions can be filled either through a company's internal hiring process or, more commonly, through the use of an external temporary agency.

There are a number of advantages that temporary workers bring to the organization, including:

- The opportunity to observe people in action, who may eventually be offered full-time employment (usually for a predetermined fee to the agency)

- Flexibility in scheduling

- Ease of termination when the work is complete

- Easy replacement of individuals who are not a good fit

- The taxes and benefits costs are shifted to the agency

There are, however, some potential downsides to using temporary workers:

- You may not get the required call center-specific skills or the level of proficiency desired

- Temporary workers sometimes have higher rates of absenteeism

- Temporary workers are usually not familiar with the organization, products or customers

- You are training a workforce who will only be there a short time

- Temporary workers may be less loyal to the organization

Temporaries often thrive in organizations with relatively short (e.g., two weeks or less) training times, flexible scheduling policies and quick calls that are relatively simple to handle. In more complex environments requiring longer training periods, temporary employees often are not the best fit.

When considering the use of temporaries, the call center manager should know the organization's policy concerning the length of time that a temporary can be employed (i.e., one year or less). Many organizations stipulate that if the worker is kept past this time period, he or she must be offered permanent employment. An over-reliance on temporary workers for too long a time can force a manager to convert them to full-time status – or let them go.

One of the most notable advantages of using temporary workers is the chance to hire those who first prove they would be valuable permanent employees. This approach – typically called a temporary-to-permanent arrangement – is generally based on a pre-determined fee to be paid to the agency. It is often a win for all parties: the organization acquires a proven employee, the employees have the chance to display their skills (and decide if the organization is a good fit for them) and the agency earns a fee for its part in making the employment possible.

**Contractors**

Not to be confused with temporary workers, contractors (i.e., consultants, freelancers, etc.) form a direct relationship with the call center. They do not come to the organization through an outsourcing company. They are hired for the expertise they can bring to a project or for a specified period of time.

Where temporary workers are generally assigned to more simple, routine tasks, contractors are often used for a small number of specialized vacancies – typically at the management or analyst level. Examples include designing a new

customer information system, managing a consolidation project, setting up a workforce management team or setting up a new quality improvement process.

The advantages of using contractors include:

- Specialized expertise that might be expensive or time-consuming for the company to develop on its own

- Applicable, outside perspectives and experiences

- Tax burdens are generally shifted to the contractor

Disadvantages of using contractors include:

- They may have multiple clients, all with urgent, competing priorities and timelines

- They may be working for your competitor, providing (even unknowingly) sensitive information

- They may have less loyalty toward your company

- They can be expensive for long-term or ongoing assignments

A prerequisite to a successful arrangement with a contractor is to ensure that the person's skills, knowledge and abilities are a fit with project requirements, and that he or she understands the organization's goals and objectives and how their contributions further them. It is also important that the project either have well-defined parameters (e.g., tasks, timeframes, milestones) or, for less defined projects, that regular reviews are scheduled to assess progress, costs and decision points.

**Managed Staffing Arrangements**

Another staffing alternative is generally known as "managed staffing." With this approach, a managed staffing company supplies all or part of the organization's employee needs, according to the organization's business rules and guidelines. Individuals hired are on the managed staffing company's payroll, and administrative responsibilities, feedback and coaching, and disciplinary actions are the responsibility of the staffing company. This staffing arrangement is a variation of outsourcing, with the outsourcing company using your facilities instead of their own.

The advantages of a managed staffing arrangement include:

- Enables the organization to focus on core functions of the business, not ongoing employee issues

- Enables the organization to benefit from the core focus (expertise) of the managed staffing company on HR and staffing issues

- Many managed staffing companies also have expertise in call center management

Potential downsides include:

- Employees may not feel as much a part of the organization

- High turnover may be a problem

- Neither the staffing company nor employees they bring may be a fit for the organization's values and direction

Managed staffing arrangements are becoming increasingly popular, especially as these organizations focus on the unique requirements of call centers. A critical success factor to this – indeed, to any – staffing solution is a call center leader who can create a supporting culture and a build cohesive team, regardless of the staffing alternatives represented.

## 8. Telecommuters

Ready? | 1 | 2 | 3 |

### Key Points

- Successful telecommuting programs can deliver compelling advantages, including:
  - The means to attract and keep good employees
  - Access to staff for peak demands
  - Increased productivity
  - Coverage for bad weather and disasters
  - Space and facilities savings (in some cases)

- Without the right planning and management approach, telecommuting programs will be hampered by unexpected costs, inadequate or misapplied technologies and difficult management issues.

### Explanation

In the early to mid-1990s, telecommuting (or telework) became a popular topic in call center circles. The potential benefits of tapping into a flexible and large labor pool and realizing space and costs savings, prompted hundreds of call centers to initiate telecommuting programs. Some were successful and are going strong. Others ran into unexpected costs, inadequate or misapplied technologies and difficult management issues. Consequently, even some of the high-profile telecommuting programs were either scaled back or tabled.

In recent years, telecommuting has been picking up steam in call centers again, and the success stories are mounting. The higher success rate this time around can be attributed to a number of factors: better planning before launch, more disciplined pilot studies, improved technologies and more and better information. In short, telecommuting can enable flexible and cost-effective staffing alternatives – but it must be set up and managed judiciously.

#### Benefits of Telecommuting

There are a number of potential benefits that a telecommuting program offers call centers, including:

- **Attract and keep good employees:** Working from home offers quality-

*Section 4*

of-life benefits that can provide a competitive advantage to call centers in recruiting and retaining high-performing staff. These quality-of-life benefits may include better balance of work/family time, reduction in stress, and an indirect pay raise through reduced needs for business clothing, food and commuting expenses. Telecommuting also allows a call center to broaden the potential employee demographic base beyond the usual constraints of tolerable commute times or availability of public transportation.

- **Access staff for peak demands:** Remote workers need not be full-time agents. Telecommuters may welcome a part-time schedule designed to bolster the call center's capacity during peak periods, and some telecommuters' shifts are scheduled in distinct intervals during the day, rather than in continuous blocks of time. Agents in remote sites may work for another part of your company but help your call center during peak periods. (See Staff-Sharing Arrangements and Service Bureaus, this section.)

- **Increase productivity:** Evidence indicates that properly selected and managed telecommuters have greater availability than onsite agents, as a result of decreased absenteeism, fewer distractions, flexibility in work hours, elimination of commuting delays, and immediate availability for overtime. Managers of telecommuters may find that their own effectiveness increases, as well, as they learn to provide clearly defined policies and procedures, make communications concise and maximize the value of every interaction with employees.

- **Provide coverage for bad weather and disasters:** Having agents available in distributed locations reduces the risk that bad weather or damage to the primary facility will disable call center operations. Emergency call-routing plans must be developed in advance and thoroughly tested.

- **Potential cost savings:** Telecommuting programs can save on facilities costs. However, this is not always the case, and careful analysis must weigh the costs of setup and applicable voice and data transmission costs with the expense of establishing a seat at the primary facility.

**Barriers to Telecommuting**

The challenges of setting up and operating a telecommuting program include:

- **Management challenges:** Remote workers do not have access to the large amount of information that is usually exchanged outside the formal processes of meetings and memos (i.e., "water cooler" exchanges).

Managers may be a tempted to focus on quantitative measurements only because they are easier to measure from a distance than qualitative measurements. Finally, there is the problem of not being able to read body language when using electronic media to communicate.

- **Individual development and career growth:** Structuring reporting relationships and teams on paper may be simple enough, but there are many hurdles to overcome in practice. Since both sides get only snapshots of each other, relationships are often more formal and mechanical. It's harder for staff to schedule time with their managers. Little "face time" with management makes evaluating, training, and coaching remote workers more difficult. For employees, remote work may hamper career development and movement, as networking and "being in the loop" are sometimes impeded by physical separation.

- **Technology obstacles:** Upgrades to the main call center's technology infrastructure may be necessary to accommodate remote workers. The high-speed, high-bandwidth access required by telecommuters may not be available where it is needed, or the service provided may be less reliable than what is available in the main faculty. Maintaining remote equipment requires additional costs, resources and planning. (For a complete discussion of telecommuting technologies, see ICMI's *Call Center Operations Management Handbook and Study Guide*.)

**Management Requirements**

There are a number of steps managers should take to maximize the success of the telecommuting program, including:

- **Compare technology and equipment costs to benefits:** Careful and thorough assessment of the total costs and benefits associated with a remote working arrangement is fundamental to success. Some benefits may be hard to quantify (e.g., disaster preparedness), so this should not be strictly a financial analysis – strategic decision-making is in order.

- **Give careful and close direction to the project:** Successful remote work arrangements often start with small pilot programs. It takes time to develop the skills to manage remote employees, as well as to work through inevitable startup problems. Controlled growth is recommended. Ongoing direct management must continue after the program is established.

- **Agent selection:** Selecting the right people for remote work is critical to success. Consequently, some centers only consider top-performing agents

for telecommuting assignments. In addition to past performance, managers need to consider how well candidates take initiative, manage change, make decisions and work independently.

- **Standard work-at-home contract:** Developing a contract that details both the organization's and the worker's responsibilities and expectations will help both sides understand how the telecommuting arrangement will work. It will also minimize risk for the company. Telecommuters are at work when telecommuting, and should provide child care and take steps to minimize other potential distractions.

- **Performance measurement and monitoring:** Consistency between the way onsite and remote agents are measured and monitored is important. The call center voice and data technologies available today can provide the same information on remote work as that being conducted onsite. Ensure that call monitoring technologies and processes are applied equitably, and ensure that remote agents receive the same feedback and support as those who work in the primary facilities.

- **Managing agent isolation:** A certain degree of isolation is an inherent part of the telecommuter's job. However, there are ways for managers to reduce feelings of isolation. The most important step is to select agents who will be comfortable working outside the traditional office environment. Some centers require that telecommuters work in the office at least several days a month.

### Using Agencies

Telecommuters can either be employees of the organization or provided through an agency. If an agency is involved, individuals can either be employed by the agency or the organization, depending on the arrangement that best suits the organization's requirements.

## 9. Staff-Sharing Arrangements

Ready? | 1 | 2 | 3 |

### Key Points

- A staff-sharing relationship is when two or more organizations share a common pool of employees, typically to meet seasonal demands.

- Successful staff-sharing requires a highly cooperative relationship between organizations, as well as similar cultures and management styles.

- Individuals who are part of a staff-sharing assignment must understand the products, services and customer expectations of the organizations involved.

### Explanation

A staff-sharing relationship is when two or more organizations share a common pool of employees, typically to meet seasonal demands. For example, an organization with a heavy summer workload may partner with an organization that is busiest in winter months to share staff. Staff-sharing relationships are, as of yet, uncommon in the call center industry. But they have been proven successful, and will likely become more widespread.

Individuals who are part of a staff-sharing assignment must understand the products, services and customer expectations of the organizations involved. However, most who are part of successful staff-sharing arrangements enjoy the variety and challenges.

The benefits of a staff-sharing relationship include:

- The ability to meet seasonal demands with minimum recruiting and retraining efforts

- Lower recruitment and turnover costs

- Higher morale (reduces the impact of "hire-and-fire" seasonal cycles)

- Greater degree of staff commitment (agents who become permanent rather than seasonal employees are more likely to develop loyalty and commitment to the organizations)

There are also obvious and significant challenges to setting up a staff-sharing

arrangement, including:

- Training for two types of organizations, two types of workloads and multiple systems

- Potential cultural differences

- Security concerns

- Contract issues (how employment and liability issues are addressed)

**Key Management Issues**

Staff-sharing arrangements require compatible partners, with products and services that don't compete and with similar cultures and value systems. A capable project team consisting of individuals from both organizations is required to establish and manage the alliance, and a detailed plan with supporting employment contracts is essential. The organization that has staff on loan to the other organization should keep those employees in the communications loop, so they continue to feel part of the culture and decisions.

It generally makes sense to have one center employ the agents full-time and invoice the partner for reimbursement. There's no need to subject the shared staff to the confusion and complication of changing employers every time their work assignment changes. The center that employs the shared staff provides the usual associated benefits.

## 10. Service Bureaus

Ready? | 1 | 2 | 3 |

### Key Points

- Today's service bureaus can handle contacts of virtually any type or degree of complexity.

- The results of working with a service bureau will only be as good as the level of integration and collaboration between the two organizations.

- The basic steps for putting a service bureau arrangement in place include:
    1. Do the strategic analysis
    2. Define the requirements
    3. Identify service bureau candidates
    4. Select the service bureau
    5. Make the transition
    6. Manage the relationship

### Explanation

A service bureau (outsourcer) is a company hired to handle some or all of the organization's contacts. In the past, service bureaus were viewed by many call center managers as call processing "factories." The prevailing wisdom was to send simple, routine calls to outsiders, but don't send complex customer service calls. For the most part, that perspective used to be accurate.

Today, service bureaus of all types and capabilities are available. Some can handle contacts of virtually any type or degree of complexity. Case in point: Technical support, financial services, insurance claims and other types of complex services are being handled by outsourcers. In fact, many service bureaus have differentiated their services based on their proficiency at handling multiple channels of contact, complex issues or contacts unique to specific vertical industries.

Despite the broad range of choices, outsourcing is not for everyone. You will need to analyze the capabilities of potential outsourcers, and the quality and depth of services they can provide. You will then need to look at comparative costs and benefits of building vs. buying these services. If you go the

Section 4

outsourcer route, you'll need to work with them closely to staff and schedule agents, ensure quality and track activity. The results will only be as good as the integration and collaboration between the two organizations.

**Benefits of Service Bureau Relationships**

Service bureaus offer a number of advantages to organizations that need help handling call center services. For example, they can:

- **Provide cost savings:** Outsourcing some or all call handling to a service bureau may be more cost-effective than handling those calls internally.

- **Increase capacity, especially temporarily:** One of the primary reasons organizations hire service bureaus is to handle call volume that is beyond their current capacity. In particular, if the increase in calls is expected to be temporary, outsourcing calls to a service bureau may be more cost-effective than increasing in-house capacity.

- **Handle certain types of contacts efficiently:** Some call centers struggle to find efficient ways to handle particular types of contacts (e.g., foreign language, late-night, email or text-chat) or consider some calls to be a waste of their skilled staff's time (e.g., simple order transactions or level-one support calls). Service bureaus can offer expertise, 24-hour operations, and/or low-cost agents.

- **Provide sophisticated technologies:** Call center service bureaus have little choice but to deploy the most current and efficient technologies in order to be competitive. Call centers evaluating the costs to upgrade their systems, or organizations that are considering establishing a new call center may find hiring a service bureau to be an attractive option. This is another form of the "build vs. buy" decision.

- **Provide redundancy:** If yours is a single-site call center, arranging for a service bureau to handle a portion of calls will provide a level of redundancy and disaster backup.

**Considerations/Challenges**

There are a number of potential considerations/challenges to having service bureaus handle part or all of the organization's contacts, including:

- **Quality concerns:** If calls cannot be handled successfully except by expert agents or if the organization does not have solid processes and documentation in place, it will be difficult for a service bureau to match the quality of in-house staff. Similarly, organizations that have robust

training processes for their own call center staff will be more likely to transfer those skills to service bureaus.

- **Control issues:** Turning your customers over to someone else inevitably reduces the amount of control you have over how those customers are treated. Service bureau contracts can provide elaborate detail specifying how the operation will be run, but in the end, you either manage the call center in-house or give up some degree of control. An important factor to consider, however, is the degree of control current call center management actually has. A competent service bureau may offer better processes and control.

- **Cost:** Depending on the variables, either solution may prove to be the most cost-effective. Setup costs, internal costs to manage the service bureau relationship, travel costs to the service bureau site, and the costs of keeping the service bureau up-to-date with the organization's plans and market must be considered.

**Putting a Service Bureau Arrangement in Place**

The basic steps for putting a service bureau arrangement in place include:

1. **Do the strategic analysis:** Carefully evaluate the need for outsourcing. What level of involvement is required (e.g., 100 percent of calls, after-hour calls, peak season, intra-day peaks, specific types of contacts, etc.)? Compare fully loaded in-house costs to expected outsource costs.

2. **Define the requirements:** Define exactly what your expectations will be of the service bureau. Consider all aspects of the relationship.

3. **Identify service bureau candidates:** Develop a request for proposal (RFP) that builds upon identified requirements. Research potential vendors and send the RFP to those that meet primary qualifications.

4. **Select the service bureau:** Evaluate RFP responses, follow up with relevant questions, visit client sites and then select the best candidates. Keep in mind that you are not just selecting a vendor, you're looking for a partner who will build customer relationships and further the mission of the organization. Before making a final decision, be sure to visit the service bureau's call center operations and spend time with the center's management and agents.

5. **Make the transition:** Put together a project team representing a cross-section of the organization's management team, and dedicate the resources required to get the relationship off to a strong start.

**6. Manage the relationship:** Once the arrangement has been established, the organization will need to maintain a team for ongoing collaboration and management. The organization will need to keep a close eye on key reports and processes, follow through on scheduled call monitoring and site visits, and take the time to maintain a strong working relationship with those handling the account. Some call centers even have their own manager on the service bureau's site for greater presence and speed in decision-making.

(For a detailed discussion of outsourcing and contractual relationships, see ICMI's *Call Center Leadership and Management Handbook and Study Guide*.)

## 11. Types and Causes of Turnover

Ready? | 1 | 2 | 3 |

### Key Points

- Turnover can be categorized as voluntary or involuntary.

- Identifying the reasons that people leave is a fundamental prerequisite to reducing and controlling turnover.

- According to industry studies, top reasons for turnover in call centers include better opportunities outside the organization, compensation issues, positive attrition (better opportunities within the organization), lack of career opportunities and job dissatisfaction related to incessant handling of complaints and problems.

### Explanation

Turnover is when a person leaves the call center. The turnover rate quantifies these employee separations as a percentage of all employees. Turnover can be categorized as voluntary or involuntary.

#### Voluntary Turnover

Voluntary turnover is when the employee decides to leave the organization or position. Examples include:

- **Internal promotions/lateral moves:** For example, taking an internal promotion, making a lateral move for development or career enhancement, or going on "special assignment" for an extended period of time. The call center experiences turnover, but the organization does not.

- **Employee quits:** People quit for many reasons, and not all of them are within call center management's control. In some cases, organizations offer employees incentives to quit, including attractive severance packages. The intent is to reduce the number of employees voluntarily.

- **Retirement:** Retirement is usually initiated by the employee unless the organization has a mandatory retirement age or encourages individuals to accept an early retirement package.

**Involuntary Turnover**

Involuntary separations occur when management makes the decision to end the employment relationship. Examples include:

- **Being fired:** This may be due to poor performance, an inadequate job fit, unethical behavior, violation of organizational policies, etc.

- **Layoffs/downsizing:** This is when the organization reduces the size of the workforce. There are a number of factors that may drive layoffs, including:

  - Economic conditions

  - Change in required skills

  - Mergers/acquisitions (resulting in redundant positions)

  - Consolidation/pooling (e.g., when several call centers are combined into one)

**Identifying the Causes of Turnover**

Turnover is a chronic problem in organizations with inadequate pay, insufficient career paths, poorly structured environments and a non-supportive culture. To manage turnover, you must understand what causes it. And causes vary from one organization to another. Steps that can help determine causes include:

- Conduct a job and salary analysis vis-à-vis market conditions

- Conduct group meetings with agents to discuss environmental factors, such as stress, management style, workload, etc.

- Review the orientation program to ensure jobs are being accurately represented to new employees

- Analyze exit interviews

- Conduct regular employee satisfaction surveys

**Causes of Turnover**

Specific causes of turnover (listed here in no particular order) include:

- Pace of effort required

- Sense of powerlessness to make a difference

- Frustration of not being allowed to do a good job

- Repetition

- Unrelenting attention necessary

- Being tied to a desk

- Over-regimentation

- Feeling of being spied on

- Feeling of not being appreciated

- Handling complaints or problems all day

- Odd work hours

- Better opportunities within or outside the organization

- Low pay

- Lack of proper tools and training

- The demand for increased skills from agents who do not want to perform those skills or who are not equipped to perform them

---

**Top Five Reasons of Agent Turnover**

- Better opportunities outside the organization

- Compensation issues

- Positive attrition: better opportunities within the organization

- Lack of career opportunities

- Handling complaints and problems all day

Excerpt from: *Agent Staffing & Retention Study Final Report*, ICMI, 2000.

---

## 12. Calculating and Tracking Turnover Rate

Ready? | 1 | 2 | 3 |

### Key Points

- Turnover rate is a key performance indicator in any call center and should therefore be tracked and managed as aggressively as other performance indicators.

- To accurately track turnover trends, call center managers should use an annualized turnover rate calculation.

### Explanation

Turnover is a fact of life in every call center. The level of turnover, however, can vary greatly from one organization to the next. Some centers operate with annual rates of less than 5 percent, while others see rates exceeding 100 percent.

Where turnover rates are high, the cost to an organization can be substantial. Beyond the obvious expense of recruiting and training, these call centers endure quality and productivity rates that are typically below expectations. Since the cost of low quality and productivity can be significant, it is important to calculate and manage turnover as aggressively as other key performance indicators.

Turnover can occur at any level of the organization and at any level of experience from trainee to seasoned agent. All types of turnover should be measured, since all can have an impact on performance; however, for the purposes of this guide, we focus here on turnover of trained agents.

To measure turnover correctly, call center managers should calculate an annualized turnover rate. (Note: See formula below.) An annualized number does not require 12 months worth of data. The annualized figure provides a consistent basis for comparison and trending. The calculation is as follows:

Turnover = (# of agents exiting the job ÷ avg. actual # of agents during the period) x (12 ÷ # mos. in the period)

Section 4

### Input for Turnover Calculation

|  | # of agents exiting the job during month | Avg. # of agents on staff during month* |
|---|---|---|
| January | 2 | 104 |
| February | 1 | 103 |
| March | 4 | 101 |
| April | 0 | 101 |
| May | 3 | 109 |
| June | 5 | 106 |
| July | 2 | 105 |
| August | 3 | 103 |
| Total/Average | 20 | 104 |

*The average number of agents on staff during the month is often calculated by taking an average of the counts at the end of each week of the month. Alternatively, an average can be taken of the trained staff count at the beginning and end of the month.

Using the data from the table above, the calculation yields the following result:

$(20 \div 104) \times (12 \div 8) = 28.8\%$

Consequently, the call center has an annualized turnover rate of about 29 percent.

While an overall annualized turnover rate is a useful number, it is of more value to further break down the number into internal/external, and voluntary/involuntary categories. Internal turnover refers to employees that leave the call center, but stay within the organization. External turnover refers to employees that leave the organization entirely. For example:

*(continued, next page)*

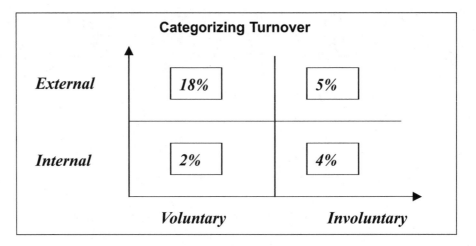

**Categorizing Turnover**

| | Voluntary | Involuntary |
|---|---|---|
| **External** | 18% | 5% |
| **Internal** | 2% | 4% |

This provides the manager with better direction on steps to be taken to address turnover. In the example, over half of the total turnover rate (18 percent out of a total of 29 percent) is external, voluntary turnover. Since the causes are usually different than those for internal or involuntary turnover, the manager can prepare an action plan accordingly.

## 13. Positive and Negative Aspects of Turnover

Ready? | 1 | 2 | 3 |

### Key Points

- Turnover is a costly and significant management issue for call centers. Costs generally include:
  - Separation
  - Recruiting and hiring
  - Training and orientation
  - Indirect

- When assessing and addressing turnover, there are a number of tradeoffs that must be considered; e.g., the cost to recruit vs. retain.

- There are also positive aspects to turnover that should be considered in the overall management approach.

### Explanation

**Costs of Turnover**

Turnover tends to be costly to the call center even if the person stays in the enterprise. Costs generally fall into a handful of major categories.

Separation costs may include:

- **Severance pay:** A lump sum or continuation of pay for a specified period of time

- **Benefits:** May continue for a specified period of time or until the person finds another job

- **Unemployment insurance rates:** Rates may go up since companies are penalized with a higher tax if more of their former employees draw benefits from the unemployment insurance fund

- **Exit interview:** Administrative costs to understand the reasons the person is leaving

- **Outplacement:** Assistance in finding a new job

- **Legal:** If the person elects to file a grievance against the organization

Section 4

Recruiting and hiring costs may include:

- **Advertising:** The cost of placing ads in various media

- **Time:** The source and pool of candidates must be identified, references and backgrounds must be checked, and interviews must be conducted

- **Travel:** These costs of the interview process could be associated with the candidate, call center manager and/or the recruiter

- **Search firms:** These companies generally charge a percentage of the employee's annual salary as a fee

- **Relocation:** This includes benefits associated with relocating new employees

Training and orientation costs may include:

- **Initial and subsequent training:** Includes orientation to the enterprise, call center, job and team

- **Travel for training:** For example, to required training programs

- **Learning curve:** Even after training classes have been successfully completed, on-the-job training effectively continues until the new employee fully masters how to apply necessary skills and knowledge

Indirect costs may include:

- **Productivity curve:** Cost of overall lower productivity and affect on service levels

- **Overtime:** Current employees may need to work additional hours to maintain call center performance

- **Loss of business:** Poor customer service can mean lost sales and customer defections to competitors

**Positive Aspects of Turnover**

Given the costs, the notion that turnover has positive implications may be counter-intuitive. But properly managed turnover goes against what most view as good management practices, and can support overall workforce management. Positive aspects of turnover can include:

- **Elimination of poor performers:** Some employees do not and will not measure up to what is defined as acceptable performance. Whether it is lack of knowledge, skill, motivation or ability, they consistently fail to

meet performance objectives. To make matters worse, they can, and often do, negatively impact call center morale, customer service and satisfaction, and revenue. Replacing poor performers with better performers not only benefits the call center, but will give the poor performer an opportunity to find positions that are a better fit.

- **Opportunity to acquire new skills quickly:** In some cases, call centers need to move quickly in a new direction and so require new skills. There may be a need to handle new markets (perhaps with foreign languages) or new technologies (e.g., with a need for written communication skills as well as spoken). It may be necessary to replace current workers with those who better fit the new profile.

- **New insights, creativity, innovation:** Outsiders bring different perspectives and may put a problem, issue or opportunity in an entirely different light, allowing you to discover new solutions.

- **Opportunity for greater diversity:** To compete both nationally and globally, call centers need a diverse workforce. Diversity can encourage a more flexible environment. Further, a diverse employee base is often more open to new ideas and change.

- **Reduce long-term costs:** New-hires are usually brought in at lower wages than tenured employees. The ideal workforce would be comprised of a balance of new-hires and higher-paid staff to provide leadership in the center. Over time, some staff may end up being overpaid for what they contribute. One solution is to transfer these individuals to other jobs that better match their interests and capabilities, and hire new staff at a lower costs.

- **Employee advancement within the enterprise:** When employees advance to other parts of the organization, the call center may suffer in the short-term, but the organization may benefit overall from the knowledge and skills former call center employees will bring to new positions. Further, the call center has an advocate in that part of the organization (and, in some cases, may still have access to that person to assist with peak loads).

- **Increased morale:** Low performers create stress, tension and reduced team cohesiveness. Other employees have to pick up the slack, and if management refuses to act, morale sinks. Replacing these workers often relieves a mountain of stress, tension and strained relationships. People can once again experience a renewal of energy and commitment to the team and call center; workloads are rebalanced and perceived equity is reestablished.

- **Geographic reorganization:** Organizations may change their structure from centralized to decentralized or vice versa, shifting the physical location of jobs. Relocating current staff may not be cost-effective, so layoffs and hiring new staff may be the best approach to implement such plans.

### Tradeoffs

When addressing turnover, there are a number of tradeoffs that must be considered. These include:

- **Cost of turnover vs. costs of retention:** While turnover is costly, steps to retain staff can also be costly. Retention costs can be difficult to quantify. The call center and organization must balance the total costs of turnover against the total costs of retention.

- **Low vs. high compensation levels:** Depending on the competition for skills in your labor market, paying below-market wages may result in higher turnover (and high costs), while paying above-market wages may lower turnover but result in unsustainable expense. Further, establishing fixed salary ranges may help control salary expenses, but also contribute to turnover. (See discussion in The Job Evaluation Process, Section 3.)

- **Cost to hire vs. retrain skilled labor:** Many call center jobs require ever-increasing levels of skills and knowledge. Where the labor market is tight, you may need to pay a premium to attract skilled and experienced people – or may not be able to find the right skills at all. In these situations, it is often most effective to retain and retrain existing staff.

## 14. Effective Agent Retention Strategies

Ready? | 1 | 2 | 3 |

### Key Points

- Solid retention strategies start with sound hiring practices. Taking time to select the right people for the agent position is the best investment a call center can make in the fight against rampant turnover.

- Agent retention is influenced by a wide variety of other factors both inside and outside the call center. Things like competitive pay, creative incentives and an overall positive call center culture are essential, and need to be accentuated by a positive enterprisewide culture to have a lasting impact on retention.

- In addition to effective hiring practices, the following factors have a significant impact on the success of agent retention programs.
  - The leadership in the call center and organization
  - The call center environment
  - Kinds of incentives and rewards offered
  - Public recognition of agents
  - Perception of internal and external compensation equity
  - Perception agents have of the environment of which they are a part

### Explanation

Agent retention ranks among the top priorities of call center managers. All the success a call center enjoys revolves around the skills and commitment of the people on the frontline. Therefore it's crucial to focus on keeping and continually developing the most qualified agents in the center.

Agent retention begins with careful selection. If you take the time to hire candidates based on job qualifications and behavioral competencies, you'll have a better chance of ensuring the right job fit and securing higher employee retention rates. In fact, if turnover rates are high, revisiting your hiring processes should be the first step to an overall retention strategy. (See Creating and Implementing a Recruiting Plan, this section.)

---

### A Focus on Job Fit

Because there is no single strategy that will solve turnover problems, Cigna Healthcare is taking a more holistic approach to employee retention, says Stephen Wood, vice president of human resources for the company's call center operations. "It requires many levers," he says.

One such lever Cigna has used since the late 1990s is a process to ensure job applicants are a good fit for call center work and the environment, and that they fully understand job expectations.

In the past, he says, the company had found a common thread among new-hires who left the company soon after training – they didn't realize what the agent job entailed. "The more we can do upfront to make it clear what the job is, the better it is for the applicant and the company," says Wood.

Before reaching the face-to-face interview, Cigna applicants undergo an assessment process to ensure they meet the call center's minimum criteria for scheduling availability. Next, they are given written materials that offer insight into the call center operation, such as the importance of schedule adherence and being available for customers, what the call center floor looks like, as well as what the working environment is like. "We want to be sure applicants understand that, unlike other jobs, this is one in which they will not be able to walk around as freely," he says.

Job applicants then take part in several simulations to evaluate how they would handle various types of calls ranging from pleasant to angry.

Agent candidates at air freight transportation company Emery Worldwide are also exposed to the call center environment during the hiring process, says Tom Burgess, director of customer service. "We take them out on the floor and let them sit with an agent to listen to calls and watch that individual work on the computer," he says. "We want to make sure they know what they're signing up for before they get started."

In the past, agents would make it through the initial training program and then, once out on the floor, suddenly realize the job wasn't really right for them. Since the company began using the new approach a few years ago, the impact on agent retention has been significant, says Burgess.

Excerpt from "Keep New-Hires Longer through Orientation and Transition Training" by Susan Hash, *Call Center Management Review*, December 2001.

---

In addition to effective hiring practices, the following factors have a significant impact on the success of agent retention programs:

- The leadership in the call center and organization
- The call center environment
- Appropriate staffing levels to reduce agent burn-out from stress
- Kinds of incentives and rewards offered

- Public recognition of agents

- Perception of internal and external compensation equity

- Perception agents have of the environment of which they are a part

A certain amount of turnover is inevitable and acceptable; the manager's challenge is to determine just what that acceptable level is. To do this, it's important to understand the full cost of turnover and compare it to the costs associated with staff retention programs. (See Positive and Negative Aspects of Turnover, this section.) The objective is to find the right balance: Managers don't want to spend more money retaining staff than it costs to replace them, but managers also don't want to spend more money replacing staff than it costs to keep them. Among the practical criteria to consider when seeking the right balance are:

- The maximum amount the company is willing to invest compensation in wages for the job

- Availability of a skilled labor pool to fill agent vacancies

- The cost (in terms of money and time) of effectively training new-hires for the agent position

- Organizational values and culture

**Retention Strategies**

There is no simple formula for agent retention that is appropriate for all call centers. However, there are certain specific strategies that will greatly enhance the chances of retaining your agents (and ensuring they perform at their best):

- **Establish effective orientation and transition-training programs.** Putting new-hires on the job without adequate training on your products/services, processes, company culture and customer expectations is a surefire way to alienate agents and increase turnover. Ease each new-hire into the job with a comprehensive initial training program that covers the fundamental aspects of the agent position, as well as the call center's mission, vision and values. Consider implementing a transition-training program as well, in which new agents handle basic customer transactions in a controlled environment with ample supervision/coaching. (See Creating and Implementing an Orientation Program, Section 5.)

- **Create a mentor program beginning with initial training.** Teaming new-hires with veteran agents as part of your initial training program is an

excellent way to enhance retention in the call center. Not only does a mentoring program help new agents find their feet in the early going, it provides experienced staff with a sense of empowerment and value as they share their expertise. Such programs often help create lasting bonds between mentor and protégé – bonds that can have a lasting impact on agent morale. (See Principles of Effective Mentoring, Section 5.)

- **Provide opportunities for ongoing skill and career development.** Agents who see their position as dynamic and evolving are more likely to remain committed to the call center. Create a skills-based pay program and, if possible, a compelling career path in the call center to encourage agents to continually expand their knowledge and capabilities. Be sure to compensate staff appropriately to enhance the value of such programs. (See Creating and Communicating Career and Skill Paths, Section 7.)

- **Provide competitive pay and benefits.** Ensure that the jobs in the call center are internally and externally equitable. (See Compensation-Related Factors, Section 7.)

- **Implement creative incentive programs that link rewards to desired behaviors/call center objectives.** Elicit agent participation in the creation of such programs – nobody knows what motivates agents better than the agents themselves. (See Types of Incentives, Section 6.)

- **Ensure that agents receive timely coaching and feedback on a regular basis.** Continually encourage the positive aspects of the agent's performance, and clearly model all other desired actions/behaviors. Work together with individual agents to create feasible action plans that will enable them to achieve objectives. Encourage agents to self-evaluate their performance during coaching/feedback sessions to help them drop their defenses. Also, take time to explain how your monitoring program works to reduce agents' fears of "big brother." (See discussions on monitoring and coaching, Section 6.)

- **Provide enterprisewide recognition for agents who consistently perform well, or who go above the call of duty.** Show agents how much they are valued by spreading the word about their good work via company memos, newsletters, intranets, etc.

- **Tap individual agent talents to create job diversity.** Your agents bring a wealth of individual backgrounds and abilities to the call center; take advantage of their skills and knowledge to make the job more alluring to them and to break up the monotony. For example, ask staff with artistic skills to create call center posters, or have staff with writing skills contribute articles to company newsletters.

- **Consider having employees sign a tenure agreement when they join the call center.** A 12- to 18-month agreement not only ensures that agents will be around for a while, it communicates to the employee just how valuable agents are to the organization, which can help to further enhance commitment and retention. (The downside is that this approach can send the message that "of course, no one would stay longer than 12 or 18 months unless we had this stipulation.")

- **Maintain consistency and eliminate agent claims of subjective treatment.** Have clear-cut policies/procedures in place (for attendance, monitoring, adherence to schedules, etc.) that every team leader, supervisor and manager understands and follows.

- **Have applicants sit side-by-side with agents early on in the selection process.** This will provide a good job preview and establish realistic expectations about the nature of the agent position.

- **Focus on good call center facility design.** Investments in ergonomics, spatial dynamics, furniture, lighting and acoustics, as well as heating, ventilation and air conditioning, can have a dramatic impact on agent satisfaction and retention rates. (Facilities and design are discussed in ICMI's *Call Center Operations Management Handbook and Study Guide*.)

- **Conduct research to determine and address causes of turnover.** (See Types and Causes of Turnover, this section.)

- **Provide as much flexibility in schedules as possible.** Offer schedule-swapping and consider agents' availability to work when designing schedules. Call center scheduling takes creativity and communication since both call arrival requirements and agent requirements must be accommodated as much as possible. (See Strategic Staff: Workforce Mix and Scheduling Alternatives, Section 3.)

- **Consider implementing a telecommuting program.** Work-at-home agent programs can help a company tap into qualified, alternative labor pools, such as workers with disabilities or individuals who, for whatever reasons, have difficulty commuting to the call center. (See Telecommuters, this section.)

## Hiring and Retention

### Exercises

#### Conducting Effective Interviews

1. Briefly answer the following questions.

   a. Why do structured interviews produce better results than unstructured interviews?

   b. Why are initial interviews by telephone and/or text chat recommended for call center positions?

   c. What are behavior-based questions?

#### Selecting Required Employees

2. What are the six steps in a sound employee selection process?

1. _____

2. _____

3. _____

4. _____

5. _____

6. _____

#### Ensuring Legally Sound Employee Selection

3. Beside each statement below, indicate whether you are legally allowed to ask about this during an interview (with an "a") or it is inadvisable (with a "i").

_____Age

_____Ethnic background

_____Credit rating

_____Educational institution

_____Family situation, childcare arrangements, marital status, maiden names

_____Military service or record

_____Past salaries and wages

_____Past work experiences

**Calculating and Tracking Turnover Rate**

4. Using the information in the table below, calculate the annualized turnover rate.

| | Number of agents exiting the job during month | Avg. Number of agents on staff during month |
|---|---|---|
| June | 4 | 84 |
| July | 0 | 87 |
| August | 3 | 87 |
| September | 1 | 89 |
| October | 2 | 85 |
| November | 2 | 88 |
| December | 0 | 87 |
| Total/Average | 12 | 87 |

The annualized turnover rate is_____.

**Positive and Negative Aspects of Turnover**

5. What are generally considered to be the four areas that comprise the costs of turnover?

_____

_____

_____

_____

**Effective Agent Retention Strategies**

6. Complete the following sentence with the appropriate phrase.

Although there are many effective strategies to keeping agents employed in the call center, agent retention begins with _____.

**Answers to these exercises are in Section 10.**

Note: These exercises are intended to help you retain the material learned. While not the exact questions as on the CIAC Certification assessment, the material in this handbook/study guide fully addresses the content on which you will be assessed. For a formal practice test, please contact the CIAC directly by visiting www.ciac-cert.org.

## Hiring and Retention
## Reference Bibliography

### Related Articles from *Call Center Management Review* (See Section 9)

Recruiting Strategies for Multimedia Call Centers

Dealing with the 'Free-Agent' Mindset: Rethink Recruiting and Rewards

Cut Agent Turnover by Hiring for Motivational Fit

The Outsourcing Evolution: Economic Trends Make It a More Viable Option

Is 'Staff-Sharing' a Viable Option for Handling Seasonal Call Volume?

The Role of Corporate Culture in Agent Commitment

Key Aspects of Successful Agent Retention Processes

Understanding the Costly Threat of Agent Turnover

Low-Cost (and No Cost) Strategies for Retaining Agents

### For Further Study

#### Books/Studies

*Agent Staffing & Retention Study Final Report.* ICMI, Inc., 2000.

*Call Center Agent Turnover and Retention: The Best of Call Center Management Review.* Call Center Press, 2002.

*Call Center Recruiting and New-Hire Training: The Best of Call Center Management Review.* Call Center Press, 2002.

#### Articles

Hansen Harps, Leslie. "Call Center Managers Turn to Employment Specialists for Staffing Solutions." *Call Center Management Review*, December 1999.

Hash, Susan. "Keep New-Hires Longer through Orientation and Transition Training." *Call Center Management Review*, December 2001.

O'Hara, Anita. "How to Develop a Retention-Oriented Agent Recruiting and Selection Process." *Call Center Management Review*, April 2001.

### Seminars

*Monitoring and Coaching for Improved Call Center Performance* public seminar, presented by Incoming Calls Management Institute.

*Call Center Hiring Web Seminar Series*, presented by Incoming Calls Management Institute.

# Training and Development

**People Management**

# Section 5: Training and Development

# Contents

**Section 5**

## 1. Definitions and Purpose of Training and Development

Ready? | 1 | 2 | 3 |

### Key Points

- Two fundamental purposes of training and development include:
  - At the individual level, increase knowledge, skills and abilities for current and future positions.
  - At the call center level, build a wide base of knowledge and increase the ability to implement strategies and achieve objectives.

- Though they are often used interchangeably, learning, training, education and development have distinct definitions.

### Explanation

Training and development benefit both the individual and the call center. From an individual perspective, training and development increases knowledge, skills and abilities for current and future positions. From a call center perspective, training and development enables the call center to implement strategies and achieve its short- and long-term objectives. The underlying purpose of training is always to increase performance, skills and/or knowledge in some area. The results of training, however, may be much broader, including increased employee satisfaction or more motivated employees.

Two trends have resulted in training becoming increasingly important in the call center environment. First, many call center managers are placing greater emphasis on finding agents who will fit into the culture of the organization and then training them on appropriate skills rather than finding those with the right skills but who may not fit into the culture and environment. Given the increasing complexity of agent interactions, new-hires often need significant training, not only in company-specific procedures, but also in general skills. Second, given the growth and turnover in many call centers, there is often an ongoing influx of new employees. As new-hires enter the employee mix, upfront and ongoing training becomes paramount to achieving high standards of quality.

#### Definition of Key Training and Development Terms

Although they are often used interchangeably, the terms learning, training,

Section 5

education and development have distinct definitions. According to HR consultant Leonard Nadler, the terms can be distinguished as follows:

- **Learning:** The acquisition of knowledge, skills and abilities.

- **Training:** Learning with job-specific objectives which enhances knowledge, skills and abilities. Training has a short-term focus.

- **Education:** Learning related to future roles or positions for which the individual is being prepared. Education should relate to career-pathing and succession planning. Education has a short- and long-term focus.

- **Development:** Learning for the general growth of the individual and/or the organization. Development has a long-term focus.

## 2. Cultivating a Learning Organization

Ready? | 1 | 2 | 3

### Key Points

- A learning organization is "skilled at creating, acquiring and transferring knowledge, and at modifying its behavior to reflect new knowledge and insights."

- Knowledge is the key sustainable source of added value in an organization and is critical to the development of strategic advantage.

- Four primary steps to becoming a learning organization include:
  1. Create an environment supportive of learning
  2. Stimulate the sharing of new ideas across internal/external boundaries
  3. Create learning forums
  4. Establish systems to capture and share learning

### Explanation

Harvard Business School professor David Garvin defines a learning organization as "skilled at creating, acquiring and transferring knowledge, and at modifying its behavior to reflect new knowledge and insights" (p. 80). Learning organizations look at the systems and processes contributing to learning as opposed to focusing primarily on specific interventions, such as a training class. This perspective leads to knowledge management and the successful development of an organization's intellectual capital.

Key assumptions and implications that drive the concept of a learning organization include:

- Knowledge is the key sustainable source of added value in an organization and is critical to the development of strategic advantage. As sources of competitive advantage disappear, the need for a highly knowledgeable, skilled and committed workforce grows. Organizational capabilities based on employee knowledge of customers, markets, products, processes, suppliers, etc., are very hard to imitate.

- Organizational and team learning is dependant upon individual knowledge acquisition. In other words, the skills, knowledge and abilities

of individuals are building blocks of organizational and team learning.

- Organizational learning makes it possible for an organization to transform itself on a continual basis in response to changing conditions (Dixon).

- To maximize success, organizations must tap into individual knowledge, identify ways in which it can be made public and transferable, and capture it so that it becomes part of the "structural capital" of the organization (Walton).

Organizational learning expert Nancy Dixon identifies three overlapping areas of organizational learning activity:

- **Individual learning:** Takes place each time an individual learns; e.g., through classroom training, reading, feedback and coaching, e-learning, job experiences, etc. Individual learning requires that people are encouraged and rewarded for their own initiative. Effective feedback is an enabler to individual learning.

- **Team learning:** Takes place when two or more individuals learn from the same activity; e.g., team activities, training, projects, games, etc.

- **System learning:** Takes place when the organization develops systematic processes to acquire, use and communicate organizational knowledge.

### Business Drivers for Organizational Learning

The need for call centers to embrace continuous learning stems from the changing requirements of the business and the marketplace. Key business drivers include:

- **Increasing emphasis on knowledge work:** In the past, work was generally 20 percent judgment and 80 percent routine; now most jobs consist much more of decision-making and judgment than routine. In call centers, many routine tasks, such as checking account balances or flight arrivals and departures, are increasingly being handled by self-service options; e.g., Web sites, interactive voice response units, etc. As self-service options continue to become more sophisticated, agents must be equipped with the ability to solve problems and exercise good judgment.

- **Demand for accelerated innovation:** Change is accelerating and most companies cannot develop new ideas and products fast enough. As a result, the call center is constantly adapting to new product lines, service options and customer access channels. The ability of call center

employees to manage change through increased knowledge sharing and development is vital to future success.

- **Flexibility of the workforce:** As businesses become increasingly unpredictable and unstable, we can no longer guarantee that the skills needed today are those that will be needed in the future. Organizations now ask employees to anticipate changes in their field and prepare themselves to work in entirely new areas. Call center managers must encourage self-development to ensure their staff is ready for new challenges.

- **Closer ties to customers and suppliers:** Today's businesses rely on customer information to drive strategic decisions. As the hub of communication for the organization, call centers must manage customer feedback well. An increasing challenge for call center managers is developing the ability to gain customer insight from each contact the center handles.

- **More global alliances:** Knowledge management and communication sharing become more challenging as organizations are distributed geographically. Call center managers must be able to facilitate organizational learning across all call center sites and the entire enterprise to ensure consistency of service and the maximum benefits from innovation.

**Steps to Becoming a Learning Organization**

Garvin suggests there are four primary steps to becoming a learning organization:

1. **Create an environment supportive of learning:** Employees must have time for reflection and analysis. It is important to provide opportunities to assess customer and system needs, problems and strengths and, as a result, invent and test new ideas. An organization that makes learning a priority effectively integrates this into planning and management processes to ensure it occurs.

2. **Stimulate the sharing of new ideas across internal/external boundaries:** Crossfunctional teams and assignments, conferences and meetings with customers and suppliers are a few ways to encourage the sharing of new ideas. As a leader in the organization, call center managers must promote dialogue and inquiry.

3. **Create learning forums:** Learning forums with explicit learning goals can be useful for strategic reviews of products, systems and competitors.

The time, resources and attention allocated to these forums can empower employees to collaborate toward new knowledge and its implications.

**4. Establish systems to capture and share learning:** In order for knowledge to be effectively communicated, technology and work processes that encourage people to engage in creating a repository of corporate knowledge must be established.

In order to sustain a learning organization, the organizational culture must support these steps. Successful organizations will encourage individuals to take responsibility for their own development, recognize and value learning, leverage the increased knowledge of individuals across the organization, and have management structures that share responsibility and decision-making.

### Benefits of Learning Organizations

Call centers are in the communication business. Unfortunately, many call center managers have not considered the implications of sharing knowledge and skills within their centers. There are many benefits of developing a learning organization, including:

- Increased speed to market
- Sustainable competitive advantage
- Stronger customer relationships
- More efficient internal systems and processes
- Lower turnover
- Higher level of individual and corporate intellect
- Improved bottom line
- Faster and more cost-effective learning

### Development Resources

Since individual professional development is vital to the growth and success of the organization, management must actively support the ongoing development of the staff. Of critical importance is the call center manager's ability to create a culture supportive of continuous learning. Management must both model and support the development of the call center's intellectual capital.

Training/development resources should be easily accessible to all employees in the call center. Many organizations develop a training library that provides a designated place for creative thinking and individual learning. The library can

be utilized by call center staff during non-peak call times and should provide development resources for a variety of individual needs. This library needs to include current information on a variety of topics that impact the call center. The library should also provide access to relevant online training programs and other electronic resources. (See Sources of Industry Information, this section.)

Call center managers should also ensure that the following resources are reasonably available:

- Time of the individual and manager for development
- Training personnel
- Budgeted dollars for training and development
- Technologies for computer-based training
- Senior managements' time for support and mentoring
- Peers' time for peer coaching

**Section 5**

## 3. Knowledge Management Issues
## [Strategic]

Ready? | 1 | 2 | 3 |

### Key Points

- Knowledge management is "the task of developing and exploiting an organization's tangible and intangible knowledge resources."

- The major barrier to knowledge management is when individuals do not have the time, support, incentives or desire share knowledge. It is essential that managers determine what methods and incentives will lead employees to contribute their own knowledge to the organization and seek out the knowledge of others.

- Call centers can contribute significantly to organizationwide knowledge management, enabling:
  - Improved quality and innovation
  - Highly leveraged marketing
  - Efficient delivery of services
  - Additional revenues/sales

### Explanation

Consultant Jenny McCune defines knowledge management as "the task of developing and exploiting an organization's tangible and intangible knowledge resources" (p. 10). An organization's tangible assets include such things as copyrights, patents, R&D, licenses and product, customer and competitor information. The intangible assets are the knowledge that the employees possess, including professional know-how, experience, skills, their own processes or methods, personal insight and creative solutions. The main objective of knowledge management is to leverage and reuse resources that already exist in the organization so people will not spend time "reinventing the wheel."

Knowledge management is not just gathering facts, but involves adding actionable value to existing data and information by filtering, synthesizing and summarizing it. Then methods must be developed to help people access the knowledge so they can take action. Employees must find it usable and in a format that is readily available.

In the final analysis, investments in knowledge can increase innovation and productivity, lead to higher return, and sustain long-term economic growth because knowledge doesn't depreciate the way raw capital does.

**Technology Issues**

Knowledge management can involve many types of technologies, including groupware programs, data warehouses, Intranets and document management software. Based on the work of McCune, the following table illustrates the major technological aspects of a knowledge management system.

| Area of focus | Tools |
|---|---|
| Connectivity | • Computer networks<br>• Email<br>• Intranet<br>• Internet |
| Containers (repositories of knowledge) | • Data warehouses, data marts and assorted databases<br>• Document management programs<br>• Electronic directories or "experts," such as corporate yellow pages and expert systems, which compile information in an intelligent database<br>• Large storage cupboards, usually on a corporate intranet |
| Locators (technology for searching and locating information) | • Browsers<br>• Search engines<br>• Knowledge maps (indices that classify information and help users locate the information they need)<br>• Electronic card catalogues (tools to summarize and categorize data)<br>• Push-and-pull Web technology (enables users to request information or organizations to send information on specific topics) |
| Learning vehicles | • Knowledge portals at employees' desktops for easy access to all useful data in the company<br>• E-learning<br>• Web collaboration software<br>• Web seminars |
| Upcoming technology developments | • Filters, browsers and locators based on natural langurage (spoken or written) CTI-enabled solutions that synthensize and interpret infomation from call center systems |

**Supporting Culture**

The major barrier to knowledge management is not one of technology, but rather of people. The capture and transmission of human intellect is critical to raising organizational capabilities. Individuals may not have the time, support,

incentives or desire to share knowledge. In some cases, they may even feel at risk by sharing knowledge and best practices. It is essential that managers determine what methods and incentives will lead employees to contribute their own knowledge to the organization and seek out the knowledge of others. This is a management responsibility that is increasingly essential for success in today's fast-changing landscape.

### The Call Center's Contribution to Organizationwide Knowledge Management

Call centers can contribute significantly to organizationwide knowledge management, by serving as a vehicle for capturing, sharing and leveraging the stream of information from customer contacts. Practical areas of impact include:

- **Improved quality and innovation:** By capturing and assessing customer experiences and input, the call center can pinpoint quality problems with products and services, and enable associated design and manufacturing operations to make necessary improvements. This same stream of information also serves as an R&D goldmine, identifying customer wishes and associated innovation opportunities.

- **Highly leveraged marketing:** By tracking buying trends, capturing customer feedback, analyzing demographic information and establishing "permission-based" marketing campaigns, the call center contributes to an increasingly well-defined understanding of customer needs and wants.

- **Efficient delivery of services:** By helping customers understand and use self-service alternatives, the call center learns how these systems can be modified for more intuitive use, and how to encourage and inform customers about these channels.

- **Additional revenues/sales:** The information call centers acquire in the normal delivery of services leads to a better understanding of customer needs and associated upselling and cross-selling opportunities. This information can enable better designed marketing campaigns, self-service systems, in-person sales and service methodologies and online information systems that key in on these opportunities.

(For a full discussion of how these areas and others contribute to the call center's value proposition, see ICMI's *Call Center Leadership and Business Management Handbook and Study Guide.*)

## 4. Principles of Effective Mentoring

Ready? | 1 | 2 | 3 |

### Key Points

- Mentoring refers to experienced employees (mentors) who support and advise less-experienced colleagues (protégés) through their personal and career development. It differs from coaching in that it does not focus on a particular set of skills or knowledge.

- For mentoring to be effective, the mentor must candidly discuss the protégé's strengths and development needs and provide guidance to meeting those needs. In turn, the protégé must accept feedback and pursue identified development opportunities.

### Explanation

Professor John Walton defines mentoring as a process whereby "experienced and often senior employees support and advise less-experienced and often younger colleagues through their personal and career development" (p. 193). Mentoring differs from coaching in that it does not focus on a particular set of skills or knowledge. Instead a mentor guides overall career objectives.

#### The Basis of the Mentoring Relationship

The relationship between the mentor and the protégé is based on mutual trust and has the capacity to develop over time. Meetings should occur on a regular basis since a good mentoring relationship requires that both parties know each other well. Both should be active listeners and agree to keep confidences. The mentor must candidly discuss the protégé's strengths and development needs and provide guidance to meet those needs. In turn, the protégé must accept feedback and pursue identified development opportunities.

Walton recommends that the two parties develop an agreement that covers:

- Confidentiality
- Duration of the relationship
- Frequency of meetings
- Specific roles of the mentor and protégé
- Desired outcomes; e.g., identifying the protégé's career ambitions and areas of interest

**The Skills and Roles of a Mentor**

Walton summarizes the characteristics of an effective mentor as follows:

- Confident of and clear about their own position in the organization and not threatened by, or resentful of, their protégé's opportunities.

- Sufficiently senior level to be well-informed about the organization and able to facilitate the protégé's opportunities.

- Knowledgeable about the protégé's area of interest.

- Supportive of the objective of learning, and perceptive of, and committed to, their own responsibilities to the protégé.

- Easily accessible to the protégé and willing to negotiate a planned timetable.

- Already in a positive professional relationship with the protégé.

- Able to treat their mentoring role as an integral part of their own job responsibilities, not an add-on.

Mentor roles encompass the functions of aiding the protégé's career development and assisting in the development of the protégé's self-awareness. To do this, mentor roles include:

- Communicator
- Counselor
- Coach
- Advisor
- Referral agent
- Advocate

Mentoring is typically associated with management positions. However, mentoring at the call center agent level can bring agents closer to the company, learn new job tasks, feel like an important part of the larger call center community and provide support during the early stages of working in a call center.

> **The Power of Peer Mentoring**
>
> Pairing inexperienced staff with a peer mentor is an excellent – though often overlooked – way to ease their transition into the fast-paced and often frightening call center environment. And by enabling experienced agents to serve as mentors, you add diversity to the job while providing them with a strong sense of value and pride in their work. The result is higher retention of and performance from both new-hires and seasoned veterans.

A formal mentoring program may be just the answer for the many call centers that perennially struggle with employee turnover. Attrition rates tend to be particularly high among agents who have only recently completed training. Why? Because that training is often insufficient in preparing them for the unique challenges associated with the agent position and the call center in general, says, Dan Lowe, president of Lowe Consulting Group. "All too often, new-hires go through an initial training session and are then thrown onto the phones where they receive little or no direct support while handling calls. It's no surprise that call centers that take such an approach often suffer high turnover right after training, as agents find they can't stay afloat on the phone floor."

**Tips for Peer Mentoring Success**

All of the peer mentoring benefits touted by managers and consultants hinge on certain key factors. A solid program requires focused planning, set up and maintenance. Following are tips to help ensure that your program gets off, and remains, on the right foot:

• **Introduce the idea to staff prior to implementation.** The level of success of any peer mentoring program is directly proportional to the level of enthusiasm of and buy-in from your existing agents. They are the ones who will carry the program, so it's essential that they fully understand and are committed to the concept.

• **Select agents with the right mix for mentoring.** Whom you choose to serve as agent mentors will have a huge impact on your program's fate. Rushing through the selection process results not only in poor mentoring, it may alienate qualified agents who should have been selected but weren't.

So, what makes an agent qualified? Certainly good performance results are an important factor, but choosing mentors solely based on individual performance is a mistake, says Lynda Cannon, manager of human resources and manpower planning for Ruppman Marketing Technologies, a service bureau that has used peer mentoring for several years. "Just because somebody is very good at what they do doesn't mean they are good at teaching what they do," explains Cannon. "We look for lead reps who not only have high performance statistics, but who have outgoing personalities and the ability to make people feel comfortable."

• **Train mentors for success in their new role.** Consider dividing your mentor training program into two major modules: 1) how to be an effective mentor, and 2) how your program works. The former needn't be too extensive, assuming the mentor selection process has been carried out with care, says Dr. Bernice Strauss, a psychologist with extensive experience in helping organizations set up mentoring programs. "A workshop on how to mentor should suffice – covering the role and function of a mentor; what the mentee might expect; how to communicate with the mentee, how to keep the relationship going and how to set boundaries."

The second phase of training is where you brief mentors on their specific responsibilities as well as how, when and where they will be interacting with new-hires.

In addition to clearly defining the mentor role, it's important to train agents to be respectful of service levels while conducting mentoring sessions. Remind them that, as

*(continued, next page)*

important as their interaction with new-hires is, customer calls and emails must take priority. Develop policies and guidelines regarding time spent off line/away from workstations and make sure that agents understand them.

• **Take care in pairing mentors and "apprentices."** Mentoring is more than just a training tool; it's a way to build relationships that can have a positive impact on call center performance. Therefore, prior to determining partners, it's a good idea to evaluate all mentors and new-hires to see who is most likely to work well together.

Forming perfect matches isn't feasible, but pairing people with similar attributes is. As Dr. Strauss recommends, "Match pairs on common points. Pair mentors and mentees according to similarities in personality, interests, regional and ethnic backgrounds, and possibly gender."

• **Monitor the relationship and provide guidance.** Lead agents may be the stars of the mentoring show, but you as manager/supervisor need to serve as the director. Be sure to keep an eye on each mentor/mentee pair to ensure that the relationship is thriving. Confirm that mentors are providing the right information and, even more importantly, that the new-hire is learning. Encourage open communication between partners to help them identify and overcome any barriers that may hinder progress. It's a good idea also to occasionally meet with each participant individually to discuss any problems or concerns they may have with the mentoring program or their partner.

Excerpt from "The Power of Peer Mentoring" by Anita O'Hara, *Call Center Management Review*, June 2002.

## 5. Self-Development

Ready? | 1 | 2 | 3 |

### Key Points

- Effective self-development requires the learner to take primary responsibility for identifying needs, setting goals and spearheading the learning process.

- Both employees and managers play an essential role in successful self-development.

- Call center managers can benefit from pursuing project assignments in other areas of the organization.

### Explanation

According to professor John Walton, self-development stresses that "the learner takes primary responsibility for diagnosing needs and identifying goals; selecting the methods, means, times and places for learning; and evaluating the results. The emphasis is on empowering the learner to act autonomously rather than expecting a third party, such as a trainer, to direct and prescribe" (p. 204).

Self-development should seek to enhance the following areas:

- Current job skills
- The next step in the career path
- Knowledge of new processes and technologies
- Personal and call center vision and direction

A self-development plan should include:

- Areas identified for development
- The goals and objectives of development
- A timeline for completing goals and objectives
- Resources required
- Proposed development activities
- The chosen training method
- A method to evaluate results

**Principles of Effective Self-Development**

Key principles that further self-development includes:

- Develop a personal mission statement.
- Conduct a self-assessment.
- Conduct a 360-evaluation. In a 360-evaluation, input on job performance is received from managers, peers, direct reports and self; these perspectives are then compiled to identify strengths and weaknesses.
- Set realistic goals and timelines.
- Take personal responsibility for career development and progression. Do not abdicate it to others.
- Make enhancing knowledge and skills a higher priority than advancement.
- Cultivate positive relationships with management; develop both internal and external networks of relationships.
- Develop and maintain a positive reputation.

**Shared Responsibility**

Who is responsible for development, the manager or the employee? The answer is both. Employees should have a vested interest in their continued training and development in order to support the call center, for their internal promotability and external marketability. They should seek feedback, accept responsibility for pursuing a training and development plan, and seek continued knowledge and skills enhancement.

The responsibility of the manager is typically dependent upon the level of the employee. Managers of front-line agents usually play a larger role in the identification of employees' strengths and weaknesses, the selection of training and the evaluation of results. Senior managers, whose direct reports consist of mid-level managers, may leave these responsibilities up to their direct reports. However, regardless of the level of employee, most managers are the ones responsible for budgeting for self-development training for their direct reports.

**Diverse Project Assignments**

Call centers frequently interact with many other areas of the organization. Assignments in these areas will broaden and deepen the call center manager's understanding of how the call center fits into the organization, and contribute

to the manager's understanding of the larger call center role. Some particularly useful to emphasize could include:

- Marketing/sales
- Operations/manufacturing
- Information technology/telecommunications
- Finance (especially budgeting)
- Corporate communications
- Legal/compliance
- Human resources
- Training

## 6. Sources of Industry Information

Ready? | 1 | 2 | 3 |

### Key Points

- Call center managers have access to a variety of helpful sources in finding call center information, including:
  - Professional associations
  - Industry conferences
  - Journals and books
  - Internet/Web research
  - Job postings

### Explanation

Access to information and education is vital to professional success in the ever-evolving customer contact industry. The following list of resources is meant as a partial guide to available call center resources. All information was accurate at the time of printing. For current industry links, visit www.icmi.com.

**Professional Associations**

Joining a professional association provides networking opportunities that can stimulate professional development by exposing you to new ideas and perspectives. Some of the major call center management professional associations are:

Association for Services Management International: www.afsmi.org

American Telemarketing Association: www.ataconnect.org

CCNG International: www.ccng.com

Help Desk Institute: www.helpdeskinst.com

Incoming Calls Management Institute: www.icmi.com

International Association of Reservation Executives: www.iare.com

International Customer Service Association: www.icsa.com

International Telework Association: www.telecommute.org

Professional Planning Forum: www.planningforum.co.uk

Society of Consumer Affairs Professionals in Business: www.socap.org

Section 5

Vercomnet: www.callcity.net/org

### Industry Conferences

Industry conferences offer large-scale networking opportunities, educational forums and a chance to learn about the latest in call center technologies and management methodologies. Some of the major call center management industry conference organizers are:

Advanstar (United States, Canada, Brazil and The Netherlands): www.callvoice.com/events.com

CIS Conference, Inc. (United States): www.cisconference.org

Customer Service Management Association (United States): www.thinkcsm.com

DCI (United States and Canada): www.dci.com

eCustomer World Institute (Canada): www.eCustomerWorld.com

Help Desk Institute (United States): www.thinkhdi.com

Incoming Calls Management Institute: www.icmi.com

International Customer Service Association (United States): www.icsa.com

Institute for International Research (United States and Canada): www.iir-ny.com

International Quality & Productivity Center (United States, Asia, Australia, Canada and Europe): www.iqpc.com

Key 3 Media Group: (United States): www.customer260expo.com

LRP Conferences (United States): www.lrp.com

Miller Freeman/CMP Media (United States): www.cmpevents.com/main.asp

Purdue University (United States): www.callcentercampus.com

Technology Marketing Corporation (United States): www.itexpo.com

### Journals and Books

Professional journals provide concise information on the latest developments in the industry, accounts of successful call center operations and coverage of

important principles and concepts. Some of the available call center management journals include:

Print Journals:

> *Business Communications Review*: www.bcr.com. Provides in-depth analysis of networking technology, trends, management issues, pricing and regulation.

> *CC News*: www.ccnews.com. A call center newspaper.

> *Call Center and CRM*: www.commweb.com/techcenters/main/3786. Offers information on call center topics, including customer relationship management.

> *Call Center Magazine*: www.commweb.com. Covers information on broad call center topics and technology.

> *Call Center Management Review*: www.ccmreview.com. Offers in-depth information on an array of call center management topics.

> *Call Center Solutions*: www.tmcnet.com/ccs/. Offers information on inbound, outbound and customer service management.

> *Customer Inter@ction Solutions*: www.tmcnet.com/cis. Covers information on management of inbound/outbound call centers, help desks, customer support services, e-commerce, e-sales and customer relationship management.

> *Customer Interface*: www.c-interface.com. Provides information on call center technology, customer relationship management and relevant call center topics.

> *Customer Service Group*: www.customerservicegroup.com. Offers information on customer service operations.

> *Customer Support Management*: www.intertec.com. Covers a broad range of customer service issues.

> *Today's Facility Manager*: www.facilitycity.com. Publishes information on facilities, design, ergonomics, etc.

Electronic newsletters:

> *All Roads Lead to Loyalty*: www.eloyalty.com. A free, monthly e-newsletter that focuses on building customer relationships in the electronic age.

> *Call Center Buzz*: www.commweb.com/forms/NewsSignUp_form.html. Free online newsletter on call center happenings.

> *CRMXchange*: www.crmxchange.com. Free electronic magazine offering call center, telemarketing and customer relationship management information.

*Customer Contact World*: www.ccworld.net.com. An e-newsletter that offers news and upcoming events.

*Customer Interaction Solutions*: www.teleplaza.com. An e-newsletter on call center technologies.

*eCustomer World Institute eNews*: www.ecustomerworld.com. Free electronic newsletter covering eCustomer and eBusiness strategies.

*ICCM Weekly*: www.cc-crmvegas.com/iccmweekly/news_join.asp. A free electronic newsletter that includes independent editorial along with headline news.

*QueueTips*: www.icmi.com. A free, interactive email bulletin with Q&A, industry news and management tips. Provided by ICMI.

The list of books covering call center management continues to grow. Online booksellers generally have a larger selection of titles than brick-and-mortar stores. Some of the best-sellers include:

*Building Call Center Culture*, Dan Coen, DCD Publishing, 2001.

*Call Center Benchmarking: How Good is "Good Enough,"* Jon Anton and David Guston, 2000.

*Call Center Dictionary: The Complete Guide to Call Center Technology and Operations*, Madeline Bodin and Keith Dawson, CMP Books, 1996.

*Call Center Handbook*, Keith Dawson, CMP Books, 1999.

*Call Center Management on Fast Forward: Succeeding in Today's Dynamic Inbound Environment*, Brad Cleveland and Julia Mayben, Call Center Press, 1999.

*Call Center Savvy: How to Position Your Call Center for the Business Challenges of the 21st Century*, Keith Dawson, CMP Books, 1999.

*Call Center Technology Demystified: The No-Nonsense Guide to Bridging Customer Contact Technology, Operations and Strategy*, Lori Bocklund and Dave Bengtson, Call Center Press, 2002.

*Customer Service on the Internet*, Jim Sterne, Wiley Computer Publishing, 2000.

*Designing the Best Call Center for Your Business: A Complete Guide for Location, Services, Staffing and Outsourcing*, Brendan Read, CMP Books, 2000.

*Maximizing Call Center Performance*, Madeline Bodin, CMP Books, 1998.

*Navigating the Customer Contact Center in the 21st Century: A Technology and Management Guide*, William Durr, Advanstar Communications Inc., 2001.

**Section 5**

*Online Customer Care: Strategies for Call Center Excellence*, Michael Cusack, American Society for Quality, 1998.

*Online Customer Service for Dummies*, Keith Bailey and Karen Leland, Hungry Minds, 2001.

*Running an Effective Help Desk*, by Barbara Czegel, John Wiley & Sons, 1998.

*The Complete Help Desk Guide*, by Mary Lenz, CMP Books, 1996.

*The Telephony Book: Understanding Systems and Services*, by Jane Laino, CMP Books, 1999.

**Internet/Web Research**

The Internet has literally revolutionized the nature of researching call center management topics. Some of the most useful Web sites useful for call center managers include:

ACD Learning Center: www.call-center.net.

Ask the Outsourcing Experts: www.outsourcing-experts.com.

CRMXchange: www.crmxchange.com.

The Call Center Directory: www.prefsolutions.com.

Call Center Depot: www.callcenterdepot.com.

Call Center eXchange: www.callcenterexchange.com.

CallCenterGuide.com: www.callcenterguide.com.

Call Center News Service: www.callcenternews.com.

CallCenterOps.com: www.callcenterops.com.

Call Center Store: www.callcenterstore.com.

Contact Center World.com: www.contactcenterworld.com.

Customer Care Institute: www.customercare.com.

Customer Contact Strategy Forum: www.ccstrategyforum.com.

eLoyalty: www.eloyalty.com.

Forrester Research: www.forrester.com.

Gartner Group Interactive: www.gartner.com.

Gil Gordon Associates: www.gilgordon.com.

Help Desk Institute: www.helpdeskinst.com.

Incoming Calls Management Institute (ICMI): www.icmi.com.

Initiatives Three Inc.: www.initiatives3.com.

Jupiter Communications: www.jup.com.

Kingsland Scott Bauer Associates: www.ksba.com.

Meta Group: www.metagroup.com.

SupportIndustry.com: www.supportindustry.com.

TARP: www.tarp.com.

Technology Marketing Corporation: www.teleplaza.com.

Teleplaza: www.teleplaza.com.

The Resource Center: www.the-resource-center.com.

Vanguard: www.vanguard.net.

### Job Postings

The following is a list of Web sites that post job openings and/or individuals looking for jobs:

Call Center Careers.com: www.callcentercareers.com.

Call Center Jobs.com: www.callcenterjobs.com.

Call Center Network Group: www.ccng.com.

Call Center News Service: www.callcenternews.com.

ContactCenterWorld.com: www.contactcenterworld.com.

Customer Contact World: www.ccworldnet.com.

CommWeb Career Center: careercenter.commweb.com.

CRMXchange: www.crmxchange.com.

Incoming Calls Management Institute: www.icmi.com.

Technology Marketing Corporation: www.teleplaza.com.

SupportIndustry.com: www.supportindustry.com.

For a complete, updated listing of the resources mentioned in this section, visit Industry Links at www.icmi.com.

## 7. Developing a Call Center Training Strategy

Ready? | 1 | 2 | 3 |

### Key Points

- Key elements of a call center training strategy include:
    - Alignment with organizational and call center objectives
    - Senior management support
    - Involvement of call center managers
    - Quality and in program design, development delivery and evaluation
    - Motivation of paticipants
    - Integration with human resource management policy
    - Inclusion in workforce management planning

- **Training is often identified as the solution to all call center ills. Training should be deemed necessary only when it has been determined that training is required to ensure employees will meet performance expectations, when the benefits of training are greater than the consequences of not training, and when training is the most cost-effective solution to the problem or opportunity.**

### Explanation

A call center training strategy determines intermediate to long-term training priorities, objectives and direction. The training strategy should align with the call center's overall objectives and strategies.

#### Elements of a Training Strategy

The following are essential elements of an effective training strategy:

- **Alignment with organizational and call center objectives:** Training initiatives must be tied to overall organizational and call center objectives. Training initiatives should be driven by business needs, contribute to the goals of the entire organization, and provide individuals with the skills and knowledge they need to improve their performance and increase their value to the organization.

- **Senior management support:** The effect of call center training on the organization's customer acquisition and retention strategy must be understood by all levels of the organization's senior management to ensure ongoing financial support.

- **Involvement of call center managers:** The best results occur when the skills acquired through training programs are practiced in a simulated environment and immediately applied to real job situations. Even if training programs are well-designed, desired results may not be achieved if the work environment does not reinforce the skills and knowledge taught in the program. Call center supervisors and managers must be held accountable to monitor and coach employees' demonstration of critical skills and knowledge acquired in training.

- **Quality in program design, development, delivery and evaluation:** A successful training program directly supports business objectives. Participants learn what was intended and knowledge is successfully transferred and demonstrated. Development should conform with the principles of instructional design and adult learning methodologies. Program delivery should include opportunities for participant interaction and for realistic application of concepts learned. Finally, the effectiveness of training should be evaluated according to actual changes in performance. (See Evaluating Training Effectiveness, this section.)

- **Motivation of participants:** Employee motivation may affect participant's ability to learn successfully. If expectations, objectives and valid reasons for the training are not communicated or if the program does not have management support or the proper facilities, participants may not be motivated to learn. Conversely, high morale encourages self-study, informal on-the-job training and enthusiastic participation in training, all of which facilitate a learning environment.

- **Integration with human resource management policy:** Training initiatives should be tied to key HR initiatives. For example, training programs must meet legal requirements, as well as fit cultural and developmental HR stardards.

- **Inclusion in workforce management planning:** The scheduling of training must be integrated into the workforce management plan. This is typically done through a rostered staff factor (or shrink factor) that includes the number of agents that will be unavailable to handle contacts because of various activities, including training. Communication between call center managers, trainers and the workforce management team is vital to providing time for training and meeting service levels.

**Strategic Decisions**

There are a number of important strategic decisions to be made when designing the training strategy, including:

- **Focus:** Who requires training – an individual, a team, a call center or the enterprise?

- **Development:** Who should direct and review the development of training materials to ensure alignment with training objectives?

- **Location:** Should the training be performed on-the-job, within the call center or off-site?

- **Provider:** Should the training be developed within the call center and/or training department or purchased from outside sources?

- **Content:** Should the content be customized or can it be generic and purchased "off the shelf"?

- **Make or buy:** Should courseware be designed and developed in-house or purchased from outside of the organization?

- **Facilitator:** Should the facilitator be a trained call center subject matter expert, an internal trainer or an external trainer?

- **Delivery:** Should the delivery be adapted to personal learning styles or can everyone learn the same way (e.g., all classroom or Web-based)?

- **Evaluation:** How will success be measured and determined?

As with other aspects of strategic planning, budgetary limitations should not be an initial consideration. Rather, the training plan should be developed first, and then the resources sought to implement the plan. If resources are unavailable, the training plan may have to be revised. However, to allow budgetary factors to drive training often leads to ineffective or unnecessary training.

**Linking the Business Needs to Needs Assessment**

Training initiatives should be linked to business requirements and supportive of management objectives. The call center training department must demonstrate how a training initiative will assist management and agents in supporting the needs and expectations of customers and the organization. Further, training should be conducted when the benefits are greater than the consequences for not training. In other words, training should support a clear business need and the training plan should be the most cost-effective solution to the identified opportunity or problem.

Many managers wisely use a return-on-investment (ROI) model to decide when training is appropriate. While ROI is an important tool in making training decisions, it should not be the sole deciding factor. For example:

- Some essential training programs expect a negative ROI (e.g., health and safety programs and government compliance issues).

- A positive training ROI does not guarantee successful implementation. An ROI analysis might indicate that additional training would enable agents to cross-sell/upsell an organization's products and services. However, if the organization is not willing to support resulting higher average handling times, training will be ineffective.

In short, a training program's ROI should not be considered in a vacuum. It must be considered within the larger context of the organization's goals and direction.

**Working with HR and Outside Providers**

A training agreement with human resources or outside firms to provide training usually contains the following elements:

- Roles and responsibilities

- Project plans and timelines

- Needs assessment to determine the gaps in performance

- Establishment of requirements for the learning experience

- Identification of necessary subject-matter experts for collaboration on content development, as well as learning strategies and delivery

- The administration and logistical responsibilities associated with training

- Followup to ensure use of knowledge and skills on the job

## 8. Drivers of Call Center Training Requirements [Strategic]

Ready? | 1 | 2 | 3 |

### Key Points

- Each training program should be viewed in the context of an overall training framework designed to provide employees with the tools they need to perform within expectations.

- There are six primary drivers of call center training:
    - Business opportunities or problems
    - Management planning
    - Changes in technology
    - Changing customer requirements
    - Political/regulatory changes
    - Labor issues

### Explanation

Each training program should be viewed in the context of an overall training framework designed to provide employees with the tools they need to perform within expectations. While some training needs are driven by internal requirements, others are prompted by external factors such as changing legal requirements or labor issues.

There are six primary drivers of call center training:

- **Business opportunities or problems:** Business opportunities often require new or additional training; e.g., for new product training or customer segmentation awareness. Industry or organizational problems often require additional or restructured training to address existing or revised work processes and systems.

- **Management planning:** The call center presents a unique environment with issues and challenges not present in other management environments. Call center managers should be trained in call center resource planning, queuing principles, real-time management, call center specific technologies and the unique people management issues associated with the environment. Ongoing training is required to ensure managers are aware of industry developments and call center trends. Supervisory staff must be trained to effectively manage daily resources, monitor contact activity for adherence and quality, and coach agents to performance objectives.

- **Changes in technology:** Today's business environment involves constantly changing technology. Call center employees must be able to understand, operate and interact with a variety of systems and technologies, including specialized telephones, online capabilities, unique desktop tools, reporting systems and others. In addition, the "softer skills," such as selling and customer service, are demonstrated differently when delivered through different contact media.

- **Changing customer requirements:** Meeting customer expectations is at the heart of providing quality service and creating satisfied customers. The increase in customer access channels and heightened customer expectations require call center management to redefine processes, technologies and objectives, and clearly communicate those objectives and corresponding expectations in the training environment.

- **Political/regulatory changes:** The call center agent is often the most frequent, if not primary, point of contact for customers. When political or regulatory mandates dictate organizational response and customer communication, it is often the call center that must handle questions, concerns or complaints regarding these initiatives. Improperly trained staff armed with incorrect information can leave an organization vulnerable to negative publicity, loss of customers and even legal action. For example, a pharmaceutical company facing a product recall must be certain agents are trained to follow recall procedures precisely.

- **Labor issues:** The competition for skilled agents (especially when coupled with high turnover) makes an organization's training strategy critical to the ongoing success of the center. Turnover and/or growth requires the organization to allocate sufficient resources to train the new employees.

## 9. Identifying Training Needs

Ready? | 1 | 2 | 3 |

### Key Points

- Training needs analysis performs three distinct functions:
  - It establishes what present practices are
  - It projects what the desired results should be
  - It provides the basis for cost justification

- The general process for identifying training needs includes the following steps:
  - Conduct a training needs analysis
  - Determine the gaps between current performance and desired results
  - Develop recommendations for decreasing or eliminating gaps
  - Identify non-training issues that may affect performance

### Explanation

According to training consultant Garry Mitchell, needs analysis is an examination of the need for training within an organization. It performs three distinct functions:

- It establishes what the present practices are.

- It projects what the desired results should be.

- It provides the basis for cost justification of training. (p. 107)

#### General Process for Identifying Training Needs

Training needs are generally identified through the following process:

1. **Assess current performance and determine future objectives:** This first step in the process involves analyzing current performance and identifying future objectives. For example, if a new product or service will be introduced in six months, determine what knowledge, skills and abilities will be required for the call center to provide sufficient support. Or, if customer satisfaction surveys are revealing that some customers are purchasing from competitors because of inadequate customer service, how does service need to change to retain customers?

**2. Determine the gaps between current performance and desired results:**
This step assesses the differences between desired performance and current
performance levels.  Once the differences have been determined, it is
critical to identify the causes for gaps.  These causes generally fall into three
categories:  those due to the individual, those due to management and
those due to the organization.  For example, if an overall objective is to
resolve 90 percent of customer requests on first contact, but current
performance levels stand at 82 percent, the reasons for this gap could
include lack of skills or knowledge at the agent level, management's failure
to provide an adequate customer problem-tracking system, or an
organizational culture that discourages frontline decision-making – or some
combination of each.

**3. Develop recommendations for decreasing or eliminating gaps:**  What
strategies and actions are necessary to close the gaps?  In making
recommendations, the following must be considered:

- Skills and experience of the target population

- Required resources

- Barriers that may mitigate the success of the initiative. (See Barriers to
  Successful Training, this section.)

**4. Identify non-training issues that may affect performance:**  If the cause
of the performance gap is primarily due to the management approach,
current processes, the organizational culture or other factors, training will
likely be ineffective. The real solution is for managers to take action to
address the specific problems.

**Sources of Information**

There are many possible sources of information that can help in conducting a
needs analysis.  Examples include:

- Organization and call center plans, goals and objectives, and the progress
  toward those objectives

- Job descriptions, which provide the tasks and duties that should be
  performed

- Industry experts, who can provide information on job requirements and
  performance standards

- Performance reviews and monitoring data, which provide specific
  information about employee and team performance trends

- Customer satisfaction data, which can point to gaps in the center's ability

to meet customer expectations

- High performing employees, who can provide input on what makes them successful

- Benchmarking data, which can identify standards and results in other organizations. (However, be cautious. Call center requirements and drivers of the benchmarked centers may be very different from those in your environment.)

**New-Hire Training**

Effective new-hire training improves morale and retention. A thorough job analysis should be conducted for each position in the call center to determine the skill and knowledge competencies required. Both general skill requirements and specific organizational knowledge should be included in the competency list. Each competency should be designated as a skill that must be present at the time of hire, or one for which the organization will train. This competency map should be translated into a training curriculum that provides new employees with the knowledge they need to succeed in their position. The following table includes some suggested general knowledge and skill requirements for several call center positions.

| Position | Example competencies |
|---|---|
| Agent | • Call center dynamics (basic understanding of how a call center operates)<br>• Data entry<br>• Telephone techniques (including verbal communication and listening skills)<br>• Online communication<br>• Customer service skills<br>• Sales skills<br>• Handling difficult customers<br>• Applicable call center technologies<br>• Time management<br>• Organization's products and services<br>• Organization's industry (e.g., regulations, vocabulary, etc.) |
| Team Leader/ Supervisor | • Agent competencies, plus:<br>• Supervisory skills<br>• Coaching<br>• Monitoring<br>• Conducting performance reviews<br>• Interviewing skills<br>• Leadership skills<br>• Queuing theory/real-time management<br>• Applicable call center technologies (including monitoring and real-time management tools) |

| Position | Example competencies |
|---|---|
| Call Center Manager | • Team Leader/Supervisor competencies, plus:<br>• Workforce management<br>• Call center planning framework<br>• Customer behavior<br>• Quality improvement techniques<br>• Budgeting process<br>• Call center technologies (including planning and reporting tools)<br>• Time management<br>• Mentoring<br>• Recruiting, interviewing and hiring skills<br>• Organization's products and services<br>• Organization's industry |
| Workforce Manager | • Queuing theory<br>• Workforce management<br>• Call center planning framework<br>• Reporting<br>• Data analysis skills<br>• Customer behavior<br>• Quality improvement techniques<br>• Applicable call center technologies (including workforce management system and desktop tools)<br>• Budgeting process<br>• Time management<br>• Organization's products and services |
| Technical Support Manager | • Call center technologies (including installation and maintenance)<br>• Queuing theory<br>• Call center planning framework<br>• Budgeting process<br>• Organization's products and services |

**Section 5**

## 10. Barriers to Successful Training

Ready? | 1 | 2 | 3

### Key Points

- Potential barriers to successful call center training include:
  - Lack of time
  - A poor physical environment
  - Conflicting policies and procedures
  - Fear
  - Poor training design or ineffective delivery
  - Unclear reasons for training
  - Objections not addressed
  - Lack of post-training support
  - Managers aren't positive role models

### Explanation

In order for a call center training strategy to be effective, the organization must value the education and training of its employees as an integral part of its culture, policies and procedures, and management decisions. Potential barriers to successful call center training include:

- **Lack of time:** Finding time to train call center agents is a challenge, given the nature of randomly arriving workloads. When service levels drop, training is often the first casualty, even when training may be the very thing that could help most! A sound resource planning and management process must be practiced diligently so that work schedules reflect the additional resources required for necessary training.

- **A poor physical environment:** Classroom training requires a separate space from the call center floor, adequate room for breakout groups and role-play activities, and technology that supports skill application (i.e., phones for practice and role-plays, computers that simulate the agent desktop and access to software in training mode). Computers with multimedia capabilities are required for computer-based training (CBT) and a technologically savvy technician should be available to troubleshoot technology problems in the classroom. Training, whether self-paced CBT, one-on-one or classroom, requires concentration and focus.

- **Conflicting policies and procedures:** Training and development initiatives must be tied to other key goals and objectives in the organization. For example, if a skills-based compensation plan is implemented but agents seldom get approval for training activities, management's objective of increasing agent skills will not be accomplished.

- **Fear:** Fear can be a subtle but powerful barrier. If employees aren't supported and encouraged during the training process or management attempts to motivate by threatening loss of pay, disciplinary action or termination, fear may hamper concentration. Other examples of fear include fear of change, discomfort with new technology, fear of appearing unintelligent or falling behind the rest of the group, and fear of ridicule or rebuke by the co-workers, trainers or supervisors. Potential fear factors must be addressed throughout training and in the organizational culture at large to free employees from this powerful distraction and encourage them to take the risks required to learn and apply new skills.

- **Poor training design or ineffective delivery:** If the training design does not clearly communicate the training objectives or if role-plays, exercises and simulations do not accurately reflect the real work environment, the training may fail to have the desired effect. Similarly, ineffective delivery in the form of poor facilitators will undermine the success of the training program.

- **Unclear reasons for training:** The objectives and goals of the training initiative must be clearly understood and embraced to gain employee buy-in and assist employees in focusing on the training goals. One requirement of adult learners is to understand why the new skill or knowledge is needed, how it will be applied and how it will benefit them. The "what's in it for me?" must be clearly communicated prior to the beginning of the training.

- **Objections not addressed:** Call center managers should anticipate some of the objections agents may have and prepare to overcome them. Common objections to training include:

  - "I don't need training, I already know and do my job well."
  - "That wasn't in my job description."
  - "I can't do this."

  One of the best ways to overcome these issues is to involve agents themselves in the training and development process.

- **Lack of post-training support:** Support, coaching and ongoing guidance is necessary for training to translate into on-the-job performance. While employees may be able to demonstrate the new skill in the training environment, supervisory and training support is imperative to ensure use of the new skill continues and is performed consistently.

- **Managers aren't positive role models:** Managers must "practice what they preach" and embrace call center training initiatives – or risk seriously diminishing the effectiveness of the training.

## 11. Adult Learning Principles

Ready? | 1 | 2 | 3 |

### Key Points

- Adults learn differently than children or adolescents. In a training environment, adults:
  - Want practical application
  - Want their real-life experiences to be recognized and valued
  - Are continuous learners and prefer to manage their own learning efforts
  - Have varied learning styles
  - Need to know why they are learning
  - Are motivated most strongly by internal pressures (themselves)

- Adult learners require a variety of learning styles that should be accommodated by call center training programs.

### Explanation

It is essential that those involved in making training policies and decisions understand how adults process information and solve problems – how they learn. Adults learn differently than children or adolescents. The following table summarizes important characteristics of adult learners and the implications to call center training programs:

| Adult learners: | Implications to call center training programs: |
|---|---|
| Want practical application | Develop task-centered and problem-centered training programs. |
| Want their real-life experiences to be recognized and valued | Use the learner's experiences and examples; develop interactive sessions. |
| Are continuous learners and prefer to manage their own learning efforts | Involve learners in development and evaluation of the programs; encourage self-discovery and action planning. |

*(continued, next page)*

Section 5

| Adult learners: | Implications to call center training programs: |
|---|---|
| Have varied learning styles | Use multimedia, varied methods of delivery, accelerated training methods. |
| Need to know why they are learning | Inform learners of the "why" behind the training before it begins. |
| Are motivated most by internal pressures (themselves) | Help learners understand the benefit of training to job satisfaction, self-esteem and quality of life. |

Note: This table is based on "What Every Trainer Needs to Know About How Agents Learn" by Laurie Solomon, published in *Call Center Management Review*, June 1999.

**Learning Styles**

Even the most well-intentioned and gifted call center trainers will fail if they focus only on *what* their participants learn and not on *how* they learn. As the Center for Accelerated Learning puts it, "Without action there is no learning. Total learner involvement is essential. Turning a presentation into an activity accelerates and enhances learning. A training course is not something you do to people, or even for people, but with people." (Solomon)

While adults share several general learning traits, they may have a variety of learning styles. The most common learning styles include:

- **Dependant, collaborative or independent:** Some people learn best as they watch a peer (dependant) or discuss possible solutions (collaborative). Other people learn better working on their own (independent). A combination of group activities and individual assignments will provide opportunities for all types of learners.

- **Visual, auditory or kinesthetic:** Learning by seeing, hearing or doing is another learning style differentiator. Classroom and computer-based training should take advantage of a variety of media to engage visual and auditory learners. Kinesthetic learners will benefit most from activities or role-plays.

- **Goal-oriented, activity-oriented or learning-oriented:** To accommodate all three styles, at the outset of training, make learners aware of the ultimate goal, the activity to be accomplished and what will be learned as a result of the training.

## 12. Instructional Design/Development

Ready? | 1 | 2 | 3 |

**Section 5**

### Key Points

- The traditional design/development model is the Instructional System Design model consisting of five phases:
    1. Analysis
    2. Design
    3. Development
    4. Implementation
    5. Evaluation

- When developing training programs, needs-assessment information should be framed in terms of course objectives, which will drive the course content.

### Explanation

Although many call center managers may not develop course content themselves, it is important that they understand principles of effective course design. The traditional design/development model is the Instructional System Design model, which consists of five phases:

1. **Analysis:** Refers to the training needs analysis and identification of the performance metric for tracking.

2. **Design:** Provides the framework for the learning experience, including the course objectives and choice of delivery method.

3. **Development:** The actual content development and instructional strategies that align with the design.

4. **Implementation:** The delivery of the learning experience.

5. **Evaluation:** The decisions and criteria to determine the effectiveness of the training.

#### Determining Course Objectives and Content

Based on the needs-assessment results and business planning requirements, the call center manager should know what training content is required to improve personnel skills and achieve call center objectives. The needs-assessment information that is to be used for a particular course should be framed in terms

of course objectives.

Course objectives are statements of what an individual should be able to do as a result of the training and what he or she should know in order to do it. They should be measurable and/or observable. Some examples include:

| Knowledge | Skill/Application |
|---|---|
| Analyze | Assemble |
| Classify | Develop |
| Describe | Calculate |
| Define | Conduct |
| Identify | Implement |
| List | Forecast |
| Recognize | Negotiate |
| Select | Plan |

Knowledge objectives become the guidelines for the content to be included or excluded in the training course. They also give guidance to the types of learning activities and assessments. For example, if an objective indicates that a person should be able to "list" the products in a product portfolio, then you can assess that knowledge by simply asking them to list them. If you only require them to "recognize" products, you can provide a matching or multiple-choice test.

The skill/application objectives lead to on-the-job application or knowledge transfer. For example, if you want a manager to "demonstrate" the steps in coaching, you can involve them in a role-play and use a behavioral checklist to see if they use those steps. If you want them to "develop" a career path or a disaster recovery plan, you can have them create a plan and assess it against a checklist.

### Principles of Effective Content Development

Important principles of effective content development include:

- **Objectives drive the course content:** The content should directly align with and support training objectives.

- **Objectives should be written in a sequence of learning, which then provides the sequence of the content:** For example, a good content structure might be:

  - Introduction

  - Link to previous module

  - Presentation of content

  - Practice content

  - Apply content

  - Review/summarize

- **Content should be directly related to the job:** The more that course content focuses on the requirements of the job and real call center situations, the greater value for participants and the greater chance of successful knowledge transfer.

## 13. Training Courseware

Ready? | 1 | 2 | 3 |

### Key Points

- The decision to purchase or develop training courseware requires the evaluation of many different factors, including expertise, cost and customization required.

- When choosing an outside training vendor, the use of a standard evaluation method, such as a weighted scorecard, will assist in determining the best company to meet the training needs.

### Explanation

Once training needs have been determined, call center managers must decide if they will purchase training from a outside training firm or develop the training internally, possibly with the help of the HR department. When considering the make or buy decision, key decision factors include:

- Does the internal organization have the time, expertise and internal credibility to develop the learning experience?

- What are the cost factors? For example, what are the initial development costs, ongoing costs for each participant, costs to keep information current?

- Who retains ownership when working with an outside training vendor?

- What degree of customization is required?

- Who will deliver the training? Do facilitators have the appropriate skills and are they credible?

- Does the vendor and organization have compatible values and culture?

- What level of quality is required?

- Is this a stand-alone course or part of a larger curriculum?

- How are skills linked to overall learning objectives?

- Does the training vendor have industry experience? Experience with your organization?

- What is the experience of the vendor's team that will be assigned to the project?

### Selecting an Outside Training Vendor

Once the decision has been made to work with an outside training company, you must decide which company best meets your needs. A traditional method of comparing vendors is through the use of weighted criteria, or a scorecard. The criteria are determined and then weighted by distributing 100 points according to the importance of each item. Finally, a scale is used to evaluate each vendor's abilities to meet the criteria.

Scale: 1 = to a very little extent, 2 = to some extent, 3 = to a great extent, 4 = to a very great extent

### Example Vendor Evaluation

| Criteria | Weight | X | Ratings | | | = | Score |
|---|---|---|---|---|---|---|---|
| Knowledge of the call center industry | 10 | 1 | 2 | 3 | (4) | | 40 |
| Knowledge of the vertical markets | 5 | 1 | 2 | (3) | 4 | | 15 |
| Credibility to the target audience | 10 | 1 | 2 | (3) | 4 | | 30 |
| Leading edge/current materials | 10 | 1 | 2 | (3) | 4 | | 30 |
| Total cost | 5 | 1 | (2) | 3 | 4 | | 10 |
| Ownership of materials | 2 | (1) | 2 | 3 | 4 | | 2 |
| Time to market | 10 | 1 | (2) | 3 | 4 | | 20 |
| Delivery methodology | 8 | 1 | 2 | 3 | (4) | | 32 |
| Delivery capability | 10 | 1 | 2 | 3 | (4) | | 40 |
| Skills of the developers | 10 | 1 | 2 | 3 | (4) | | 40 |
| Compatibility of cultures | 10 | 1 | 2 | 3 | (4) | | 40 |
| Qualified facilitators | 10 | 1 | 2 | 3 | (4) | | 40 |
| Totals | 100 | | | | | | 339 |

To determine the score of each vendor, the weighted amount is multiplied by the rating for each item. All of the scores are added together to get each vendor's total evaluation. The vendor with the highest score is typically awarded the project.

## 14. Training Delivery Methods

Ready? | 1 | 2 | 3 |

### Key Points

- Deciding which training method is best requires the consideration of many different factors including:
  - Classroom training
  - Coaching, mentoring and peer-teaching
  - Self-paced (hard copy, Web-based, CD-Rom)
  - On-the-job training

### Explanation

Today's training landscape provides many different delivery options. Different options are appropriate for different types of training needs and it is important to understand the strengths and weaknesses of each. Deciding which method is best requires consideration of many of the following:

- Costs

- Content

- Learner preferences and styles

- How often the content needs updating (also called "shelf-life")

- Availability of resources (technology, instructors and facilities)

- Organizational culture, goals and objectives

- The geographic dispersion of the learners

- How much time is available for training development

**Classroom Training**

Classroom training brings participants face-to-face with facilitators. Knowledge and skills are taught through a variety of formats including lectures, multi-media presentations, individual and group activities, and role-plays. Classroom delivery can be centralized, requiring learners to travel to one location, or decentralized, delivering training in multiple locations or via teleconferencing.

Strengths include:

- Highly interactive

- Effective for almost any type of content

- Allows the facilitator to conduct "status checks" to ensure participants are learning and to adjust delivery accordingly
- Can be easily customized to accommodate learner preferences and styles
- Easy to change content from session-to-session
- Training content, participant materials and testing methods can be standardized and reviewed for quality

Weaknesses include:

- Quality is dependent on the availability and skills of facilitators
- Costs may be high (e.g., time, travel and material development)
- Time-of-delivery dependent; may be difficult to train all shifts and absent employees

**Coaching, Mentoring and Peer-Teaching**

Coaching, mentoring and peer-teaching are appropriate for individual development training needs. Each has a slightly different focus:

- **Coaching:** A performance management technique, which may be performed by a manager or trainer. Through informal, one-on-one discussions, creatively designed activities and frequent monitoring, the coach helps an employee improve performance in a specific skill area. (See Principles of Effective Coaching and Feedback, Section 6.)
- **Mentoring:** A long-term relationship between a tenured employee (mentor) and a less-experienced worker (protégé). The mentor advises the protégé on issues relating to his or her skill or career path. (See Principles of Effective Mentoring, this section.)
- **Peer-teaching:** The peer-teaching approach pairs an employee, often a new-hire, with a peer knowledgeable in call center policies, procedures and protocol. The peer is a source of knowledge, coaching and support as the employee learns essential aspects of his or her job.

Strengths include:

- Appropriate for specific, targeted skills
- Provides frequent on-the-spot coaching and reinforcement of desired skills
- Promotes relationships that are likely to contribute to overall organizational communication and employee satisfaction
- Low cost

Weaknesses include:

- Results dependent on coaching skills and relationship
- Less formal approach is difficult to monitor for effectiveness
- Not feasible for relaying a large body of material to many participants

**Self-Paced Study**

This method allows individuals to study training materials at their own pace. In many cases, it allows employees to "test out" of material or to study specific aspects of the content at their own choosing. Self-paced delivery methods include:

- Printed materials and workbooks
- A reading program of books and articles
- Online or Web-based training
- CD-Rom based training
- Video or cassette based programs

Strengths include:

- Appropriate for reinforcing existing skills or providing remedial training
- Easy to reach many employees; e.g., part-timers, shift workers, geographically disbursed workforce
- Can ease classroom space requirements
- Can present all learners with the same, standardized experience
- Effective for independent learners
- Web-based or online training allows frequent content updates

Weaknesses include:

- Often not the best option for teaching complex skills
- Self-motivation may be an obstacle for some employees
- CD-Rom training can be difficult and costly to update
- May be difficult to track and monitor progress and on-the-job skills implementation
- E-learning modules and videos are costly to develop

---

### Using Technology-based Training (TBT): Take a Look at the Call Center Environment

When considering the use of TBT in the call center, managers and trainers should keep in mind its limitations and the realities of the call center environment. For example:

**1. The call center can be distracting.** While agents are used to working in the call center environment, training requires concentration. This can be hard to do at the workstation.

**2. Agents may benefit more from a break rather than training.** Some companies like TBT because it enables them to integrate training into a call center agent's workday, fitting training in between phone calls. That may be a mixed blessing, says Todd Beck of AchieveGlobal. Agents who have been taking call after call all day with just a few minutes in between may not be able to quickly shift their mindsets when training is routed to them.

In addition, training may be the last thing an agent wants to do with extra time, Beck says. While the training program provides a change of pace, it takes place at the same workstation, using the same screen the agent has looked at all day. In some cases, the agent might be more refreshed and re-energized by standing and stretching, or a quick change of scenery.

**3. Off-line practice is important.** Don't have agents complete a Web-based seminar or a CD-ROM program, then immediately try their new skills and knowledge out on the phone, Beck advises. "Do you really want their first practice to be with a live customer?" It's more effective to build in opportunities for agents to practice their new skills and knowledge, perhaps during team or shift briefings or by bringing in a facilitator for role-play or practice.

On the plus side, an effective and balanced TBT approach can break up the monotony of static classroom training. The more diverse, individualized and interactive your training program is, the more motivated agents will be to learn — and the better they'll retain information.

Excerpts from "Tap the Potential of Technology-based Call Center Training" by Leslie Hansen Harps and Laurie Solomon, published in *Call Center Management Review*, March 2000.

### On-the-Job Training

This method attempts to expose the employee to realistic job situations through observation, guided practice and while working on the job. Through constant feedback and monitoring, the employee is encouraged to take risks and add to his or her body of knowledge with each experience. As part of a formal program, the trainee actually works under the guidance of someone performing the job. Less structured programs may have a looser approach; e.g., supervisor is available to answer questions as needed.

Strengths include:

- Knowledge transer to the job is virtually guaranteed
- Addresses needs of kinesthetic learners, who learn by doing
- Low cost

Weaknesses include:

- Difficult to monitor the effectiveness of unstructured programs
- May leave new employees feeling lost and unsupported
- Employees may be practicing untested skills on customers

## 15. Training Facilitators

Ready? | 1 | 2 | 3 |

### Key Points

- Training for the call center should be done by individuals who are credible to that audience and have solid facilitation skills.

- When equipping call center subject matter experts with facilitation skills, it is important to have an established process to ensure the quality of the instructor.

### Explanation

Training for the call center should be conducted by individuals who are credible to that audience. Credibility stems from a combination of education, work experience and facilitation skills. You must decide if it is more appropriate for an individual in the training department or call center to conduct the training. Trainers must have sufficient knowledge of call center dynamics and processes in order to effectively communicate call center-specific information. Call center personnel, on the other hand, must be equipped with facilitation skills (not just presentation skills). Not all call center personnel will be effective trainers, so you must carefully select and train those expected to do the training. More often, it will be easier to equip the trainer with the appropriate call center knowledge than to equip the call center personnel with training expertise.

Another option is to team someone from the call center with a trainer to gain the advantages of each. However, this approach is more costly and requires coordination to ensure learners receive a consistent message.

#### Facilitator Requirements

Important facilitator requirements include:
- In-depth knowledge of the topic
- Practical experience in topic areas
- Appropriate facilitation skills, including small and large group management, understanding of adult learning methodologies, adherence to training objectives, time management, sense of humor, etc.
- Credibility with the target audience and management

Section 5

- Commitment to the training process
- Knowledge of the organization
- Knowledge of the industry

**Train-the-Trainer Process**

When equipping call center subject matter experts with facilitation skills, it is important to have an established process to ensure the quality of the instructor. Steps that should be incorporated into a train-the-trainer process include:

- Select facilitators with at least some proven facilitation skills. If call center personnel are chosen, they should attend facilitation skills training.

- Provide a separate customized training session to train facilitators on the course content, learning strategies and assessments.

- Allow facilitators to co-teach the course with a trained instructor. The trained instructor should observe the new facilitator and provide feedback and coaching.

- Evaluate the facilitator until he or she demonstrates competency to deliver the course.

## 16. Evaluating Training Effectiveness

### Key Points

- Training evaluation should result in:
  - Determining the effectiveness of the training program
  - Deciding whether to change, stop or expand the program
  - How to improve the program for future delivery

- When assessing a training program, there are four levels of evaluation:
  - Level 1: Reaction
  - Level 2: Learning evaluation
  - Level 3: Application to job
  - Level 4: Evaluating the impact and ROI

### Explanation

Call center training requires precious time away from handling customer contacts, so it is important to ensure that the program meets the objectives of the call center. A thorough and systematic evaluation process is needed to assess the effectiveness of training.

At a basic level, evaluation consists of defining objectives, specifying those objectives measurably, and then assessing the extent to which learners have mastered those objectives. Evaluation should result in:

- Determining the effectiveness of the training program

- Deciding whether to change, stop or expand the program

- How to improve the program for future delivery

**Four Levels of Evaluation**

Training programs should be evaluated on four levels:

**Level 1 – Reaction:** Reaction comes primarily from evaluations filled out by attendees at the conclusion of the training program. In survey format, it usually covers such items as program methodology, group and individual exercises, quality of materials and media, facilitator capabilities, facilities, etc.

**Level 2 – Learning evaluation:** This is the process of collecting, analyzing and

reporting information to assess how much the participants learned and applied in the learning experience.

**Level 3 – Application to the job (also called transfer):** This step assesses the degree to which the knowledge, skills and abilities taught in the classroom are being used on the job. It includes identification of enablers and barriers that facilitate or inhibit successful application. (See Barriers to Successful Training, this section.)

**Level 4 – Evaluating the impact and ROI (also called results):** This is the process of determining the impact of training on organizational productivity, improved customer satisfaction, and the organization's strategic business plan. There are two aspects to Level 4 evaluation:

- **Impact:** What is the change in business metrics attributable to training?

- **ROI:** What is the return on the training investment (calculated by dividing the net dollar value of the benefit by the costs of training)?

### Identify the Performance Metrics Required for Success

To determine the results of training, management must first establish baseline performance metrics based on the needs assessment. That is, "What measurement is used to identify the gap?" The measurement could be adherence to schedule, accuracy of information, compliance to policies and procedures, etc. (See Measuring and Tracking Performance Objectives, Section 6.)

### Decisions from Evaluation Information

Managers should make changes to the training program based on feedback from the evaluation process. Key issues include:

- Effectiveness of the facilitator to determine if a change in instructors or additional training for the instructor is required (from Levels 1 and 2).

- Effectiveness of the materials to see if content, sequence or priority need to change (from Levels 1 and 2).

- Effectiveness of the instructional/learning strategies to see if they reinforce the content and allow for practice and application (from Levels 1 and 2).

- The extent of the use of new knowledge and skills on the job to determine if there needs to be a change in the content, instructional/learning strategies, delivery method – or whether training should continue (from Level 3).

- The environmental factors that support or hinder the use of the knowledge and skills on the job, to decide if changes in system support tools are needed (from Level 3).

- The extent of the impact on the business or enterprise metric to determine if training should continue (from Level 4).

- The ROI to determine if training should continue (from Level 4).

## 17. Aligning Call Center Training with Organizationwide Initiatives [Strategic]

Ready? | 1 | 2 | 3 |

### Key Points

• The role of the call center is to support the organization's mission and help the organization meet its strategic objectives. This effort requires the development of targeted call center training to improve the effectiveness and increase the contribution of each worker.

• To ensure call center training objectives are in alignment with organizationwide initiatives, call center training managers should:
  • Operate in tandem with larger training initiatives
  • Maximize call center employees' knowledge and skills as resources for the organization
  • Make training valuable by providing solutions to critical business issues
  • Develop relationships across the organization
  • Understand the corporate culture
  • Ensure training initiatives keep pace with change

### Explanation

The role of the call center is to support the organization's mission and help the organization meet its strategic objectives. This effort requires the development of targeted call center training to improve the effectiveness and increase the contribution of each worker.

To ensure call center training objectives are in alignment with organization wide initiatives, call center training managers should:

• **Operate in tandem with larger training initiatives:** Call center training cannot be developed and implemented in a vacuum. Eliminate the duplication of efforts by sharing resources and materials between call center and corporate trainers and determine if any training initiatives can be jointly developed. Every effort should be made to design call center programs that complement and align with larger training initiatives.

• **Maximize call center employees' knowledge and skills as resources for the organization:** The call center's value lies in the vast knowledge and skills of individual employees. With primary responsibility for the

development of the call center's workforce skills and knowledge, training managers have the responsibility to design training programs that will leverage each employee's potential.

- **Make training valuable by providing solutions to critical business issues:** Proactive training initiatives should identify strategic business issues (through frequent needs assessment) and be designed to target these critical areas. (See Aligning Structure and Strategy, Section 3.)

- **Develop relationships across the organization:** The actions of other divisions influence the performance of the call center and vice versa. Training managers should develop and maintain relationships in other departments within the organization to share ideas and formulate call center training strategies that are in alignment with the rest of the organization. Cross-departmental training and work assignments can facilitate relationship development.

- **Understand the corporate culture:** Though the call center may be geographically located far from "corporate headquarters," the call center's culture should reflect the culture of the larger organization. Call center training, especially new-hire orientation, should reflect the organization's brand messages and image so that they are conveyed to customers.

- **Ensure training initiatives keep pace with change:** The call center is the eye of the hurricane in most organizations, making it adept at adjusting to change. Call center training should keep pace with change in the organization and industry and flexibly adapt training initiatives to address change. To stay ahead of the curve, call center training management should be able to look into the organizational horizon and anticipate future training needs to support organizational objectives.

## 18. Creating and Implementing an Orientation Program

Ready? | 1 | 2 | 3 |

### Key Points

- An orientation program introduces new employees to the call center industry, organization, job and team.

- Goals of orientation include:
  - Reduce the anxiety and stress for new-hires
  - Reduce the burden that the orientation process places on management and peers
  - Provide a favorable first impression of organization

### Explanation

An orientation program introduces new employees to the call center industry, organization, job and team. Key goals of orientation include:

- Reduce the anxiety and stress for new-hires

- Reduce the burden that the orientation process places on management and peers

- Provide a favorable first impression of organization

#### Orientation to the Call Center Industry

Working in the call center environment requires all employees to learn specialized vocabulary and unique operating practices. Performance measurement in call centers is different than most other types of business units, so it is important for all employees to understand the "why" behind the practices of the call center. An orientation to the call center industry should include:

- The people who comprise the call center

- The call center as hub of communication for the organization

- Three driving forces of call centers:
  - Random call arrival
  - The psychology of queues
  - Factors of caller tolerance

- A basic understanding of staffing and scheduling, including:

- Service level
- Forecasting
- How base staff is calculated
- Scheduling considerations
- Adherence to schedule
- Quality contact handling
- Monitoring and coaching
- Meeting customer expectations

### Orientation to the Organization

Orientation to the organization usually contains:

- Orientation to general organization rules; e.g., start/stop times, basic procedures, use of equipment for personal use, etc.
- Management philosophy
- Organizational structure
- Information about the organization and industry
- Benefits the organization provides
- Emphasis on health and safety
- Behaviors resulting in corporate discipline
- Information regarding how the call center fits into the enterprise and its strategic direction

### Orientation to the Job

Orientation to the job provides information about the realistic demands of the job, the organization's expectations and the work environment. The orientation should include:

- A copy of the job description
- Identification of a peer to act as a mentor and the value of a mentor for long-term success
- An orientation job aid including what to read and who to contact about certain issues
- Manuals regarding products, procedures and processes
- A discussion concerning management expectations and reporting

procedures

- Performance expectations, guidelines and criteria

- Compensation policies; e.g., performance reviews, timing of merit increases, pay periods, etc.

- Grievance procedures

- How agent groups are structured and contacts are routed

**Orientation to the Team**

Many times turnover occurs because the individual is not oriented to the team. The issue is not one of ability to do the work, but of not feeling included. Therefore, management should take steps to quickly build team acceptance of the new employee.

# Training and Development

## Exercises

### Definitions and Purpose of Training and Development

1. Match the following terms with their definitions. You will use each definition only once.

_____ Development

_____ Education

_____ Learning

_____ Training

a. Learning with job-specific objectives which enhances knowledge, skills and abilities; has a short-term focus.

b. The acquisition of knowledge, skills and abilities.

c. Learning related to future roles or positions for which the individual is being prepared; has a short- and long-term focus.

d. Learning for the general growth of the individual and/or the organization; has a long-term focus.

### Cultivating a Learning Organization

2. Fill in the blanks to complete each sentence.

_____ is the key sustainable source of added value in an organization.

Organizational and team learning is dependant upon _____ knowledge acquisition.

### Knowledge Management Issues [Strategic]

3. True or false

_____ The biggest barrier to knowledge management is finding technology that enables easy access to gathered knowledge.

_____ Knowledge maps and electronic card catalogs are examples of knowledge management containers.

**Self-Development**

4. Select the most appropriate answer to each question.

Who is responsible for self-development?

     a. Employee

     b. Manager

     c. Both employee and manager

Which of the following should be a higher priority in a self-development plan?

     a. Career advancement

     b. Enhancing knowledge and skills

**Developing a Call Center Training Strategy**

5. True or false

_____A positive return on investment (ROI) is sufficient to determine that training should be conducted.

_____The training plan should be developed before budgetary limitations are considered.

**Identifying Training Needs**

6. What are the three functions of a training needs analysis?

_____

_____

_____

7. What are generally considered to be the three causes for gaps between current performance and desired results?

_____

_____

_____

**Adult Learning Principles**

8. Beside each statement below, indicate whether it is a characteristic of most adult learners (with an "a") or not a characteristic of most adult learners (with an "n").

_____Are motivated most strongly by external pressures

_____Have varied learning styles

_____Learn best when their learning efforts are mandated by others

_____Need to know why they are learning

_____Want practical application

_____Want their real-life experiences to be recognized and valued

**Instructional Design/Development**

9. What are the five phases of the Instructional System Design model?

   _____

   _____

   _____

   _____

   _____

**Training Delivery Methods**

10. Select the most appropriate answer to each question.

   Which of the following is a strength of classroom training?

   a. Easy to reach many employees, e.g., part-timers, shift workers, geographically-disbursed workforce

   b. Effective for almost any type of content

   c. Knowledge transfer to the job is virtually guaranteed

   d. Low cost

Section 5

Which of the following is a strength of self-paced study?

a. Appropriate for reinforcing existing skills or providing remedial training

b. Can be easily customized to accommodate learner preferences and styles

c. Easy to change content from session-to-session

d. Promotes relationships which are likely to contribute to overall organizational communication and employee satisfaction

### Evaluating Training Effectiveness [Strategic]

11. When assessing a training program, what are the four levels of evaluation?

Level 1: _____

Level 2: _____

Level 3: _____

Level 4: _____

**Answers to these exercises are in Section 10.**

Note: These exercises are intended to help you retain the material learned. While not the exact questions as on the CIAC Certification assessment, the material in this handbook/study guide fully addresses the content on which you will be assessed. For a formal practice test, please contact the CIAC directly by visiting www.ciac-cert.org.

## Training and Development
## Reference Bibliography

### Related Articles from *Call Center Management Review* (See Section 9)

Ensuring New-Hire Success via 'Transition Training'

Develop a Coherent Training Process for Multiple Sites

Training and Support for Frontline Supervisors

Tap the Potential of Technology-based Call Center Training

Measuring the Effectiveness of Customer Service Training in Call Centers

### For Further Study

#### Books/Studies

*Call Center Recruiting and New-Hire Training: The Best of Call Center Management Review.* Call Center Press, 2002.

Dixon, Nancy. *Organizational Learning.* The Conference Board of Canada, 1993.

Mitchell, Garry. *The Trainer's Handbook: The AMA Guide to Effective Training.* AMACOM, 1998.

Nadler, Leonard and Zeace Nadler. *Designing Training Programs, The Critical Events Model.* Gulf Professional Publishing Company, 1994.

Walton, John. *Strategic Human Resource Development.* Financial Times Management, 1999.

#### Articles

Garvin, David. "Building a Learning Organization." *Harvard Business Review,* July 1993.

Hansen Harps, Leslie and Laurie Solomon. "Tap the Potential of Technology-based Call Center Training." *Call Center Management Review,* March 2000.

Levin, Greg. "The Power of Peer Mentoring." *Call Center Management Review*, June 2002.

McCune, Jenny. "Thirst for Knowledge." *Management Review*, April 1999.

Solomon, Laurie. "What Every Trainer Needs to Know About How Agents Learn." *Call Center Management Review*, June 1999.

## Seminars

*Monitoring and Coaching for Improved Call Center Performance* public seminar, presented Incoming Calls Management Institute.

# Measuring and Improving Performance

**People Management**

# Section 6: Measuring and Improving Performance

## Contents

Section 6

## 1. Measuring and Tracking Performance Objectives

Ready? | 1 | 2 | 3 |

### Key Points

- Call center performance objectives serve as goals/targets for individuals, teams, the call center and the organization.

- Some objectives are appropriate in all environments; e.g., quality, first call resolution, customer satisfaction and adherence to schedule. Some are appropriate in certain types of call centers; e.g., average call value and revenues produced. And others – notably occupancy and contacts handled – are usually counterproductive.

- Performance measures are captured by many different systems and retrieval methods vary according to the technologies that are in place. Reporting formats and usage also vary, depending on the implications of the information and the time-sensitive nature of the data.

### Explanation

Call center performance objectives serve as goals/targets for individuals, teams, the call center and the organization. They are often based on the call center's key performance indicators (KPIs). However, whereas KPIs are high-level measures of actual performance, performance objectives are results that the call center is striving to achieve. Also, KPIs tend to be limited to high-level results, while performance objectives can be broken into as many specific goals/objectives as necessary to support KPIs, and the call center's vision and mission.

Performance objectives – and how they are applied – tend to vary significantly from one organization to the next, depending on the mission, focus, culture and size of the call center (as well as management experience and know-how). Further, some objectives, though commonly used, can be counterproductive. (See Avoiding Conflicting Objectives, this section.) Choosing appropriate performance objectives is an important management responsibility.

Performance measures are captured by many different systems, and retrieval methods vary according to the technologies that are in place. Acquiring the data required to track some objectives is straightforward, and comes directly

from common system reports (when available); other performance objectives require many more data sources and much more assembly.

The following table summarizes:

- Common call center performance objectives
- The formula or approach for measuring each objective
- Sources of data and tracking methodologies
- A summary of suggested applications and relevant role

| **Objectives Related to Quality:** | |
|---|---|
| **Call (Contact) Quality** <br><br> Approach: Assigns a value to the quality of individual contacts. <br><br> Data typically comes from samples via monitoring and/or recording contacts; however, some criteria may also be generated from ACD-based call coding or reports from customer information systems. Either supervisors or quality assurance specialists review monitored/recorded contacts for initial data capture. | Application: Appropriate in all environments as both a high-level objective (overall summary of the results of individual contacts) which is generally tracked monthly, and as the basis for specific objectives for agents and supervisors, contact by contact. <br><br> Notes: The quality of each contact is essential to successful call center performance. Quality should be defined to reflect the needs and objectives of both the organization and customers. Criteria generally include such things as interpreting customer requirements correctly, entering data accurately, providing the correct information, accurate call coding, capturing needed and useful information, etc. These criteria should be an inherent part of monitoring and coaching processes. |
| **First-Call Resolution** <br><br> Formula: Calls resolved upon initial contact ÷ total calls. <br><br> First-call resolution is generally tracked through a database system (customer information system) or by ACD call coding. How first-call resolution is defined drives tracking – e.g., does it refer to a call not being transferred or to an issue that is resolved even if it must be escalated or transferred? Ideally, first-call resolution should be defined as an issue resolved on first contact (the caller doesn't have to con- | Application: Appropriate in all environments as a high-level objective, which is generally tracked monthly (however, with the right systems, can be viewed at any time). Components that lead to first-call resolution should also be built into specific quality objectives for agents (however, because not all aspects are within their control, these components must be selected carefully). <br><br> Notes: Studies indicate that organizations incur many types of additional expenses (some hidden and difficult to track) when |

| | |
|---|---|
| tact the center again or vice versa), even if escalated or transferred during the contact; transferred/escalated calls can be tracked as supporting data. | callers' issues are not fully resolved with the first contact. There is significant value in analyzing relative increases and decreases in first-call resolution, in response to changes in call center processes, systems and customer requirements. |
| **Errors and Rework**<br><br>Approach: The percent (and types) of errors and rework that are occurring.<br><br>Data generally comes from a database system (customer information system) and/or by ACD call coding. | Application:  Appropriate in all environments as high-level objective, reported monthly or (with the right systems) as often as the manager chooses.  Specific components of errors and rework are often built into quality objectives for agents (however, because not all errors are within their control, variables must be selected carefully).<br><br>Notes:  Errors lead to rework, unreliable data and potential interpretation problems downstream.  As with first-call resolution, there is significant value in analyzing increases and decreases in errors and rework, in response to changes in processes, systems and other factors. |
| **Objectives Related to Accessibility:** | |
| **Service Level and Response Time**<br><br>Formula, service level: X percent of contacts answered in Y seconds.<br><br>Formula, response time: 100% of contacts handled within N days/hours/minutes.<br><br>Service level is available directly from ACD reports.  Response time reports may come from additional systems, e.g., email response management systems (ERMS), Web servers, workforce management systems (WFMS), etc. | Application:  Service level and response time are key accessibility measures and are appropriate high-level objectives.  They should be reported by "reporting intervals" (e.g., the number of half-hours within, above and below objectives) NOT as averages across days, weeks or months.  Managers should be able to identify recurring problematic intervals.  These objectives are also key planning targets, used for base staff calculations.<br><br>Notes:  Establishing concrete service level and response time objectives is a prerequisite to the solid planning necessary to ensure that the organization is accessible through whatever channel customers use. |
| **Average Speed of Answer (ASA)**<br><br>Formula: Total delay ÷ total number of calls.<br><br>Available directly from ACD reports and the WFMS. | Application: ASA comes from the same set of data as service level.  It is not necessary to have both service level and ASA objectives.  If service level data is not available, ASA can be a substitute.  ASA does have important operational applications; e.g., it is a component of trunk load. |

*(continued, next page)*

| | |
|---|---|
| | **Notes:** ASA is often misinterpreted as a "typical" experience, but the average is skewed by many callers who get answered before ASA and some who wait far longer than ASA. |
| **Abandoned and Blocked Calls**<br><br>Formula, abandoned calls: Calls abandoned ÷ calls received.<br><br>Formula, busy signals: Number or percent of attempts that received busy signals.<br><br>Abandoned calls are available directly from ACD reports.<br><br>Reports on busy signals may come from the ACD (if using ACD controlled busies), the local telephone company and the inter-exchange (long distance) company (IXC). | **Application:** Abandoned and blocked calls are caused by insufficient staffing or trunking resources. They should be supporting information to service level and response time reports, not primary objectives.<br><br>**Notes:** Abandonment rate, though often a primary objective, is not a concrete measure of call center performance, because it is driven by caller behavior which the center cannot directly control; it should be of secondary importance to service level. Busy signals may be due to insufficient trunks, but are often the result of inadequate staffing and the resulting queues of waiting callers. |

## Objectives Related to Efficiency:

| | |
|---|---|
| **Forecasted Call Load vs. Actual**<br><br>**Approach:** The percent variance between the call load forecasted and the call load actually received.<br><br>Forecasted call load is available from the system used for forecasting, e.g., workforce management system or spreadsheets.<br><br>Actual call load is tracked by the WFMS, ACD, ERMS, fax servers, Web servers, etc. | **Application:** Appropriate in all environments as a high level objective, reported by interval; it is also used for ongoing tactical adjustments.<br><br>**Notes:** Forecasting the workload is a high-leverage activity that is fundamental to managing a call center effectively. Underestimating demand will mask and defeat all other efforts to provide good service. And overestimating demand results in waste. As a high level objective, forecasting accuracy should NOT be reported as a summary of forecasted versus actual calls across a day, week or month, but an illustration of accuracy for each reporting interval (typically, half-hours). |
| **Scheduled Staff vs. Actual**<br><br>**Approach:** A comparison of the number of agents scheduled versus the number actually in the center.<br><br>Scheduled staff is available from the system used for scheduling, e.g., WFMS or spreadsheets. | **Application:** Appropriate in all environments as a high level objective for a center and for teams. As with forecasts, reports should show each interval.<br><br>**Notes:** The purpose of the objective is to understand and improve staff adherence and schedules. |

| | |
|---|---|
| Actual staff available is reported primarily by the ACD. May also be tracked by the WFMS, with some components available from ERMS and other systems. | |
| **Adherence to Schedule**<br><br>Approach: A measure of how much time and when, during the agents' shifts, they are taking or available to take calls.<br><br>Data comes from the WFMS and/or ACD reports. | Application: Appropriate in all environments as a high-level objective. Is also a common and recommended objective for individuals and teams.<br><br>Notes: Adherence consists of time spent in talk time, after-call work, waiting for calls to arrive, and placing necessary outbound calls. The two terms most often associated with adherence include availability (how much time agents were available) and compliance (when agents were available to take calls). In today's environment, it is more important than ever for agents to be "in the right places at the right times, doing the right things." The measure is independent of whether the call center actually has the staff necessary to achieve a targeted service level and/or response time; it is simply a comparison of how closely agents adhere to schedules. |
| **Average Handling Time (AHT)**<br><br>Formula: The sum of average talk time + average after-call work.<br><br>Available from ACD reports for incoming calls, and from ERMS and Web servers for those contacts. May also be available from a WFMS. | Application: Appropriate in all environments for high-level purposes and for ongoing tactical planning; it is generally not recommended as a strict agent standard.<br><br>Notes: In many centers, AHT is increasing as contacts become more complex and as objectives focus on building relationships and capturing needed and useful information. However, all things equal, reductions in AHT through better processes, technologies and training will create significant efficiencies. Creating strict AHT targets at the individual level often backfires, resulting in repeat calls, lower quality or in agents using work modes incorrectly (which skews reports). |
| **Occupancy and Productive/ Nonproductive**<br><br>Approach, occupancy: The percentage of time agents spend handling calls. The rest of the time agents are waiting for calls to arrive. The inverse of occupancy is often | Application: These figures are not appropriate objectives, other than as a part of high-level analysis, because occupancy and contacts handled are driven by random call arrival, call type, caller communication skills and many other variables outside the |

*(continued, next page)*

| | |
|---|---|
| referred to as idle time, available time or availability. | control of agents. It is important that the manager understand and account for the influence of occupancy in these measures. |
| Approach, productive and nonproductive: Generally measures the volume of work (e.g., number of contacts) that agents produce. | Notes: When adherence to schedule improves (goes up), occupancy – as well as average contacts handled per person – goes down. Adherence to schedule is within the control of individuals, whereas occupancy is determined by the laws of nature, which are outside of an individual's control. |
| Reports on occupancy and contacts handled come directly from the ACD and ERMS, as well as the WFMS. | |

### Objectives Related to Cost Performance:

| | |
|---|---|
| **Cost Per Call (Cost Per Contact)**<br><br>Formula: Total costs ÷ total calls.<br><br>Volume of contacts requires ACD reports, and potentially other systems that track contacts, e.g., the ERMS, fax servers, Web servers, etc.<br><br>Cost data comes from several reports/sources; e.g., payroll for staffing costs; budget for equipment, building depreciation, etc.; telecommunications reports for toll and line usage costs. | Application: Appropriate in all environments as a high-level objective, but must be interpreted carefully' e.g., a climbing cost per call can be a good sign (process improvements may result in fewer calls, spreading fixed costs over fewer calls and driving up cost per call).<br><br>Notes: Cost per call should ideally be differentiated by each channel or combination of channels of contact (i.e., inbound call, IVR only, IVR to agent, Web only, Web to agent, etc.). |
| **Average Call Value**<br><br>Formula: Total revenue ÷ total number of calls.<br><br>Revenue information requires data from several reports/sources; e.g., sales reports, total orders, CRM system reports, etc. In other words, any report that indicates revenue generated by the call center.<br><br>Volume of contacts requires ACD reports, and potentially other systems that track contacts; e.g., the email ERMS, fax servers, Web servers, etc. | Application: Appropriate for revenue-generating environments, such as reservation centers and catalog companies, where calls have a measurable value.<br><br>Notes: Average call value is tough to apply (and generally not recommended) in call centers where the value of calls is difficult to measure; i.e., customer service centers and help desks. |
| **Revenue**<br><br>Approach: Tracks revenues attributed to call center services.<br><br>Revenue information requires data from several reports/sources; e.g., sales reports, total orders, CRM system reports, etc. In other words, any report that indicates revenue generated by the call center. | Application: As with average call value, is appropriate for revenue-generating environments.<br><br>Notes: Results are often correlated with other variables such as call center costs, market conditions and revenues through other channels of contact (e.g., retail or direct sales force) to gauge the call center's impact on the organization's profits. |

| | |
|---|---|
| **Budget/Cost Objectives**<br><br>Approach:  The difference between projected and actual expenditures, for various budget categories.<br><br>Budget vs. actual information can be formulated from corporate accounting systems, or developed in a spreadsheet. | Application:  Is appropriate in all environments as a high-level objective, assuming it is considered within the context of changing workload variables and call center responsibilities.<br><br>Notes:  Is generally produced both quarterly and annually, and is available monthly in some environments. |
| **Objectives for Outbound** [1]<br><br>Approach: The number or percentage of attempted calls, connected calls, contacts, abandoned calls, contacts per hour, contact rate, cost per contact, cost per minute and penetration rate. | Application:  These objectives are appropriate and necessary in outbound environments.<br><br>Notes:  Call blending literally combines inbound and outbound work, making integrated KPI measures for inbound and outbound work a necessity. |

### Objectives Related to Strategic Impact:

| | |
|---|---|
| **Customer Satisfaction**<br><br>Approach:  Measures the percentage of all customers who felt satisfied with the service they received.<br><br>Data can come from a variety of sources; e.g., customer satisfaction surveys, mystery shopping, automated IVR surveys, focus groups, etc. | Application:  Appropriate in all environments as an overall objective. Customer satisfaction data is often presented quarterly or monthly, broken down by channel of contact and customer segment.<br><br>Notes: Studies have linked customer satisfaction to customer loyalty, repeat purchases and word-of-mouth advertising.  If customer satisfaction drops, both customers and agents are great sources of information on how to improve results. Customer satisfaction has greatest value as a relative measure and in conjunction with other objectives (e.g., when policies, service level performance, system enhancements and other changes take place, what happens to customer satisfaction). |
| **Employee Satisfaction**<br><br>Approach: Assigns a value to how satisfied call center employees are with their jobs.<br><br>Data is captured via surveys, focus groups or one-on-one interviews. | Application:  Appropriate in all environments as a high-level objective.   Generally produced once or twice per year.<br><br>Notes:  Studies have demonstrated that customer satisfaction increases as agent job satisfaction increases.  Further, retention, productivity and quality often have a definable, positive correlation to agent satisfaction. Results of surveys to gauge agent satisfaction should be compared to job satisfaction levels in other parts of the organization. Results are typically provided in summarized hard copy, and are often compiled by parties outside of the call center. |

*(continued, next page)*

| **Turnover**<br><br>Formula: (number of agents exiting the job ÷ avg. actual number of agents during the period) x (12 ÷ number of mos. in the period).<br><br>Data is captured via a entry into a HR records and/or a WFMS, and retrieval is typically a manual calculation or a report from the WFMS. | **Application:** Appropriate in all environments as a high-level objective. Turnover reports are often produced monthly (calculated on an annualized basis), and should be categorized as voluntary (natural) or involuntary (unnatural).<br><br>**Notes:** Retention is an increasingly important objective as call centers become more complex and agent and management skill and experience requirements escalate. Reductions in turnover can typically be translated into financial savings for the organization, and overall improvements in quality and productivity. |
| --- | --- |
| **Overall Call Center ROI**<br><br>Approach: Objectives related to the call center's overall return on investment (ROI) seek to identify, measure, track, improve and communicate the call center's impact on the organization. These objectives include:<br><br>• Customer satisfaction<br>• Improved quality and innovation<br>• Innovative products and services<br>• Highly leveraged marketing and CRM initiatives<br>• Efficient delivery of services<br>• Supporting self-service systems<br>• Revenue/sales (in commercial organizations)<br><br>These measures are a synthesis of samples and analysis, and data comes from a variety of sources. | **Application:** ROI-related objectives are appropriate in all environments as high-level objectives.<br><br>**Notes:** Revenue and profit related measures will not apply to non-commercial organizations (e.g., government, non-profits) but the call center's impact on things like innovation, quality, etc., can and should be measured through samples and analysis. |

*(1) Outbound is categorized with cost performance, but can feasibly fall in any other area depending on the reasons for and effectiveness of outbound.*

*These measurements/objectives are covered in detail in ICMI's* Call Center Operations Management Handbook and Study Guide.

## 2. The Contribution of Roles/Responsibilities to Objectives [Strategic]

Ready? | 1 | 2 | 3 |

### Key Points

- Given the many interrelated activities inherent in the call center, there is almost always overlapping responsibilities for meeting high-level objectives.

- The interplay between roles can leave individuals feeling like there is little direct connection between their roles and what the call center is trying to achieve; however, each individual has a significant impact on overall call center results.

- An important management responsibility is to ensure people understand the contribution they make to call center's – and organization's – direction.

### Explanation

Call center activities are inherently interrelated and there are almost always overlapping responsibilities for meeting high-level objectives. For example, agents, supervisors, managers, workforce planners, information technology (IT) staff, trainers and others all have a role in improving customer satisfaction. But who is responsible for what? The interplay between roles can leave individuals feeling like there is little connection between their roles and what the call center is trying to achieve.

Nothing could be further from the truth. Though impact and responsibilities are shared – and heavily influenced by the process – it's important to understand the contributions individuals and teams make to the call center's objectives. The following table provides a summary of the connections between key roles, and the call center's major objectives. While not every possible position/role is included, the table illustrates the broad impact that each role has on the results the call center is producing.

| Objectives | Contribution of Roles |
|---|---|
| **Quality Objectives**<br>• Call (Contact) Quality<br><br>• First-Call Resolution<br><br>• Errors and Rework | **Agents:** Agents have a direct impact on call-by-call quality, which contributes to overall quality, first-call resolution and a low rate of errors and rework.<br><br>**Supervisors:** Supervisors contribute to quality objectives by ensuring that individuals in their teams have the resources, coaching and feedback they need to handle each contact with quality. The experience supervisors have in handling frontline work, as well as their proximity to it, make them invaluable in quality improvement initiatives.<br><br>**Quality Specialists:** Manage a centralized repository of quality data captured contact by contact (by the quality specialist or by supervisors). Analysis of this information leads to process, system, training and coaching improvements.<br><br>**Workforce Planners:** Workforce planners impact quality by forecasting the call center's workload accurately and ensuring that schedules match requirements accurately (resulting in the right contacts going to the right places at the right times). They also are responsible for identifying the best times for people to work on quality initiatives and training.<br><br>**Technical Support (IT):** IT enables quality by equipping the call center with appropriate tools and technologies. For example, information systems that provide agents with accurate, real-time data on customers, products, services and policies contribute enormously to call quality and first-call resolution. Similarly, capable systems that are thoughtfully programmed ensure the right contacts are routed to the right places at the right times.<br><br>**Managers/Directors:** Managers contribute to quality first and foremost by ensuring agents, supervisors, planners and others have the training, skills, tools and processes that enable them to be successful in their positions. They ensure the call center is an inherent part of organizationwide processes (e.g., marketing and product development). They also are generally responsible for cultivating culture that values quality from top to bottom. |
| **Accessibility Objectives:**<br>• Service Level and Response Time<br><br>• Average Speed of Answer (ASA)<br><br>• Abandoned and Blocked Calls | **Agents:** Agents contribute to accessibility by being in "the right places at the right times, doing the right things."<br><br>**Supervisors:** Supervisors contribute to accessibility by ensuring that individuals are in the right places at the right times, doing the right things. They help resolve adherence problems and often serve as liaison between real-time workforce managers and teams.<br><br>**Quality Specialists:** Quality specialists are inherently close to processes that impact handling times and other key accessibility drivers.<br><br>**Workforce Planners:** Accessibility is a primary workforce management responsibility. Workforce planners impact accessibility by forecasting the call center's workload accurately and ensuring that schedules match workload requirements. |

| | |
|---|---|
| | **Technical Support (IT):** IT enables accessibility by ensuring systems are structured well, responsive and support real-time call-handling requirements. IT also has the responsibility to ensure systems are up and running and that technical problems are quickly resolved.<br><br>**Managers/Directors:** Managers contribute to accessibility by ensuring that the call center's priorities – and supporting operational decisions – support accessibility. They ensure that employees have the resources they need, and that processes and systems support consistent accessibility. They ensure that departments across the organization that may impact the call center's workload collaborate with call center planners. |
| **Efficiency Objectives:**<br>• Forecasted Call Load vs. Actual<br><br>• Scheduled Staff vs. Actual<br><br>• Adherence to Schedule<br><br>• Average Handling Time (AHT)<br><br>• Occupancy and Productive/ Nonproductive | **Agents:** Agents contribute to efficiency objectives not only by how they handle contacts, but also by how they code work. For example, when they use talk time, after-call work and other work modes consistently and accurately, they contribute to more stable, reliable data for forecasting, scheduling and other objectives. Agents also have a direct impact on adherence to schedule.<br><br>**Supervisors:** Supervisors ensure that work is being handled as required, which leads to stable results and reliable data for planning purposes. They also usually serve as coordinators/liaisons for planning meetings and when schedules are adjusted to accommodate changing workload requirements. They have a key role in coaching agents to achieve adherence results.<br><br>**Quality Specialists:** Quality specialists have a responsibility not just for quality, but for associated efficiencies; e.g., if it takes one agent seven screens to do the same thing another can do in three, quality specialists can drive relevant training and coaching improvements.<br><br>**Workforce Planners:** As with accessibility, objectives related to efficiency are primary workforce planning responsibilities. Accurate forecasting, staffing and scheduling, as well as competent real-time adjustments, contribute enormously to efficiencies.<br><br>**Technical Support (IT):** IT contributes to efficiency by ensuring that workload tracking tools are correctly programmed and ensuring that trainers and supervisors teach agents their proper use. They also have a role in supporting systems that provide reports and data essential to the planning process (e.g., ACD, WFMS, reporting tools, ERMS, etc.).<br><br>**Managers/Directors:** Managers impact efficiency not only by ensuring that the center has the right tools, methods and training in place, but also by establishing a culture of collaboration – and one that emphasizes the importance of accurate and comprehensive planning. And, as with accessibility, ensuring that data information and plans other departments have are shared with the call center. |

*(continued, next page)*

| Cost-Performance Objectives: | **Agents:** Agents have an indirect but significant impact on cost-performance objectives. By doing the right things at the right times and handling contacts with quality, they contribute to accessibility and quality, which, in turn, have a bearing on cost performance. Also, in revenue producing environments, sales skills significantly impact revenue results. |
|---|---|
| • Cost Per Call (Cost Per Contact)<br><br>• Average Call Value<br><br>• Revenue<br><br>• Budget/Cost Objectives<br><br>• Objectives for Outbound | **Supervisors:** As with agents, supervisors have an indirect but significant impact on cost-performance objectives. By enabling their teams to do the right things at the right times and handle contacts with quality, they contribute to accessibility and quality, which, in turn, have a bearing on cost performance. Coaching and monitoring should also support overall budget and revenue objectives. |
| | **Quality Specialists:** Important aspects of quality include those things that lead to revenue and cost-performance objectives (e.g., efficient processes, seeing cross-selling opportunities, etc.). |
| | **Workforce Planners:** Virtually every cost-performance objective is impacted by the accuracy of workforce planning and effectiveness in carrying out those plans. For example, forecasts and schedules that are improved by just one or two percent can translate to thousands of dollars of daily savings in a medium to large call center. Appropriate schedules reduce overtime costs, and accurate planning ensures contacts are going to the right agent groups at the right times – which impact revenue and cost results. |
| | **Technical Support (IT):** The technologies available to the call center – their functionality and how they are programmed and used – have a significant impact on cost-performance objectives. This is true both for customer-facing systems (e.g., to what degree will they use self-service channels?), information systems agents need to handled contacts with quality, and reporting systems used by management to leverage call center efficiencies and effectiveness. Efficiency of systems, uptime, technical support response times all contribute to cost objectives. |
| | **Managers/Directors:** Managers have primary responsibility for identifying budgetary requirements and ensuring the call center gets the resources necessary to fulfill its mission. They also have a significant impact on cost performance, by ensuring that the right people, processes and technologies are in place and working in sync. |
| Strategic Impact Objectives:<br><br>• Customer Satisfaction<br><br>• Employee Satisfaction<br><br>• Turnover<br><br>• Overall Call Center ROI | **Agents:** Agents contribute to customer satisfaction through their contributions accessibility and quality, on a contact-by-contact basis. But agents also have a much larger strategic impact; for example, the information captured during contacts – assuming it is complete and accurate – becomes the basis for product and service improvements and innovations, better marketing campaigns and quality improvements (inside and outside the call center). Agents are also key in educating customers on the availability and use of self-service access channels. |
| | **Supervisors:** Supervisors contribute to the call center's strategic impact by helping to facilitate their teams' success. Supervisors are also frequently involved in projects and initiatives to identify, |

measure, track, improve and communicate the call center's impact on the organization (e.g., through data analysis teams and as liaisons between other groups/departments and frontline activities).

**Quality Specialists:** Typically, quality specialists are involved in assembling information captured during contacts, analyzing it and getting it to other departments for which it would be useful. Quality specialists also are responsible for recommendations on process improvements that would contribute to higher levels of customer satisfaction and agent support.

**Workforce Planners:** Workforce planners have a similar impact on both customer satisfaction and employee satisfaction. For example, when the call center is accessible, due to accurate forecasts and schedules, customers are happier because they can reach the services they require quickly and easily. Similarly, good service levels mean occupancy levels that are not too high, giving agents the chance to "breathe" between contacts and to work with callers who aren't angry from waiting in a long queue. Again, accurate planning matches right resources with right contacts, enabling the highest quality services and customer satisfaction.

**Technical Support (IT):** Technologies first impact customer satisfaction at the user interface – e.g., are customer facing systems (IVRs, Web, etc.) easy to use and do they enable customers to accomplish what they want? But back-end systems also have a huge role; e.g., do agents have the information and support they need? Are capabilities in place to capture data from contacts that can be used to improve products, services and marketing, as well as to better understand customers? The answers to these questions impact customer satisfaction, employee satisfaction and the call center's overall ROI. Technical support also has a key role in developing and maintaining disaster recovery plans.

**Managers/Directors:** Managers ensure the culture, environment, tools and resources are in place to support a high-value environment. They also work with managers across the organization to use data captured during call center contacts to improve the organization's overall effectiveness in meeting the needs of customers. They ensure that call center staff remain focused on the vision of the organization and that behaviors are within company guidelines and support the company's brand and direction.

In short, agents, supervisors, quality specialists, workforce planners, IT, managers and other call center positions all have an impact on overall results. Consequently, it is essential that management:

1. Ensure that the interrelated nature of call center objectives and responsibilities is understood at all levels.

2. Establish the right objectives for the right groups of people. (See Setting Performance Objectives, this section.)

3. Differentiate between the responsibilities of individuals and teams, and the role of processes, technologies and strategies.

**Section 6**

## 3. Setting Performance Objectives

Ready? | 1 | 2 | 3 |

### Key Points

- Managers are inherently responsible for achieving results through other people. Consequently, call center managers/directors are generally held responsible for a broad range of objectives.

- Supporting roles and agents generally have accountabilities directly associated with the areas in which they have primary responsibility.

- There are two general methods for establishing individual performance objectives:
  1. Minimum standard
  2. Acceptable range

### Explanation

How does the reality of overlapping responsibilities translate into specific performance standards for individuals and teams? After all, on one hand, every person has a bearing on call center performance objectives. On the other, is it fair to set performance standards on things that are outside the direct control of an individual?

In principle – and in practice – the answer is fairly simple. Managers are inherently responsible for achieving results through other people. Consequently, the senior-level call center managers/director are generally held responsible for the full repertoire of call center performance objectives that the organization establishes. Of course, they shouldn't be held accountable for objectives that are in conflict or that are mutually exclusive. (See Avoiding Conflicting Objectives, this section.) And they can only accomplish what is possible within the context of the resources they have to work with. But, by nature, they answer for overall results.

Managers and analysts in supporting roles are in a similar situation; however, with more specific responsibilities, accountabilities are generally associated with the areas in which they have primary responsibility. For example, the workforce manager in charge of forecasting and scheduling is generally accountable for the accuracy of the forecast (among other things) even though it is influenced by many variables, people and departments outside of their immediate control.

Even so, if the forecast is way off the mark, they need to have answers as to why – and recommendations on how it can be improved.

In the best-managed organizations, agents have an accountability to their teams (and the larger organization), as well as for the results of their own work. However, with primary responsibility to the specific work to which they are assigned, performance standards must be selected with care and foresight. (See Key Objectives for Agents, this section.)

**Performance Standards/Accountabilities**

Given overlapping responsibilities in call centers, high-performance centers put much more emphasis on processwide improvements than strict output quotas (e.g., handling X number of calls or keeping handling time under N seconds). They work hard to educate everyone on the interrelated nature of processes and the impact each person has on results. And, they establish key areas of accountability.

Of course, some standards apply to everyone, such as attendance, punctuality and quality of workmanship. However, well-managed call centers also establish areas of accountability for each call center position, which stem from job descriptions. (See Call Center Roles and Responsibilities, Section 3.) These typically include the following:

**Agents:**

- Adherence to schedule
- Quality (contact by contact), including:
    - Identify and handle customer inquiries
    - Apply customer service policies
    - Perform business retention activities
    - Resolve customer problems
    - Educate customers on products and services offered
    - Match product benefits with customer needs
    - Enter coding and tracking information completely and accurately

Note: Many call centers also set standards on average handling time or after-call work (a component of average handling time). However, focusing on these outputs as strict quotas can backfire, in the form of incorrect mode usage, and degradations of required service. (See Key Objectives for Agents, this section.)

**Supervisors:**
- Team adherence to schedule
- Quality of the team
    - Ensure team meets quality objectives
    - Provide monitoring and coaching to individuals
    - Work with management to identify systemic quality problems
- Effectiveness of performance reviews and team meetings
- Performing the work of the agents during peak periods (as applicable)
- Representing team on special projects/initiatives

**Quality specialists:**
- Leading and managing monitoring processes
- Ensuring consistent calibration
- Synthesizing monitoring input and preparing timely reports
- Identifying individual and process improvement opportunities
- Tracking and analyzing monitoring results vs. customer satisfaction measures

**Workforce Planners:**
- Creating accurate workload forecasts
- Organizing schedules that fit well for workload and agent requirements
- Assessing budgetary needs and implications of resource requirements
- Taking the initative to coordinate plans with other departments
- Ensuring proper use of work modes (e.g., after-call work, auxiliary modes, etc.)
- Present key performance results to executive management

**Technical Support:**
- Maintaining existing systems with minimum downtime
- Addressing usability issues (e.g., configuration, programming, etc.)
- Updating call-routing tables and systems as required
- Troubleshooting technical problems
- Recommending system improvement opportunities

**Section 6**

**Managers/Directors:**

- Ensuring the call center meets key objectives related to:
  - Quality
  - Accessibility
  - Efficiency
  - Cost performance
  - Strategic impact
- Establishing clear objectives for employees
- Maintaining morale
- Preparing budgets, illustrating budgetary tradeoffs
- Overseeing hiring and training efforts
- Aligning call center objectives with enterprise and customer objectives
- Maximizing the call center's strategic impact on the organization

## Two Approaches to Setting Standards

Since performance standards impact everything from pay and promotions to training and coaching, they must be chosen carefully. It is important not to focus on average performance when setting performance expectations at the job level. For one thing, average performance may or may not meet the objectives of the call center. Further, by nature, about half of a group will be performing above average and about half below – regardless of the actual proficiency with which the group is performing.

Instead, call center managers should generally use one of the following two methods to set individual performance objectives:

**1. Minimum standard:** Determine the minimum performance standard that will achieve call center objectives. Then, use this method for establishing objectives in areas such as quality and adherence to schedule.

**2. Acceptable range:** Determine a range of acceptable performance. The range then becomes the guide to establishing objectives. Training or other actions will be necessary for individuals who fall below the acceptable range. Those above the range are either shortchanging the process, or are role models for training and process improvement efforts that can be applied to the rest of the group.

A common acronym used to describe performance metrics is that they should

be SMART:

    (S)pecific

    (M)easurable

    (A)ctionable

    (R)elevant

    (T)imely

### Shifting Performance Curves

Some managers advocate a process of "shifting performance curves" – turning average performers into top performers. The steps they generally take include:

- Identify competencies (knowledge, skills, abilities, behaviors) of top performers

- Identify current competencies of moderate performers and determine training and development needs

- Set performance expectations based on top performers

- Track annual performance of moderate performers against baseline of top performers

In short, this process actively "raises the bar" to encourage better performance from "average" performers. In the right context – e.g., with the right leadership and culture – this approach can work well. However, it's important to note the downsides of this approach. For one, in any group of people, there will be distribution of talents and skills. Constantly pushing average performers can disenfranchise those who, for whatever set of reasons, are in the middle of the pack.

Further, top performers may be neglected when it comes to training and development. Although they are currently performing well, individuals need to be challenged and encouraged in order to sustain their performance and grow in their career. Without sufficient training and development time, your top performers may begin to pursue other job opportunities in search of career growth.

Finally, an age-old complaint workers have against management is that they receive an unwelcome reward for pushing hard to meet objectives: The bar is raised and expectations are reestablished at a new level. Great leaders bring out the best in people and tap into an innate desire to constantly improve; but when pay, promotions and general well-being are gauged on a constantly moving target, this approach can backfire. It takes the right environment, leadership and buy-in to work as a sustainable approach to setting standards.

Section 6

## 4. Key Objectives for Agents

Ready? | 1 | 2 | 3 |

### Key Points

- Contacts handled has been a traditional productivity measurement. However, as a measure of performance, contacts handled is, and always has been, problematic.

- The two recommended performance objectives for agents include adherence to schedule and quality.

- Adherence to schedule and qualitative measures are becoming even more important as increasingly sophisticated and varied call-handling routines proliferate.

### Explanation

Performance measurements are usually tied to expectations and standards, and raise issues about fairness, what agents can and can't control, why people have different capabilities and drives, and the processes that they are working within. Consequently, few subjects elicit such strong and varied opinion.

There are about as many different sets of performance measurements and standards for agents as there are call centers. However, three types of performance measurements – contacts handled, adherence to schedule and qualitative measurements – are common, albeit in various iterations. Contacts handled is fading, while the other two types of measurements continue to gain acceptance.

#### Contacts Handled (Calls Per Agent)

Traditionally, contacts handled (also referred to as calls/contacts per agent or calls/contacts per hour) has been an almost universal productivity measurement. In fact, many call center managers have viewed contacts handled as virtually synonymous with "productivity." There have always been concerns about sacrificing quality for quantity. But in practice, contacts handled has been the more widely used benchmark for establishing productivity standards, comparing performance among agents and groups, and assessing the impact of changes and improvements to the call center.

However, as a measure of performance, contacts handled is and always has

Section 6

been, problematic. Many of the variables that impact contacts handled are out of agents' control: call arrival rate, type of calls, knowledge of callers, communication ability of callers, accuracy of the forecast and schedule, adherence to schedule (of others in the group), and absenteeism.

There are also mathematical realities at work that are not within the control of an individual agent. For example, smaller groups are less efficient (have lower occupancy) than larger groups, at a given service level (see table). Since the number of calls changes throughout the day, so does average calls per agent for a group or an individual in the group.

| Calls in 1/2 Hour | Service Level | Agents Required | Occupancy | Avg. Calls Per Agent | True Calls Per Agent |
|---|---|---|---|---|---|
| 50 | 80/20 | 9 | 65% | 5.6 | 8.6 |
| 100 | 80/20 | 15 | 78% | 6.7 | 8.6 |
| 500 | 80/20 | 65 | 90% | 7.7 | 8.6 |
| 1000 | 80/20 | 124 | 94% | 8.1 | 8.6 |

Assumption: Calls last an average 3.5 minutes.

Further, if contacts handled is over-emphasized, quality can suffer. Agents may even "trick" the system to increase their call count and achieve a set standard.

**True (Normalized) Calls/Contacts Per Agent**

Some call center managers convert raw contacts handled into an adjusted measurement that is more fair and meaningful. For example, occupancy, which is not within the control of an individual, can be "neutralized" by dividing contacts handled by percent occupancy. Using the numbers in the table above, 5.6 average calls per agent divided by 65 percent is 8.6 "normalized" calls, as is 6.7 calls divided by 78 percent, 7.7 calls divided by 90 percent and 8.1 calls divided by 94 percent. Others go a step further and develop statistical control charts to determine whether the process is in control, what it's producing and which agents, if any, are outside of "statistical control."

But even with further analysis, calls per agent begins to lose meaning as technologies such as CTI, skills-based routing and Web integration, which enable increasingly sophisticated and varied call-handling routines, proliferate. Thus the growing acceptance and use of adherence and qualitative measurements.

**Adherence Measurements**

Adherence to schedule, or signed-on time, is a measurement of how much time an individual is available to handle calls vs. the time he or she was scheduled to handle calls. If adherence to schedule is 85 percent, an agent would be expected to be in adherence .85 x 60 minutes, or 51 minutes on average per hour. Adherence consists of all plugged-in time including talk time, after-call work (wrap-up) time, time spent waiting for the next call and making necessary outgoing calls. Lunch, breaks, training, etc., are not counted as time assigned to handle calls. Adherence to schedule should be established at a level that is reasonable and that reflects the many things that legitimately keep agents from the phones. The same adherence to schedule goal may not be appropriate for all agent groups since the nature of the contacts in each group may lead to more or less legitimate reasons to be away from the phones. It should also be flexible (adjustable downward) when call volumes are low.

Some have developed adherence to schedule into a more refined measurement that also incorporates timing – when was a person available to handle contacts, in addition to how much time they were available. The idea here is to ensure that people are plugged in mid-morning when calls are barreling in, and are saving special projects for Thursday and Friday afternoons when calls slow down. ACD and forecasting/scheduling software has improved adherence reporting significantly in recent years.

The advantage of adherence to schedule is that it is reasonably objective. Agents cannot control variables such as the number of staff scheduled to handle contacts, the number of contacts coming in, the distribution of long and short contacts or the distribution of easy and difficult contacts. But they can generally control how available they are to take contacts.

**Qualitative Measurements**

In most call centers, qualitative criteria, which focus on knowledge of products and services, customer service and call-handling skills, and the policies of the organization, continue to become more refined and specific. Most use some form of monitoring (i.e., remote, side-by-side or call recording) to evaluate individual performance and identify training and coaching needs. (See Developing a Monitoring and Coaching Program, this section.)

An important and developing aspect of quality is that agents take the necessary time to do the job right — no more, no less. This means not rushing calls, but also not spending excess time on calls over and above what is necessary to

satisfy callers and handle them completely and correctly. If qualitative measurements are refined enough to ensure that agents are spending the appropriate amount of time handling calls, then adherence and qualitative measurements make a powerful pair. In fact, measuring contacts handled becomes unnecessary and quotas on average handling time are also unnecessary.

Many managers still believe that tracking production outputs, such as calls per hour or average handling time, is necessary. But the trend is clear: well-defined qualitative measurements are beginning to erode reliance on measurements that are after-the-fact outputs. Contacts handled, which used to be an almost ubiquitous productivity measurement, is fading. It is increasingly being replaced by focused and specific qualitative and adherence measurements. Agents can concentrate on being available and on handling each transaction according to its individual needs. If implemented well, qualitative and adherence measurements can cultivate a better working environment, better quality and higher productivity.

**Other Performance Objectives for Agents**

In addition to the two major objectives of qualitative and adherence measures, there are a number of other performance objectives that may be appropriate supporting objectives. Examples include:

- Attendance (or absenteeism)
- Initiative/creativity
- Team orientation
- Sales/orders as a percent of contacts
- Others, depending on the environment

## 5. Avoiding Conflicting Objectives

Ready? | 1 | 2 | 3 |

### Key Points

- Many call centers have expectations and standards that are at least partially in conflict, either with each other or with call center realities.

- Common conflicting standards include:
  - Average handling time vs. quality
  - Occupancy vs. service level and schedule adherence
  - Calls handled per agent vs. queue behavior
  - Cost per call vs. process improvement
  - Service level vs. service level
  - Service level vs. average speed of answer
  - Resources vs. mission

- An important management responsibility is to weed out conflicting objectives and focus on the things that really matter.

### Explanation

Conflicting objectives are, unfortunately, common in call centers. While no call center manager intentionally sets performance objectives that are diametrically opposed, many do have expectations and standards that are at least partially in conflict, either with each other or with call center realities.

The following examples produce troublesome symptoms: unclear priorities, misunderstandings, inconsistent results and hampered performance.

**Average handling time vs. quality:** An important aspect of quality is that agents take the necessary time to handle transactions correctly. This, of course, means not rushing calls. But it also means not spending time on calls over and above what is required to satisfy callers and handle transactions completely and correctly.

The nature of the calls, the processes you have in place, and the skills and knowledge of your agents determine how long calls are. If qualitative measurements are refined enough to ensure that agents are spending the appropriate amount of time handling calls, then average handling time

objectives are redundant and potentially counterproductive.

**Occupancy vs. service level and schedule adherence:** Occupancy is the percent of time during a half-hour that those agents who are on the phones are in talk time and after-call work. The inverse of occupancy is the time they spend waiting for inbound calls, plugged in and available. Some industry benchmarking reports have suggested that 90 percent occupancy is an appropriate target.

The problem is, occupancy is a phenomenon of random call arrival and is heavily influenced by service level and group size. If you staff correctly to handle the call load at your service level objective, occupancy will be what it will be. It's dictated by the nature of the workload and the service level objective you establish.

| | | | | |
|---|---|---|---|---|
| **Avg. Talk Time: 180 sec; Avg. Work Time: 30 sec; Calls: 250** | | | | |
| Agents | SL%<br>in 20 Sec. | ASA | Occ. | Trunk Load<br>(in hours) |
| 30 | 24% | 208.7 | 97% | 54.0 |
| 31 | 45% | 74.7 | 94% | 35.4 |
| 32 | 61% | 37.6 | 91% | 30.2 |
| 33 | 73% | 21.3 | 88% | 28.0 |
| 34 | 82% | 12.7 | 86% | 26.8 |
| 35 | 88% | 7.8 | 83% | 26.1 |
| 36 | 92% | 4.9 | 81% | 25.7 |
| 37 | 95% | 3.1 | 79% | 25.4 |
| 38 | 97% | 1.9 | 77% | 25.3 |
| 39 | 98% | 1.2 | 75% | 25.2 |
| 40 | 99% | 0.7 | 73% | 25.1 |
| 41 | 99% | 0.5 | 71% | 25.1 |
| 42 | 100% | 0.3 | 69% | 25.0 |

Consequently, setting objectives on occupancy – 90 percent or otherwise – is likely to conflict with about everything else you want to achieve. For example, when service level goes up, occupancy goes down. And when schedule adherence improves, occupancy goes down. Solution: Don't set occupancy targets.

**Calls handled per agent vs. queue behavior:** Many of the variables that impact calls handled per agent are out of their control (e.g., call arrival rate, call types, callers' knowledge, callers' communication abilities, the accuracy of the forecast and schedule, and the adherence to schedule of others in the group). As with occupancy, calls handled per agent looks better when service level and schedule adherence deteriorate (see table in this section).

The solutions is to eliminate this objective and instead focus on schedule adherence and quality. Calls handled will take care of itself within the context of your processes and the nature of queues.

**Cost per call vs. process improvement:** There are various ways to calculate cost per call, but the basic formula is to divide total costs by total calls for a given period of time. Conventional wisdom is, the lower the cost per call, the better. However, a climbing cost per call can be a good sign, depending on the variables driving it up. For example, better coordination with other departments may help reduce the number of times a customer has to contact your center. As a result, the fixed costs (in the numerator) get spread over fewer calls (in the denominator), driving cost per call up. But total costs will go down over time because eliminating waste and rework will drive down the variable costs.

**Service level vs. service levels:** A widely distributed benchmarking report recently suggested that setting a single standard for service level is "problematic" because for a service level of, say, 80 percent answered in 20 seconds, you are ignoring the business impact of the 20 percent who have to wait longer than 20 seconds. The proposed solution was to have two standards: one, to answer 80 percent of calls in 20 seconds; and the second, to answer the remaining 20 percent within 50 seconds. The problem: 100/50 is a very different service level than 80/20! You can no more hit both than you can adjust the pull of gravity.

When you establish 80/20, 90/15 or anything else, you are inherently dictating what longest wait will be. Choose one objective that is appropriate, then concentrate your energies on hitting it consistently.

**Service level vs. average speed of answer:** A similar problem stems from establishing objectives for both service level and ASA; e.g., our service level objective is to answer 90 percent of calls in 20 seconds, and our ASA objective is 15 seconds. Although service level and ASA calculations are based on the same set of data, they are very different reports (please refer to the table in this section). Choose one or the other, but don't have objectives for both. (Of the

two, service level tends to be a more stable and accurate, and less prone to misinterpretation.)

**Resources vs. mission:** Probably the most common and recurring case of incompatible objectives is between resources and mission. For example, be it too many or too few people, what you have and what you're asked to accomplish may be at odds. This issues goes to the heart of call center management and the ongoing challenge of matching resources to the workload. A characteristic of a well-managed call center is the ability to sort through and address any incompatibilities between available resources and desired results, on an ongoing basis.

No one purposely establishes objectives that are contradictory. But it's easy to do, given the many interrelated activities and processes, and the nature of random call arrival and the behavior of queues. An important management responsibility is to weed out conflicting objectives and focus on the things that really matter.

**Section 6**

## 6. Improving Call Center Processes

Ready? | 1 | 2 | 3 |

### Key Points

- A call center is a highly interrelated system of causes.

- Setting performance objectives and standards for individuals will have little positive impact, without also making improvements to call center processes.

### Explanation

As illustrated by the figure, a call center is a highly interrelated system of causes.

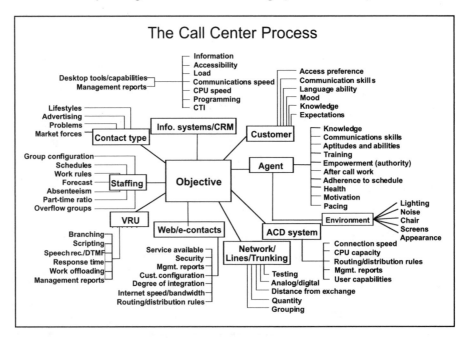

The central focus of the process can be any key performance indicator, or virtually any other measure or objective. Since just about everything is interrelated, the causes of performance problems are often difficult to isolate and measure. There is little use exhorting agents (or individuals in other positions) to improve quality and productivity, without also making improvements to the system of causes (the process) itself.

Without the appropriate methodology and tools, identifying the root causes of productivity and quality problems in a call center is a significant challenge. Consider a recurring problem, such as providing incomplete information to callers. Maybe the cause is insufficient information in the database. Or a need for more training. Or maybe a lack of coordination with marketing. Or carelessness. Or agent stress from a chronically high occupancy rate. Or a combination of any of these factors, coupled with many other things.

To make improvements and leverage opportunities, you need to have a systematic approach for improving quality, such as:

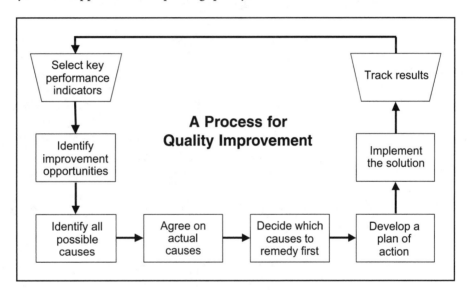

Further, there are a number of quality analysis and improvement tools that are useful in understanding processes and locating the root causes of problems, for example:

- **Check lists:** Lists of process steps; e.g., key procedures

- **Flow charts:** Used to analyze and standardize procedures, identify root causes of problems and plan new processes (e.g., system programming or steps to handle a contact)

- **Cause and effect diagrams:** Illustrate the relationships between causes and a specific effect you want to study; e.g., long calls or repeat calls

- **Scatter diagrams:** Assess the strength of the relationship between two variables; is used to test and document possible cause-and-effect; e.g., average handling time versus quality scores

- **Pareto charts:** Bar charts that rank events in order of importance or

frequency; e.g., transactions by type and errors by type

- **Control charts:** Provide information on process variation; e.g., average handling time or schedule adherence

- **Benchmarking:** The process of measuring your products, services and procedures against other organizations

Note: The point here is that setting performance objectives and standards will have little positive impact, unless you also work on making improvements to call center processes. Quality improvement tools and processes are covered in detail in ICMI's *Call Center Leadership and Business Management Handbook and Study Guide.*

---

### Using Control Charts

One of the reasons that quality problems in the call center are challenging and often confusing is because they are a part of a complex process, and any process has variation from the ideal. For example, the first chart is a simple view of group performance.

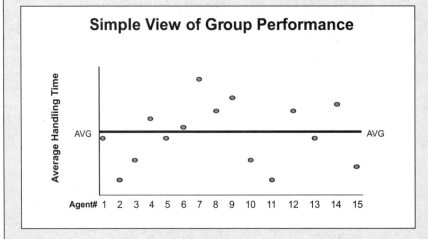

**Simple View of Group Performance**

A control chart is a tool that provides information on variation and is based on specific statistical calculations. There are two major types of variation: special causes and common causes. Special causes create erratic, unpredictable variation. For example, an agent with degenerative hearing loss, unusual calls from unexpected publicity or a computer terminal with intermittent problems are special causes. Common causes are the rhythmic, normal variations in the system.

A control chart enables you to bring a process under statistical control by eliminating the chaos of special causes. You can then work on the common causes by improving the system and thus, the whole process. Special causes show up as points outside of the upper control or lower control limits, or as points with unnatural patterns within the limits.

---

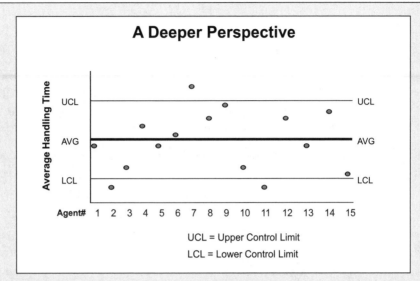

**A Deeper Perspective**

UCL = Upper Control Limit
LCL = Lower Control Limit

A control chart cannot reveal what the problems are. Instead, it reveals *where and when* special causes occur. Once special causes are eliminated, improving the system itself will have far more impact than focusing on individual causes. Improvements to the system will move the entire process in the right direction.

In short, control charts can:
- Control and reduce variation
- Prevent you from chasing the wrong problem
- Give early warning of changes in the process
- Improve predictability
- Improve planning

There are dozens of books and seminars on this subject. The best book we've found to describe the mechanics of producing and using control charts is *AT&T Statistical Quality Control Handbook* (Western Electric Company, Inc.). This classic was written in 1956 for internal use, and is easy to use and understand. For a more philosophical discussion of quality control and insight into the colorful life of W. Edwards Deming, read his pivotal work, *Out of the Crisis* (Massachusetts Institute of Technology, Center for Advanced Engineering Study).

**Example Applications:**

- Average handling time
- Percent adherence
- Percent defective calls (from monitoring)
- Requests for supervisory assistance (transfers)

Excerpt from *Call Center Management on Fast Forward: Succeeding In Today's Dynamic Inbound Environment* by Brad Cleveland and Julia Mayben, Call Center Press, 1999.

**Section 6**

## 7. Developing a Monitoring and Coaching Program

Ready? | 1 | 2 | 3 |

### Key Points

- Monitoring and coaching are fundamental to maintaining and improving agent performance quality, identifying training gaps and customer needs, and evaluating the level of customer satisfaction.

- Use these steps to develop an effective monitoring and coaching program:
    1. Identify the monitoring program goals/objectives
    2. Determine the program requirements
    3. Create standards for performance
    4. Create the monitoring scoring system including forms, scorecards, etc.
    5. Develop a calibration strategy
    6. Determine a coaching strategy and standards
    7. Share program details with employees

- Monitoring and coaching go hand-in-hand. An effective monitoring program provides a solid basis for a productive coaching program. Coaching is one of the most effective ways to act on monitoring results.

### Explanation

Monitoring and coaching are fundamental to maintaining and improving agent performance quality, identifying training gaps and customer needs, and evaluating the level of customer satisfaction. According to a recent ICMI study on monitoring, approximately 90 percent of call centers in North America monitor agent calls, using various methods (with most centers using a combination), including real-time remote and side-by-side monitoring, call-taping and mystery shopping. (See Types of Monitoring, this section.)

#### Monitoring

Monitoring is a call evaluation process that appraises the qualitative aspects of call handling. Monitoring programs include the tracking and analysis of data to identify individual agent and overall call center performance trends, anticipated

problems, and training and coaching needs.

### Objectives and Uses of Monitoring

The major objectives and uses of a monitoring system include:

- Provides the basis for organizationwide quality improvement and innovation
- Measures the quality of interaction and accuracy of information provided
- Measures adherence to the call-handling processes
- Contributes to consistency and effectiveness of call center processes
- Provides data for trend analysis to look for patterns of effectiveness across call contact types, teams and centers
- Supports coaching by providing specific examples for feedback
- Identifies additional training needs for individual agents
- Evaluates the effectiveness of training
- Identifies customer needs/expectations
- Supports a tactical deployment of call center and enterprise vision
- Evaluates customer satisfaction
- Refines the selection process in that monitoring helps in the development of a profile of skills and competencies
- Provides legal compliance and mitigates liability
- Ensures agents follow organization's policies

### Coaching

Monitoring and coaching go hand-in-hand. An effective monitoring program provides a solid basis for a productive coaching program. Coaching is one of the most effective ways to act on monitoring results.

Through informal, one-on-one discussion, creatively designed activities and frequent monitoring, coaching is designed to encourage employees to continue positive behaviors and provide constructive feedback.

### Objectives and Uses of Coaching

Coaching provides a number of complementary benefits to monitoring:

- Provides individualized feedback in a supportive environment

- Clarifies performance goals and developmental needs
- Provides customized practice or activities tailored to the individual
- Provides on-the-spot feedback
- Reinforces effective performance
- Recommends specific behaviors in which the employee needs improvement
- Models successful professional behavior
- Facilitates communication and encourages relationship-building

**Developing a Monitoring and Coaching Program**

The agent monitoring and coaching program is the foundation of interaction quality in the call center. An effective program takes time to develop. The rewards, however – in terms of an increase in contact quality and employee morale – are significant.

To develop a monitoring and coaching program the following steps should be included:

- **Identify the monitoring program goals/objectives:** Program goals and objectives should be defined in terms of what you want the program to accomplish; e.g., processwide improvements, ensuring legal compliance, call center skill trending, standardization of the monitoring and coaching process.

- **Determine the program requirements:** Review the call center environment to decide what types of monitoring will be used, how often representatives will be monitored, if your contact types require new monitoring technologies, how monitoring results will be tied to pay-for-performance programs.

- **Create standards for performance:** Performance standards may be divided into base requirements (behaviors that represent the minimum level of acceptable performance) and expectations (behaviors that can be continually refined and improved). All performance standards should be specific, observable, realistic and valid. (See Setting Performance Objectives, this section.)

- **Create the monitoring scoring system including forms, scorecards, etc.:** Every monitoring program should include a written record (electronic or hard copy) of each monitored call which details the standards for performance being rated during the call. The monitoring form should have fields for identifying information (agent name, call ID, date, time)

with room for notes to record specific behaviors (quotes, memory jogs) and a checklist or numerical rating system for each behavior.

- **Develop a calibration strategy:** Calibration ensures that supervisors and other employees who engage in monitoring activities rate agent interactions consistently and fairly. (See Scoring and Calibration, this section.)

- **Determine a coaching strategy and standards:** Decide who will have responsibility for coaching activities. It is not a recommended practice to have monitoring and coaching responsibilities separated. The individual who monitors the interaction should provide the coaching and feedback. (See Principles of Effective Coaching and Feedback, this section.)

- **Share program details with employees:** Clearly inform agents about the purpose of monitoring, how it will be conducted, and how the results will be used. Employees should have access to written monitoring policies, the criteria on which they will be monitored and monitoring forms and scorecards. Take employee feedback into account during the design of the monitoring program and process revisions.

**Getting Agent Buy-in**

There is an important test monitoring programs must pass in order to be effective: Agents should like the program. If they don't see the value in monitoring or, worse, feel victimized or spied upon, that's a signal the monitoring methods need improvement. Agents generally will like monitoring if it is helping them identify areas that need improvement, while recognizing the things that are going well.

To gain agent support for a monitoring program, you should position it as:

- A tool that focuses on behaviors that affect customer satisfaction

- A process to develop agent skills

- The means to improve the training curriculum

Getting agent buy-in and input to the monitoring program will result in three key benefits:

- The better the agents understand and buy into the quality criteria, the easier it will be for them to excel

- Agents will become their own "in-process inspectors," correcting problems before they happen, not afterward

- Results become the basis for organizationwide process improvements

**Section 6**

### Requirements of Electronic Contacts

As electronic contacts (e.g., email, text-chat, Web collaboration, etc.) proliferate, principles of sound monitoring and coaching are essential to maintain quality. While many principles and objectives apply across any contact channel, written correspondence has its own requirements:

- Those doing the monitoring must be proficient in written communication.

- Monitoring forms and criteria unique to written correspondence must be developed, not simply replicated from call monitoring.

- In addition to content requirements, monitoring and coaching should concentrate on completeness, brevity, logical flow, grammar, tone, appropriate use of "netspeak" and anticipation of customer needs.

---

### Monitoring Practices Recommended by ICMI

- Inform job candidates of monitoring and coaching policies.

- Share the purpose and details of the program with employees and inform agents of when and how they are monitored.

- Tell agents which phone lines can be monitored and where unmonitored lines are for personal calls.

- Monitoring equipment should monitor what is said on the line, not what is said by agents between calls at their workstation.

- Permit only qualified personnel to monitor and evaluate for quality or to provide feedback and coaching.

- Do not publicly post monitoring results by name or other data that could identify an individual agent.

- Do not single out agents for unsatisfactory performance that is common to a group of agents; more than likely the poor performance is the result of a management/training problem – not an individual performance problem.

- Use standardized and consistently applied evaluation forms and monitoring techniques.

- Use objective criteria in evaluation forms and monitoring techniques.

- Monitor all agents periodically to determine where the performance level of the group is centered.

- Permit only personnel with a legitimate business need to monitor calls for orientation purposes (i.e., new call center personnel who will be involved with call handling, consultants working on call center improvements, etc.).

Excerpt from *Call Center Management Review's* Monitoring and Coaching Special Issue, 1999.

---

## 8. Types of Monitoring

Ready? 1 2 3

### Key Points

- There are several ways to monitor agents' performance, each with its own advantages and disadvantages:
  - Silent monitoring
  - Call recording
  - Side-by-side monitoring
  - Peer monitoring
  - Mystery shopping

### Explanation

There are several ways to monitor your agents' performance, each with its own advantages and disadvantages.

**Silent Monitoring**

The supervisor or person who is responsible for conducting the monitoring session listens to an agent call in real-time from another location. In some call centers, the supervisor can also monitor the agent's keyboard activities to ensure quality and system navigation while the agent is handling the call.

Advantages of silent monitoring include:

- The calls are selected randomly, ensuring a good call sample
- Since agents are unaware of being monitored, they perform more naturally
- Silent monitoring allows for uninhibited interaction between the agent and the customer
- The monitoring can be done from a variety of locations

Disadvantages of silent monitoring include:

- It is difficult to provide immediate feedback
- This method can be inefficient since the person doing the monitoring can experience unproductive time waiting for a call to arrive
- Telephone calls cannot be repeated unless they are taped; it's easy to miss critical information

Section 6

- This method may create a fear among agents that "Big Brother" is watching

- Some states laws may restrict silent monitoring; e.g., require a beep tone notifying agents and/or customers that monitoring is taking place. (See Legal Considerations of Monitoring, this section.)

### Call Recording

The supervisor or automated system records a sampling of calls. The person conducting the monitoring then randomly selects calls for evaluation of agent performance. (See Monitoring Technologies, this section.)

Advantages of call recording include:

- Agents can listen to their own calls to see how they handled the customer

- An automatic system provides more flexibility and control since it can be pre-programmed

- Eliminates the unproductive time experienced with the silent monitoring method

- The agent and supervisor can review the conversation as many times as necessary

Disadvantages of call recording include:

- Can be cumbersome if it is done with ordinary electronic taping devices; i.e., portable tape recorders

- Fully automated systems can be expensive and require appropriate training to use effectively

### Side-by-Side Monitoring

The person conducting the monitoring sits beside the agent and listens while the agent handles a call.

Advantages of side-by-side monitoring include:

- The agent can receive immediate feedback and coaching

- Allows the agent to practice new behaviors with the undivided attention and support of a supervisor/coach

- The supervisor or person conducting the monitoring can observe the agent using the system, reference materials and other workstation job aids

- For new-hires, this method provides an interactive and supportive environment.
- Enhances the relationship between the agent and supervisor

Disadvantages of side-by-side monitoring include:

- Direct observation can impact performance. The agent may feel nervous resulting in a negative impact on performance. Alternatively, the agent may follow the standards more closely while being monitored, resulting in behavior that is not typical.
- It is time-sensitive and time-consuming for those who do the monitoring

### Peer Monitoring

Call center agents monitor peers' calls and provide feedback on their performance.

Advantages of peer monitoring include:

- Involves agents in the quality process
- Reduces resistance and fear of monitoring when monitoring and coaching is performed by a "friendly face"
- Supports an environment of empowerment and job enrichment
- Management's time is reduced as agents take on some monitoring responsibilities

Disadvantages of peer monitoring include:

- Management must carefully select top performers to provide the peer monitoring or the agents may be passing on poor skills and behaviors
- Peer monitors must be trained in giving feedback
- It takes time away from the top performers' work with customers
- The recognition/reward system must be aligned to support the peer monitoring system

### Mystery Shopper

A form of unobtrusive observation in which a designated "mystery shopper" initiates a call to the center and monitors the skills of the agent.

Advantages of the mystery shopper approach include:

- The calls are selected randomly, ensuring a good call sample

Section 6

- Since agents are unaware of being monitored, they perform more naturally

- Can test specific call types or skills

- Eases some time requirements associated with monitoring in the call center

Disadvantages of the mystery shopper approach include:

- Does not allow for immediate feedback to the agent

- There is the danger that the evaluation will be miscommunicated or misunderstood as feedback is communicated to the supervisor and then to the agent

- Mystery shoppers must be carefully selected and trained, resulting in increased time and expense

Agents' performance may be monitored using a combination of these methods to provide variety and capitalize on the advantages of each.

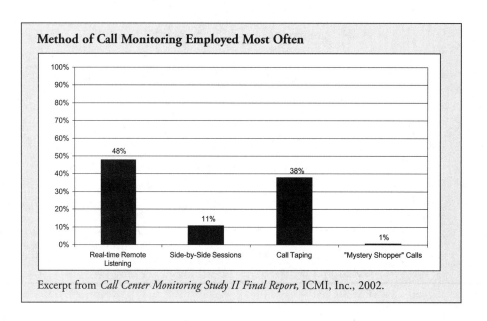

**Method of Call Monitoring Employed Most Often**

| Method | Percentage |
| --- | --- |
| Real-time Remote Listening | 48% |
| Side-by-Side Sessions | 11% |
| Call Taping | 38% |
| "Mystery Shopper" Calls | 1% |

Excerpt from *Call Center Monitoring Study II Final Report*, ICMI, Inc., 2002.

## 9. Scoring and Calibration

Ready? | 1 | 2 | 3 |

### Key Points

- Effective scoring and calibration are necessary to ensure consistency and fairness in the monitoring process. Scoring provides a context in which to view improvements or trends in the quality of transactions. Calibration provides the opportunity to test the process and confirm that consistent standards are applied to each monitored call.

- The cornerstone of the monitoring process is documenting specific, observable behaviors and tailoring agent coaching to the individual call. It is, however, helpful to use scoring or other quantitative methods to support a rating system.

- For a monitoring process to succeed, it is essential to integrate calibration into the planning, implementation and ongoing maintenance of your monitoring program.

### Explanation

Effective scoring and calibration are necessary to ensure consistency and fairness in the monitoring process. Scoring provides a context in which to view improvement or trends in the quality of transactions. Calibration provides the opportunity to test the process and confirm that consistent standards are applied to each monitored call.

**Scoring Customer Interactions**

The cornerstone of the monitoring process is documenting specific, observable behaviors and tailoring agent coaching to the individual call. It is, however, helpful to use scoring or other quantitative methods to support a rating system. There are as many types of monitoring forms and evaluation methods as there are scoring systems. A single monitoring form should include a variety of rating systems to address the different skills being evaluated. Some examples of rating systems include:

- **Yes/no scoring:** Some organizations use a yes/no – alternately indicated by 1/0, Y/N, checkboxes – to indicate which behaviors were completed

Section 6

satisfactorily. Results may be expressed by the number of yes's and no's (8 Y and 2 N), a fraction (8/10) or a percentage (80%).

Yes-or-no scoring is beneficial in environments where behaviors are "cut and dry"; e.g., they did or did not provide accurate information, correct opening or conclusion steps. It is less effective for behaviors that may be measured in degrees; e.g., questioning skills or rapport building.

- **Numerical scoring:** To rate more subjective skills, a numerical system may be used. Numerical systems often present a range (e.g., 1-5) of possibilities, which scorers can use to rate the agent's proficiency in demonstrating the skill. Numerical scoring allows for more variation in indicating the employees skill level and is appropriate for skills that affect the quality of the interaction. A range of scores addresses the individuality of each interaction and takes the agent's current skill level and experience into account. Numerical scoring is often weighted to reflect the call center objectives and the value and importance of each skill being scored.

  The wider variation of scores possible with a numerical scoring method reveal subtle skill improvement; e.g. an employee may have improved a skill but not achieved full mastery. A weighted scoring system assigns values to each monitored objective; e.g., providing correct information is rated higher than the correct greeting. A weighted scoring system can help reflect which objectives are most important

Other variations or combinations in scoring are possible. You may choose to indicate N/A (not applicable) or exempt specific skills during certain types of calls. N/As are either counted as yes's or another agreed-upon score, or are not counted at all.

**Scoring Considerations**

Before you implement a scoring system, consider the following:

- The scoring system should be easy for the scorer to use.

- A scoring system should emphasize the award of points for positively demonstrated skills, rather than deductions for negative behaviors.

- Call center management and agents should thoroughly understand how the scoring system works.

- Advise management and agents to keep scores in context. Specific feedback and coaching is the most essential part of the monitoring and coaching process and is the component of the monitoring process that

improves quality. Don't overemphasize scores.

- Resist the temptation to coach to scores. Scores don't improve the quality of an interaction; specific feedback and coaching to behaviors do. Some call centers do not share scores with agents until after the coaching session.

- The scoring system should reflect call center objectives, call objectives and the behaviors you want to encourage. A flawed system may underemphasize critical behaviors and overemphasize non-essential skills.

- Confirm the mathematical validity of the scoring system, especially if a total score is compiled or the system is weighted.

- Establish the validity of the system by testing it before it impacts individuals; e.g., before scores are included as part of performance-based pay.

- Understand agents become very interested in scoring systems if they are tied to bonuses, performance evaluations and salary reviews. Be prepared handle their questions and concerns.

- When possible, define variations in specific behaviors associated with a skill and the corresponding scores; e.g., what behaviors earn a 1 or a 3 or a 5?

**The Need for Calibration Sessions**

For a monitoring process to succeed, it is essential to integrate calibration into the planning, implementation and ongoing maintenance of your monitoring program. In a call center, calibration is the process in which variations in the way performance criteria are interpreted from person to person are minimized.

The calibration component of a monitoring program is crucial because it:

- Provides consistency
- Reduces the likelihood of agents questioning fairness
- Continuously develops and assesses monitoring criteria

Proper calibration is the best preventative maintenance against allegations of inequity and favoritism. It eliminates perceived biases by ensuring consistent application of call standards and scoring. When calibration is achieved, it will not matter who did the monitoring and scoring; the outcome will be the same. Once agents understand this, the coaching process can focus on recognizing achievements and identifying opportunities for improvement, instead of whether a particular score is accurate.

Calibration is not a quick or easy process; it takes a considerable commitment. It may take many hours of discussion and practice before a team begins to score a call the same way. While it is difficult, the rewards will be worth it in the end.

**How to Conduct a Calibration Session**

The following basic steps are prerequisites to consistent calibration:

- Every employee responsible for monitoring and scoring calls should have an excellent working knowledge of the call center's services.

- Those doing the monitoring must understand how the stardards are administered.

- Those doing the monitoring should be given formal training in the program, as well as relevant criteria and definitions.

The following describes a typical calibration session:

- Schedule at least one hour of uninterruptible time.

- Prepare recorded calls to get the most from the calibration time. If recorded calls are not available, prepare to listen to live calls during the session.

- Choose a facilitator. The role of the facilitator is to direct discussions, take notes and keep the team focused.

- Listen to a call and have all participants use your evaluation form to make notes and score the call.

- After the call, ask one person to verbally recap what he or she just heard. Recapping the call reinforces listening skills and attention to detail; take turns doing this so that everyone learns how. During the recap, the monitor will identify the areas in which he or she awarded points.

- The facilitator should direct a discussion to review scores. Be prepared — these debates can be passionate, but need to be played out. The point is to come to an understanding and apply that understanding to evaluating calls in the future.

- At the end of the session, the facilitator should review the notes, highlighting any changes or group decisions that have been made. These notes should be distributed quickly to all people who actively monitor calls.

Use a phased approach to best achieve a successful level of calibration. When you're just beginning the calibration process, set an attainable goal; e.g., strive for overall call scores to be within, say five points or 10 percent of each other –

as more sessions are conducted consistency should improve. The goal should never be to agree on an exact score. Rather, the emphasis should be on acheiving a common understanding of how performance is measured.

Once initial goals have been achieved, raise the bar by lowering the scoring variation goal from five points to three points (or a comparable variation percentage). It may take between two to four hours a month to keep the team calibrated, depending on the complexity of the program.

### Facilitating Calibration Sessions

Following are key ground rules for conducting calibration sessions:

- Create an environment in which everyone can feel comfortable sharing his or her opinion.

- Avoid being confrontational. Allow your team to finish explaining their thoughts before you begin to explain your position. It is important that everyone's opinions are heard.

- Talk about the facts, not feelings. The performance criteria are (or should be) defined by measurable tasks, so keep the discussion focused on what can be taught, not thought.

- When making decisions, consider what would be best for the overall success of the program. Do not make a decision just because everyone has grown tired of discussing the issue!

- Enforce compliance. It is critical to your overall program to identify and warn any person who monitors using their own standards, and not the standards agreed upon during calibration.

- Do not give up or become frustrated when the process gets difficult and some people seem ready to quit. The calibration process is not a sprint; it is a marathon.

**Section 6**

## 10. Monitoring Technologies

Ready? | 1 | 2 | 3 |

### Key Points

- As call center contact channels have expanded and evolved, so has monitoring technology. The most advanced monitoring systems are able to record not only traditional phone calls, but also Web-based contacts such as Voice over Internet Protocol (VoIP) calls, email transactions and text-chat sessions.

- Automated call monitoring systems can significantly reduce monitoring time and effort, thus enhancing the effectiveness of your overall quality improvement program.

- Gaining agent buy-in is paramount in any successful quality program. To reduce agent fears and concerns about transaction recording and tracking practices, managers should explain how the center's monitoring technology works, what kind of data it collects, and how this information will be used to improve training and systems in the call center.

### Explanation

As call center contact channels have expanded and evolved, so has monitoring technology. The most advanced monitoring systems are able to record not only traditional phone calls, but also Web-based contacts such as voice over Internet protocol (VoIP) calls, email transactions and text-chat sessions.

The quality monitoring systems on the market today are, for the most part, adjunct systems from a variety of manufacturers. There are a few automated call distributor (ACD) providers that incorporate this functionality (in a limited way) into their products, but the adjunct systems offer the most complete set of features and connectivity.

The big attraction of the new generation of systems is their ability to record and review both the voice and data; e.g., agents' keyboard activity, customers' interactive voice response (IVR) menu choices, number of transfers, etc. This capability, known as voice and data synchronization, allows the manager to factor in and verify the activity happening on the agent's screen.

Most users of computer screen monitoring conclude that it enhances training and quality significantly.

**Key Features and Functionality of Today's Monitoring Systems**

Most monitoring technology includes the ability to:

- Schedule call monitoring randomly.

- Program system to record contacts for later review.

- Record the agents' interactions with the computer. This may involve recording keystrokes, use of screens or Web/email transactions.

- Schedule call recording based on a variety of factors such as agent experience level, time of day or special promotion/specific campaigns.

- Record calls on agent demand. This allows agents to initiate recording of complex calls, irate callers or any call that the agent deems important for the supervisor to hear.

- Follow the call through the entire transaction, from IVR prompts to the final termination of the call. This is extremely useful when calls are routinely escalated to second-level support. Computer telephony integration (CTI) can also enable the recording of calls based on certain customer identifiers, such as automatic number identification (ANI) or account number.

- Embed the performance evaluation forms into the recording. This creates a link between the recording session and the evaluation that can be saved for later review with the agent.

- Automatically evaluate performance results, rate individual agents/calls (based on the call center's pre-defined performance objectives), trend data and even provide training suggestions. This information helps managers see abnormal highs and lows that may uncover a need for additional training and/or system adaptations (e.g., clarification of queue announcements or IVR menu options).

- Attach the recording to email or embed it in a word-processing document. This allows easy distribution of the recording.

**Using Technology Judiciously**

Today's monitoring systems can vastly enhance a call center's quality program, but only if combined with a well-defined monitoring strategy. Relying solely on technology will not help to improve customer satisfaction nor agent acceptance of monitoring in your call center.

In fact, over-reliance on technology may cause even more problems than not monitoring at all. Because of the ability of advanced monitoring technology to easily record all activity that takes place during a customer transaction, agents may feel they are being over-scrutinized, which can lead to burnout and center-wide morale problems. It's important to use monitoring systems appropriately and to clearly explain to agents how this technology fits into the call center's overall quality program. Make sure agents understand that these systems are not intended to catch them doing things wrong, but rather to help the center improve employee performance and the customer experience.

(Monitoring technologies are covered in depth in ICMI's *Call Center Operations Management Handbook and Study Guide*.)

## 11. Legal Considerations of Monitoring

Ready? | 1 | 2 | 3 |

### Key Points

- Call monitoring in the United States requires consent of one or both parties to the call, depending on the law of the applicable states. Federal law, in the form of the Electronic Communications Privacy Act (ECPA), permits monitoring if you establish consent from one party in the call. The Act also allows states to enact stricter legislation, such as two-party consent.

- The ECPA permits recording with the consent of one party, and provides states with the option to require more stringently worded legislation.

### Explanation

Call monitoring in the United States requires consent of one or both parties to the call, depending on the law of the applicable states. Federal law, in the form of the Electronic Communications Privacy Act (ECPA), permits monitoring if you establish consent from one party in the call. Agent consent fulfills this requirement.

In two-party consent states, callers should hear a monitoring and recording announcement and the agents in the call center must sign a consent form. Some state statutes include the words "overhear" or "record," whereas others use the term "intercept a communication." There are also different rules to govern interstate vs. intrastate calls.

In regard to the recording of phone calls, the ECPA permits recording with the consent of one party, and also allows states to enact stricter legislation. Further, Federal Communications Commission (FCC) regulations require either:

- A beep tone audible to both parties when recording
- Prior consent of all parties to recording of the conversation, or
- Notification of the other party up front that you are recording (known as the one-party notification option previously described)

However, some states specifically require two-party consent to record.

Section 6

The Direct Marketing Association (DMA) maintains a State Government Relations division whose purpose is to keep on top of state statute information. Similarly, the American Teleservices Association (ATA) has a Legislative Alert Warning Service (LAWS), to provide its members with updated information on legislation pending in any state.

For Canadian legal guidelines, see Managing within Legal Guidelines – Canada, Section 7.

## 12. Principles of Effective Coaching and Feedback    Ready? | 1 | 2 | 3 |

### Key Points

- Coaching and feedback needs to:
  - Be timely
  - Be specific
  - Be focused on agent development
  - Consist of two-way communication and participation
  - Balance positive and negative feedback

- Coaching and feedback sessions should be agent-centric, taking individual backgrounds and experience into account and providing agents with the opportunity to evaluate themselves and the support they are given.

### Explanation

The coaching and feedback process involves managers and supervisors meeting with agents – after observing specific aspects of their work - to discuss performance strengths and areas that need improvement. During the process, agents should be given the opportunity to provide feedback on their personal performance as well as the resources and support they currently receive in the center.

#### Role of a Coach

Coaches provide identification of skills and behaviors (positive and negative), support and encouragement for agents to improve. A coach:

- Helps to clarify performance goals and developmental needs
- Reinforces effective performance
- Recommends specific behaviors in which the agent needs improvement
- Serves as a role model to demonstrate successful professional behavior

Good coaches must be able to effectively:

- **Observe and evaluate agent performance:** Coaches need to take the time to observe and evaluate agent performance via formal monitoring sessions, report analysis and informal observation on the call center floor.

**Section 6**

Coaches should explain when and why monitoring takes place to ensure that agents don't feel they are being micro-scrutinized.

- **Provide useful feedback:** This is the crux of any call center quality program. Coaches should apply the principles of coaching and feedback (as summarized below).

- **Listen:** This refers not only to paying close attention to agents during customer interactions, but to listening to agents' opinions and concerns during coaching and feedback sessions. Coaching is not a one-way process, but rather an interactive learning experience for both the agent and coach.

- **Understand the diverse nature of people:** To be effective, coaches need to consider the specific personality, background and experience level of each agent, and adapt their feedback methods accordingly.

- **Communicate and motivate:** Coaches need to have excellent communication skills, both verbal and written, to ensure that agents not only fully understand what is expected of them, but become inspired to work on continually improving their performance.

**Principles of Coaching and Feedback:**

Employee performance issues may be averted through focused coaching and feedback. Such coaching and feedback should:

- **Be timely:** Giving feedback immediately or very soon after an observed customer contact ensures not only that the event is fresh in the agent's mind (thus enhancing the significance of the feedback), but also ensures that the agent doesn't make similar mistakes with hundreds of customers before being informed of his or her performance problem.

- **Be specific:** Ambiguous feedback leaves agents in the dark regarding their performance and what they need to focus on to improve. Good feedback is clear, concise and directed at specific performance issues and demonstrated skills.

- **Be focused on agent development:** It's not enough to merely tell agents what they need to work on; coaches must demonstrate desired skills/behaviors and work with agents to develop clear-cut and feasible performance plans. Such plans should include detailed steps to help the agent obtain necessary skills and overcome specific performance problems. In addition, the plan should discuss rewards for achieving desired results and possible consequences of not achieving results.

- **Consist of two-way communication and participation:** Coaching sessions that merely involve coaches calling the shots are static and demotivating. Agents know the intricacies of their job better than anybody, and thus should be encouraged to evaluate their own performance and offer ideas for improvement.

- **Balance positive and negative feedback:** A good mixture of both praise and constructive criticism is essential for fostering continuous improvement among agents.

**Section 6**

## 13. Steps to Effective Coaching and Feedback

Ready? | 1 | 2 | 3 |

### Key Points

- Coaching presents rich opportunities for developing and motivating staff. Use the SAFE model to deliver structured coaching that achieves results:

  - (S)ummarize one to two observed behaviors and consequences
  - (A)sk for input, if necessary
  - (F)ormulate plan of action and desired consequences
  - (E)xpress gratitude

- While coaching is typically provided by dedicated call center trainers and/or supervisors, many call centers find self-evaluation (with supervisor feedback) and peer evaluation programs (agents helping agents) to be highly effective and empowering.

### Explanation

Coaching presents rich opportunities for developing and motivating staff. After interactions have been monitored, coaching should be provided in a timely manner. A coaching session may be used to offer praise so that behavior continues, to provide instruction on how to improve undesirable behavior, or to give the agent an opportunity to practice behavior that may be especially difficult for them to master.

Using a structured approach or model provides coaches with the necessary guidelines for delivering effective, consistent feedback to agents. Although there are many effective models available, ICMI has developed the SAFE model. This model is designed to offer a structured format that places coaching in the context of a "safe" environment, in which risk is minimized and employees feel supported and secure in their attempts to develop and grow new skills. It consists of four components including:

**(S)ummarize one to two observed behaviors and consequences**

This first step involves selecting one or two behaviors on which to focus the coaching session. Trying to coach on too many skills at once can overwhelm the agent with too much to try to improve or continue. Since coaching

sessions should happen frequently, there will be time to cover other behaviors at a later date.

Be sure to explain the behavior and the consequences of that behavior in specific and objective terms. It is a good practice to use actual quotes from the monitored call to help the agent understand the skill they need to improve or the behavior they did well.

### (A)sk for input, if necessary

This step can be helpful in some situations, but is not always necessary. While a coach never wants to discourage agent input, coaching should include quick reminders and frequent praise, which may not allow time for a two-way discussion with the agent.

However, two-way collaboration is necessary when an undesirable behavior is persistent or has not shown improvement over several prior coaching sessions. The coach should use questions that clarify the agent's understanding of the desired behavior, test the agent's desire to improve, and allow the agent time to practice the required skill.

### (F)ormulate plan of action and desired consequences

Once the positive or negative behavior has been identified and clarified, it is the coach's job to suggest ways to change undesirable behavior or to offer encouragement to continue desired behavior. The suggested actions should be specific and measurable, and the coach must ensure the agent has the tools necessary to implement the ideas. If the suggestions include practicing a certain skill, it may be helpful for the coach to model the desired behavior or provide the agent with the opportunity to practice while the coach is present.

The coach should also communicate the benefit of changing negative behavior or continuing positive behavior. It should not be assumed that the agent knows this connection without explanation. Since it is the agent's job to focus on his/her specific task at hand, he/she may not realize how a procedure or process may affect overall call center objectives. Communicating the reasons why the behavior needs to be changed or continued will increase agent buy-in to the plan of action.

### (E)xpress gratitude

Finally, close the coaching session with an expression of gratitude. Whether the agent is struggling to meet expectations or is exceeding expectations continually,

it is important to communicate appreciation for his/her time, reflection, effort and attention. This step conveys sincerity and encouragement to the agent, and reinforces the important role of the agent in the call center.

### Empower Agents with a Peer-Monitoring Program

Consider a peer-monitoring program to bolster your traditional coaching practices. Teaming veteran agents with less-experienced employees for coaching sessions is a great way to enhance performance while empowering staff. Employees are often more relaxed working with peers than with supervisors, and are thus more open to the feedback provided. Good peer-monitoring programs are usually overseen by supervisors to ensure that effective and consistent feedback is provided.

---

**Overcoming Common Coaching Quagmires**

Development of specific coaching skills is necessary to adapt your approach to the situation and to the individual you are coaching. Here are three specific challenging situations you may face whenever providing feedback in coaching situations (based on Peter Quarry's training programs: *Feedback Solutions and Performance Excellence*):

• The agent disagrees with the feedback received: I'm sure we've all experienced it. The agent we are coaching disagrees with us. Now what? In order for the outcome to be constructive – avoiding an argument or a conflict spiral – we must get to the root of what the agent is disagreeing with. Listen carefully to what he or she is saying. If the comments are focused around whether or not the problem is occurring, they are disagreeing with the facts. You must provide specific examples and evidence that the situation is in fact occurring. Perhaps the agent may say, "You're right, that is happening but it's not a problem because..." This agent disagrees with the outcome or result. In this situation, you need to point out the negative effects on service that may occur if the agent's behavior remains unchanged.

• The agent lacks flexibility regarding change: A highly effective method for helping an agent who resists change is to use a skill called "reframing." It's likely that the agent is focusing on the disadvantages of changing and the advantages of not changing.

Take a computer change, for example. Disadvantages of changing may be expressed by the agent as, "Now I'll have to learn the new system," or "What if I need additional training?" or "My proficiency may go down," or even "Will the new system eliminate jobs?" Advantages of not changing may be expressed by the agent as, "It works well enough," "I know what I am doing," or "I can focus more on the customer if I'm not focusing on a new system."

You can help this agent by getting him or her to reframe the situation and see the advantage of changing and the disadvantage of not changing. For instance, enhancing the computer system may mean that, after the realistic time it may take everyone to get up to speed, the call flow may be streamlined and help to provide better customer service or minimize paperwork. The disadvantage of not changing could be that the competition

---

already is providing easier access to information or answers and therefore have streamlined the call handling making them easier to do business with. Not changing could cost us customers.

• The agent has low motivation: Declines in an agent's performance, customer service or tolerance are just signs of low motivation. We may get short-term results by motivating with praise, recognition, new responsibilities or raises/incentives, but these results will be limited in impact or duration. Why? Because lasting motivation comes from within; we can not truly motivate another person. However, we can help create an environment that is motivating.

One problem is the tendency to try motivating others by giving or offering advice. "Why don't you...?" "Have you tried...?" "What I do is..." "Maybe the problem is..."

The person on the receiving end of this advice responds with the classic "Yes, but..." It is far more effective to use a questioning style to allow agents to come up with their own suggestions, ideas and solutions. Ask "what" and "how" questions. "What would it take to help you feel better about your job? How can you do this?" Stay silent when you've asked the question; allow the agent to think. When we ask these questions, it's easy to become impatient waiting for the answer, so we tend to jump in and answer the question for the agent. We're now back to giving advice, and guess what's next? That's right – "Yes, but..." Wait for the agent to respond and then, if relevant, push for more detail. Use open questions with words like who, what, when, where and how.

Excerpt from "Proven Tips for Effective Feedback and Coaching," by Laurie Solomon, Monitoring and Coaching Special Issue, *Call Center Management Review*, 1999.

## 14. Purposes and Benefits of Performance Reviews   Ready? | 1 | 2 | 3 |

### Key Points

- A performance review is "the specific and formal evaluation of an employee in order to determine the degree to which the employee is performing his or her job effectively."

- There are two primary and two secondary purposes of most performance reviews:
  - Primary purposes: employee development and financial
  - Secondary purposes: motivational and informational

- Performance reviews benefit both employees and management:
  - Employees receive detailed feedback about their performance and contribution to the call center, well-deserved recognition and rewards, as well as career/skills path clarification and guidance.
  - Management gets the opportunity to identify and document employee strengths and weaknesses – information that is essential, not only for enhancing individual performance, but for improving hiring practices, training programs and overall performance in the call center.

### Explanation

A performance review is "the specific and formal evaluation of an employee in order to determine the degree to which the employee is performing his or her job effectively." (DeNisi and Griffin, p. 232) Performance standards are measures or levels of achievement (based on quality, quantity and/or timeliness) established by a manager for the responsibilities expressed in a job description.

Performance reviews give employees information they need to enhance their professional development and contribution to the enterprise. Timely reviews help to motivate employees and correct performance problems before they have a lasting effect on customer satisfaction and loyalty. Performance reviews also enable the organization to make key financial decisions regarding the value of each employee and his/her contribution to the success of the organization.

Note: The performance review is not a monitoring session. Monitoring sessions

are more frequent and focus on the particular knowledge and skills involved in handling specific customer contacts. Performance reviews should measure overall job performance based on the employee's total job responsibilities. (See Developing a Monitoring and Coaching Program, this section.)

**Purposes of Conducting Performance Reviews**

Performance reviews accomplish much more than merely evaluating the performance of an employee. There are two primary and two secondary purposes for most performance reviews. The primary purposes are:

1. **Employee development:** Performance reviews should include a personalized development plan based on the identified strengths and weaknesses of each employee, as well as on the needs (current and future) of the call center. The plan should contain:

   - Positive reinforcement (what actions should continue)

   - Areas/skills that need improvement

   - Expected results

   - Actions and plans to accomplish those results

   - A timeframe for performance improvement with specific dates

   - Consequences, if results are not achieved

   - Rewards, if desired results are achieved

The manager needs to provide the support necessary to help the employee improve performance: focused coaching and training sessions; the tools and technology the employee needs to achieve results; regular feedback on progress; and time for an employee to complete development plan activities.

However, employee development should not be delayed in order to wait for a formal performance review. Employees who ask for more challenging tasks or request help in specific areas should receive timely action from their supervisor.

2. **Financial:** The second primary purpose of the performance review is the allocation of merit pay or salary dollars. The manager must decide if merit pay is to be given and if so, the amount (usually a percentage based on the salary grade midpoint) as well as the effective date. In most organizations, the HR department or finance department issues salary guidelines that include the amount of merit pay available. This may require the manager to evaluate the individual employees based on their personal performance as well as that of their peers.

The secondary purposes include:

**1. Motivational:** The performance review enables the manager to provide employee recognition based on objective data and results of work performed. Use specific work examples and recognize the positive actions performed by the employee to reinforce the desire for good performance. Often, the work or job content itself can be a motivator; many employees respond to challenges requiring commitment and expertise. The performance review process should foster mutual respect and trust to build a stronger manager/employee relationship.

**2. Informational:** Performance reviews provide opportunities to discuss relationships, work styles and values, as well as goals and objectives. During the review, the call center manager and employee should discuss such things as:

- Mutual expectations regarding support, behavior, communication, accessibility, performance, etc.

- Why the end result of goal accomplishment is so important

- The compatibility of the employee's values with those of the call center and the organization

- The manager's management style

**Benefits of Performance Reviews**

From the employee's perspective, the performance review:

- First and foremost, provides feedback on performance and contribution to the call center

- Provides recognition for accomplishments

- Consistently allocates rewards for employees, using the same system for everyone to ensure objectivity and fairness

- Assesses performance to see if and where there is need for improvement

- Provides a source of motivation

- Ensures that management is accountable for the evaluation and provides useful feedback

From management's perspective, the performance review:

- Identifies the more talented or high-potential employees

- Distinguishes and documents top, moderate and poor performers

- Validates the hiring and selection process, and reveals ways to improve these practices

- Provides information for training needs assessments, development plans and the effectiveness of training

- Provides a method for distribution of rewards based on the organization's compensation system

- Links individual performance with business unit performance

- Provides legal documentation of promotions, demotions and terminations based on performance as opposed to discriminatory factors such as race, gender, age, etc.

- Ensures that management is accountable for the evaluation and provides feedback

## 15. Conducting Performance Reviews

Ready? | 1 | 2 | 3 |

**Section 6**

### Key Points

- Conducting effective performance reviews requires careful planning and preparation. Managers need to gather key documents and additional input on agent performance from supervisors, team leaders and trainers prior to conducting any review.

- Managers should develop a consistent review format to ensure a smooth appraisal process and employee acceptance of feedback.

- Treating employees as unique and valuable individuals during performance reviews is essential for fostering enthusiasm and the desire for continual improvement.

### Explanation

In many organizations, HR policy dictates the timeframe for the performance review, which may be annually based on an employee's hiring or promotion anniversary date, annually at a specified time (i.e., all employees are evaluated in December), semi-annually, quarterly or other timeframe. The annual timeframe may not be appropriate in the call center environment due to high turnover or the need to cultivate improvement opportunities for individual performance. Call center managers should work with the HR department to determine the best timeframe for performance reviews and communicate clearly to the call center staff if this timeframe differs from the rest of the organization.

**Plan and Prepare for the Review**

The following are steps managers should take to prepare for performance reviews:

- **Gather the documentation:** The primary tools and sources of information for the performance review include:

  - The agent's job description

  - The agent's performance objectives and standards

  - Documentation of actual performance against objectives. Gather input from individuals – i.e., supervisors, team leaders, trainers – who have observed and interacted with the agent on a consistent

basis over an extended period of time.

- The performance file, including observation notes (both positive and negative), letters or input from others, and previous performance reviews
- A 360-review from peers, direct reports and supervisors (if used)
- A self-assessment (if used)
- The call center's goals and objectives

Be sure the documentation and observation of performance covers the entire review period and all performance areas.

- **Develop a format for the review:** To ensure a smooth appraisal process and to enhance agent understanding of the feedback provided, it's important to have a clear agenda for the performance review. This should include the following elements:
  - A statement of purpose
  - Input from the employee
  - Identification of performance standards
  - Methods of measuring performance
  - Identification of an employee's strengths and weaknesses
  - A check for understanding and agreement
  - A plan for followup meetings

- **Evaluate your own performance:** During the employee performance review process, effective managers take a close look at their own behaviors/actions and consider the impact they have on employees. Good questions to ask yourself include: What is the relationship of the agent's performance to your performance? Are your work styles and leadership styles compatible? Have you provided adequate supervision, tools, resources, materials, etc.? How can you change to improve your relationship with the agent? What support can and will you be providing to assist the employees in reaching the goals?

- **Review the current job description:** Is it still accurate? Is the agent working within or beyond the job description? Do the agent's skills and knowledge align with those in the job description? Is the agent meeting the minimum requirements of the job?

- **Review the performance file:** Evaluate current performance standards and the individual's performance against those goals. Include statements indicating the quality and timeliness of work performed. Organizations

**Section 6**

too often focus only on results; it's important to also pay close attention to how the goals were accomplished so that work style and relationship issues can be addressed.

- **Review the call center's objectives:** Place the agent's job and accomplishments in the context of the call center's goals and the organization's mission and goals.

- **Determine new performance goals and standards:** Based on call center objectives and past performance, start the process of setting performance goals and standards for the next review period. (See Setting Performance Objectives, this section.)

- **Determine the amount of merit pay:** Prior to the performance review, determine the amount of merit pay allowable under the organization's current compensation policy.

- **Prepare a preliminary review:** Just prior to the performance review, it's a good idea to have all the forms in order with some notes and preliminary ratings. However, do not complete the performance rating nor make merit pay decisions prior to the review with the employee. This will send the message that there is no room for input and change during the review process.

- **Determine the time and place for the review:** The review is a confidential conversation that requires honest dialogue. Since call centers tend to be open, visible workplaces, consider holding the reviews in a separate place away from daily operations. Ensure that the facility is appropriate for serious conversation and is free from outside interruptions. Sufficient time should be allowed so the review is not rushed.

- **Prepare for the individual's response:** Considering the unique nature of each agent is important for conducting a successful review. Think through the sequence of the information to be presented, anticipate the employee's response and how that response should be addressed. Plan to be open and seek collaboration. Ask the employee to prepare a self-evaluation, and provide the format to do so.

### Conduct the Review

Performance reviews will be most effective if the employee is at ease. Consider ways to reduce stress and anxiety. Offer coffee and a comfortable chair, and arrange to sit at a round table or on the same side of a desk to reduce "spatial power." Provide sufficient time for a thorough discussion. The employee will be

able to sense if you are rushed or distracted and may interpret that as a lack of interest in their performance.

Begin the review by stating the general purpose of the meeting, which may be to:

- Review performance based on objective data
- Allocate salary
- Provide a development plan based on identified strengths and weaknesses
- Clarify job expectations
- Initiate new goals and standards
- Seek feedback on your management style

The performance review should result in a development plan that identifies the area(s) for development and the methodology for development, actions, timeframe and resources. The plan should also provide a statement of outcomes with expected results.

Avoid the following when conducting performance reviews:

- Interruptions of any kind
- General criticism that cannot be substantiated
- Overwhelming the agent with comments on positive or negative behavior
- Doing all the talking and not actively listening
- Becoming irritated or defensive if the employee disagrees
- Arguing
- Focusing on any factors that are not job-related or are out of the employee's control

**Section 6**

## 16. Motivation Theory and Principles

Ready? | 1 | 2 | 3 |

### Key Points

- There are several theories on motivation that can help call center managers create and sustain an environment that fosters high levels of employee enthusiasm and the desire to continually improve.

- Herzberg's Hygiene-Motivation Theory outlines that some aspects of an employee's job directly influence job satisfaction, referred to as motivators, while others only create dissatisfaction if they are missing, referred to as hygiene factors. Both motivators and hygiene factors are necessary for a motivated work environment.

- Locke's goal-setting principle states that, because motivation is goal-directed, we can motivate agents by providing clear and challenging, yet attainable, goals.

- The Job Characteristics Theory states that jobs containing certain core elements, such as skill variety, task completion and autonomy, result in higher employee satisfaction, which is closely linked to motivation and performance.

- Maslow's Hierarchy of Needs theorizes that individual motivation is driven by a desire to satisfy a range of needs.

### Explanation

To be successful, call center managers need to create and sustain an environment that fosters high levels of employee enthusiasm and the desire to continually improve. Several theories on motivation exist that – when appropriately applied to the center – can help managers build and maintain such a healthy and dynamic environment.

#### Herzberg Two-Factor Theory

Psychologist Frederick Herzberg developed the Hygiene-Motivation Theory in the 1950s and 60s. In his studies, he discovered that some aspects of an employee's job directly influence job satisfaction, referred to as motivators, while others only create dissatisfaction if they are missing, referred to as hygiene

factors. Hygiene factors must be present to avoid dissatisfaction, but they alone will not motivate employees. Motivators are those aspects of the job that directly result in greater job satisfaction.

Examples of motivators include:

- **The work itself:** Make sure that agents understand how valuable the call center and, in particular, the agent position, is to the entire organization. When agents fully understand the impact they can have on customer satisfaction and revenue generation/containment, they're likely to approach the job with more pride and dedication.

- **Recognition:** Providing positive feedback and recognition for work performed well is a huge motivator. The more public the recognition, the more motivated the agent will be, so be sure to share positive experiences and results with the entire enterprise.

- **Achievement:** During feedback sessions and performance reviews, show agents/teams how they have improved over time. Focus on former areas of weakness in which the agent/team has made significant strides. A sense of progress and achievement is highly motivating and builds on itself.

- **Responsibility:** Provide agents with a strong sense of value and responsibility by implementing training modules on the impact that issues, such as adherence to schedule, occupancy and attendance, have on service levels and overall call center performance.

- **Chance for growth and advancement:** Even the best agents can burn out quickly without opportunities for skill development and career advancement. Implement skills-based pay and career path programs that provide room for both lateral and vertical movement within the center. (See the discussions on career and skill path models, Section 7.)

Examples of hygiene factors include:

- **Compensation:** If pay doesn't equal or exceed what's being offered at similar call centers, or if it doesn't match up with what agents feel they deserve for the work being done, poor morale and high turnover will result.

- **Company policies/procedures:** Without clear policies/procedures on things like monitoring, adherence to schedule, attendance, etc., claims of subjective treatment and favoritism may run rampant in the call center. Make sure that straightforward procedures/policies are not only in place, but that agents are aware of and understand them.

- **Job security:** Agents deserve to know that their jobs are safe provided

they continue to perform to expectations. Make this point clear to them. In the case of contract/seasonal workers, be upfront and honest about expected length of employment. Fear and doubt among agents about job security will have detrimental affects on the service they provide.

- **Relationships with supervisors and peers:** Create an atmosphere rich in cooperation and teamwork. Encourage open communication. The rapport among agents, supervisors and managers has a big influence on morale and, consequently, motivation and performance.

- **Work environment:** In addition to a healthy team-oriented environment, focus on the physical design of the call center. Studies have shown how things like poor ergonomics, lighting and spatial arrangement can drain agents and cause service to suffer.

- **Personal life:** While the call center's objectives are important, so are the personal lives of agents. Inflexible schedules and excessive overtime are sure ways to demotivate employees and damage service levels.

- **Status:** If agents simply view themselves as merely "the people on the phones" and the call center as an insignificant back-office operation, morale and performance will sink. It's up to the call center manager to create a positive call center culture in which agents can feel proud to work, and where other members of the organization would like to work.

- **Feedback:** The failure to provide regular feedback – both positive and negative – sends the message to agents that "it just doesn't matter." This can be highly contagious – spreading from agent to agent and, even more costly, from agent to customer.

- **Objectives:** Without clear objectives and performance standards in place, agents will be in the dark about what is expected of them. This will lead to staff frustration and doubts about the leadership in the call center.

### Locke's Goal-Setting

Professor Edwin Locke has written several books to explain his motivational theory of goal-setting. Because motivation is goal-directed, we can motivate agents by providing clear and challenging, yet attainable, goals. Keep in mind that the effect will be enhanced if goals are set collaboratively with agents. Conduct interviews or surveys with staff to determine what they feel are fair and attainable objectives, and which factors they feel are essentially out of their control (i.e., number of calls handled).

Frequent feedback on goal progress also plays a big part in fostering motivation

and performance. Hold regular coaching and feedback sessions with agents, and be sure to ask them for their input. (See discussions on coaching and feedback, this section.)

### Job Characteristics Theory

Richard Hackman and Greg Oldham proposed their Job Characteristics Theory in 1976. Its three-stage model includes job characteristics that impact critical psychological states, which influence a set of affective and motivational outcomes.

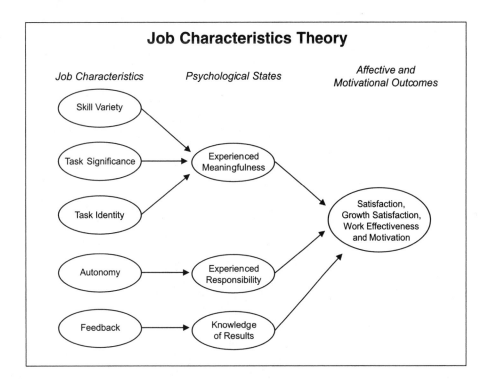

Jobs that contain these core elements result in higher employee satisfaction, which is closely linked to motivation and performance. These core job characteristics include:

- **Skill variety:** Employees are motivated by jobs that require doing a diverse range of tasks and using a variety of skills and abilities. Don't view your agents as mere call-handlers. Mix things up by having them work on interesting off-phone activities and team-based projects. Provide continuous training and opportunities for new skills acquisition.

- **Task completion:** Employees want the opportunity to see a task through to completion, and to be held accountable for the final results. Empower your agents to take ownership over projects and assignments, and recognize their successes publicly.

- **Significance:** Employees want to know how their job affects others. Show agents how their work impacts the success of the call center and enterprise as a whole, as well as the satisfaction and well-being of customers.

- **Autonomy:** The more independence, freedom and accountability employees have, the more motivated they will be. Consider implementing a team-based environment in which agents are empowered to solve problems, make decisions and work together on important projects with minimal supervision. If you aren't comfortable offering autonomy to agents, perhaps it's time to review your hiring practices.

- **Feedback:** While agents like autonomy, they also like receiving clear, concise information about how they are performing. Provide agents with such information during regular coaching/feedback sessions, as well as during performance reviews. In addition to recognizing agents' strengths, let them know what areas they need to work on and provide guidance on how to close performance gaps.

**Maslow's Hierarchy of Needs**

Abraham Maslow published his theory of human motivation in 1943. Maslow theorizes that individual motivation is driven by the desire to satisfy needs. He developed the following needs hierarchy, which is listed from most basic (at the bottom) to most complex:

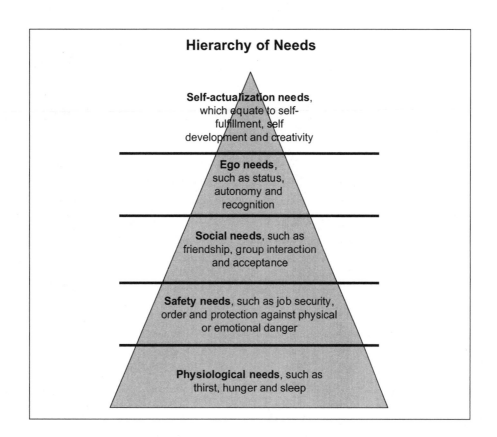

**Hierarchy of Needs**

**Self-actualization needs**, which equate to self-fulfillment, self development and creativity

**Ego needs**, such as status, autonomy and recognition

**Social needs**, such as friendship, group interaction and acceptance

**Safety needs**, such as job security, order and protection against physical or emotional danger

**Physiological needs**, such as thirst, hunger and sleep

Lower-level needs must be satisfied before an individual can attend to higher-level needs. The lower-level needs are predominant and must remain satisfied. Management should seek to ensure that lower-level needs are met (through breaks, safety regulations and social interaction) and provide opportunities for all employees – even entry-level personnel – to meet higher-level needs (through such things as empowerment programs and opportunities for creativity).

Empirical research has confirmed the first three levels of basic needs, but has not done so for the fourth and fifth levels of esteem and self-actualization.

## 17. Enabling a Highly Motivated Environment

Ready? | 1 | 2 | 3 |

### Key Points

- The responsibility of creating a highly motivated work environment falls squarely on the shoulders of the call center manager.

- There are a variety of practices to help managers create an atmosphere in which agents are inspired to serve customers and continually improve. These practices center around key areas such as training, coaching/feedback, advancement, recognition/rewards, empowerment and teamwork.

- Managers pave the way for high levels of employee motivation and performance when they strive to create a work environment in which they themselves would be proud to be an agent.

### Explanation

Creating a stimulating and dynamic call center environment is paramount to agent motivation. The more effort a manager makes to create and maintain such a positive atmosphere, the greater the chance of having enthusiastic and high-performing agents who are committed to the job and to customers.

#### Maximizing Agent Motivation

Here are some key practices to help managers maximize motivation:

- **Provide a comprehensive initial training program:** This is essential for ensuring that agents begin their journey in your call center with a high level of confidence and enthusiasm. A solid training program shows new-hires that the call center is willing to invest in people and set them up for success. Before sending new agents out to the floor, be sure that they successfully complete all key training modules and gain at least some experience handling common customer transactions in a controlled setting. Throwing unprepared agents on the phones is a sure way to destroy confidence and increase turnover. (See Identifying Training Needs, Section 5.)

- **Provide timely coaching and feedback:** Whether a new-hire or a seasoned veteran, agents need continuous encouragement, guidance and

support to perform consistently at high levels. Immediately after monitoring sessions, supervisors/managers should meet with agents to praise strengths and provide suggestions on how to improve. Regular coaching and feedback, like training, shows agents that the call center cares about their success and development. (See Principles of Effective Coaching and Feedback, this section.)

- **Work with agents to set challenging, yet attainable, goals and standards:** Setting objectives shouldn't be a top-down process. Utilize your agents' experience and knowledge to help determine the most important and appropriate performance goals for the call center. Eliciting their participation will help to foster agent buy-in and enhance their sense of value to the organization. (See Setting Performance Objectives, this section.)

- **Provide meaningful recognition:** Agents want to know that their hard work and successes get noticed by management. Implement rewards and recognition practices that keep agents striving to do their best. Be sure to recognize individual as well as team accomplishments, and spread the word enterprisewide via memos and/or company newsletters.

- **Strive to create a strong sense of team among agents:** Agents spend most of their time handling customer transactions alone at their workstations. To fend off feelings of isolation and alienation, it's important to help agents develop a group identity. This can be accomplished by things such as implementing a team-based environment. (See Implementing Teams, Section 7.)

- **Challenge agents to continually develop their capabilities:** Agents can become stagnant if they aren't encouraged to develop their skills and knowledge on an ongoing basis. It's up to the call center manager to provide them with ongoing training and career path opportunities. Consider a skills-based pay program in which agents increase their compensation by acquiring key skills that can help the call center. Such programs can be extremely motivating: Agents not only get the chance to earn more money, they continually expand their capabilities, which helps to add diversity to the job and reduce burnout. (See Types of Compensation, Section 7.)

- **Find ways for agents to use their creative abilities:** Sitting on the phones all day can cause burnout among even the most dedicated agents. Break up the monotony by letting agents work on projects that enable them to use their individual talents. For example, let agents with excellent speaking skills make presentations at meetings, have agents with strong

writing skills contribute a column to the company newsletter, or tap the artistic talents of some of your staff by giving them the opportunity to create posters or materials for special events in the call center. The possibilities are endless, and the approach is invaluable to agent motivation.

- **Elevate the image of the agent position (and the call center):** Make agents aware of the impact they have on the call center, the enterprise, and customers' lives. Agents have their fingers on the pulse of the organization. Few other employees have as much daily influence on revenue generation/retention, operational costs and customer loyalty. Communicate this point clearly to agents, and explain how things like quality service, adherence to schedule and attendance can have a dramatic impact on call center/organizational success.

- **Empower agents to take ownership of projects and customer relationships:** One of the best things a call center manager can do with skilled staff is leave them alone. When agents are given the power and trusted to make decisions and see tasks through to completion – without (excessive) supervisory intervention – they are able to realize their true value. The payback is huge: enhanced agent confidence, performance and commitment to the call center and customers. Consider allowing agents to work on projects in teams where they can develop positive autonomy. (See Cultivating Empowerment, Section 7.)

- **Implement creative incentives based on agent input:** Nobody knows what motivates agents more than agents themselves. Encourage agents to come up with ideas for captivating incentives and contests that will inspire them to perform while helping the call center meet key objectives. (See Types of Incentives, this section.)

- **Ensure the center is adequately staffed with skilled agents:** A call center manager needs to be – or have somebody in place who is – an expert in forecasting and scheduling. Centers that are continually understaffed or "underskilled" cause both customers and agents to grow frustrated and lose interest.

- **Conduct employee satisfaction surveys or interviews:** Just taking the time to ask agents if they are satisfied with their jobs is a huge step in enhancing motivation in the call center. It shows agents that their welfare, and their opinions, matter to the company. (See Employee Satisfaction Surveys, Section 7.)

- **Inspire people to excel through modeling excellence and enthusiasm:** A manager's leadership skills are crucial to agent motivation. If the manager

merely goes through the motions, agents will likely do the same. Don't just tell agents what great perfomance is; demonstrate these sentiments through consistent action.

- **Create a work environment where people enjoy what they do and for whom they do it:** The call center environment is dynamic and challenging by nature. When poorly managed, the intensity can be a heavy burden on staff. When managed well, the energy flows from agent to agent and fosters commitment. Managers pave the way for high levels of motivation and performance when they take time to create a work environment in which they themselves would like to be an agent – an environment that incorporates diversity, empowerment, opportunity and fun.

## 18. Types of Incentives

Ready? | 1 | 2 | 3 |

### Key Points

- A well-designed, well-implemented incentive program is paramount to sustained agent motivation and productivity.

- Good incentive programs are aligned with the call center's specific objectives, as well as customer expectations and agent interests. It's up to the call center manager – with input from staff – to determine what incentives will have the biggest impact on call center/agent performance and customer satisfaction.

- Awards can be based on either team or individual results, as well as on productivity or quality measures – with each incentive type having its own advantages and possible drawbacks to consider. A solid incentive program usually incorporates a healthy combination of several different incentive types.

### Explanation

Call center managers are constantly challenged to enhance agent performance and productivity. Staff motivation is essential if the manager is to succeed in this regard. One of the best tools to help managers foster sustained high levels of motivation among agents is an effective, well-rounded incentive program.

Good incentive programs are intended to supplement – not replace – a competitive base salary. And each incentive should reward behavior that is linked to the achievement of specific call center/organizational goals. For example, call centers that aim to achieve a specific service level objective might consider rewarding agents who demonstrate solid adherence to schedule results.

Call centers need to ensure that these goals align well with customer expectations. For example, centers that base incentives solely on productivity measurements (e.g., total calls handled, average talk time) may meet their objectives only to see quality crumble and customers leave.

To enhance the effectiveness of any incentive program, managers should seek input from staff. Agents know what motivates them and will be able to shed light on the types of incentives that will inspire them to perform.

Section 6

Incentives come in many different shapes and sizes. Sometimes they represent only a small portion of an agent's total compensation; other times they can contribute to a significant amount of an agent's take-home pay.

There is a variety of incentive types that, when well-implemented, can be highly effective in the call center:

- **Merit pay:** The increase in a person's base pay as a result of good performance. The amount is usually determined by the supervisor or manager and communicated to the agent during the performance review. This amount should correspond to the relative value of the agent's contribution to the call center.

- **Bonuses:** A one-time lump-sum payment that is completely separate from base pay. Bonuses are often given when an agent or team achieves a significant call center objective; i.e., a specific quality or productivity goal. Bonuses can also be used to encourage agents to strive for short-term objectives. For example, managers may give quick cash awards to agents/teams whenever they sell a particular product during a special promotion.

- **Awards:** One-time, non-monetary rewards presented to agents and teams in recognition of good service, sales or support. Examples of popular awards include small gifts, theater tickets, dinner coupons, special privileges, paid time off, points accumulated for merchandise, etc. Other ways to provide agent recognition through non-financial incentives include: a verbal thank-you at a group/team meeting, write-ups in organizational newsletters, desirable assignments with visibility, special training sessions, certificates, etc.

- **Commissions:** Usually a monetary amount given to agents for meeting or exceeding sales goals. Sales agents may be paid on a straight commission, or salary plus commission (although some call centers pay sales agents on a straight salary basis).

*(continued, next page)*

**Section 6**

According to a recent ICMI study, the most common incentives are illustrated in the following table.

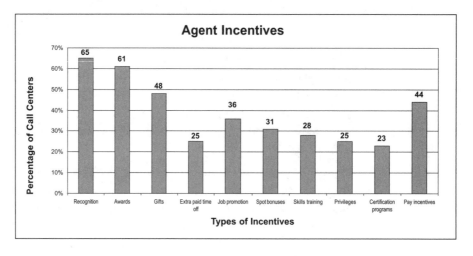

**Team-Based vs. Individual Incentives**

Incentives can be either team-based or individual. Team incentives reward all members equally based on the performance of the team. Advantages to team-based awards include the following:

- Build/support team cohesiveness as team members have the same goals. Team ownership of results encourages cooperation among agents in the group.
- Link the team to call center and business unit goals, thus enhancing performance consistency throughout the enterprise.
- Pave the way for the use of "higher level" objectives that are more closely related to overall performance success than some individual statistics.

Individual incentives are often used when managers feel that higher levels of performance are needed from each member of the team. Advantages to individual incentive plans include:

- Performance that is rewarded individually will most likely be repeated by the agent.
- Helps the call center to achieve internal equity (through assessing performance of individuals and allocating rewards based on that performance).
- Individuals don't feel dependent on others to meet their objectives.

- Enhances level of self-reliance and empowerment among agents.

When carefully planned and implemented, an incentive program can have a dramatic impact on call center/agent performance, customer satisfaction/loyalty, as well as employee morale and retention. In today's competitive demanding environment, managers can ill afford to ignore the importance of powerful incentives in the call center.

**Union Considerations**

Managers of unionized call centers are often restricted in how they can reward performance. During contract negotiations, it is important to work with union leaders to construct a structure that is fair to employees, but gives managers the ability to motivate agents appropriately. Of course, once the contract is in place, incentive programs should be designed according to contract specifications.

**Section 6**

## 19. Pros and Cons of Incentives

Ready? | 1 | 2 | 3 |

**Section 6**

### Key Points

- While incentive programs can have a big impact on call center and agent performance, managers need to familiarize themselves with the potential pitfalls of specific types of incentives to ensure that the center's rewards and recognition efforts don't backfire.

- Potential problems of incentive programs include a lack of teamwork and cooperation among agents, as well as an obsession with performance targets at the expense of customer satisfaction.

- As effective as some incentive programs may be, they cannot replace solid leadership skills and management practices.

### Explanation

Most call center professionals are familiar with the positive impact that a well-designed incentive program can have on agent performance and morale. Many centers have developed and implemented comprehensive programs that offer extra compensation or non-monetary awards for agents that achieve objective goals and standards.

### The Pros

Successful incentive programs bring with them the following potential benefits:

- They inspire the call center and organization to determine and meet key performance objectives.

- They clarify for agents what's important and what's not.

- They provide high performers (both individuals and teams) with the opportunity to earn more money and recognition, resulting in lower turnover rates.

- They help to reduce the subjectivity inherent in less-structured compensation models.

- They ensure that the company "gets what it pays for."

- They help to make the job interesting and challenging for agents.

**The Cons**

If not carefully implemented and evaluated, some incentives can become obstacles to real gains in quality and efficiency. Here are some of the potential problems and challenges:

- Agents may focus too much on achieving performance targets and not enough on customer needs. For example, an agent may rush a caller through a transaction in hopes of meeting a talk-time objective prescribed by a particular incentive. Or an agent striving to meet an objective for "number of calls handled" might be inclined to "drop" calls as soon as they are received.

- Individual reward programs may discourage teamwork.

- Organizations often use incentives in an effort to continually increase results, rather than focusing on the true causes of inefficiency and poor quality. (See Quality and Performance Improvement Process, this section.)

- Supervisors may pay less attention to coaching and development under the assumption that the incentive program will provide all the motivation that agents need.

- When agents become dependent on incentives, it is often difficult to get them to successfully complete a project or assignment that doesn't offer an incentive. Agents may ask themselves is "What's in it for me?"

**Key Principles and Elements of Effective Incentive Programs**

There are several key principles that call center professionals should consider when planning an effective incentive program:

- If the incentive program is not well-thought out and closely developed and monitored, it will likely fail.

- Incentives that focus solely on productivity metrics will likely cause quality and customer satisfaction to fall.

- Incentives that focus solely on quality metrics will likely cause service levels and overall call center efficiency to fall.

- A combination of team- and individual-based incentives will greatly enhance general agent acceptance of the program.

- Most employees find the concept of higher pay for better results to be appealing. However, it's important to also include non-monetary rewards and recognition in the incentive program.

- Incentive programs that provide a substantial payout are difficult to change or eliminate.

- Performance that is rewarded is likely to be repeated.

- Call centers differ in mission and in the types of agents employed – what works in one center may or may not work in another.

For any incentive program to be successful, managers need to ensure that the following elements exist:

- **Management and executive buy-in:** Clearly explain to upper management how a well-implemented incentive plan will help to enhance performance and revenue while cutting costs associated with turnover.

- **Agent buy-in:** You get this by seeking agent input regarding the types of incentives that they feel are inspiring, fun and fair.

- **Clear definitions and easily calculated formulas:** It should be easy to determine when someone is eligible for a reward and how payouts are made. This will eliminate agent claims of subjective treatment down the road, and will help to enhance buy-in.

Remember: No incentive program, regardless of how well it is planned and implemented, can ever replace solid leadership skills and key management practices. An incentive program is just one aspect of an effective manager's performance improvement arsenal.

---

**12 Steps to Develop an Effective Incentive Program**

Regardless of the type of incentive program you decide to implement, follow these 12 steps to make sure that it motivates and energizes agents and gets the results that you seek:

1. Identify goals and objectives of the incentive program.

2. Put together a team that will plan and design the program.

3. Develop the planning process and schedule.

4. Identify budget for the year.

5. Review previous reward and recognition efforts, and research other call centers' experiences.

6. Seek employee feedback through team or staff meetings, focus groups and confidential surveys. Find out what motivates the greatest number of people, and what the de-motivators are.

---

7. Design the program so that it meets your goals and objectives. What will the criteria include? Should it reward individual and/or team performance? Will it be inclusive or selective? How will potential equity and popularity contest issues be addressed? What will be the process for nomination and selection? How will the awards be distributed? Get professional advice on any tax and legal issues.

8. Test it out. Make sure that it will get the results you seek. Solicit feedback from agents, team leaders and supervisors. View it through the eyes of the employees who will participate in the program.

9. Revise the program as necessary.

10. Develop a communications strategy that covers how you will announce the program, maintain interest, announce the winners, etc. Put together supporting materials, including answers to frequently asked questions.

11. Roll out the program. Watch it carefully. Try to keep interest up throughout the program. If participation lags, find out why.

12. Evaluate results. Did you get the results you expected? If not, why not? Seek agent feedback: What did they like; what didn't they like? Incorporate these findings in your next incentive program.

Excerpt from "Incentives that Rev Up and Retain Agents" by Leslie Hansen Harps, published in *Call Center Management Review*, February 2000.

**Section 6**

## 20. Addressing Poor Performance

Ready? | 1 | 2 | 3 |

### Key Points

- How call center managers address poor performance can make the difference between a team of motivated, ever-improving agents and a team of continually poor performers riddled by low morale.

- Gaps between current and desired performance must be clearly and sensitively communicated to employees, and specific development plans must be created to help employees close these gaps.

- Typical performance problems can usually be divided into one of two categories:
  1. "Can't do" (the employee lacks the ability to perform the task effectively)
  2. "Won't do" (the employee lacks the motivation to perform the task effectively)

### Explanation

Performance is a function of the person's ability, motivation and situational, or environmental factors. All three elements must be considered during performance assessments. Situational factors includes things such as: tools, processes, recognition/reward programs, management support, organizational culture, quality of materials, technology, coordination among workers and quality of supervision. The lack or ineffectiveness of these factors can have a detrimental effect on employee performance and customer satisfaction. It's crucial to note that these factors typically are out of the employee's control and need to be rectified by management, not the employee.

#### Causes of Poor Performance

Some of the most common causes of poor performance in the call center include:

- Employee's lack of knowledge, skill or ability
- Organizational or situational barriers
- Lack of or ineffective incentives in the call center
- Low employee motivation

- Lack of or poor feedback on performance
- Unknown performance expectations

**"Can't Do" vs. "Won't Do"**

One of the key challenges in addressing poor performance is determining whether the employee can't (lack of ability) and/or won't (lack of motivation) perform the task in question. The table below illustrates the actions that can be taken in each of the above circumstances.

|  | Will | Won't |
|---|---|---|
| Can | No problem | Collaboratively explore ways to motivate the employee |
| Can't | Train, give feedback and provide opportunities for practice | Determine if the employee is appropriate for the job and, if not, search for other jobs that may be a better fit |

**Guidelines for Managing Poor Performance**

Here are several guidelines to help managers address poor performance:

- **Deal with the situation immediately:** As soon as you realize performance is slipping, start the process of constructive feedback with the employee.

- **Seek the assistance from your HR team:** These people are often trained experts in dealing with performance problems and may offer invaluable advice on providing effective feedback and facilitating behavioral change.

- **Inform the employee that you are going to evaluate his or her performance:** Make sure they understand that you are not trying to merely catch them making mistakes, rather to identify how you can help them perform to the best of their ability.

- **Critique the behavior, not the person:** Providing constructive criticism of specific behaviors helps employees see where they need to improve and, when done well, provides them with the confidence and motivation to improve. However, criticizing the employee as a person will likely lead to feelings of anger, frustration and incompetence – all of which are detrimental to performance improvement.

- **Provide affirmation of the person and any desired behaviors:** It is important to balance negative feedback on specific behaviors with positive affirmation of the person as an individual. Praising those behaviors that are positive will help prevent the individual from

becoming demoralized by the criticism.

- **Avoid comparing an employee's performance to that of other individual employees:** Feedback comments like, "Well, Mary can do it, why can't you?" don't take individual experiences and backgrounds into account. It's better to focus more on the employee's personal potential and how he or she can improve to help the call center.

- **Collaboratively develop a plan of action with known consequences:** The plan of action should be a detailed account of areas the employee should focus on, along with steps that need to be taken to achieve results. The plan should include a list of how the call center can assist the employee (i.e., training and coaching sessions with supervisors or team leaders, etc.).

- **Maintain complete records of all correspondence, observations, input and conversations:** Keep accurate and up-to-date feedback and performance files.

- **Keep senior management informed about systemic problems:** Senior management needs to know about ongoing, frequently occurring problems so they can allocate resources, revise hiring practices and improve crossfunctional processes.

- **Be realistic:** You may have to let some people go.

One the of the tests of effective leadership is: "How are low performers dealt with?" A sensitive approach is necessary to help individual employees develop the skills and desire to improve poor performance. Individual performance problems that go unaddressed can infect a call center. Not only will low performers continue to provide poor service and support, but high performers may become de-motivated by the lack of action being taken.

## 21. Disciplinary Principles and Practices

Ready? | 1 | 2 | 3 |

### Key Points

- All call center disciplinary programs should include the following basic practices:
  - Clear communication of the rules that call center employees are expected to follow.
  - Documentation of the facts involved in specific disciplinary cases that occur in the call center. This documentation should include clear-cut evidence that is difficult to refute.
  - Consistent and unbiased disciplinary action following the violation of any rules.

### Explanation

"Discipline is a formal organizational action taken against an employee due to rules violation, unacceptable performance or other dysfunctional behavior" (DeNisi and Griffin, p. 442). It is not a tool to be used by managers to demonstrate power, rather a tool that managers can use to show an employee that he or she needs to change his or her behavior to help the call center maintain optimum performance.

Typical situations resulting in discipline include:

- Unacceptable performance
- Poor attendance and tardiness
- Sexual harassment or negatively impacting others' well-being or performance

#### Processes for Disciplining Employees

Progressive discipline is the process most often used in call centers. This involves a sequence of penalties that increase in severity with each successive violation. A typical progressive discipline process may include:

- First offense:    Verbal warning
- Second offense:   Written warning
- Third offense:    Suspension
- Fourth offense:   Termination

After each offense, the employee should be given a specific period of time in which to change his or her behavior. If the behavior continues, then the consequences become more severe. The manager must document all aspects of the process, including the verbal warning.

**Reasons for Employee Termination**

While each organization makes its own decisions about what is cause for immediate employee termination, here are some of the most common reasons:

- Use of drugs or alcohol on the job

- Insubordination

- Illegal activities such as theft or fraud

- Providing confidential information to others, especially to competitors

- Workplace violence

---

**Document All Disciplinary Action**

Employers no longer have an option of whether to document disciplinary matters and regularly maintain personnel files. Whenever a wrongful discharge or discrimination claim is filed, your documentation of the entire employment relationship is critical. It can literally make the difference between winning and losing a lawsuit. More importantly, good documentation can prevent a lawsuit from being filed in the first place.

All supervisors should maintain a disciplinary file on each employee they supervise. Those files should be kept separate from personnel files in the supervisor's office. They should contain written documentation on each incident where the supervisor had to warn or admonish the employee, especially when he or she thinks the incident isn't severe enough to be documented in her permanent personnel file. The documentation can be informal – for example, written on notebook paper – but it should reflect the reasons for the discipline.

All files should be regularly reviewed to make sure that the information is current and accurate. Review your employees' files at least annually; semiannual review is even better.

Excerpt from *Employment Law Letter*, M. Lee Smith Publishers, 2000. Found at http://www.hrhero.com:/q&a/discipline.shtml

---

## Measuring and Improving Performance

### Exercises

**Measuring and Tracking Performance Objectives [Strategic]**

1. True or false

_____Service level and response time should be summarized into average daily results.

_____If service level data is not available, average speed of answer can be a substitute.

_____Abandonment rate is a good measure of call center performance because it is in the direct control of the call center.

_____Adherence to schedule is independent of whether the call center actually has the staff necessary to achieve its service level and/or response time objectives.

_____Average handling time is better used to analyze current processes, technologies and training than as an individual performance objective.

_____Occupancy should be managed by each agent to ensure adequate productivity levels.

_____A climbing cost per call can be a good sign.

_____Customer satisfaction has greatest value as a relative measure.

**Key Objectives for Agents**

2. Select the most appropriate answer to the question.

Which of the following performance metric is NOT appropriate for call center agents?

    a. Adherence to schedule

    b. Calls per agent

    c. Quality (contact by contact)

    d. Sales/orders as percent of contacts

**Avoiding Conflicting Objectives**

3. Select the most appropriate answer to the question.

Which of the following are potential conflicting objectives?

    I. Adherence to schedule vs. quality

    II. Average handling time vs. quality

    III. Occupancy vs. service level

    IV. Service level vs. average speed of answer

    V. Turnover vs. employee satisfaction

        a. I, II, III

        b. I, II, IV

        c. II, III, IV

        d. III, IV, V

**Developing a Monitoring and Coaching Program**

4. Fill in the blanks with the appropriate word or phrase to complete seven steps to an effective monitoring and coaching program.

1. Identify the monitoring program _____

2. Determine the program _____

3. Create _____ for performance

4. Create the monitoring _____

5. Develop a _____ strategy

6. Determine a _____ strategy

7. Share program details with _____

**Types of Monitoring**

5. Select the most appropriate answer to each question.

Which is NOT an advantage of silent monitoring?

    a. Agents perform more naturally

    b. The agent receives immediate feedback and coaching

    c. The calls are selected randomly, ensuring a good call sample

    d. The monitoring can be done from a variety of locations

Which is NOT an advantage of call recording?

    a. Agents can listen to their own calls to see how they handled the customer

    b. Can test specific skills

    c. Eliminates unproductive time waiting for a call to arrive

    c. The agent and supervisor can review the conversation as many times as necessary

Which is NOT an advantage of side-by-side monitoring?

    a. Agents perform more naturally

    b. Allows the agent to practice new behaviors with the undivided attention and support of a supervisor/coach

    c. Enhances the relationship between the agent and supervisor

    d. The agent receives immediate feedback and coaching

**Scoring and Calibration**

6. Choose one of the words (or phrases) after each statement to correctly fill in the blanks.

_____ is best used to measure subjective skills. (Yes/no scoring | Numerical scoring)

A scoring system _____ include deductions for negative behaviors. (should | should not)

Coaching and feedback _____ emphasize scores. (should | should not)

It is generally a better practice to listen to _____ calls during a calibration session. (live | recorded)

**Legal Considerations of Monitoring**

7. What do the following acronyms (that relate to legal monitoring practices) represent?

ECPA _____

FCC _____

**Steps to Effective Coaching and Feedback**

8. What are the steps in the SAFE model of effective coaching?

S _____

A _____

F _____

E _____

**Purposes and Benefits of Performance Reviews**

9. What are the two primary purposes of performance reviews?

_____

_____

10. What are the two secondary purposes of performance reviews?

_____

_____

**Motivation Theory and Principles**

11. Beside each statement below, indicate which of the following is a hygiene factor (with an "h") or a motivator (with an "m"), according to Herzberg's Hygiene-Motivation Theory.

_____Achievement

_____Chance for growth and advancement

_____Company policies/procedures

_____Compensation

_____Feedback

_____Job security

_____Recognition

_____Responsibility

_____The work itself

_____Work environment

12. Put the following list of Maslow's hierarchy of needs in order by placing a number (1 for the most basic through 5 for the most complex) in the blank beside each one.

_____Ego

_____Physiological

_____Safety

_____Self-actualization

_____Social

**Addressing Poor Performance**

13. Complete the following table with the phrases below.

No problem

Collaboratively explore ways to motivate the employee

Train, give feedback and provide opportunities for practice

Determine if the employee is appropriate for the job and, if not, search for other jobs that may be a better fit

|        | Will | Won't |
|--------|------|-------|
| Can    |      |       |
| Can't  |      |       |

### Disciplinary Principles and Practices

14. What are the disciplinary practices typically associated with a progressive discipline process?

First offense: _____

Second offense: _____

Third offense: _____

Fourth offense: _____

**Answers to these exercises are in Section 10.**

Note: These exercises are intended to help you retain the material learned. While not the exact questions as on the CIAC Certification assessment, the material in this handbook/study guide fully addresses the content on which you will be assessed. For a formal practice test, please contact the CIAC directly by visiting www.ciac-cert.org.

## Measuring and Improving Performance
## Reference Bibliography

### Related Articles from *Call Center Management Review* (See Section 9)

Measuring Individual Agent Performance

Maximizing the Value of Your Call Monitoring Program

Creating a Successful Peer Monitoring Program for Your Call Center

Monitoring Quality in the Multi-Channel Interaction Center

Principles of Effective Motivation (Three Parts)

Keeping Absenteeism to a Minimum in the Call Center

Use Incentive Programs to Link Desired Behaviors with Rewards

### For Further Study

#### Books/Studies

*Call Center Agent Motivation and Compensation: The Best of Call Center Management Review.* Call Center Press, 2002.

*Call Center Monitoring Study II Final Report.* ICMI, Inc., 1999.

*Call Center Sample Monitoring Forms.* Call Center Press, 2001.

Cleveland, Brad and Julia Mayben. *Call Center Management on Fast Forward: Succeeding in Today's Dynamic Inbound Environment.* Call Center Press, 1999.

DeNisi, Angelo, and Ricky Griffin. *Human Resource Management.* Houghton Mifflin Company, 2001.

#### Articles

*Call Center Management Review: Monitoring and Coaching Special Issue.* ICMI, Inc., 1999.

Hansen Harps, Leslie. "Incentives that Rev Up and Retain Agents." *Call Center Management Review,* February 2000.

**Section 6**

Solomon, Laurie. "Proven Tips for Effective Feedback and Coaching." *Call Center Management Review: Monitoring and Coaching Special Issue.* 1999.

### Seminars

*Monitoring and Coaching for Improved Call Center Performance* public seminar, presented by Incoming Calls Management Institute.

*Essential Skills and Knowledge for Effective Call Center Management* public seminar, presented by Incoming Calls Management Institute.

*Call Center Monitoring Web Seminar Series,* persented by Incoming Calls Management Institute.

*Call Center Coaching Web Seminar Series,* presented by Incoming Calls Management Institute.

### Web sites

Employment Law Letter, M. Lee Smith Publishers, 2000, www.hrhero.com:/q&a/discipline.shtml

# Maximizing Human Resources

# Section 7: Maximizing Human Resources

## Contents

## 1. Differentiating Career and Skill Path Models

Ready? | 1 | 2 | 3 |

### Key Points

- Career paths involve structured tracks or levels through which employees can progress, while skill paths focus on an individual's acquisition of skill sets.

- The basic career path process involves three key phases:
    1. Assessment phase
    2. Direction phase
    3. Development phase

- Because the historical corporate-ladder approach to staff development can be limited for call centers (due to the finite amount of supervisory and management positions available), a more effective staff development approach may be the skill path model.

### Explanation

Most centers follow one of two basic approaches to employee development. Career paths involve structured tracks or levels through which employees can progress, while skill paths focus on an individual's acquisition of skill sets. These terms are often used interchangeably since the differentiation is only one of emphasis: career paths focus on progressing to new positions while skill paths are associated with acquiring new skills and responsibilities without necessarily changing job titles.

#### Career Paths

Career paths guide individual development through structured advancement opportunities within the call center and/or organization. Most career paths require specific tasks to be successfully accomplished in order to move from one level to the next. In most career path programs, base pay increases are dependant on advancement to the next position and variable pay is linked to performance.

A typical career path model requires the development of job families, which are comprised of a number of jobs arranged in a hierarchy by grade, pay and responsibility; e.g., agent, team leader, supervisor, manager, senior manager,

**Section 7**

director. The career path then indicates the requirements for each job within the family; e.g., education, experience, tenure, knowledge, skills, behavioral competencies, etc. Many organizations also require crossfunctional experience to provide a broader, organizational perspective. Generally, this involves a job rotation in other functions, such as marketing, sales or finance. (See Self-Development, Section 5.)

The basic career path process involves three key phases:

**1. Assessment phase:** Individual assessment through performance appraisals, coaching/mentoring, skills assessment and interests evaluation, which identifies the strengths and weaknesses of the individual.

**2. Direction phase:** Direction and goal-setting, in which the employee decides on the type of career he or she wishes to pursue and identifies the necessary steps to attain it.

**3. Development phase:** Development, which includes taking the necessary steps or actions to increase skills to prepare for promotions, such as job rotation, special projects/assignments, seminars/workshops and self-paced training.

**Skill Paths**

Because the historical corporate-ladder approach to staff development can be limited for call centers (due to the finite amount of supervisory and management positions available), a more effective staff development approach may be the skill path model. Skill paths seek to prepare agents for the future of the organization's business by taking into consideration individual staff needs and organizational goals. Individuals often receive more compensation as they acheive new skill levels within their position. It is easier to get executive-level support and funding for skill paths if they are aligned with overall business needs.

Skill paths focus on the development of specific skills rather than the progression of positions through the center and/or organization. Skill paths can move laterally; e.g., a printer technical support agent can be crosstrained to handle technical support on fax machines, as well, or upward; e.g., an agent can acquire leadership and coaching skills add peer coaching responsibilities to his or her current position. The difference between skill paths and career paths is a focus on the skills that are acquired instead of focusing on promotion to a new position.

## 2. Creating and Communicating Career and Skill Paths

Ready? | 1 | 2 | 3 |

### Key Points

- The basic career or skill path strategy includes the following components:
  1. Competency model for each position
  2. Professional career development model for each position
  3. Standards and expectations for each position
  4. Skills assessment for each individual
  5. Professional development plan for each individual
  6. "University-style" training curriculum

- One of the most critical components of career and skill path programs is the employees' access to training. Call center managers must use sound workforce management processes to develop schedules that include time for agent training.

- The most significant career pathing obstacle for employees is an organizational culture that doesn't support growth.

### Explanation

According to consultant Elizabeth Ahearn, a comprehensive career or skill path strategy includes the following components:

**1. Competency model for each position:** This document should define the necessary skills and behaviors and describe each level of performance (i.e., no indication of behavior, some indication, proficient or expert). Hire only those individuals who can demonstrate the critical competencies of the job.

**2. Professional career development model for each position:** Identify where individuals can move both within the call center and externally. If opportunities for such movement do not currently exist, a partnering plan should be developed and "sold" within the organization.

**3. Standards and expectations for each position:** This consists of the minimum level of performance and the skills, knowledge and experience required for each position.

Section 7

**4. Skills assessment for each individual:** This involves using the competency model-both self-assessment and manager assessment-for each individual in the call center.

**5. Professional development plan for each individual:** This document should include realistic timeframes for movement based on business needs and the individual's demonstration and application of the competencies required for the new position.

**6. "University-style" training curriculum:** This curriculum should include courses (from internal and/or external sources) specifically targeting core competencies for the call center and each job within it, and electives that will enable staff to achieve their professional goals.

### Critical Success Factors

The following are critical success factors when establishing career and skill path programs:

- **Involve employees:** Career and skill path programs should not be developed in a vacuum. Begin the development process with a cross-functional team that includes call center agents, supervisors, managers, the HR department and others. Input from those affected by the program will result in an approach that balances the needs of employees with the needs of the organization.

- **Market the plan to employees:** Since employees drive the career and skill path process, it is vital to educate employees on how the program works and how it benefits them as individuals.

- **Establish a scheduled feedback process:** Create a scheduled feedback process that includes the measurement of progress and sharing of results. Take time during monitoring and coaching sessions to discuss the skills the agent is developing. Link skills development to performance reviews. (See Principles of Effective Coaching and Feedback, Section 6.)

- **Make training available:** One of the most critical components of career and skill path programs is access to training. Training often gets postponed or even canceled when service levels are low, and it is impossible to train all call center agents at the same time during business hours. Call center managers must use sound workforce management processes to develop schedules that include time for agent and management training.

- **Provide opportunities for a variety of employee interests and organizational needs:** An effective career or skill path model synchronizes employee interests and organizational needs. For example, an organizational requirement that can be addressed through career or skill pathing is the challenge of handling multichannel contacts. Attractive advancement opportunities to handle more types of contact channels, such as email or Web transactions, can give agents the incentive to learn new skills required by these channels.

- **Integrate plans with other management processes:** Once career and skill paths are in place, call center managers should examine other management processes, such as selection and hiring, training, coaching, mentoring, performance feedback and incentives. These processes should be aligned with career and skill paths.

- **Consider the impact of call center size:** A large center may want to target growth plans on specific career or skill paths that create experts in focused areas. Smaller centers need agents and managers with the capacity to handle a wide variety of responsibilities.

- **Consider the impact of transaction types:** In environments where customer contacts are relatively simple and repetitive, growth opportunities may need to be focused on more career paths; e.g., supervisory, coaching and quality positions. In contrast, environments with a wide variety of complex transactions have many skill path alternatives.

**Obstacles to Successful Programs**

The most significant career pathing obstacle for employees is an organizational culture that doesn't support growth. Other obstacles, include:

- Lack of a solid model that includes detailed skill requirements, a variety of advancement options and a structured feedback process

- Insufficient crossfunctional opportunities

- Absence of available positions when turnover is low

- Limited access to coaches and mentors

- Little time dedicated to training

- Inadequate funding for training and compensation

- Flat organizational structures

- Lack of senior management support

- Lack of agent envolvement

- Counter-productive human resources policies

The ICMI study, *Agent Staffing and Retention Study Final Report,* identified organizational obstacles to developing career or skill paths. Results are summarized in the graph:

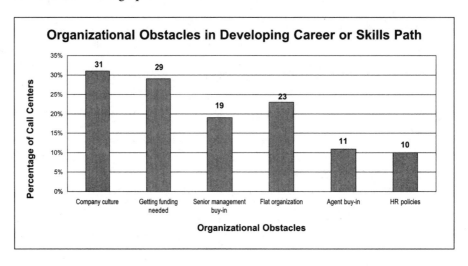

**Organizational Obstacles in Developing Career or Skills Path**

## 3. Succession Planning
## [Strategic]

Ready? | 1 | 2 | 3 |

### Key Points

- Succession planning is the identification and preparation of high-potential individuals for senior-level positions.

- There are a number of factors critical to effective succession planning efforts. Succession planning should be:
  - Customized to the call center
  - Based on key leadership criteria
  - Supported by top executives
  - Focused on development with shared responsibility
  - Driven by future direction and strategy
  - Determined by objective assessments
  - Focused on a small group of capable individuals

### Explanation

Succession planning is the identification and preparation of high-potential individuals for senior-level positions. Succession planning is needed to ensure that leadership growth keeps pace with organizational growth. It is more than simply finding the right person for an open position. Today, organizations are learning that the focus must also be on the context of these individuals to the leadership team. Effective succession planning examines how each succession candidate would add value to team performance.

**Succession Planning Process**

As the flowchart illustrates, the first step in succession planning is determining the leadership criteria. These criteria consists of both general leadership qualities and call center specific requirements. Then managers should be evaluated based on several objective measurement methods to determine which individuals exhibit leadership potential. The readiness of the identified managers should be assessed and then appropriate development plans, coaching and mentoring should be established. The results from the evaluation of each manager should be made available to appropriate coaches and mentors to facilitate the employee's development. When an executive position becomes available, succession candidates should be evaluated against that position's specific requirements and the most appropriate person should be selected.

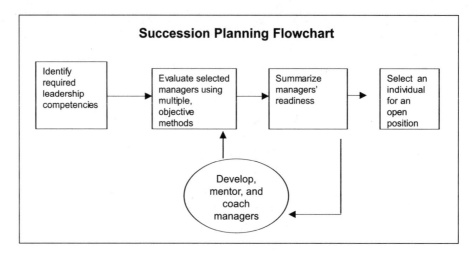

**Factors Critical to Success**

There are a number of factors critical to effective succession planning efforts. Succession planning should be:

- **Customized to the call center:** There is no "right" way to develop a succession plan. It must be tailored to the unique needs of the call center.

- **Based on key leadership criteria:** The leadership qualities and background required for senior-level positions in the call center should drive the selection process. A candidate's profile and criteria could include:

  - Kind of experience, including call center, leadership/management, fiscal responsibilities, accomplishments and strategic planning

  - Knowledge of the industry, organization, customers, trends, etc.

  - Education

  - Leadership qualities

  - Demonstrated performance

- **Supported by top executives:** Senior executives must model and support the succession planning process.

- **Focused on development with shared responsibility:** Individual development plans should be identified for each person in the succession plan. Development opportunities that expose the employee to different leadership styles and situations (e.g., crossfunctional job assignments,

executive coaching and mentoring, and job rotation) will have the greatest impact.

- **Driven by future direction and strategy:** Succession planning must align with and support the call center's future strategic direction. It should be aimed at developing a leadership group whose competencies align with the strategic mission. Succession plans that only focus on identifying a group of candidates for positions that may open in six to 12 months are short-sighted.

- **Determined by objective assessments:** The most effective way to assess the individual is by using a variety of methods including 360-reviews, simulations, project leadership experiences, etc.

- **Focused on a small group of capable individuals:** Succession planning is not about developing the entire workforce, or all call center managers. Instead, the focus should be on a select number of identified individuals who have the potential to assume future executive positions.

### Benefits of Succession Planning

Succession planning benefits the call center in a number of ways. Succession planning:

- Encourages senior management to review its leadership capabilities in a disciplined, consistent way

- Guides key executives' development plans

- Assures continuity of leadership and avoids transition problems

- Can prevent premature promotion of managers into senior, strategic roles

### Challenges of Succession Planning

Many companies see the value in succession planning, but have difficulty implementing those plans because of the challenges, including:

- Executives have little available time for development and succession planning.

- Executives will likely choose and develop successors who are similar to themselves, perpetuating the status quo and limiting diversity.

- Individual development is generally not compensated or rewarded.

Today's call center environment requires that succession planning be a continual process and integrated with the organization's strategic plan. It takes time and must be a long-term commitment, but the benefits are significant.

**Section 7**

## 4. Types of Compensation

Ready? | 1 | 2 | 3 |

### Key Points

- An employee's total compensation has three components:
  1. Base pay (the fixed amount a person receives; i.e., salary)
  2. Incentives (rewards for performance; e.g., bonuses)
  3. Benefits

- Job-based pay determines compensation according to the value of the job. Skills-based pay places value on an employee's abilities, potential and flexibility to handle multiple job responsibilities or duties.

- Because of the often limited advancement opportunities in call centers, skills-based pay can be an effective way to provide agents with room to grow professionally.

### Explanation

An employee's total compensation has three components:

1. Base pay (the fixed amount a person receives; i.e., salary)

2. Incentives (rewards for performance; e.g., bonuses)

3. Benefits

#### Types of Base Pay

Employees can be compensated based on a specific job they perform or based on knowledge and skills that they apply to their role in the organization. Compensation should support career and skill paths. (See Differentiating Career and Skill Path Models, this section.)

- **Job-based pay:** Compensation is determined by the value of the job, not how well a person performs in that job. Job-based pay assumes that work is completed satisfactorily by employees who are paid to perform a well-defined job. Through job analysis and job evaluation, the value of a job (base pay range) is determined independently of the individuals performing the job. Specific individuals are then paid within the range established for the job.

Note: With this approach, there is a problem when employees reach the top of the pay grade. They must either move to another job, settle for cost-of-living adjustments or request to have the job re-evaluated. (See The Job Evaluation Process, Section 3.)

- **Skills-based pay:** This approach places value on an employee's abilities, potential and flexibility to perform multiple job responsibilities or duties. Employees are paid on the basis of the skills they can do or the talents they have that can be applied to a variety of tasks and situations. They advance by acquiring additional knowledge and skills. Because of the often limited advancement opportunities in call centers, skills-based pay can be a way to provide agents with room to grow professionally.

Note: Organizations pay for knowledge and skills that a person has, but may (or may not) use. The organization may experience increased training costs as employees seek to improve their skills to gain higher compensation. However, this approach provides greater staffing flexibility and crosstraining opportunities.

Studies have shown that most call centers choose to compensate employees based on specific jobs, not skills. However, as shown by the graph from the *Agent Staffing and Retention Study Final Report,* published by ICMI, skill-based pay is more prevalent in some industries than in others.

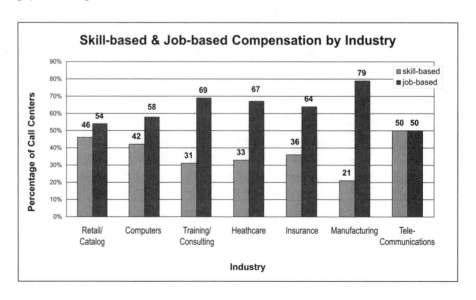

### Incentives

Incentives also play an important part in compensation issues. (See Types of Incentives, and Pros and Cons of Incentives, Section 6.)

### Benefits

Employee benefits, or indirect compensation, provide security for employees and their family members. There are four legally required benefits that the organization must offer. These include:

- Social Security

- Unemployment insurance

- Workers' compensation

- Family and medical leave (depending on company size)

Other benefits, such as health and medical insurance, retirement and time off are not legally required but help an organization recruit, retain and motivate employees. Some of these benefits impact scheduling; e.g., vacations, holidays, and sick leave. Since agent scheduling is so vital to a call center's ability to meet service levels, call center managers should work with HR to establish benefits policies that will meet both employees needs and the organization's requirements.

## 5. Compensation-Related Factors

Ready? | 1 | 2 | 3

### Key Points

- A number of factors must be considered when setting salaries, including:
  - Economic forces
  - Pay differentials
  - Deferred compensation
  - Cost of living
  - Living wage requirements
  - Supply and demand (including competition)

- In the call center industry, supply and demand is poised to be the biggest driver of salary increases, as organizations focus on finding, training and keeping top-notch employees, and as competition for employees becomes more acute.

### Explanation

Compensation plays a vital role in the recruitment, retention and motivation of call center employees. To determine appropriate salary levels, managers should conduct a detailed job evaluation and consider a number of other factors, including:

- **Economic forces:** In the larger context, economic forces set the upper and lower limits of jobs and the amounts of increases. In a recession, organizations tend to establish wages and increases that are more conservative. In boom times, wages and increases are often more aggressive. If wages and increases are set too high, based on a strong economy, there are significant employee cost issues when the economy slows. Likewise, if increases are too conservative in a slow economy, employees will likely seek other opportunities as they become available.

- **Pay differentials:** One common pay differential is based on hours. For example, in many 24x7 centers, those working night and weekend shifts receive a pay premium. Premiums may also be established for agents who are on-call or work holidays.

Another common pay differential, based on location, is called a geographic differential. Geographic differentials recognize cost-of-living differences in various parts of the country and world. For example, it is more expensive to live in Boston or San Francisco than Memphis. Usually, the organization will make pay adjustments upward to reflect higher costs of living.

- **Deferred compensation:** Deferred compensation can take the form of bonus deferrals or supplemental retirement payments. The idea is to maximize the individual's after-tax income by reducing his or her tax burden and postponing the payment of taxes until he or she is in a lower tax bracket. The goal of deferral income is to retain the employee and is usually reserved for executives of the organization.

- **Cost of living:** Cost-of-living adjustments are usually pegged to the rate of inflation, as tracked by the Consumer Price Index (CPI). While a cost-of-living adjustment is usually part of the compensation strategy, there may be situations in which some employees receive salary adjustments and others do not. For example, in a union environment, cost-of-living adjustments may be built into a long-term contract. In addition, some labor contracts contain a clause permitting the renegotiation of wages. Others use escalator clauses that provide for automatic wage increases (in many cases, quarterly) in times of rapid inflation.

- **Living wage:** The concept of a "living wage" is gaining popularity with lawmakers in some regions of the country. Living wage laws require employers to set wages at levels that permit the employees to maintain a certain standard of living. The wage is set above the national minimum wage and is based on what local officials determine to be an appropriate minimum standard of living. In some cases, the cost is offset by local subsidies and employer incentives.

- **Supply and demand:** Supply and demand impacts call center viability. When compensation is established at a level below what supply and demand dictate, the call center will not be able to attract and retain required staff. If compensation is well above what supply and demand dictate, the organization's high cost structure will harm its ability to compete. Call center managers must be aware of and operate within these boundaries.

Supply and demand is an overarching factor that is ever evolving and is influenced by variables such as agents with both verbal and written

Section 7

communication skills, managers with e-commerce experience, technicians trained in today's open, multisystem environment or competition vying for the same employees. In the call center industry, supply and demand is poised to be the biggest driver of salary increases, as organizations focus on finding, training and keeping agents who excel in the multichannel environment, and as competition becomes more acute.

## 6. Implementing Compensation Plans

Ready? | 1 | 2 | 3 |

### Key Points

- As the role of call centers has evolved to be mission-critical, strategic and a competitive advantage, the pay of call center employees must evolve to attract the best employees.

- Compensation plans should be based on performance objectives that are in the control of the employee and result in the accomplishment of call center goals.

- Effective compensation plans will avoid the following problems:
  - Incentives that undermine teamwork
  - Compensation plans that focus on performance objectives only
  - Compensation plans based on inappropriate performance objectives
  - Performance objectives that are inaccurately measured
  - Compensation planning without the input of union representatives

### Explanation

As the role of call centers has evolved to be mission-critical, strategic and a competitive advantage, the pay of call center employees must evolve as well to attract the best employees. Call center managers must be advocates for appropriate pay, recognition and career opportunities for employees.

**Implementing Compensation Plans**

There are a number guidelines to consider when implementing effective compensation plans:

- Consider workforce demand; i.e., availability of workers.

- Take into account budgetary restraints.

- Focus the plan around job or skill requirements.

- Apply the plan consistently since inconsistent compensation practices lead to mistrust between management and employees.

**Section 7**

- Base the plan on appropriate performance objectives that are in the control of the employee and result in the accomplishment of call center goals.

- Don't place too much emphasis on benchmarking data or industry averages. The employees in your call center should be compensated based on the skill requirements and compensation-related factors unique to your environment. (See Compensation-Related Factors, this section.)

- Consider incentives. Since base pay and benefits may be dictated by organizational policy, incentives can provide greater flexibility to meet the needs of the call center. (See Pros and Cons of Incentives, Section 6.)

- Involve employees. A good way to increase acceptance of compensation is to include employees in the design of the pay plan and the administration of incentives.

**Problems to Avoid When Implementing Compensation Plans**

There are a number of potential problems when implementing compensation plans that, when identified, can be addressed. These include:

- **Incentives that undermine teamwork:** If call center agents are structured in teams, care must be taken to ensure team members are not competing for "scarce" resources. Consider implementing team-based incentives to foster collaboration and teamwork. (See Types of Incentives, Section 6)

- **Compensation plans that focus on performance objectives only:** If a compensation plan focuses too narrowly on a specific set of objectives, other important, though less tangible, parts of the job may be neglected. Agents may get the message that those activities not tied to compensation are not worth doing.

- **Compensation plans based on inappropriate performance objectives:** Call center agents do not have control over all factors that impact their performance. For example, they cannot control when calls arrive, the speed of computer systems or the accuracy of workforce management decisions. Therefore, objectives that are within the agent's control, such as adherence to schedule and quality contact handling, should be the ones used to determine compensation. (See Key Objective for Agents, Section 6.)

- **Performance objectives that are inaccurately measured:** Assessing individual and team performance accurately is difficult, especially if

inadequate data collection or analysis tools exist. Agents should not be expected to meet performance objectives that are not accurately and objectively measured. For example, those conducting monitoring must be well-trained and participate in frequent calibration sessions to diminish individual biases. (See Scoring and Calibration, Section 6.)

- **Compensation planning without the input of union representatives:** Unions often require cost-of-living adjustment or across-the-board salary increases for union members. Therefore, any reward being considered should be consistent with the union contract.

---

### Companies Ignore Customer Service Agents' Impact on Revenue

According to Laura Sikorski, managing partner of Sikorski-Tuerpe & Associates. "Most companies still feel that the customer service agent position is at the low end of the spectrum, just an entry-level position. They don't realize the impact these agents have on revenue." Sikorski points out that a sales rep may bring in new customers with a sale, but it's the support provided by the customer service agent that so often creates customer loyalty and repeat business. "I'm not saying that sales reps don't deserve the good money that they make, I'm saying that management needs to realize the important role that dedicated customer service agents play, and pay them accordingly," says Sikorski.

Few are as impassioned over inadequate agent compensation as Mary Beth Ingram, president of the call center training consultancy PHONE PRO. "As the role of the call center has evolved, the job classification and resulting pay scale of the frontline staff – the people who we ask to know the most in the call center – has lagged behind," says Ingram. "I believe that wages for call center agents are woefully low and must be reevaluated."

Ingram alludes to a study conducted by SOCAP (Society of Consumer Affairs Professional in Business) to support her claims that customer service agents deserve better compensation. According to the Executive Summary of SOCAP's *Consumer Loyalty Study*, call centers "not only excel in delivering service quality, but are significantly affecting the consumers future buying patterns." (Ingram explains that consumer affairs call centers are typical of many customer service centers – they handle mostly compliment, complaint and inquiry calls from existing or prospective customers.) Specifically, the study revealed that the typical consumer affairs agent contributed an average of $1,359,745 per year of what SOCAP refers to as "lifetime consumer loyalty dollars." The value of a typical phone call from a customer to a consumer affairs call center was found to be $95.

Ingram points out that many consumer affairs calls are about small-end products like toothpaste, food items, etc., and that, therefore, $95 is probably a low figure for call centers that support higher-end goods and services (computers, banks, etc). Even still, she gladly uses the figure uncovered by the SOCAP study in her calculations.

"Say your typical agent handles 50 calls a day – a conservative number," says Ingram. "That agent handles $4,750 ($95 x 50) a day for the company. In a week, the agent handles $23,750. In a year, $1,235,000! And we all know that it's not uncommon for

---

*(continued, next page)*

agents in many call centers to handle 100 calls a day or more. The point is that the amount of loyalty dollars frontline staff contribute to is astounding, but these figures are overlooked by most senior managers."

Given these numbers, how much should a qualified customer service agent be paid? Ingram's response: a wage/salary more comparable to that of sales staff. To get a rough idea of what this might be, she suggests taking the $1,235,000 figure above to determine how much of that a typical outside sales rep would be paid. Average commission for sales reps is about 5 percent, meaning that they would receive $61,750 a year. "Even if we give experienced customer service agents only 3 percent commission," Ingram explains, "they would still be making over $37,000 a year. That's a darn sight better than most are making now."

Like Sikorski, Ingram isn't trying to reduce sales reps' salaries. "I don't have a problem with sales staff making a lot of money –they work hard and earn it. But let's pay the customer service folks – the people who are in the position to ensure years of repeat business – what they are truly worth, too."

Excerpt from "Call Center Professionals Speak Up for Underpaid Agents," by Greg Levin, *Call Center Management Review*, April 1999.

## 7. Contributors to Employee Satisfaction

Ready? | 1 | 2 | 3 |

### Key Points

- Employee satisfaction in the call center has a profound impact on absenteeism and retention, customer satisfaction and overall call center performance. Many factors that influence employee satisfaction are within the organization's and, specifically, the call center manager's direct control.

- Studies have revealed key contributors to employee satisfaction in the call center. Among these are:
  - Effective communication
  - Professional development
  - Trust, respect and fairness
  - Challenging and diverse projects and tasks
  - A healthy balance of personal and work lives

- Even small adjustments to a call center's policies, procedures and direction can have a positive impact on employee satisfaction levels.

### Explanation

Optimizing employee satisfaction is an important success factor in any call center. How employees feel about their jobs can have a significant impact on:

- Absenteeism

- Turnover

- Customer satisfaction

- Productivity

- Overall call center performance

Creating a culture that fosters employee satisfaction is the responsibility of the call center manager. To ensure that employees are happy with the environment and the work they do, managers need to conduct satisfaction surveys on a regular basis, analyze the results and act upon them quickly. (See Employee Satisfaction Surveys, this section.)

According to a recent study by The Radclyffe Group, there are four common fac-

Section 7

tors within call centers that negatively impact the way agents feel about their jobs:

- The rules are perceived as stringent and inflexible

- The work is stressful by nature

- Call centers tend to assess overall performance using solely quantitative, not qualitative, measures

- Schedules and phone time are "managed in the moment"

However, call center managers can mitigate the factors contributing to these negative feelings and perceptions by focusing on creating a positive culture (i.e., demonstrating effective leadership skills, empowering agents, implementing the right supporting processes, etc.).

### Key Contributors to Employee Satisfaction

Several industry studies have identified the following contributors to a positive call center culture:

- **Effective communication:** Managers who regularly seek agent input and encourage them to challenge and improve how things are done pave the way for a center filled with empowered and motivated staff dedicated to serving customers. Managers further enhance employee satisfaction by being upfront and honest about call center processes and objectives.

- **Professional development:** High levels of agent satisfaction are likely in a call center that provides timely coaching and feedback, as well as opportunities to continually enhance skills and to advance their careers. To do this, managers should strive to implement effective training and quality assurance practices, as well as skills-based pay and career-path programs.

- **Trust, respect and fairness:** Once agents sense that they are being micro-managed, under-valued or subjectively treated, the call center is doomed. Managers need to ensure that staff feels trusted and respected by call center and senior management, and are given the opportunity to work with dignity. This can be accomplished by implementing self-directed teams and empowering agents to solve problems and create change, as well as by having clear and consistent policies regarding pay, incentives, monitoring and adherence to schedule.

- **Challenging and diverse projects and tasks:** Employees in general seek work that is diverse and rewarding. On the surface, the work in some call centers appears to be repetitive and monotonous. However, there are

many opportunities to enhance and expand tasks and reduce burnout. For example, put agents in charge of special projects, create assignments for individuals with specific skills, and inject fun and inspiring incentives into the mix. Be sure to ask agents what could be done to make their jobs more dynamic and interesting to them.

- **A healthy balance of personal and work lives:** Call centers that go out of the way to help employees achieve equilibrium in their personal and professional lives are rewarded with higher levels of staff commitment, performance and retention.

---

**Alternatives for Improving Employee Satisfaction**

- Set up a planned program of skills acquisition for agents as a regular part of on-the-job training. Reward them for each level of achievement.

- Hold lunch break seminars on any topic of interest. Ask in-house experts to share info on work-related and nonwork-related subjects. Get agents involved with planning and running the seminars.

- Provide Web-based training or computer-based training to improve customer service skills and/or knowledge sets.

- Provide tuition reimbursement for any outside course, whether or not it's related to work.

- Meet regularly with agents to share information on work-related issues, or to research and solve a problem that's been bugging you.

- Provide continuing education unit credit instruction in enterprise-related fields.

- Use your company's Web page or intranet to link to sites that relate to your business. Encourage agents to explore whats going on in your industry.

- Create a list of subject-matter experts in your organization – encourage agents to gain the skills required to be included on the list.

- Incent agents to share learning.

Excerpt from "The Role of Corporate Culture in Agent Commitment" by Jean Bave-Kerwin, *Agent Development and Retention Special Issue, Call Center Management Review*, 2000.

---

Creating a call center environment where employees are proud to work requires commitment on the part of the call center manager. A positive call center culture doesn't suddenly appear; it's a gradual process, one which involves frequently seeking employee input and making improvements based on that input. Remember, even small adjustments to a call center's policies, procedures and direction can have a positive impact on employee satisfaction levels.

## 8. Employee Satisfaction Surveys

Ready? | 1 | 2 | 3 |

### Key Points

- Employee satisfaction surveys are instruments designed to determine which aspects of employees' work situations contribute to or impede their job satisfaction.

- To conduct a successful employee satisfaction survey, the call center manager should:
  - Tell employees the purpose of the survey
  - Tell employees how the results will be used
  - Inform employees of the results and actions to be taken
  - Use data for stated purpose only
  - Use the results as a baseline for trending employee satisfaction
  - Use a third party to conduct and analyze the survey

### Explanation

Employee satisfaction surveys are instruments designed to determine which aspects of employees' work situations contribute to or impede their job satisfaction. Typical areas of measurement include management effectiveness, peers/team members effectiveness, career opportunities, equity of salary, level of appreciation, satisfaction with benefits and quality of training, feedback and coaching.

**Principles of Conducting Effective Employee Satisfaction Surveys**

To conduct a successful employee satisfaction survey, the call center manager should:

- Tell employees the purpose of the survey

- Tell employees how the results will be used

- Inform employees of the results and actions to be taken

- Use data for stated purpose only

- Use the results as a baseline for trending employee satisfaction

- Use a third party to conduct and analyze the survey

## 10 steps to preparing effective employee surveys:

1. Identify your goals. What do you need to know? What information are you trying to gather? How will you use the output from the survey?

2. Determine who will see the results. Survey designs can change based on who will be seeing the final report. In general, senior executives are presented with complete results, department heads view breakout reports from their departments and staff see summary results.

3. Plan the assessment. Determine if you want a quantitative (numerical) or qualitative (word) response – or a combination. Both have advantages. With quantitative responses, employees pick from numerical rankings from a multiple-choice list. Qualitative answers do a better job of capturing the themes and ideas of employees but require subjective evaluation and the results are more difficult to track.

4. Select a delivery method. Whether the survey is delivered by paper, telephone, email or Web site depends on the type of survey, the need for anonymity and the technical capabilities of your staff.

5. Prepare and test the survey. It's important that the survey's questions be specific and easy to interpret. Quantitative questions such as, "I understand my company's mission," are easy to answer.

6. Consider an incentive. Incentives can substantially increase response rates. You might want to offer participants an inexpensive incentive, such a lottery ticket, free lunch coupon or opportunity to enter a drawing.

7. Publicize the survey. Let your staff know why you're conducting a survey, what you hope to accomplish and when they will be contacted. Don't surprise them by enclosing a survey with their paycheck or sending unexpected email. Be sure to let employees know what you intend to do with the results and when the results will be available.

8. Tabulate and evaluate the results. Look at the results carefully to identify what themes emerge. What are your organization's strengths and weaknesses? What could be made better? What is surprising? What opportunity is there for quick fixes that would make big improvements? What problems existed that surprised you?

9. Change your organization. There's nothing more demoralizing for employees than being told their opinion is important, only to discover that nothing has changed as a result of the survey. Decide what you can do – and then do it.

10. Measure the results. Once you've made changes, evaluate the results. Perhaps you'll want to conduct another survey for comparison purposes. Then use this data to determine if you're improving. Look to see if any new problems are emerging that require your action.

Remember, paying attention to the needs of employees will increase employee satisfaction and improve retention, which has a direct impact on your organization's profitability. Although knowing what your staff thinks is always important, it's essential if you're going to retain employees in today's tight job market.

Excerpt from "Use Surveys to Assess Your Employees' Satisfaction" by Ingrid Marro Botero, *The Business Journal of Phoenix*, November 12, 1999.

**Section 7**

**Using the Data**

The evaluation of survey data is key to taking action toward improved employee satisfaction. Important considerations include:

- Decide which items to address first. After a survey has been conducted, employees will expect to see changes as a result. In determining which items should be addressed first, consider the following:

    - Identify those items that will have the greatest impact on improving employee satisfaction.

    - Divide these items into those that can be done quickly and those that will take more time and/or resources. Begin with several items that can be implemented quickly so that employees will see positive changes soon. Establish and communicate plans to accomplish longer-term objectives.

- Segment the data by critical groupings, such as position or tenure. Include employee profile questions as part of the survey so that you can segment the data.

- Analyze the content of open-ended questions (qualitative) for consistent themes or issues.

- Form a team to explore reasons for low employee satisfaction. The team should be made up of a diverse group of employees that is representative of the call center as a whole.

**Reporting the Results**

Survey results should be reported to both management and employees. Open sharing of positive and negative feedback will let employees know that they have been heard and give everyone a clearer picture of the prevailing concerns. The survey report should include the following:

- Gratitude to employees for their participation.

- The purpose of the survey.

Tip: No survey – or any other marketing research technique for that matter – is foolproof. People may not tell the whole truth and survey techniques are fallible – just look at the times when political polls don't predict the outcome of elections. It is always important to temper decisions with common sense and experience. Survey data should aid you in decision-making, not make decisions for you.

-Perseus Development Corporation, www.perseus.com

- The findings. Be objective and identify potentially controversial subjects. If the majority of low employee satisfaction results are from employees of only one or two managers, do not single him or her out. Meet with each manager individually to review results.

- Initial decisions regarding what policies, procedures and practices need to be changed to improve employee satisfaction.

## 9. Cultivating Empowerment

Ready? | 1 | 2 | 3

### Key Points

- Empowerment of staff doesn't reduce the importance of the call center manager, rather it moves him or her into an even more important role – that of mentor and enabler.

- There are numerous potential benefits of employee empowerment, namely enhanced call center efficiency, customer satisfaction, staff motivation and retention.

- Managers increase the chances for empowerment success when they:
  - Encourage autonomy
  - Openly share information
  - Redesign policies, procedures and systems
  - Provide focused training and coaching
  - Obtain employee buy-in
  - Trust employee to make decisions
  - Give recognition for good work

### Explanation

To empower someone is to give him or her the official authority to accomplish something. Empowering agents to take ownership of projects, make key decisions and create positive change can transform a static call center into a dynamic, efficient and profitable entity. Once individuals are given the opportunity and resources to take control of customer relationships, enhance processes and procedures, and continually improve, they become career-minded professionals who remain committed to the mission of call center and the organization.

Giving people more power and authority does not undermine the authority of the call center manager. Empowerment encourages individuals to expand their knowledge and involvement, and to work with the manager in a quest to enhance performance and customer loyalty. The manager becomes more of a coach, mentor, enabler – focusing on giving the individual what he or she needs, then stepping out of the way to let them do their job. The manager is still, ultimately, accountable for call center performance, but responsibility and authority are shared.

In general, empowerment in the call center is based on the recognition that – assuming good hiring and training programs are in place – individuals have the skills and knowledge to effectively identify and address unique problems and opportunities.

### Benefits of Empowerment

Empowerment benefits employees, managers and customers, as well as the call center and organization as a whole. Here are some specific advantages:

- Empowered agents provide more effective and efficient service. Armed with the tools, knowledge and authority to quickly provide solutions and make decisions, agents are able to increase first-call resolution results. This improves customer satisfaction and loyalty, and brings significant savings to the bottom line.

- As individuals in all roles take on more responsibility, their commitment to the call center's and the organization's success increases.

- The transition from a passive to an empowered environment often requires jobs to be re-evaluated and redefined, which may provide advancement opportunities for staff.

- In empowered environments, creativity and initiative are encouraged, resulting in better solutions for the organization and customers.

- Empowered individuals are typically more motivated and feel more appreciated than those in traditional top-down environments. This leads to higher performance, enhanced morale and improved employee retention.

### Management Actions to Support Empowerment

Too often, managers attempt to create an empowered environment without fully understanding the implications to themselves, the employees and the call center. Empowerment requires a change in the call center's culture, including work processes, performance measurements and the way managers and employees relate to one another.

To ensure an effective transition from a traditional to an empowered call center environment, managers need to take the following actions:

- **Encourage autonomy:** Managers must create opportunities for employees to experience empowerment. Identify projects and tasks where they can exercise their decision-making authority and responsibility while

**Section 7**

enhancing call center performance and customer satisfaction.

- **Openly share information:** Empowerment requires more disclosure of information so that individuals can make appropriate decisions. Keep employees up-to-date on the latest developments affecting the call center, the customer and the enterprise at large.

- **Redesign policies, procedures and systems:** In an empowered environment, employees need clear decision-making guidelines and boundaries for dealing with customers. Performance measurements must reflect the new goals and support empowerment by allowing room for mistakes. Managers must also provide systems and tools that enable success.

- **Provide focused training and coaching:** Empowered individuals must receive the necessary training and support to make good decisions. Ongoing coaching and mentoring will provide the skills, knowledge and confidence for challenging situations. Note: Managers may need training to help them adapt to their new role as coach and mentor.

- **Obtain employee buy-in:** Managers must communicate the advantages of empowerment to ensure that employees are eager and willing to accept more responsibility and learn additional skills. If employees perceive the empowerment program as "more work," the benefits will be lost.

- **Trust employees to make decisions:** If managers and supervisors interfere with autonomy, employees will begin to view the center's empowerment efforts as mere rhetoric, and thus lose interest. Be sure that individuals truly are given the opportunity to take ownership of tasks and customer relationships. And let them know early on that mistakes will be made, but not punished, as they find their feet in their new roles.

- **Give recognition for good work:** Employees are more likely to embrace empowerment if they receive credit for their sound decisions and ideas for improvement. Create opportunities to publicize their accomplishments. Tell people inside and outside the call center about their good work.

**Agent Actions to Support Empowerment**

Agents who are fortunate enough to work in an empowered environment need to take their new roles seriously. There are certain general guidelines that empowered agents should follow to ensure that they maintain their autonomy and help the call center to continuously improve. It's up to the manager to

remind agents of these guidelines and encourage agents to embrace them:

- Take initiative and make decisions within the context of specified guidelines

- Bring solutions to – rather than merely identify – problems affecting the call center, customers and agents' ability to do their jobs well

- Recognize when additional expertise is needed, and secure it

- Foster a spirit of cooperation and collaboration with fellow agents, supervisors and managers

---

**Ideas for Agent Emancipation**

Here are suggestions on how to expand agent roles to help them and the call center continually evolve and improve:

• **Create agent-led task forces.** Agents respond in big ways when they are given some control over issues that directly affect them in their jobs. Letting them lead special task forces that focus on improvements to key processes – monitoring, scheduling, call center design, etc. – is the best way to turn problem-finders into problem-solvers, says Laura Sikorski, managing partner of consulting firm Sikorski-Tuerpe and Associates in Centerport, N.Y.

"Use the task-force approach for selecting 'complaining agents' to solve an issue," she says. "If an agent doesn't like the current monitoring process, ask him or her to find better ways to evaluate calls. Or create a general task force in charge of creating ways to make agents' jobs easier and more fun. If you give agents the opportunity to change the system, you will be amazed at how motivated and committed they will become."

• **Implement a formal mentoring program.** Adding a mentoring component – in which veteran staff are paired with new-hires – to your initial training program is a great way to enhance learning and enrich the job for your top agents. A good mentoring program not only raises the comfort level of trainees and ensures that they develop good customer contact habits, it helps to foster cohesive bonds among agents that enhance overall morale in the center.

• **Add peer evaluation to the monitoring mix.** Change the perception of monitoring as a "supervisor vs. staff" battle in your call center by making agents an integral part of your quality assurance team. Call centers that supplement supervisor-led monitoring programs with peer-observation and evaluation often see a noticeable improvement in agent commitment to the center's quality efforts.

• **Get agents involved in the hiring process.** Consider creating an agent-led hiring team to help enhance your center's recruiting and selection practices. Ask members to write a detailed job description and an "ideal agent" profile. Have them interview job candidates (after the candidate has interviewed with a manager/supervisor), and take them on a tour of the call center. Later, give members of the hiring team the opportunity to convene as a group to evaluate each candidate and present their selections to supervisors.

---

*(continued, next page)*

- **Tap individual agents' talents.** The opportunities to allow agents to use their unique experiences and capabilities are endless. For example, offer agents who have strong writing skills the opportunity to contribute articles – even a monthly column – to the company newsletter. Let the artists among your staff create posters or other visual aids for special events/contests in the call center. And if you have an agent with outstanding organizational and speaking skills, give him or her the chance to make occasional presentations at call center or interdepartmental meetings.

- **Create "specialist" positions.** Over time, experienced agents become experts on specific products and services, or in specific skills such as cross-selling or dealing with irate customers. Reward these agents by making them a centerwide "specialist" in their area(s) of expertise. Let specialists lead training modules, and encourage other staff members to arrange tutorials with them to improve performance.

- **Immerse agents in the enterprise.** The more your entire staff knows about the inner workings of each department, the better they can serve customers and the more clearly they will see how the call center fits into the enterprisewide picture.

As part of initial and ongoing training, send agents on tours of marketing, sales, IT, finance, shipping – and any other departments that interact with the call center directly or indirectly. Encourage agents to conduct informational interviews with managers or supervisors from other areas to further enhance their knowledge.

### Set Them Free, Why Don't You?

Merely *telling* agents that they are highly valued employees who play an important role isn't enough to raise retention and performance. Agents need to *see* and *feel* how valued they are and the importance of what they do.

Set agents free on occasion to let them spread their skills and knowledge throughout the call center and enterprise. Otherwise, they'll look to spread those skills and that knowledge someplace else.

Excerpt from "Enhance Agent Retention by Turning Them Loose" by Greg Levin. *Call Center Management Review*, February 2002.

## 10. Building Trust

Ready? | 1 | 2 | 3 |

### Key Points

- Building a high degree of trust in an organization is essential to sustainable success.

- Trust cannot be bought or mandated – it must be earned.  Trust is based on both integrity and competence.

- Organizational structures, as well as policies and procedures, can positively or negatively impact trust.

### Explanation

At an individual level, trust is reliance on the integrity and competence of another person; it is an expression of confidence in the behavior of that person. Integrity is largely based on the person consistently keeping their commitments and doing what they say they will do, when they say they will do it.  Trust in competence stems from demonstrated skills and abilities (e.g., he consistently produces reports that are accurate and useful) or credentials (e.g., she is a licensed commercial pilot and can therefore fly us safely to Chicago).

Building a high degree of trust within an organization is essential to sustainable success.  But it is not an easy or automatic process.  In their classic work, *Leaders*, leadership experts Warren Bennis & Burt Nanus contend that in today's complex business environment, "There are too many ironies, polarities, dichotomies dualities, ambivalences, paradoxes, confusions, contradictions, contraries, and messes for any organization to understand and deal with" (p. 8). The authors go on to assert that trust is the "lubrication that makes it possible for organizations to work" (p. 43).  In short, complexity tends to create environments in which trust is difficult to cultivate – and yet, trust is the very thing that keeps complex organizations glued together.

Trust in an organization (as well as between individuals) cannot be bought or mandated.  It must be earned.  There is no fool-proof, step-by-step formula for achieving trust.  It's like leadership itself – hard to define and defies a specific recipe for those who want to create it.  There are, however, tangible, conscientious steps you can take to create an environment where trust is cultivated and becomes a bedrock principle:

Section 7

- Be consistent in your values, actions and decisions, and encourage others to do so
- Communicate clearly and honestly by:
    - Using open, sincere statements to clearly state positions and views
    - Admitting mistakes
    - Providing honest and complete answers to questions
    - Keeping people informed
    - Seeking feedback from others
- Keep your promises; ensure those you make are realistic
- Protect confidences
- Be careful about changing objectives midstream
- Treat others with dignity and respect; be open to divergent views
- Do not tolerate any breach of honesty in the organization
- Give the bad news, as well as the good
- Discuss the vision and purpose of the call center often

**Structure and Policies**

It's important that leaders consider the implications of the environment they create. For example, organizational structure can impact trust. In hierarchical structures, functions can become silos with conflicting objectives or competition for scarce resources. Flatter, more collaborative style organizations tend to create an environment in which trust can flourish. (See Forms of Organizational Structures, Section 3.)

Policies and procedures can also impact trust. For example, monitoring and coaching programs with a bent toward demerits or discipline (e.g., only catching things that are wrong) tend to create mistrust – mistrust in the approach, the organization and those who are part of the process. But programs that tangibly contribute to the growth and well-being of individuals and the organization, help to build trust.

(For a discussion on the importance of integrity and values to effective leadership, see ICMI's *Call Center Leadership and Business Management Handbook and Study Guide*.)

### Trust in Time of Change

Times of change often threaten the trust that organizations have built. The following sidebar provides a four-stage change process model to help managers navigate change.

---

#### A Four-Stage Change Process Model

Change is certain, but not always easy. That's why successfully leading an organization through a transition is one of the greatest challenges facing executives today. Fortunately, some 50 years or more of research into managing organizational change has converged on a few key concepts that hold strong promise for guiding today's leaders.

**Transitions Model**

Successful organizational change passes through four stages:
I. Acknowledging/Knowing
II. Reacting/Responding
III. Investigating/Exploring
IV. Implementing/Doing

An organizational transition is successfully moved through these four stages by the appropriate application of four key leadership skills:
• Informing
• Supporting
• Encouraging
• Reinforcing

Each skill is most appropriately used in one of the four different stages of the Transitions Model. Each skill also helps leaders deal most effectively with tensions created among persons of varied Change Style preferences, that is, Conservers, Pragmatists and Originators. Leaders who act skillfully in concert with an understanding of Change Style preferences can rely on the Transitions Model to help guide them through a change process perhaps more successfully than ever before.

**Stage 1. When a change is announced or revealed . . .**

all three Change Styles face the same challenge of becoming consciously aware of it. Sometimes people must overcome some level of denial. Moreover, leaders sometimes struggle with what information to share at the front end of a transition cycle. But, all information is critical. It helps all members of the organization – Conservers, Pragmatists and Originators alike – to acknowledge the change as a reality.

**Stage 2. When people react and respond, . . .**

emotions can sometimes dominate actions. Some people are excited about new opportunities; others are anxious about facing uncertainty. Conservers are most likely to linger in this stage the longest. They are also the ones most interested in carrying forward

---

*(continued, next page)*

the best of what was working before the change. Originators, on the other hand, may skip through this stage and may move quickly into Stage 3, Investigating/Exploring, where they are most comfortable dealing with possibilities and ideas. It is, in fact, the tension created between Originators and Conservers in the movement from Stage 2 to Stage 3 that is most immediately noticeable in a changing organization.

**Stage 3. When people are creating and exploring, . . .**

all relevant concerns and suggestions should be considered by all stakeholders. The Conservers in Stage 2, who are reviewing and salvaging, may be seen by Originators as "resistors"; and, the Originators in Stage 3 may be seen as "zealots" by the Conservers. With the organization straddling this interface of Stages 2 and 3, effective leaders provide both Support for the Conservers and Encouragement for the Originators. The Support given for those in Stage 2 slows down the Originators' interest in racing ahead and it keeps issues expressed by Conservers on the table for consideration. The Encouragement given for those in Stage 3 endorses the investigation and exploration of new ideas by the Originators and it encourages the Conservers to become involved in the dialogue necessary to bring about inevitable change. However, some Originators are likely to linger too long is this stage.

**Stage 4. When people are implementing new ideas, . . .**

new challenges arise. Moving from investigating and exploring to actual execution creates another point of tension revealed by the Transitions Model. Originators in Stage 3 are busily inventing new ideas and diverging their thinking. This is where they are most comfortable. Getting them to move into Stage 4 can be difficult because that move involves the converging actions of deciding, planning and detailing. These converging actions are the strengths of Conservers, who may be eager to put any new system into order and to return to a predictable, routine operation. Consequently, Conservers who may have spent a long time in Stage 2, Reacting and Responding, may move quickly through Stage 3 in the interest of getting involved with implementing, testing and documenting the new system in Stage 4. Originators, however, may want to linger in Stage 3 continuing to revise ideas and coming up with new ones before actually implementing anything. They may be reluctant to leave Stage 3 because every decision to do one thing is a decision not to do all the other things they also have been considering.

Excerpt from "Staging Change" by Randell Jones. Published in *Excursions*, Volume 5, No. 2, Summer 2002 by Discovery Learning Inc. at www.discoverylearning.com.

## 11. Conflict Resolution

Ready? | 1 | 2 | 3 |

### Key Points

- Effective leadership and open lines of communication are the best defense against disruptive conflicts in the call center. Management teams who solicit employee input and promote empowerment are less likely to encounter situations that require formal conflict resolution procedures.

- Conflict may be topical, personal or relational. Some of the most common sources of conflict in the organization include:
  - Competition for scarce resources (e.g., people, dollars, time)
  - Different or conflicting goals
  - Different ideas or interpretation of ideas
  - Different values
  - Personality conflicts
  - Unclear or unrealistic performance expectations
  - Balance of work and personal life

- Grievance procedures, open-door policies, peer review and mediation are formal policies designed to resolve grievances or disputes between individuals or groups within the organization.

### Explanation

When employees feel their contributions to the organization are not valued or that they have no avenue to effectively express their grievances, conflict within the organization is inevitable. Conflict can occur between any employee or group of employees and may be expressed in a variety of ways. However, it is always disruptive to the organization because it impedes positive working relationships and strong communication. Therefore, call center managers need to be able to support and implement actions for positive conflict resolution.

Before exploring the best methods to address conflict in the call center, recognize that the best way to avoid a reactionary approach to handling conflict is to promote effective leadership, a positive environment and open lines of communication. Management teams that solicit employee input and promote empowerment are less likely to encounter situations which require formal

**Section 7**

conflict-resolution procedures.

### Types of Conflict

A prerequisite in determining resolution steps is to identify the type of conflict or what the employee causes for dissatisfaction are. Types of conflict include:

- **Topical:** These conflicts result from different approaches to what, why and how something is done; e.g., events, priorities, methods, style, processes and use of time.

- **Personal:** These concerns affect how employees view themselves and what they want; e.g., self-esteem, values, goals, recognition, success, appearance and health.

- **Relational:** Relational conflicts stem from interpersonal issues; e.g., trust, support, commitment, control and jealousy.

### Sources of Conflict

Some of the most common sources of conflict in the organization include:

- Competition for scarce resources (e.g., people, dollars, time)
- Different or conflicting goals
- Different ideas or interpretation of ideas
- Different values
- Personality conflicts
- Unclear or unrealistic performance expectations
- Balance of work and personal life

Understanding the true source of conflict is essential before determining the best course of action for resolution. The source is not always apparent to everyone involved and may be shrouded by other issues.

### Managing Conflict

Some call center managers exacerbate conflict within the center by failing to address the situation or handing down dictatorial decisions without taking into account employee viewpoints and feelings. The following actions can help address conflict in the call center:

Conflict control:

- Stay in contact with your team and create an environment that allows them to freely air problems and grievances.

- Listen for potential problems, such as conflicting objectives and shortage of resources.

Conflict management and resolution:

- If you learn of the potential for conflict, take immediate steps to investigate it, whether in informal meetings or a more formal investigation.

- Actively listen to complaints; ask questions and clarify verbal statements.

- Let the employee know what you plan to do to address the situation or when you will update them with a course of action.

- Keep written documentation of all meetings and statements.

- Ask the employee to document and sign statements detailing critical events.

- Set a timeline for the investigation and implementation of actions to resolve the problem.

- Do not make assumptions without all the facts. Be impartial and discreet when conducting research.

- Implement your action plan and followup.

Conflict-resolution reflection:

- Reflect on the course of events. What components of the conflict-resolution process or your actions were effective? What could be improved the next time?

- Get feedback from participants and observers.

**Open-Door Policy**

In an attempt to keep the lines of communication open, an organization may encourage an open-door policy. This approach assures employees that any managers' door is open, without restriction, to any employee who wants to discuss a problem with a member of the management team.

The practice of open-door policies varies by organization. Some open-door

policies are characterized by a lack of boundaries. Employees are encouraged to communicate grievances however they feel most comfortable, without regard to channel or hierarchy. Other organizations implement a more structured approach, requiring the employee to raise the issue with his or her direct supervisor before approaching another manager within the organization. Regardless of the structure, the door must really be open; that is, without an intimidating hierarchy or scheduling problems.

**Grievance Procedure**

An essential component of labor union contracts, grievance procedures are developed to provide employees with a framework to formally raise complaints with management. The process, however, can also be useful in a non-union environment as an effective way to settle disputes over management interpretation or implementation of established policies; e.g., job requirements, working hours, wages and benefits, or company procedures.

A grievance procedure is a step-by-step process that is agreed on by all affected parties as the formal process to settle employee-management disputes. As part of this formal process, there is usually a limited timeframe for each step and a clear explanation of responsibilities.

**Mediation**

Opposing sides are brought together and work toward a resolution with the help of an intermediary who is called a mediator. Mediation is often used when positive conflict-resolution steps have reached an impasse and communication between the parties is stalled. The mediator is not a judge and does not announce a decision or ruling on the matter at hand. He or she is responsible for assisting the disputing parties toward resuming communication and coming to a mutual agreement.

Union environments have a formal mediation process, with assigned roles and responsibilities included as part of the contract. In non-union organizations, HR representatives or peer review panels often mediate unresolved disputes.

An effective mediator exhibits the following qualities:
- Impartial, non-judgmental, bias-free
- Flexible
- Self-aware
- Good listening skills

- Strong interpersonal communication skills

An effective mediation process will include the following steps:

1. Find a mutually agreed upon time and place to talk

2. Prevent interruptions and distractions

3. Set ground rules for the discussion

4. Express appreciation for each person's participation and optimism for the success of the mediation process

5. Support conciliatory gestures

6. Discuss the how and what of specific behaviors

7. Test for agreement

**Peer Review**

The peer review panel is comprised of a select group of the employee's peers and managers (but not the employee's immediate manager). The panel may be assembled on a regular basis to handle grievances, or be chosen to address a specific problem and then disassembled after a resolution is determined. Peer review panels may be used as part of the appeals process when a manager's decision is in dispute.

The selected panel reviews the complaint and the proposed resolution and goes about independently investigating the grievance. The panel then renders a final decision – either in support of the initial ruling or with a revised decision.

---

**Managing a Union Call Center**

Negative perceptions and poor communication between the union and management often present the greatest challenges in managing a union call center. For example, electronic monitoring may be viewed as a quality assurance method by call center managers, but as a violation of worker rights by the union. The union may also frown upon certain quantitative goals set by managers, claiming that asking agents to meet such objectives causes undue stress.

The best way for call center managers to eliminate the friction that often exists between unions and call centers is to develop a relationship where open and honest communication prevail.

**Read and Understand the Union Contract**

Do not assume that union contracts will align with call center goals. When a new contract

---

*(continued, next page)*

**Section 7**

is negotiated, ask how it will affect your center's ability to meet its mission. Identify any challenges or roadblocks related to the call center's goals and then plan accordingly. Ask questions regarding key call center issues, such as workforce management. For instance, does the contract give you the flexibility to shift resources as required? Do you have the ability to move agents between call answer groups, which could effect their tours of duty and daily schedules? Do you have the ability to hire temporary or seasonal agents to help out during high-demand periods? Also look at what the contract says about your ability to analyze and evaluate work flow, individual performance, and technical enhancement issues. The key here is to proactively address the union regarding any potential roadblocks to your center's effectiveness.

### Educate Union Officials/Employees on the Dynamics of the Call Center

Often, union officials and agents don't fully understand the business needs of a call center or how the center behaves. Managers of any unionized call center should invest in training union officials and employees, highlighting the dynamics behind service levels, forecasting, planning, adherence, and other call center issues.

### Improve Communication Channels and the Level of Accountability

One of the most common union/management problems is that discussions between the two entities are often victim- or blame-based. What's worse is that most discussions don't take place until there is a crisis or significant conflict.

A "silence is golden" approach doesn't work. Call center managers should initiate and foster a process of continuous improvement designed to address perceived challenges. Doing so will require an honest and open discussion of issues as well as the use of objective tools to gauge the level of accountability between all participants.

One way to enhance communication is to create teams composed of both union officials/agents and call center managers/supervisors to regularly address topics and work on projects. Both the union and management stand to benefit from this process.

Excerpt from "Managing a Union Call Center: Eliminating the 'Us vs. Them' Mentality" by Darryl Elliot. *Call Center Management Review*, December 1998.

## 12. Diversity in the Workforce

Ready? | 1 | 2 | 3 |

### Key Points

- Valuing diversity means viewing differences as assets rather than liabilities. Managing diversity means utilizing those differences in the workforce to accomplish organizational goals.

- To successfully build and leverage diversity in the workforce, diversity must have support at both from the organization and individuals.

### Explanation

Diversity is the result of characteristics that make us different from each other. There are two basic categories of diversity:

1. Characteristics over which we have no control: gender, age, race, physical characteristics, handicapped/disabled, etc.

2. Characteristics over which we have some control: income, education, marital status, work history, political persuasion, etc.

Valuing diversity means viewing differences as assets rather than liabilities, seeing stereotypes for what they are, and getting beyond prejudices to appreciate differences. Managing diversity means utilizing those differences in the workforce to accomplish organizational goals, finding the delicate balance between developing shared organizational values and valuing diversity, and challenging assumptions that limit opportunities. (Davis, p. 246)

#### Benefits of Diversity

Benefits of diversity include:

- Increase the organization's creativity and problem-solving ability

- Improve relations among diverse groups

- Improve product innovation for specific markets

- Increase the recruiting pool of candidates

Valuing diversity in the workforce can also translate into better service for

Section 7

customers. Employees who appreciate the differences in their co-workers will also be more likely to appreciate differences in the customers that they serve. Organizations that do not cultivate a diverse workforce may need to spend more time training call center staff on how to tolerate cultural differences of the customers they serve.

**Building Diversity**

To successfully build and leverage diversity in the workforce, diversity must have support at both from the organization and individuals. Organizations can encourage and enable diversity at the corporate level:

- Demonstrate top management's support and commitment to diversity. Senior level executives must communicate and model the value of diversity.

- Introduce diversity as a part of new employee orientation programs.

- Develop internal support groups to help assimilate diverse workers.

- Develop programs that help meet family needs; e.g., through day care, flexible work schedules and flexible benefits.

- Establish mentoring and coaching initiatives that support diversity efforts.

- Develop communication styles and standards that are sensitive to the diverse workforce.

- Instill management reward systems that encourage diversity.

- Recruit for diversity. (See Sources and Methods for Recruiting, Section 4.)

Ways individuals can encourage and enable diversity include:

- Develop relationships with individuals of different races, ages, genders, education level and backgrounds.

- Seek help from others to understand their perspectives, experiences and culture.

- Actively seek input from a diverse group when making decisions.

- Become active in community initiatives that involve learning or working with diverse groups.

- Learn about the contributions that are being made from individuals in diverse groups.

- Consider decisions, actions and policies from others' perspectives.

- Confront unacceptable behavior regarding intolerance for diversity.

- Self-examine personal biases to ensure sensitivity to diverse groups.

## 13. Implementing Teams

Ready? | 1 | 2 | 3 |

### Key Points

- A team is a group of individuals with complementary skills who are committed to a common purpose and performance goals to which they hold themselves mutually accountable.

- Factors to consider when deciding whether or when to use teams include:
  - Analyze the business drivers for using teams
  - Evaluate the restraining forces
  - Determine what work is appropriate for teams
  - Examine the readiness of employees, supervisors and managers
  - Allow sufficient time for training and team meetings
  - Consider appropriate compensation, incentives and performance metrics

- Generally, the team leader is the person who is accountable for achieving a set of objectives that require the coordinated efforts of the team. Team member responsibilities generally fall into task roles and maintenance roles.

### Explanation

A team is a group of individuals with complementary skills who are committed to a common purpose and performance goals to which they hold themselves mutually accountable. The purpose of creating a team is to bring together people whose work is related and interdependent. The team enables them to work in a more collaborative manner to achieve individual, call center and organizational objectives.

The subject of teams in call centers is not a firmly defined issue. Depending on the size of the center, the types of contacts that are handled and the organizational culture, one agent team may be a subset of an agent queue group or may include several agent queue groups. Supervisors may be responsible for several agent teams or there may be several supervisors responsible for different members of one team. The scenario that is most effective in your environment can only be determined through careful consideration of the culture, workload and

objectives of your center.

There are several types of teams, which can be categorized by function, structure and skill:

- **Function:** A functional team is based on the purpose for forming the team. For example, a task force could be a functional team formed to study a particular situation such as inaccurate forecasts or innovation opportunities.

- **Structure:** Team types may also be categorized according to their structure. The crossfunctional team is an example of a team structure. In this case, team members are comprised of individuals from several organizational functions. This team structure brings different perspectives and expertise to bear on an organizational problem or opportunity.

- **Skill:** In this type of team, it is the commonality of skill sets that form the basis for the team. For example, call centers may organize coaches into quality teams to facilitate consistency and shared team focus on quality objectives.

These types of teams are not mutually exclusive. For example, you could easily have a crossfunctional task force to address a problem or opportunity.

**The Case for Teams**

The use of teams has grown in call centers as the demands on the call center increase and the nature of the employee/employer relationship evolves. Some of the reasons that call centers are using teams include:

- Competitive pressures require doing more with less; e.g., driving down costs while providing quicker responses to customer needs

- The emphasis on customer relationships has shifted employee accountability from narrow job duties to interrelated contributions

- Many projects require crossfunctional resources

- Employees expect empowered and collaborative work environments

- Proliferating customer access channels require more collaboration and coordination in the call center

While there are many reasons to implement teams in the call center, some managers are hesitant to do so for the following reasons:

Section 7

- Lack of conviction

- Personal discomfort

- Unclear goals

- Unconfirmed return on investment

- Low trust to delegate

- Fear of loss of control/status/power

Advocates for team structures should address these concerns early in the implementation process.

**Decision Factors**

Because of the impact of teams on work processes and relationships, managers should carefully consider many factors when deciding whether and when to use teams. Some of these factors include:

- **Analyze the business drivers for using teams:** Teams should only be implemented if they help accomplish call center objectives, such as better service, increased productivity, cost savings or increased morale. Beginning with the business drivers provides a basis to determine if teams are being effective.

- **Evaluate the restraining forces:** Examine what may impede the formation of teams in the call center. Seek the support and buy-in of senior management, agents, supervisors and union personnel early. Consider the costs of time and training. Look into cultural issues as well, such as willingness to change and previous teamwork experiences.

- **Determine what work is appropriate for teams:** The following are criteria that will assist in deciding whether or not to develop teams for a specific process or activity. "Yes" answers suggest teams are appropriate.

  - **Judgment:** Does the work call for complex decision-making? Are employees expected to be able to make judgment calls on key customer issues and problems?

  - **Complexity:** Is the work itself complex? Does it require employees to master many technologies, product/service details and processes without significant ongoing instruction or supervision?

  - **Shared accountability and responsibility:** Are satisfactory results contingent on more than one process? Do employees need assistance

and support from others to do their jobs?

- **People-intensive:** Do results/outputs, in terms of both quality and quantity, rely more heavily on the actions of people rather than on technologies or routine processes?

- **Examine the readiness of agents, supervisors and managers:** Clearly, the success of any team is dependent upon the people involved. They must be ready for teams in order to support the initiatives and drive change. One of the best ways to assess the readiness of people is to observe the actions taking place today. Do agents, supervisors and managers currently cooperate and collaborate in their day-to-day activities? Are managers and supervisors actively seeking input into decisions? Are supervisors acting more like coaches and less like traffic cops? Have you successfully utilized teams in the past for specific projects?

- **Allow sufficient time for training and team meetings:** Given the call center's variations in workload, the time spent in training and meetings to ensure team success must be considered. The call center must be prepared to commit the additional resources that may be required to train agents, managers and supervisors on team skills. Time for team meetings must be included in resource management plans.

- **Consider appropriate compensation, incentives and performance metrics:** Are you able to revise these processes to include both individual- and team-based metrics and incentives? Do you have the systems/technological capabilities to track both team and individual performance?

The use of teams is not an "either/or" decision. In some situations it makes more sense to team employees for certain activities, such as developing a new quality monitoring process, than to form daily work teams. An example of this might be individual account representatives in a brokerage call center. Each agent might continue to work their territory or customer base individually, but team up to strategize on new opportunities or solve shared problems.

**Team Success Factors**

Even though there are different types of teams with different objectives and priorities, there are several factors that are common to effective teams. These success factors include:

- A shared purpose

- Mutual accountability

- Broadly defined job descriptions

- Team members work inter-dependently

- Team members bring a mixed set of skills that benefit the team as a whole

### Advantages and Disadvantages of Teams

Key advantages of using teams in the call center include:

- Enables the sharing of knowledge and skills

- Higher employee motivation

- Diversity in perspectives and better decisions

- Faster adoption and integration of new technologies and processes

- Increased quality of work and efficiency due to team ownership

- Accelerated crosstraining, which leads to greater call center efficiency

Some disadvantages of teams include:

- Longer decision-making processes due to consensus-building

- One strong personality may dominate the team

- Recognizing and rewarding individuals becomes a challenge

- Some members may not pull their weight

- Schedules must accommodate team training and meetings

One cautionary note when considering the advantages and disadvantages of teams in the call center. Larger teams typically realize fewer advantages and feel a greater impact from disadvantages than smaller teams. Teams that are too large to allow team members to know one another can result in team members that do not recognize their value to the team. These members may fall prey to the idea that the performance of other team members will outweigh their poor performance.

### Aligning Team Goals with Organizational Objectives

In call centers, effective teams create and achieve objectives that benefit not only the center and the customer, but also the organization as a whole. Each team must not only work well as a unit, but also work well with other teams

throughout the call center. Mutual respect, shared objectives, open communication and flexibility are indications that teams are working well together. Aligning team goals with organizational objectives promotes performance and cultural consistency throughout the organization.

**Section 7**

## 14. Team Roles and Responsibilities

Ready? | 1 | 2 | 3

### Key Points

- Generally, the team leader is the person who is accountable for achieving a set of objectives that require the coordinated efforts of the team. The best team leaders understand the interpersonal dynamics of teams and are willing to share power and control with team members.

- Team member responsibilities generally fall into two categories:
  - Task roles
  - Maintenance roles

### Explanation

Part of any effective team is clearly defined roles and responsibilities of members. Each member should understand their role in decision-making, leadership and accomplishing shared objectives. As the team is formed, the team leader should ensure that all required skills are represented among the members of the group.

**Roles and Responsibilities – Team Leader**

Generally, the team leader is the person who is accountable for achieving a set of objectives that require the coordinated efforts of the team. In addition to fulfilling the responsibilities of being a team member, the team leader must:

- Define the team mission, vision and strategy collaboratively with the team, including the work limitations, team member roles and responsibilities, and operating guidelines of the team

- Provide resources, including current technology and information to enhance the work of the team

- Report team activity to management

- Coordinate team activities, including:
  - Ensure that team activities complement other initiatives in the call center
  - Keep the team up-to-date on call center and organizational issues

- Facilitate team meetings

- Establish processes for information-sharing within the team and with other teams

  - Plan staffing and workload to allow for team meetings and improvement activities

  - Balance daily workload with team building requirements

- Set team performance goals

- Develop team members for improved performance through coaching and feedback, strengthening diversity, allowing for risk taking, holding members accountable and building commitment and confidence

- Motivate team members and provide recognition and rewards (both formal and informal recognition)

- Manage the work processes

- Share power and control

### Roles and Responsibilities – Team Members

Team member responsibilities generally fall into two categories:

- **Task roles:** Activities required for completing a team task, objective, goal, etc.

- **Maintenance roles:** Activities and attributes needed to build and sustain the group as a functioning team; e.g., communication, commitment, flexibility, etc.

### Process Skills

Teams need to be comprised of individuals who collectively possess all of the following the skills:

- Technical skills

- Functional skills

- Performance management skills

- Problem-solving and decision-making skills

- Administrative skills

- Interpersonal skills

## 15. Building Team Effectiveness

Ready? | 1 | 2 | 3 |

### Key Points

- Teams develop through a four-stage process: form, storm, norm and perform.

- Teams require effective collaboration. While consensus is not always possible, a sound decision-making process is essential. There are a number tools available that can foster teamwork and agreement:
  - Responsibility charting
  - Brainstorming
  - Nominal group technique
  - Multi-voting
  - Fishbowl
  - Force field analysis

### Explanation

Today's realities require that the enterprise and call center find more effective ways to get things done. The call center, like other business units, is being asked to do more with less, to be nimble in the face of escalating customer demands, and respond to competitive pressures. Employees must be more interdependent and empowered to meet those demands. Effective teams help address these issues.

#### The Team Development Process

Teams develop through a four-stage development process, popularly referred to as form, storm, norm and perform. The time and intensity of each stage varies by team. The faster a team can move from "form" to "perform," the shorter the cycle time to produce results. Training and regular team meetings are essential to a team's development progress.

- **Form:** Team members learn about each other, set goals, define tasks and actions to accomplish these goals and set ground rules. Individuals may express excitement, anticipation and optimism about working in the team. Others may experience suspicion, fear and anxiety about the task ahead. During the forming stage, members only have a tentative attachment to the team.

Call center teams typically experience the forming stage when they are first initiated and, to a lesser extent, as new-hires are integrated into the team. If high turnover persists in a call center with teams, it may be difficult for teams to go far beyond the forming stage as they continually learn how to work with new members. Some call centers choose to organize new-hires into their own teams with leadership by more experienced agents. These new-hire teams allow team members to get acclimated to the call center and ensure team members are well-suited for their responsibilities.

- **Storm:** The forming stage can be a "honeymoon" period for team members until they enter the storming stage. As people learn to work with one another, it is inevitable that conflicts will arise and goals, tasks and responsibilities will need clarification. Team members should be prepared for the storming stage through training that includes conflict resolution, negotiation skills and communication principles.

- **Norm:** As conflicts are resolved and personalities are better understood, teams transition to the norm stage. This stage is characterized by open communication, shared leadership and a spirit of cooperation. The team has reached the norm stage when team goals take precedence over individual ambitions.

- **Perform:** Teams that work well together reach the performing stage. Team members come to understand and appreciate the strengths and weaknesses of other members. They experience interdependence, synergy and a high level of performance. Reaching this stage often results in increased work satisfaction.

### Making Team Decisions

Teams require effective collaboration. While consensus is not always possible, a sound decision-making process is essential. There are a number tools available that can foster teamwork and agreement:

- **Responsibility charting:** A matrix is created in which each team member is assigned a role in the decision-making process. For example, some team members are responsible for making the decision while others simply provide input.

- **Brainstorming:** This well-known approach is useful for generating ideas that can lead to better decisions.

- **Nominal group technique:** This weighted ranking technique is effective

**Section 7**

for determining priorities. Team members individually rank issues by importance. The issues receiving the highest votes are worked on first. Since ranking is done individually and then combined, the nominal group technique is a way to give all team members an equal voice in problem selection.

- **Multi-voting:** When a decision has an abundance of possible solutions, it can be useful to conduct a series of votes to continually reduce the number of options.

- **Fishbowl:** A seating configuration where there are two circles, the inner circle (invited group) of persons who discuss the topic/issue and the outer circle (host group) of those who observe. This allows those in the invited group to discuss the topic in an uninterrupted way while the host group observes, listens and learns. When the invited group concludes its discussion, the host group explains what they heard.

- **Force field analysis:** This process involves identifying the factors that support (driving forces) or work against (restraining forces) a proposed plan. This tool is appropriate for determining if the positives outweigh the negatives. Strategies are then developed to strengthen the driving forces and to diminish or eliminate the restraining forces.

## 16. Leading Crossfunctional and Distributed Teams

Ready? | 1 | 2 | 3 |

### Key Points

- Although computer, telecommunications and Internet capabilities have enabled people to link resources and skills in new, imaginative ways, technology hasn't eliminated the natural barriers that exist between people who work in distributed environments.

- To maximize chances for success, leaders of distributed and crossfunctional teams should take steps to align goals and objectives and build solid communication, including:
  - Create a compelling mission
  - Build trust among members
  - Establish appropriate communication tools
  - Eliminate unnecessary bureaucracy and rules
  - Establish a communications agreement
  - Consistently communicate progress
  - Listen actively and regularly
  - Ensure a common understanding of call center dynamics
  - Celebrate accomplishments

### Explanation

Computer and telecommunications technologies have spawned organizations that span geography and have enabled people to link resources and skills in new, imaginative ways. The world – and organizations – are truly becoming "connected."

Many of the trends in call centers reflect these developments. Distributed call centers, telecommuting, crossfunctional teams and 24x7 operations are common examples of people working across sites and time. If you are a call center manager or director, you will most likely have responsibility of getting results from people who work in different locations, don't report to you or don't work the same hours.

For example, a team formed to spearhead the organization's customer relationship management initiatives may include members from marketing, IT, HR, training, telecommunications and the call center. These members bring

*Section 7*

their own departmental objectives and perspectives to the overall organizational goals and may be dispersed geographically.

While technology has enabled enormous opportunities, it hasn't eliminated the natural barriers that exist between people who work in distributed environments. For example, people who work in different places and/or at different times often have trouble seeing themselves as an integral part of a larger team. Informal opportunities that people have for getting to know each other in traditional settings (such as around the coffee pot or in the hallway) may be rare; these experiences can be tough to replicate by phone or email. Further, in any organization a large amount of information is exchanged outside the formal context of memos and meetings which, without extraordinary effort on the part of all group members, is often unevenly distributed among individuals.

There is no fool-proof formula for leading a distributed group. Like leadership in general, building a cohesive virtual team defies a specific recipe. There are, however, tried-and-true principles that will significantly increase the odds of success:

- **Create a compelling vision:** Begin by asking key questions; e.g., Why does the distributed group exist? What is it going to collectively achieve? What's in it for the participants? A clear focus that is championed by the leader is a prerequisite to pulling people in and aligning actions. And it is essential to creating goals and purposes that are not in conflict.

- **Build trust among members:** Trust builds open and honest communication and mutual respect, essential ingredients to crossfunctional and distributed teams. Start by creating opportunities for the people in your distributed group to get to know each other; e.g., one call center manager set up a Web page profiling the members of a multisite team, then gave everyone a short quiz on the interests and backgrounds of the other members. It's also important to ensure that everyone gets key information at the same time and that all are abreast of major decisions.

  Part of building trust is developing an environment based on collaboration, not competition. This culture will promote the sharing of strengths, ideas and best practices that will ultimately improve the performance of everyone involved.

- **Establish appropriate communication tools:** A prerequisite to a productive distributed workgroup is that the members of the group have

Section 7

compatible communications technologies. Telephone, email, intranet, and collaboration and conferencing tools offer enormous potential when available to the entire group; it's important that all individuals have access to the same communications tools. Further, creating an online directory of contact numbers and addresses just for the distributed workgroup gives people the basic information they need to collaborate, and also adds to the symbolism that will help the members of the team identify with each other.

- **Eliminate unnecessary bureaucracy and rules:** Peter Drucker, respected management consultant, has insisted that "So much of what we call management consists of making it difficult for people to work." Distributed groups in particular are prone to encounter unworkable rules, policies and procedures. The result can be project gridlock.

  It's important for the leader to regularly and vigilantly look for ways to scrap (or, at least, minimize) the impact of unnecessary hierarchies and cumbersome bureaucracies. That's easier said than done, but is one of the most important steps you can take to facilitate the progress of your distributed team. Help the members of your group accomplish their tasks by eliminating stumbling blocks, such as interdepartmental barriers. And, ensure that sufficient flexibility exists for the team to operate effectively as conditions unfold.

- **Develop a communications "agreement":** Distributed work groups need ground rules that stipulate levels of priority and appropriate responses for: a) urgent messages requiring immediate response, b) routine messages requiring response any time that day, and c) non-urgent informational messages that require no response.

- **Consistently communicate progress:** Hazy objectives and vaguely defined tasks will destroy the productivity and morale of a distributed work group. The objectives of the group should be as concrete as possible, and projects should have clearly defined milestones, with beginning and ending points. Since projects tend to take on a life of their own as they develop, it's important to keep the group updated and on the same track.

  Project tools such as Gantt charts and flow charts can be useful for identifying resources required, showing the interrelated nature of individual tasks and tracking progress. They give a tangibility to the mission of the workgroup, and can help address questions such as: Where are we? How far have we come? What's next? They should be updated

**Section 7**

and distributed as often as something substantial changes in the ongoing direction and plans.

- **Listen actively and regularly:** There is a common myth that great leaders create compelling visions from "gifted perspectives" or "inner creativity" that others don't posses. But many studies on the subjects of leadership and strategy (e.g., from the work of Warren Bennis, Peter Senge, Michael Porter and others) have shown the visions of some of history's greatest leaders often came from others. The leaders may have selected the best vision to focus on, shaped it and communicated it to others in a compelling way, but they rarely originated the vision. The point: Be a superb listener. Develop both formal and informal channels of communication to gain access to the ideas and insights of others. The added benefit of being a good listener is that when people have a stake in an idea, they tend to work much harder to bring about its success.

- **Ensure a common understanding of call center dynamics:** The call center is an important part of a much bigger process, and call center managers who consistently get the best results know that. They take the initiative in coordinating with other departments, they work hard to integrate call center activities with developments in other parts of the organization, and they have an incessant focus on strengthening the call center's support of the organization.

  To reduce misunderstanding of varying results among teams, management should initiate an awareness program on call center dynamics. The program should identify and explain important variables, and illustrate their influence on results. An effective program will provide a solid base of understanding and ensure that members of cross-functional and/or distributed environments understand the drivers of results.

- **Celebrate accomplishments:** As the distributed group reaches critical milestones, it is important to acknowledge the accomplishments and celebrate! A shared vision is motivating. But, the manager has to keep the vision alive, and one of the best ways to do that is to actively recognize accomplishments along the way.

## 17. Managing Within Legal Requirements - U.S.

Ready? | 1 | 2 | 3 |

### Key Points

- In the United States, the federal government prescribes legal guidelines for such issues as overtime, employee status and family and medical leave. Call center managers should be aware of the following compensation-related laws:
  - The Fair Labor Standards Act
  - Equal Pay Act
  - Family and Medical Leave Act

- Discrimination in the workplace based on a person's race, color, religion, gender or national origin is prohibited in the United States. Laws regarding discrimination include:
  - Title VII of the Civil Rights Act
  - Age Discrimination in Employment Act
  - Americans with Disabilities Act
  - Vietnam Era Veterans Readjustment Act
  - Pregnancy Discrimination Act
  - Negligent Hiring and Retention Laws

- Sexual harassment, prohibited by law, includes unwelcome sexual advances, requests for sexual favors and other verbal or physical conduct of a sexual nature.

- Call center managers are responsible for understanding the basic legal context of managing human resources, seeking guidance before acting in potentially litigious situations, and promoting compliance within their teams through education and open communication channels.

### Explanation

When it comes to conforming with legal regulations, ignorance is no excuse for noncompliance. Managers are held accountable for operating within the boundaries of federal, state and local laws. In many cases, both the organization and individual managers can be held accountable.

**The Fair Labor Standards Act**

The Fair Labor Standards Act (FLSA) of 1938, which has been amended numerous times, is designed to protect workers from unfair wage and compensation practices and outlines detailed guidelines for ensuring employees are compensated fairly for the time they work. Far-reaching in scope, the FLSA covers:

- Standards for employee vs. contractor status

- Standards for exempt and nonexempt employee status

- Federal minimum wage and overtime requirements

- Restrictions on the employment of children

- Requirements for human resources record keeping

**Employee vs. Contractor**

The federal and state governments in the United States have established laws to govern the definition of employees and contractors. The call center manager should be aware of these laws to ensure the compliance of their staffing decisions.

An employment relationship is distinguished from a contractual relationship based on the "economic reality" of that arrangement. There is no single rule or test for determining if an individual is an employee or independent contractor. The U.S. Supreme Court has held that it is the total activity or situation that controls employment status.

According to the U.S. Department of Labor, factors which the court has considered significant are:

- The extent to which the services rendered are an integral part of the principal's business

- The permanency of the relationship

- The amount of the alleged contractor's investment in facilities and equipment

- The nature and degree of control by the principal

- The alleged contractor's opportunities for profit and loss

- The amount of initiative, judgment, or foresight in open-market competition with others required for the success of the claimed

independent contractor

- The degree of independent business organization and operation

Factors such as the place where the work is performed or the absence of an employment agreement do not have a bearing on the determination of employee status.

### Exempt vs. Nonexempt

According to the FLSA, there are two categories of employees:

1. **Exempt:** Exempt employees, commonly referred to as salaried, are not covered by FLSA. As a result employers are not required to pay overtime exempt staff. This category includes most administrative, professional, executive and sales jobs.

2. **Nonexempt:** Nonexempt employees, often called hourly workers, must receive at least the minimum wage and may not be employed for over 40 hours in a week without receiving at least one and one-half times their regular rate of pay for the overtime hours. In this case, employ means to permit to work and includes work that is not requested but permitted. Employees who clock out and continue to work or work through lunch may have good intentions. However, legally and ethically, they must be compensated for all time worked.

Management cannot simply "decide" if a job is exempt or nonexempt. There are guidelines established by FLSA that determine job status, including the nature of the work; e.g., decision-making authority, appraising the work of others, amount of autonomy, how routine are the duties, etc. You should consult these specific guidelines when determining the exempt vs. nonexempt status of positions.

### Full-time vs. Part-time

Part-time employees carry the same legal status as full-time employees and as such are protected by all organizational and legal policies and requirements related to employment laws and FLSA. However, the FLSA does not define the number of hours that distinguishes part-time from full-time.

### Equal Pay Act

The Equal Pay Act of 1963 mandates that men and women are to receive the same pay for doing the same job. Jobs that are the same in terms of skill,

effort, working conditions and responsibilities should be compensated equally regardless of the employee's gender. However, individuals can receive different pay for the same position based on one of the following:

- **Merit:** You can compensate an individual more if he or she is performing better.

- **Productivity:** Pay differences are allowed for differences in quality and quantity of work.

- **Seniority:** Compensation plans based on the length of time an employee's tenure are permitted.

- **Other:** Factors such as extra job responsibilities, work shifts and different geographical areas can be compensated differently, as long as gender is not considered.

### Family and Medical Leave Act

The Family and Medical Leave Act (FMLA) of 1993 requires employers to provide up to 12 weeks of unpaid leave for:

- Childbirth or adoption

- Care of a sick spouse, child or parent

- Serious health problems that interfere with job performance

### Title VII of the Civil Rights Act

Title VII of the Civil Rights Act of 1964 prohibits employment decisions based on a person's race, color, religion, gender or national origin. Employment decisions include terms, conditions or privileges of employment. In essence, it applies to hiring, compensation, disciplinary action, termination, demotion, promotion and training.

A protected class is a group of people who have suffered past discrimination and are given special protection by the judicial system. Under Title VII, protected classes include such groups as African Americans, Asian Americans, Latinos, Native Americans and women.

Types of discrimination include:

- **Disparate treatment:** Whereby an employer treats a person differently because of his or her protected class status.

- **Adverse impact:** When the same standard, applied to all applicants or

employees, affects a protected class more negatively. Job requirements such as education and employment tests are especially susceptible to this.

There are basically four defenses an organization can use to defend itself against a charge of discrimination:

- **Job-relatedness:** Demonstrate that the decision was made for job-related reasons. It is best to support this claim with a job description and job analysis.

- **Bona fide occupational qualification:** This is a characteristic that must be present in all employees for a certain job; e.g., a female role in a play.

- **Seniority:** This includes employment decisions made within the context of a formal seniority program.

- **Business necessity:** This is when the employment practice is necessary for safe and efficient business operations and where there is an overriding business purpose.

### Age Discrimination in Employment Act

Providing similar coverage to Title VII, the Age Discrimination in Employment Act of 1967 prohibits employers from discriminating against an applicant or employee based on his or her age.

### Americans with Disabilities Act

The Americans with Disabilities Act (ADA) of 1990 forbids employment discrimination against individuals with disabilities who can perform the essential functions of the job with or without reasonable accommodations. The disability must be physical or mental and not due to cultural, economic or environmental conditions. Important definitions include:

- **Essential functions:** Job duties that must be performed by any employee to be effective.

- **Reasonable accommodations:** Actions to accommodate known disabilities so that a disabled employee or candidate can enjoy equal employee opportunity.

Types of disabilities include impaired walking, breathing, speaking, lifting, hearing, seeing, reading and performing manual tasks. Those with communicable diseases (including HIV) are also protected.

### Vietnam Era Veterans Readjustment Act

The Vietnam Era Veterans Readjustment Act of 1974 prohibits discrimination against Vietnam-era veterans by federal contractors.

### Pregnancy Discrimination Act

The Pregnancy Discrimination Act of 1978 requires that employers treat a pregnant job applicant or employee the same as they would any employee with a medical condition.

### Negligent Hiring and Retention

More than half of U.S. states legally recognize that an employer is responsible for, and can be held accountable for, checking the background and references of any job applicant before placing that applicant within the organization. An employer can be held responsible for negligent hiring or negligent retention if it hired or retained an employee that the employer knew or should have known was "unfit" for the position.

The issue of liability focuses upon the adequacy of the employer's pre-employment investigation into the employee's background. Any information regarding past convictions should be judged relevant if they place the employee in a position where he or she would have the opportunity to exhibit the same pattern of behavior. For instance, if an applicant had been convicted of a financial impropriety or fraud and was then given access to customer's credit card or other financial information by his or her employer, this could expose the organization to accusations of negligent hiring

### Sexual Harassment

In the text *Managing Human Resources*, sexual harassment is defined as follows:

Unwelcome sexual advances, requests for sexual favors, and other verbal or physical conduct of a sexual nature constitute sexual harassment when:

- Submission to such conduct is made either explicitly or implicitly a term or condition of an individual's employment

- Submission to or rejection of such conduct by an individual is used as a basis of employment decisions affecting such individual

- Such conduct has the purpose or effect of unreasonably interfering with an individual's work performance or creating an intimidating, hostile or

offensive work environment. (Gomez-Mejia p.99)

Categories of sexual harassment include:

- **Quid pro quo:** When sexual favors/activities are demanded in return for keeping or getting a job-related benefit.

- **Hostile work environment:** When the behaviors of supervisors, managers, coworkers, suppliers, customers or anyone in the work environment is sexual in nature and the employee perceives the behavior as undesirable and offensive.

Management has two defenses against a sexual harassment charge, and must prove two things:

1. That the employer exercised reasonable care to prevent and correct the problem in a timely fashion.

2. That the employee failed to use internal processes for reporting sexual harassment. If the employee did not use the organization's internal processes because of the nature of the complaint (e.g., the complaint is against the supervisor to whom the employee is required to report the offense), the employer cannot use this defense.

**Preventing Discrimination and Harassment**

The entire organization is responsible for understanding employment laws that apply to your organization and ensuring practices are in compliance with legal regulations. The HR and legal departments are responsible for disseminating information throughout the organization and providing management with the information needed to guide their practices and actions. Management is responsible for understanding the basic legal context of managing human resources, seeking guidance before acting in potentially litigious situations, and promoting compliance within their teams through education and open communication channels.

As a call center manager, there are some actions you can take to prevent discrimination and harassment. Some of these actions include:

- Provide training for your management staff on the various laws and the legal aspects of discrimination as they relate to employee decision-making

- Continually communicate to your management staff and call center employees your commitment to a discrimination-free work environment

- Document all employee-related decisions

- Develop and implement a process for internal resolution of employee complaints

- Develop and conduct a survey on workplace issues to acquire some baseline data

These preemptive measures do not always work. Therefore, if you suspect any form of discrimination is taking place, actions you should take include:

1. Contact your HR representative. HR can help you contain and resolve the problem.

2. Carefully document the situation, the nature of any HR decisions, and the rationale for those decisions.

3. Talk to the offended party. Many times employees file charges against the organization because they perceive they are being mistreated. Open dialog regarding the complaint may result in a resolution of the issue without legal action.

4. In cases of harassment, talk to the person demonstrating the undesirable behavior, and explain the corporate stance and implications for individuals and the team. Provide direct, honest feedback including the potential consequences if the behavior continues.

5. Meet with the call center team to review the corporate and call center stance on discrimination. Do not leave any doubt regarding your expectations for fair treatment. Indicate that all persons have the right to be treated with dignity and respect.

Note: This section is designed to provide a summary only. Please direct specific legal questions to your HR and legal departments.

Section 7

## 18. Managing Within Legal Requirements - Canada

Ready? | 1 | 2 | 3 |

### Key Points

- Most call centers in Canada fall under the jurisdiction of the provincial labor legislation. Only those call centers in the "federally regulated" sector of the labor force are governed by the federal Canada Labour Code, the Canadian Human Rights Act, and the Employment Equity Act.

- The Canada Labour Code details the required guidelines for compensation, vacations, sexual harassment and individual and group terminations of employment. While companies not included under the jurisdiction of the Canada Labour Code are not required to comply with the Code, each territory and province has enacted a set of laws which address these issues.

- Other legislation covering workplace health, safety and human rights issues, such as Occupational Health and Safety (OHS) Regulations, the Employment Equity Act and the Canadian Human Rights Act, bind employers who fall within federally designated groups. Each territory and province has enacted legislation which regulates employers who operate within their geographic region and are not federally regulated.

- The call center industry's practices are primarily regulated by province, although recent federal legislation enacted by the Canadian Radio and Television Commission places new national restrictions on outbound telemarketing activity.

### Explanation

Canadian employment issues are either federally or provincially regulated, depending on the category of employer. Federal regulations guide employers in designated industries, while the rest of the employers are divided into regional territories and provinces, each of which enact and enforce their own legislation. The table on the following page describes the laws which govern Canadian employment.

Section 7

Federally regulated industries include:

- Interprovincial and international services such as railways, telephone systems and shipping services

- Radio and television broadcasting, including cablevision

- Air transport, aircraft operations and aerodromes

- Banks

- Undertakings for the protection and preservation of fisheries as a natural resource

- Other undertakings declared by Parliament to be for the general advantage of Canada

Most federal Crown corporations, such as the Canada Mortgage and Housing Corporation and Canada Post Corporation, are covered by federal legislation. The Government of Canada has stated, however, that the minimum standards of the Code will be met in the public service as a matter of policy.

| | Federally Regulated | Provincially Regulated |
|---|---|---|
| Wage & Hour, Minimum Age, Sexual Harassment, Leave, Termination | • Canada Labour Code | • Provincial Legislation |
| Workplace Health & Safety | • Occupational Health and Safety Regulations | • Provincial Legislation |
| Discrimination & Accomodation | • Canadian Human Rights Act<br>• Employment Equity Act | • Provincial Legislation |

**Canada Labour Code**

Most public sector and designated private sector organizations, regardless of geographic location, are governed by a comprehensive set of regulations called the Canada Labour Code. This is approximately only 10 percent of the labor force. The Canada Labour Code details the required guidelines for dealing with the minimum age for employment, hours of work and overtime pay, minimum wages, part-time employees, equal pay, the weekly rest-day, general holidays with pay, annual vacations with pay, parental leave, sexual harassment and individual and group terminations of employment.

In most cases, the above guidelines should indicate whether your call center is

covered by federal, territorial or provincial legislation.

Companies not included under the jurisdiction of the Canada Labour Code are not required to comply with the specifics of the code and are governed by territorial and provincial labor regulations based on their geographic location. For more information regarding individual territory and province legislation visit, www.hrdc-crhc.gc.ca/.

### Occupational Health and Safety (OHS) Regulations

Canada's Occupational Health and Safety (OHS) Regulations apply to federally regulated industries and are intended to prevent accidents and injury in the course of employment. Three fundamental rights of workers underlie the legislation:

- The right to know about known or foreseeable hazards in the workplace

- The right to participate in identifying and resolving job-related safety and health problems

- The right to refuse dangerous work if the employee has reasonable cause to believe that a situation constitutes a danger to him/herself or to another employee

Each territory and province has enacted health and safety legislation that binds employers who operate within their geographic region and are not federally regulated. These regulations address specific industries, such as mining, construction or farming, or potential hazardous workplace situations; e.g., laws covering noise limitations, ventilation requirements, chemical handling and explosives safety. For more information, contact the individual territory or provincial labor department.

### Employment Equity Act

The Employment Equity Act requires employers to identify employment barriers against certain groups and determine the degree of under-representation. The Employment Equity Act was enacted in 1986 and is enforced by the Canadian Human Rights Commission (CHRC).

The Act applies to federally regulated employers with 100 or more employees. The purpose of the legislation is to ensure that employers achieve a workforce that is equitable and representative of four designated groups – women, Aboriginal peoples, members of visible minorities and persons with disabilities. Employers are required to develop and implement employment equity plans

and programs, and to report annually to Human Resources Development Canada on their progress in achieving a representative workforce. Contact the CHRC (www.chrc-ccdp.ca/) for more information. For provincial guidelines concerning equity and disability concerns, contact the provincial labor department.

### Canadian Human Rights Act

The Canadian Human Rights Act entitles all individuals to equal employment opportunities without regard to race or color, national or ethnic origin, religion, age, family or marital status, sex (including pregnancy or childbirth), pardoned conviction, disability (either physical or mental or as the result of dependence on alcohol or drugs), or sexual orientation.

The Act covers employment under federal jurisdiction. All provinces and territories have similar laws forbidding discrimination in their areas of jurisdiction

Note: The information above was compiled from Human Resources Canada, http://employers.gc.ca/. It is provided as an overview of the material and should not be used to create organizational policies. Contact your organization's legal counsel for specific guidance on these issues.

### Call Center Legislation

Telemarketing restrictions have historically been issued according to province and service provider category, resulting in a patchwork application of rules across Canada. Regional legislation regulates many issues associated with outbound and inbound contacts. Increased focus on federal call center legislation is concerned with issues relating to the growing outbound telemarketing industry and the public's dissatisfaction with this the practices of some organizations.

The federal Canadian Radio and Television Communication Commission has recently standardized its rules on telemarketing and extended them to include all telephone companies in Canada – including resellers and cell phone providers.

The rules include:

- Restricted calling hours

- Guidelines for identifying information

- "Do Not Call" list guidelines

- Ban on sequential dialing

- Ban on contacts to emergency and healthcare facilities

There is national interest in expanding this legislation to cover all outbound calling, regardless of industry. The Canadian Marketing Association has established a Code of Ethics and Standard of Practice for their members, in which members agree to maintain Do Not Call lists, restrict calling hours, limit the number of contacts to an individual, and to use customer opt-in lists for calling campaigns.

For more information, contact the Canadian Radio and Television Communication Commission (www.crtc.gc.ca) and the Canadian Marketing Association (www.the-cma.org).

Note: This section is designed to provide a summary only. Please direct specific legal questions to your HR and legal departments.

## 19. Privacy-Related Issues

Ready? | 1 | 2 | 3 |

### Key Points

- Privacy is the expectation that confidential or personal information disclosed in a private setting will not be made public.

- The Federal Electronic Communications Privacy Act prohibits employers from deliberately eavesdropping on an employee's personal conversation.

- According to the Communications Decency Act of 1996, an employer can be held liable for the activities of its employees, including activities that are not work-related, but are done while an employee is at work.

- Under federal law, sending and receiving email on an employer's computer is no different than writing a memo on company letterhead.

### Explanation

Privacy is the expectation that confidential or personal information disclosed in a private setting will not be made public. In the United States, privacy is not guaranteed to workers by law. Organizations are free to monitor their workers unless they are bound otherwise by a union or employee contract.

**Telephone Usage**

United States law does provide protection to the employee concerning private telephone conversations. The Federal Electronic Communications Privacy Act prohibits employers from deliberately eavesdropping on an employee's personal conversations. This legislation is limited to telephone calls and audio-equipped video devices. It does not extend to means other than the spoken word, such as email or other Web-based forms of communication.

**Email and Internet Usage**

According to the Communications Decency Act of 1996, an employer can be held liable for the activities of its employees. For example, other employees could construe someone accessing pornographic Web sites as sexual harassment

and the employer would be responsible.

Under federal law, sending and receiving email on an employer's computer is no different than writing a memo on company letterhead. Organizations have been sued for sexual harassment and racism based on offensive email postings by their employees. Call center managers should work with the organization to ensure appropriate policies and procedures are in place to safeguard the organization from such liability.

**Drug Testing**

Privacy is not limited to employees' conversations and emails. Random drug testing creates privacy concerns for employees and liability concerns for employers. Random drug testing screens employees for drug use, without suspicion or cause. Employees may consider this an invasion of privacy. Yet, employers have the right, and in some cases, the obligation to perform drug testing.

**Personnel Files**

Another sensitive privacy issue is the maintenance of the employee's personnel file. Because this file contains critical information such as performance reviews, disciplinary actions, salary history, and career progression, access to it should be managed carefully and ethically. Clearly, employees should have access to their personnel files so they can review the information to ensure its accuracy. Access should be denied to all other people except managers who have a job-related "need to know" situation.

**Privacy Policies**

Call center managers should develop policies that address privacy-related issues. Important aspect of this responsibility include:

- Communicate your policy regarding privacy. Employees and call center managers need to have a clear, mutual understanding of what each may and may not do. This should be part of every orientation program, in the employee handbook and disseminated to all employees.

- Make employees aware of any electronic surveillance devices that are being used. Generally, undisclosed monitoring should be avoided and separate, unmonitored phone lines should be made available if personal phone calls are allowed during breaks.

- Ensure that agents understand that the primary purpose of monitoring in the call center is to improve quality and individual performance, not to spy on employees.

- Develop and communicate your policy regarding access to personnel files.

Note: This section is designed to provide a summary only. Please direct specific legal questions to your HR and legal departments.

**Section 7**

# Maximizing Human Resources

## Exercises

### Differentiating Career and Skill Path Models [Strategic]

1. What are the three phases of a typical career path program?

_____

_____

_____

### Creating and Communicating Career and Skill Paths

2. Select the most appropriate answer to each question.

The most significant career pathing obstacle for employees is:

    a. An organizational culture that doesn't support growth

    b. Insufficient cross-functional opportunities

    c. Lack of access to training

    d. Lack of a solid model which includes detailed skill requirements, a variety of advancement options and a structured feedback process

Which model is typically more appropriate in environments where customer contacts are relatively simple and repetitive?

    a. Career path

    b. Skill path

**Succession Planning [Strategic]**

3. Insert the appropriate text to complete the following succession planning flow chart.

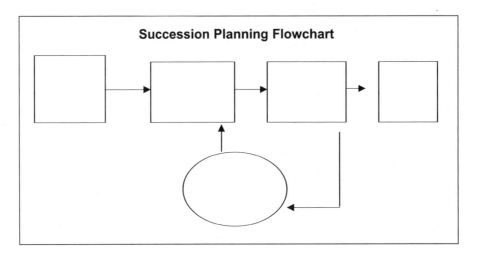

4. True or false

_____Succession planning is needed to ensure that leadership growth keeps pace with organizational growth.

_____The most effective succession plans will focus on identifying a group of candidates for positions that may open in six to twelve months.

**Types of Compensation**

5. What are the three components of compensation?

_____

_____

_____

6. Select the most appropriate answer to the question.

Which of the following is NOT a legally mandated employee benefit?

    a. Family and medical leave

    b. Sick leave

    c. Unemployment insurance

    d. Workers' compensation

**Employee Satisfaction Surveys**

7. Briefly answer the following questions.

    a. When deciding what improvements to make as a result of employee satisfaction surveys, is it better to begin with those items that can be implemented quickly or those that will have the greatest impact?

    b. Do qualitative or quantitative questions do a better job of capturing the themes and ideas of employees?

**Building Trust**

8. True or false

_____Trust is most easily achieved in bureaucratic organizations where job hierarchies are clearly defined.

_____It is easier to cultivate trust in less complex, more straightforward environments.

**Conflict Resolution**

9. What are the three types of conflict?

_____.

_____

_____

10. Match the following terms with their definitions. You will use each definition only once.

_____Conflict control

_____Grievance procedures

_____Mediation

_____Open door policy

_____Peer review

a. Assures employees that management is always available to discuss a problem with any employee.

b. Management listens for potential problems, such as conflicting objectives and shortage of resources.

c. Often used as part of the appeals process when a manager's decision is in dispute.

d. Often used when positive conflict resolution steps have been unsuccessful.

e. Provides employees with a framework to formally raise complaints with management; often a part of union contracts.

### Diversity in the Workforce

11. Fill in the blanks to complete each sentence.

a. Valuing diversity means viewing differences as _____ rather than _____.

b. To successfully build and leverage diversity in the workforce, diversity must have support from the _____and _____.

### Implementing Teams

12. Select the most appropriate answer to each question.

Which of the following is NOT an advantage of teams?

a. Faster adoption and integration of new technologies and processes

b. Faster decision-making processes

c. Higher employee motivation

d. Increased quality of work and efficiency

Which of the following is NOT an indicator that teams may be appropriate?

    a. Complex decision-making is required

    b. Employees need assistance from others to do their job

    c. Employees require minimal supervision

    d. Results/outputs rely heavily on routine processes

**Building Team Effectiveness**

13. What is the typical four stage team development process?

    _____

    _____

    _____

    _____

14. Match the following terms with their definitions. You will use each definition only once.

_____Brainstorming

_____Fishbowl

_____Force field analysis

_____Multi-voting

_____Nominal group technique

_____Responsibility charting

a. A matrix is created in which each team member is assigned a role in the decision-making process.

b. A useful technique to reduce the number of options.

c. This approach allows those in the invited group to discuss the topic in an uninterrupted way while the host group observes, listens and learns.

d. This tool is appropriate for determining if the positives outweigh the negatives.

e. This weighted ranking technique is effective for determining priorities.

f. This well-known approach is useful for generating ideas that can lead to better decisions.

**Section 7**

**Managing Within Legal Requirements – US**

15. Select the most appropriate answer to each question.

The Fair Labor Standards Act covers the following:

    a. Standards for employee vs. contractor status

    b. Standards for exempt vs. non-exempt

    c. All of the above

    d. None of the above

The following applies to nonexempt employees:

    a. May not be employed for over 40 hours in a week without receiving at least one and one-half times their regular rate of pay for the overtime hours

    b. Must be compensated for any work that is permitted, even work completed at home.

    c. All of the above

    d. None of the above

The Equal Pay Act allows individuals to receive different pay for the same position based on:

    a. Merit

    b. Seniority

    c. All of the above

    d. None of the above

The Family and Medical Leave Act requires employers to provide up to how many weeks of unpaid leave?

    a. 6 weeks

    b. 12 weeks

    c. 16 weeks

Which of the following is NOT a defense that an organization can use against discrimination charges?

    a. Adverse impact

    b. Business necessity

    c. Job-relatedness

    d. Seniority

**Privacy-Related Issues**

16. True or false

_____In the United States, privacy is not guaranteed to workers by law.

_____The Federal Electronic Communications Privacy Act prohibits employers from deliberately eavesdropping on an employee's personal conversations.

_____Under federal law, sending and receiving email on an employer's computer is no different than writing a memo on company letterhead.

**Answers to these exercises are in Section 10.**

Note: These exercises are intended to help you retain the material learned. While not the exact questions as on the CIAC Certification assessment, the material in this handbook/study guide fully addresses the content on which you will be assessed. For a formal practice test, please contact the CIAC directly by visiting www.ciac-cert.org.

**Section 7**

## Maximizing Human Resources
## Reference Bibliography

### Related Articles from *Call Center Management Review* (See Section 9)

Agent Compensation Evolving as Industry Growth Continues

Effective Career Progression Programs Balance Both Staff and Business Needs

Understand the Employee-Customer Satisfaction Link for Positive Impact

Empower Agents with the Resources and Authority to Satisfy Customers

### For Further Study

**Books/Studies**

*Agent Staffing & Retention Study Final Report.* ICMI, Inc., 2000.

Bennis, Warren and Burt Nanus. *Leaders: Strategies for Taking Charge.* Harper Perenial, 1997.

*Call Center Agent Motivation and Compensation: The Best of Call Center Management Review.* Call Center Press, 2002.

*Call Center Culture: The Hidden Success Factor in Achieving Service Excellence.* The Radclyffe Group, 1999.

Davis, Brian, Susan Gebelein, Lowell Hellervik, James Sheard and Carol Skube. *Successful Manager's Handbook: Development Suggestions for Today's Managers.* Personnel Decisions International, 1992.

Gomez-Mejia, Luis R., David Balkin and Robert Cardy. *Managing Human Resources.* Prentice-Hall, Inc., 2000.

**Articles**

Ahearn, Elizabeth. "Designed Turnover: A Different Approach to Retention." *Call Center Management Review,* January 2001.

Bave-Kerwin, Jean. "The Role of Corporate Culture in Agent Commitment." *Call Center Management Review: Agent Development and Retention Special Issue,* 2000.

Elliot, Darryl. "Managing a Union Call Center: Eliminating the 'Us vs. Them' Mentality." *Call Center Management Review,* December 1998.

Levin, Greg. "Call Center Professionals Speak Up for Underpaid Agents." *Call Center Management Review,* April 1999.

Levin, Greg. "Enhance Agent Retention by Turning Them Loose." *Call Center Management Review,* February 2002.

Marro Botero, Ingrid. "Use Surveys to Assess Your Employees' Satisfaction." *The Business Journal of Phoenix,* November 12, 1999.

### Web sites

Canadian Radio and Television Communication Commission, www.crtc.gc.ga

Canadian Marketing Association, www.the-cma.org

Perseus Development Corporation, www.perseus.com

**People Management**

## Glossary

**360-Evaluation.** Also called a 360-Review. Peformance review that incorporates assessments from managers, peers, direct reports and self. These perspectives are compiled to identify strengths and weaknesses.

**Abandoned Call.** Also called a Lost Call. The caller hangs up before reaching an agent.

**Adherence to Schedule.** A general term that refers to how well agents adhere to their schedules. Can include both a) how much time they were available to take calls during their shifts, including the time spent handling calls and the time spent waiting for calls to arrive (also called Availability), and b) when they were available to take calls (also called Compliance or Adherence). See Occupancy.

**Adverse Impact.** When the same standard, applied to all applicants or employees, affects a protected class more negatively. Legally defined in Title VII of the Civil Rights Act of 1964.

**After-Call Work (ACW).** Also called Wrap-up and Post Call Processing (PCP). Work that is necessitated by and immediately follows an inbound transaction. Often includes entering data, filling out forms and making outbound calls necessary to complete the transaction. The agent is unavailable to receive another inbound call while in this mode.

**Agent.** The person who handles incoming or outgoing calls. Also referred to as customer service representative (CSR), telephone sales or service representative (TSR), rep, associate, consultant, engineer, operator, technician, account executive, team member, customer service professional, staff member, attendant and specialist.

**Automatic Call Distributor (ACD).** The specialized telephone system used in incoming call centers. It is a programmable device that automatically answers calls, queues calls, distributes calls to agents, plays delay announcements to callers and provides real-time and historical reports on these activities. May be a stand-alone system, or ACD capability built into a CO, network or PBX.

**Average Call Value.** Total revenue divided by total number of calls for a given period of time.

**Average Handling Time.** The sum of Average Talk Time and Average After-Call Work for a specified time period.

**Average Speed of Answer (ASA).** Also called Average Delay. The average delay of all calls. It is total delay divided by total number of calls.

**Base Pay.** The fixed pay an employee receives on a regular basis for work performed. Also referred to as salary or hourly rate.

**Blocked Calls.** A call that cannot be connected immediately because a) no circuit is available at the time the call arrives, or b) the ACD is programmed to block calls from entering the queue when the queue backs up beyond a defined threshold.

**Bonuses.** A one-time lump-sum payment that is completely separate from base pay.

**Bureaucratic Organizational Structure.** The traditional pyramid structure, or hierarchy, typically with many layers of management and based on functional divisions of labor.

**Calibration.** The process in which variations in the way performance criteria (especially monitoring criteria) are interpreted from person to person are minimized.

**Call Taping.** A type of monitoring in which the supervisor or automated system records a sampling of calls. The person conducting the monitoring then randomly selects calls for evaluation of agent performance.

**Calls per Agent.** See Contacts Handled.

**Career Path.** A set of structured career advancement opportunities within the call center and/or organization. See Skill Path.

**Coaching.** Feedback given during ongoing meetings (formal and/or informal) between an individual and his/her manager to discuss performance, development, career, etc. Coaching can be thought of as one-on-one interactive training.

**Commissions.** Monetary compensation given to agents for meeting or exceeding sales goals. Sales agents may be paid on a straight commission, or salary plus commission (although some call centers pay sales agents on a straight salary basis).

**Compensable Factor.** Work-related criteria that an organization considers important in assessing the relative value of different jobs.

**Compensation.** Base pay, incentives and benefits given to an employee in return for services rendered.

**Computer Telephony Integration (CTI).** The software, hardware and programming necessary to integrate computers and telephones so they can work together seamlessly and intelligently.

**Contacts Handled.** Also called Calls per Agent. An agent productivity metric typically expressed as contacts per hour. Contacts handled is not a recommended agent performance objective since many of the variables that impact contacts handled are out of agents' control. For comparison, see True (Normalized) Contacts per Hour.

**Contractors.** These self-employed individuals form a direct relationship with the organization for specific projects or predefined periods of time. Since the tax burden is shifted from the organization to the contractor, there are legal guidelines for distinguishing contractors from employees.

**Customer Relationship Management (CRM).** The process of holistically managing a customer's relationship with a company. It takes into account their history as a customer, the depth and breadth of their business with the company, as well as other factors. CRM generally uses a sophisticated applications and database system that includes elements of data mining, contact management, and enterprise resource planning, allowing agents and analysts to know and anticipate customer behavior better.

**Delay.** Also called Queue Time. The time a caller spends in queue, waiting for an agent to become available. Average delay is the same thing as average speed of answer.

**Development.** Learning focused on long-term growth in the individual's or organization's capabilities and skills.

**Development Plan.** This document outlines the areas/skills of an employee's performance that need improvement. It includes expected results, actions and plans to accomplish the results and a timeframe for performance improvement. Creating a development plan is typically part of the performance review process.

**Disparate Treatment.** When an employer treats a person differently because of his or her protected class status. Legally defined in Title VII of the Civil Rights Act of 1964.

**Education.** Learning that prepares an individual for a specific future role or opportunity. This should relate to career pathing and succession planning.

**Empowerment.** A business strategy that gives ownership and responsibility to the individuals who have direct contact with the product, service, and customer. Empowerment shifts the direction and control from the supervisor (an external force) to the individual (with an internal force or desire to perform).

**Exempt Employee.** A salaried employee not covered by the overtime requirements in the Fair Labor Standards Act. Includes most administrative, professional, executive and sales jobs; however, the Act should be consulted for specific guidelines on determining exempt employees.

**Flat Organizational Structure.** A structure that has few levels of management and emphasizes decentralization.

**Full-Time Equivalents (FTEs).** A term used in scheduling and budgeting, whereby the number of scheduled hours is divided by the hours in a full work week. The hours of several part-time agents may add up to one FTE.

**Incentive.** Compensation designed to reward behavior that is linked to the achievement of specific call center/organizational goals.

**Interactive Voice Response (IVR).** Also called Voice Response Unit (VRU) or Audio Response Unit (ARU). An IVR responds to caller-entered digits or speech recognition in much the same way that a conventional computer responds to keystrokes or clicks of a mouse. When the IVR is integrated with database computers, callers can interact with databases to check current information (e.g., account balances) and complete transactions (e.g., make transfers between accounts).

**Job Aid.** Sources of information pertinent to specific job roles and tasks that can be accessed quickly by employees as needed.

**Knowledge Management.** Treating individual and collective knowledge within the organization as a strategic resource meriting management planning and attention.

**Section 8**

**Learning.** The acquisition of new skills, attitudes, and knowledge.

**Learning Organization.** Learning organizations look at the systems and processes contributing to learning as opposed to focusing primarily on specific interventions, such as a training class. This perspective leads to knowledge management and the successful development of an organization's intellectual capital. See Knowledge Management.

**Mentoring.** When an experienced employee (mentor) meets with a less-experienced employee (protégé) to advise and provide guidance related to the protégé's career development.

**Merit Pay.** The increase in a person's base pay as a result of good performance.

**Monitoring.** The process of listening to agents' telephone calls for the purpose of maintaining quality. Monitoring can be: a) silent, where agents don't know when they are being monitored, b) side-by-side, where the person monitoring sits next to the agent and observes calls or c) record and review, where calls are recorded and then later played back and assessed.

**Mystery Shopper.** A type of monitoring in which a person acts as a customer, initiates a call to the center and monitors the skills of the agent.

**Needs Analysis.** A systematic and comprehensive process of assessing what training is needed in an organization.

**Negligent Hiring.** When an employer fails to use reasonable care and judgment in hiring an employee who later commits a crime during employment.

**Nepotism.** Hiring or giving unfair advantages to relatives in an organization.

**Net Rep.** A call center agent trained to handle Internet transactions such as email, text chat, web callbacks, co-browsing, etc.

**Netspeak.** Abbreviated spelling and colloquial phrasing employed by experienced Internet users. For example, "BTW" for "by the way," and "IMHO" for "in my humble opinion."

**Nonexempt Employee.** Often called hourly workers, these employees are legally required to receive at least the minimum wage and may not be employed for over 40 hours in a week without receiving at least one and one-half times their regular rate of pay for the overtime hours.

**Occupancy.** Also referred to as agent utilization. The percentage of time agents handle calls versus wait for calls to arrive. For a half-hour, the calculation is: (call volume x average handling time in seconds) / (number of agents x 1800 seconds). See Adherence to Schedule.

**Open Door Policy.** A verbal grievance procedure where the manager's door is open any time an employee want to discuss a problem. This is a way management encourages employees to discuss their problems and issues with their immediate supervisor, with the right of appeal to upper management.

**Organizational Structure.** See Organizational Design.

**Organizational Design.** Organizational design refers to the structure of jobs, positions and reporting relationships in an organization.

**Peer Monitoring.** Call center agents monitor peers' calls and provide feedback on their performance.

**Performance Review.** A systematic assessment of an employee's job performance to evaluate the quality and effectiveness of his/her work against performance objectives.

**Protected Class.** A group of people who have suffered past discrimination and have been given special protection by the judicial system. Defined and designated in Title VII of the Civil Rights Act of 1964.

**Quid Pro Quo.** A type of sexual harassment in which sexual favors/activity is demanded in return for keeping or getting a job-related benefit.

**Recruitment.** The process of developing a pool of qualified candidates for a given job.

**Response Time.** The time it takes the call center to respond to transactions that do not have to be handled when they arrive (e.g., correspondence or e-mail). See Service Level.

**Retention.** The continued employment of staff. Retention is the opposite of turnover. See Turnover.

**Rostered Staff Factor (RSF).** Alternatively called an Overlay, Shrink Factor or Shrinkage. RSF is a numerical factor that leads to the minimum staff needed on schedule over and above base staff required to achieve your service level and response time objectives. It is calculated after base staffing is determined and before schedules are organized, and accounts for things like breaks, absenteeism and ongoing training.

**Service Bureau.** A service bureau (outsourcer) is a company hired to handle some or all of the organization's contacts.

**Service Level.** Also called Telephone Service Factor, or TSF. The percentage of incoming calls that are answered within a specified threshold: "X% of calls answered in Y seconds." See Response Time.

**Sexual Harassment.** Under certain circumstances, unwelcomed sexual advances, requests for sexual favors, and other verbal or physical conduct of a sexual nature.

**Side-by-Side Monitoring.** A type of monitoring in which the person conducting the monitoring sits beside the agent and listens while the agent handles a call.

**Silent Monitoring.** A type of monitoring in which the person conducting the monitoring session listens to an agent call in real-time from another location. In some call centers, the supervisor can also monitor the agent's keyboard activities to ensure quality and system navigation while the agent is handling the call.

**Skill Path.** Skill paths focus on the development of specific skills rather than the progression of positions through the center and/or organization. See Career Path.

**Skills-Based Routing.** An ACD capability that matches a caller's specific needs with an agent who has the skills to handle that call, on a real-time basis.

**Staff-Sharing.** When two or more organizations share a common pool of employees, typically to meet seasonal demands.

**Succession Planning.** A form of career development involving activities related to identifying and preparing people for executive positions.

**Talk Time.** The time an agent spends with a caller during a transaction. Includes everything from "hello" to "goodbye."

**Team.** A group of individuals with complementary skills who are committed to a common purpose and performance goals to which they hold themselves mutually accountable.

**Telecommuting.** Using telecommunications to work from home or other locations instead of at the organization's premises.

**Temporary Staff.** Employees who are usually assigned to short-term projects or seasonal workloads. In most cases, they are employees of a staffing agency, but may become a source for employee recruitment.

**Training.** Instruction which places an emphasis on job-specific objectives and enhances learning (knowledge/skills/abilities) for the current job.

**True (Normalized) Calls/Contacts per Hour.** Actual calls an individual or group handled divided by occupancy for that period of time.

**Turnover.** When a person leaves the call center. Turnover is typically calculated at an annualized rate.

Section 8

# Reference Articles

The following articles are from the pages of *Call Center Management Review* (formerly *Service Level Newsletter*), the journal for ICMI members. They were selected to provide you with further information on some of the key areas of people management.

# From The Field with Jay Minnucci

# Maximizing the Value of Your Workforce Management Team

**Success depends on clear roles, a focus on planning and management support.**

At one time, forecasting, staffing and scheduling formed the nucleus of the call center manager's job. Not today. Many organizations have evolved these functions into their own entity. While sometimes that role encompasses just those three key tasks, other times, they're combined with related functions that can best be handled in a more centralized environment (see box, below).

Most often, a team is assigned to this role, rather than one individual. While the functions vary and the names of the group differ from one company to the next (e.g., Workforce Management Team, Resource Management Team, Command Center, etc.), there is a common thread that ties them together. The teams are dedicated to forecasting workload and scheduling staff to meet service level commitments with the fewest possible resources. It has never been an easy assignment, but in light of the increased complexity of the call center environment over the past decade, today it can be particularly onerous. Skills-based routing, multimedia queuing and other

## Potential WMT Responsibilities

- Forecasting
- Staffing
- Scheduling
- Vacation administration
- Real-time traffic control
- Budgeting
- Reporting
- Call routing
- Voice-technology support
- Trunk provisioning
- Internal consulting

advancements have created a mathematical nightmare that can baffle even a skilled statistician.

However, given the current multi-channel environment, the decision to create (or upgrade) a workforce management team (WMT) is one of the most significant moves an organization can make in the quest to consistently meet service level and response time objectives. But pulling together a team is not enough to guarantee improved performance results. Creating the ideal WMT takes time, money and dedication. A poorly constructed WMT, which is not supported appropriately throughout the organization, can have a detrimental impact on results.

## Building a Team Structure

A WMT must decide how best to use resources that report to others in the organization. It's inevitable that questions concerning control and organizational power arise when the concept is introduced. This potential for conflict can ruin an otherwise strong and valuable team. To avoid killing your team effort at the start, make sure the organization can clearly distinguish the roles and responsibilities of the WMT vs. those handled by the call center floor. That's the single, most important success factor.

So how do you decide which responsibilities to assign to the WMT? I recommend that the organization views this team as the planning arm of the call center. The WMT creates the blueprint that assures the best chance for success. The call center floor is responsible for the execution of that plan, which, in a call center, is determined by adherence. Obviously, both parties have to meet their objectives in order for service level goals to be met.

Within the WMT, make sure the focus is on planning. The team must constantly look ahead to the next minute, the next day, the next month and the next year to ensure that the center has the required

resources. But keep in mind, this kind of planning takes time, which is often in short supply. Too many call centers waste valuable time and WMT resources over-analyzing historical results. History is important, but only to provide lessons on how to improve on past performance. A good rule of thumb is "spend more time planning for tomorrow than explaining away yesterday."

## The One Key Activity

While the WMT will have a pretty full plate with forecasting, staffing and scheduling tasks, there is one activity that is crucial to consistent service level delivery – developing a report to show the gap between required staff and scheduled staff by interval for the next day.

This information allows the center to create a plan to address staff shortages (and surpluses) in the most effective manner possible. And while looking ahead one week or a month is a good practice, there's no substitute for running a gap analysis for the very next day. That allows you to capture all but the last-minute activities that will affect staff availability, thereby ensuring the most accurate analysis. And you will still have time to respond to any projected staffing gaps.

A final thought: While a well-constructed WMT is a valuable asset to centers dedicated to consistently meeting service level objectives, success doesn't happen by accident. If you want the team to reach its potential, call center leaders must organize it well, carefully train its members, clearly define its roles and fully support the concept. If you are willing to make that type of investment, the payoff can be substantial. *CCMReview*

### Jay Minnucci

*Jay Minnucci, Senior Consultant, Incoming Calls Management Institute, has more than 15 years experience running mission-critical call center and customer services operations. He can be reached at 610-502-9876 or jaym@icmi.com.*

Section 9

April 2001 ■ Reprinted with permission from *Call Center Management Review*®, www.icmi.com.

1

# Recruiting Strategies for Multimedia Call Centers

*by Greg Levin*

## Internet-savvy agents play an increasingly key role in call centers. Do you know how, and where, to find them?

While advanced technology has certainly enhanced today's call center capabilities, there is no argument that agents are still the most important resource for call center success. Unfortunately, there is also no argument that finding those crucial resources is getting more difficult.

According to the Customer Contact Strategy Forum — a Toronto-based association for North American call center executives, recruiting skilled staff is, by far, the biggest challenge for today's call center manager. "Our members come in all the time saying they can't find people," says Sarah Kennedy, president of the forum. "The skill demand in the call center industry is going through the roof."

True, higher customer expectations and new customer contact channels — particularly email and the Web — have certainly raised the bar for agent recruiting. But top call centers are learning that, by adding ample muscle to their hiring strategies, finding agents who can handle the multimedia blitz doesn't have to be a Herculean task.

The problem is that many multimedia call centers are still using the same tired recruiting techniques they used back when traditional phone agents were all they needed. They have done little to attract and attain the type of staff they need today — agents with the skills to effectively handle the customer email and Web-based transactions now flowing into the center.

### In Search of Net Reps

While everybody is talking about how crucial Net reps are today, few are talking about how to find them. According to Wanda Sitzer, executive vice president of Initiatives Three, a consulting firm specializing in phone and Web initiatives to improve customer support, managers in search of quality Net reps need to go through a formal process that includes four essential steps.

■ **Define Net rep requirements.** Before you can begin looking for Net reps, you have to know exactly what you're looking for. A Net rep at one call center may have quite different responsibilities than a Net rep at another. It's up to you to carefully define the position: Will they handle email only or Web-chat, as well? Will they also handle voice-based transactions online, e.g., voice over Internet protocol (VoIP) and/or Web call-backs? Do they need page-push and/or collaborative browsing skills? Will they be primarily sales, service or tech support agents? Does (or will) video come into play at your center?

The answers to these questions will serve as the guide to your entire Net rep hiring process. Without it, it's easy to get lost during the "e-cruiting" and skills assessment stages.

■ **Implement a progressive "e-cruiting" strategy.** Placing traditional employment ads in the local newspaper is not the best way to find top online agents. To find candidates with the written and technical skills you're seeking, you need to recruit using the same medium in which agents will be working — the Web. Post Net agent job openings on your corporate Web site and intranet (for recruiting internally), as well as on at least one of the growing number of online career centers and recruiting sites that exist on the Web today.

"Applicants who search sites like ours demonstrate Net savvy — a good start when looking for online reps," says Tara Thorne of Web recruiter CareerBuilder. There are even a few online recruiting sites dedicated specifically to call centers, such as CallCenterCareers.com. In addition, several call center consultancy Web sites now feature pages where companies can post job openings.

Encourage all Net rep applicants to respond to online job ads via email, and take note of those who comply with these instructions. "If candidates call to ask about the job, you may have just learned their preferred communication style — vocal, not written — and they may not be the right person for the Net agent job," Sitzer points out. Be sure to include a detailed job description as part of your online ad to ensure that applicants are aware of the skills they'll need to succeed.

Applicants who follow the online application procedure, who have no problem attaching documents (i.e., resumé, cover letter) and who demonstrate good writing skills should be invited to participate in the next phase of the hiring process.

■ **Assess candidates' customer support skills online.** Here's where you ask applicants to put their money where their mouse is. Sitzer recommends starting off by sending applicants an interactive "e-roleplay" scenario online to assess how they respond to a challenging customer email inquiry. Be sure that the e-roleplay you create reflects the types of inquiries your center typically receives; i.e., sales-related, service-related, etc. When evaluating responses, take note of whether or not the applicant correctly interpreted the inquiry, provided a concise, well-written response, and demonstrated other appropriate skills (i.e., upselling, personalization). Also, check to see that he or she is familiar with the rules of "netiquette."

If your center handles Web-chat transactions, schedule a chat-based interview with applicants. This will enable you to learn more about each candidate while evaluating their real-time, interactive writing skills. In addition to the interview, call centers such as Goodwill Toronto conduct chat-based e-roleplays to see how candidates respond to a live customer support transaction online.

"I play the customer and give [applicants] a situation," explains Sharon

Myatt, director of program development and Innovation at Goodwill Toronto. "Here I test the skills they need to succeed in chat: grammar, keyboarding, critical thinking, paraphrasing and questioning."

Don't forget to assess Net rep applicants' ability to handle voice-based customer transactions via a telephone interview. This is important even if your Net reps aren't responsible for handling VoIP contacts and/or Web call-backs. Why? The phone is still the primary mode of contact in most call centers, thus having Net reps who can help out on the phones when necessary is an added bonus.

*As a manager of a multimedia operation, it's important not to get so caught up in the search for Net reps that you forget your need for dedicated phone staff.*

■ **Conduct face-to-face interviews.** Once you've found candidates who have the core Net rep skills you're seeking, invite them into the call center. This gives each applicant a chance to see the center and gives you a chance to evaluate his interpersonal skills.

"There's more to being a Net rep than managing and establishing online relationships," Sitzer explains. "Online agents will also need to integrate successfully with your entire operation. That means responding to coaching and working well with peers. Face-to-face interviews ensure that your top choices can thrive in your dynamic environment."

## Don't Forget the Phones

While email and Web-based transactions are certainly increasing in most call centers, the phone is still — and will likely remain to be — the primary mode of customer contact. As a manager of a multimedia operation, it's important not to get so caught up in the search for Net reps that you forget your need for dedicated phone staff. As already mentioned, finding Net reps who can effectively handle online as well as phone transactions can be very difficult. Therefore, you will likely need to have a separate recruiting program in place to acquire quality phone agents.

Considering the exorbitant demand for skilled phone staff in our industry, relying solely on traditional recruiting methods isn't sufficient for finding and assessing quality candidates. While newspaper ads and references from existing agents can be effective, progressive call center managers incorporate some of the following recruiting and assessment techniques into their hiring programs.

■ **Partnerships with local educational institutions.** Numerous colleges, universities and trade schools have created special call center/customer service certificate programs into their curriculum. Forming alliances with such institutions can provide you with a continuous supply of qualified staff who are serious about call center careers. These schools are always looking for call center partners that can help out with course development and provide students with agent internships during the academic year. In return, the schools give the call centers first crack at new graduates.

■ **Internet job postings and IVR applicant screening.** The Web isn't just useful for attracting Net reps. Most serious job seekers spend the majority of their time on the Internet today, as they are allured by the speed in which they can find jobs opportunities and respond online. Thus posting phone agent openings on your Web site, online career centers and call center-specific Web sites is a wise strategy.

Ask all phone agent applicants to email their resume and cover letter, but don't use the Web for screening purposes with these candidates. You are looking for phone agents, not email and chat experts, so why not use the phone channel as an initial screening device? This can be done quickly and effectively via the call center IVR system, says Anne Nickerson, editor and publisher of the *Call Center Insider* electronic newsletter.

"Screening applicants via the IVR is

one of the biggest time savers for human resource and call center managers," says Nickerson. "You determine the minimum qualifications you are looking for — what you would usually peruse in a stack of resumes — and, instead, ask those questions with voice or keypad responses." She adds that the IVR system can be programmed to rank top candidates based on their responses. (Several vendors provide IVR profiling services; check out www.Wonderlic.com or www.TelServe.com.)

■ **IVR job postings.** The IVR unit is not only ideal for screening applicants, it's a cost-effective tool for advertising job openings. Your call center receives thousands of calls each day. Many of your customers may be in the job market or know of somebody who is. Many call centers have found that a simple announcement in the IVR greeting can be a more efficient recruiting method than placing an ad in the local paper (i.e., "Press '5' for job opportunities"). Callers who choose this option can then be immediately routed to the automated applicant screening system described previously.

As with Net rep applicants, further

**Section 9**

May 2001 ■ Reprinted with permission from *Call Center Management Review*®, www.icmi.com.

3

assessment of phone agent applicants' skills is best done via interviews and role plays. The difference is that these assessment methods should be voice-based, not text-based, from the start. Conduct phone interviews with quality applicants to better assess their phone voices and personalities. Here's your chance to ask more detailed questions than were asked during the IVR screening process. Be sure to present each applicant with a challenging customer situation and ask them how they would handle it. Do the applicant's responses sound genuine or do they seem scripted — lacking thought and creativity? Does he or she sound confident, friendly and professional? Is humor used appropriately?

Invite candidates who fare well during the phone interview in for a face-to-face interview. Conduct realistic customer role plays, with the applicant seated at a computer. Take note of his or her customer support/sales skills, as well as his or her ability to quickly and accurately fill in basic customer information screens.

## Revamped but Realistic Recruiting

In today's multimedia call center environment, you can't expect all agents to be all things to all customers all the time. However, you can develop strategic recruiting strategies to ensure that all customer contacts — whether via email, Web or phone — are handled by skilled agents all the time.

The quest for universal agents — those who can effectively handle any transaction type — is a noble one, but don't expect a high percentage of your staff to fill such oversized shoes. Online customer support is quite a different animal than traditional phone support, and there's nothing wrong with using separate teams to tame the two beasts.

However, there is something wrong with clinging to yesterday's staid hiring methods to find staff who can manage today's multichannel mix. The Web-savvy staff you need exists, you just need to peek around a few new corners when recruiting. _CCMReview_

May 2001 ■ Reprinted with permission from *Call Center Management Review*®, www.icmi.com.

4

# Dealing with the 'Free-Agent' Mindset: Rethink Recruiting and Rewards

*by Susan Hash*

The Generation X mindset became a strong force in the workplace in the early 1990s, challenging corporate cultures and rejecting the traditional button-down management policies and procedures.

Just when companies were learning how to adjust to their Generation X workforce (now 24 to 39 years of age), along comes the next wave of call center agents – Generation Y.

Generation Y includes 68 million Americans born between 1977 and 1994 (16 to 24 years of age), 40 million of whom are already in the workforce.

"All of those disconcerting attitudes and behaviors that Corporate America had to learn to work with for Generation X have been challenged. It's created even more of a necessary mind-meld for managers to work with the emerging generation," says Eric Chester, author of *And You Thought Generation X Was Tough*, and founder of Generation Why. Chester coined the phrase "Generation Why" to better describe this generation, which "is typified by youth who continually question the standards and expectations imposed by society," (i.e., "why does it matter?" and "why should I care?").

Like the preceding generation, Generation Y is changing the way business has to function and operate, says Chester.

Generation Y can be described as "similar to Generation X – only on fast forward," says Bruce Tulgan, author of *Managing Generation Y* and founder of Rainmaker Thinking Inc., a research firm focused on the working lives of Americans born after 1963. "They're the self-esteem generation. Their independence isn't fierce, it's casual. They know they'll have to take care of themselves and they're not worried at all."

## The Staffing Crisis Is Not Going to End

While the Generation Y workforce will surely impact businesses in upcoming years, Tulgan points out that some 20 million older Gen Xers are now managers. "They're already doing things differently," he says.

He adds that the key changes in business were brought about by business leaders and management experts who began to change the employer-employee relationship more than a decade ago through reengineering, downsizing and restructuring. "It's not just young workers who know they have to fend for themselves in this environment. Employers no longer offer job security, so employees of all ages are starting to think like free agents." The free-agent mindset is possibly the biggest challenge that employers have ever had to deal with, he says.

"That means managing people is going to be much harder than it's ever been. You won't be able to retain people; we're going to have a staffing crisis on our hands forever. Instead, you need to change the way you do business," he says.

Bill Peters, VP of reservations for Outrigger Hotels in Denver, agrees. "There's really no commitment [among younger staff] to the business for the long term," he says. However, he attributes part of that to the job market. "If the economy was down, people would spend more time trying to achieve more in their current positions instead of just jumping ship with the first confrontation or poor performance review."

## Rethinking Recruiting Strategies

Recruiting is the key process call center managers should consider revamping right away. "In the workplace of the future, you're not looking for people to join the family or climb the ladder," says Tulgan. "Rather, you need people who bring specific skills to the table, who are

## Understanding the Generational Perspectives

|  | Baby Boomers 1946-1960 | Generation X 1961-1976 | Generation Why 1977-1994 |
|---|---|---|---|
| The Future | "Is ours!" | "Sucks!" | "Ain't gonna happen." |
| Wealth | "I'll earn it." | "I don't want it." | "Gimme, or I'll take it." |
| Employment | "Lucky to find." | "Only if I have to." | "Jobs are a dime a dozen." |
| Loyalty | "To the end!" | "For a while." | "Until a better offer." |
| Instruction | "Tell me WHAT to do." | "Show me HOW to do it." | "Why do I need to know!" |
| Communication | Via parent's phone | Via personal phone | Pager/cell phone/ e-mail |
| Change | Dislike | Accept | Demand |
| Technology | Ignorant | Comfortable | Masters of |
| Video Game | Pong | PacMan | Mortal Kombat |

Source: Eric Chester, Generation Why, Web site: www.generationwhy.com

December 2000 ■ Reprinted with permission from *Call Center Management Review*®, www.icmi.com.

5

able to get up to speed quickly and who can begin making valuable contributions right away."

Outrigger Hotels is changing its recruiting process to focus on agents who fit a particular profile – specifically, candidates attending local technical or travel schools, or those interested in getting into the hospitality industry. "We focus on those people trying to get their degrees – sending the message that this would be a great job for them for a year or so," says Sandy Schuster, Outrigger's director of human resources.

"It's not fair to say this would be a great career for you," adds Peters. "But if we can identify that profile during or prior to the interview process, we have a better chance of retaining that employee for at least a year." The call center's goal is to retain 65 to 70 percent of its agents for a year.

### Reaching the Right Candidates

Because of the tight labor market, many call centers are so desperate to hire agents, the main selection criterion appears to be whether or not they have a pulse, says Tulgan. Besides changing the recruiting focus to a more short-term outlook, "the goal of developing a compelling recruiting message and running an effective campaign is to attract an applicant pool that's large enough to allow you to be selective," he says.

At FurstPerson, a call center outsourcing firm in Chicago, recruiting has become a sales and marketing strategy, says Vice President Michelle Cline.

"We've had to take a hard look at the marketing tactics we use to go after candidates in the younger age groups. It has forced us to reallocate some of our resources away from traditional recruiting mechanisms to investing in more Internet and grassroots type of recruiting."

FurstPerson's agent recruiting campaign targets places that Gen

## Build a Fluid Talent Pool to Leverage Staffing ROI

The demand for talent will continue to outpace the supply for the foreseeable future, says Bruce Tulgan. And "there's no doubt that most employers are experiencing the staffing crisis most acutely with their youngest workers."

To combat high turnover, Tulgan suggests call center managers work on developing a "fluid talent pool."

"When agents leave, don't let them leave altogether. Put them in your reserve army," he says. "Offer them the chance to continue adding value on a part-time basis, as flex-timers, telecommuters, periodic temps or consultants. Let them leave and come back in three months, six months or a year." Keep a list of names and phone numbers of high-performing agents. When you have a staffing gap, call your former employees and ask if they would like to come in and work – full time or on a temporary basis.

Then, welcome them back with open arms. "After all," he says. "You've already invested in recruiting and training them, why not leverage your investment?"

Xers and Yers frequent, such as coffee houses, movie theaters and outdoor activities like beach volleyball.

"It does take a little more effort to shake out the right candidates," says Outrigger's Schuster. Her company has expanded its recruiting sources from just using newspaper ads to including radio advertising, job fairs, local community colleges and Internet ads.

An effective recruiting campaign must be both aggressive and year-round, adds Tulgan. "That means all company materials, even sales materials should be developed with your recruiting goals in mind." He offers the following four basic elements and suggestions for developing an effective campaign:

■ Unpaid media (news or quasi-news coverage). Develop concrete news stories or events to pitch to editors and reporters by building a list of all the potential angles and events that are newsworthy about your recruiting program. Don't dismiss unconventional tactics such as letters to the editor and calls to phone-in talk shows.

■ Paid media (advertising). The key to an effective ad in any media is being disciplined about sticking to the message. Don't just consider print ads. Write a script for a 60-second radio spot, buy a 30-second spot on cable

television or place your ad online at a job posting Web site.

■ Direct contact (mail, telephone, fax, e-mail). Identify and secure available databases with accurate contact information. Decide which means of direct contact will be most effective for reaching those people.

■ Events (sponsored by you or someone else). When planning events, keep in mind: 1) What can you do to make the event special to your target market, and 2) What is the potential news/publicity tie-in?

### Immediate Gratification is Key

When it comes to compensation, both Gen X and Y expect to be paid what they think they're worth. The main difference between the younger generations and their Baby Boomer predecessors is the period or intervals at which incentives or rewards are expected.

"These groups don't tolerate annual bonuses or reviews," says FurstPerson's Cline. "They want instant gratification from a financial standpoint, as well as with feedback on performance."

Cline says that bonuses at her company have dropped from yearly to quarterly or even monthly. In addition to monetary compensation, Gen X and Y agents value frequent pay-outs

December 2000 ■ Reprinted with permission from *Call Center Management Review*®, www.icmi.com.

6

on motivational programs, such as monthly, weekly or even daily.

A roundtable discussion of Outrigger Hotel's agents revealed that, while they like having incentives to shoot for, they prefer those that have monetary value, says Assistant Director of Operations Eric Boyd. "We've offered movie tickets, gift certificates of varying amounts, plus drawings for trips."

## What Works Besides Money?

While incentives are great, it takes more than that to motivate the younger workforce, says Chester.

"This is a generation who wants to have contact with a superior to let them know on an ongoing basis what they're doing is good."

Also, he says, given the choice between money and flexibility, they would take the freedom – wider parameters, more responsibility, less

structure.

Surveys by Rainmaker Thinking found the six top choices of non-monetary rewards among 20-somethings to be:

■ Control over their work schedules.

■ Training opportunities.

■ Exposure to decision makers.

■ Credit for projects.

■ Increased responsibility.

■ Opportunities for creative expression.

"In a call center environment, where it's hard to give agents control over their own schedules, the style of the manager also makes a huge difference," says Tulgan. "Managers need to be right in there, rolling up their sleeves and engaging people."

That's true, says Schuster. Younger agents "are looking more at their man-

agers, making sure they walk the talk – in other words, don't ask me to do something you wouldn't do."

And Bill Peters suggests managers readily accept the questioning they're likely to get from their staff. "There's a lot of thought that goes into that questioning," he says. "It used to be that agents were accountable to their managers. But in today's business, managers have to be accountable to their staff." *CCMReview*

December 2000 ■ Reprinted with permission from *Call Center Management Review*®, www.icmi.com.

7

Section 9

## From The Field with Michelle Cline

# Cut Agent Turnover by Hiring for Motivational Fit

**Do job candidates have the motivation it takes to work in your call center? Screen for "will do" attitudes.**

Do you have an agent in your call center who has the experience, knowledge and skills for the job, but who still performs below his or her potential? What about an agent who has the right skills, but is frequently tardy or absent? Have you ever hired someone who just didn't fit with your corporate culture? Just about every manager can answer "yes" to at least one of these questions.

The harder question to answer is "Why?" How can an employee possess the right skills for the job, yet not succeed? An elusive, yet key, recruiting component is *motivational fit* — understanding whether or not the candidate's motivations match your call center's needs.

Screening resumes, conducting traditional interviews and other typical assessment tools have limited success in consistently and accurately pinpointing a candidate's skills and abilities that pertain to the job. However, attempting to measure motivation and attitude accurately with these methods is even more difficult.

Determining a candidate's fit for the job with traditional interviews, general personality tests or references is as accurate as flipping a coin. So how do you accurately determine a candidate's skills, abilities and, importantly, motivation to do the job?

Developing a hiring system that accurately measures job success factors, especially motivation and attitude, is the key to hiring the right people — the top performers — for your call center.

### Understanding your needs

To know exactly whom you should hire, you must first understand the skills, attitudes, interests and motivations that make an agent successful in your call center. This is much more involved than writing a job description with job requirements. It includes understanding the type of work that is done, the skills and motivations it takes to complete this work, the expectations that are set for agents and the cultural aspects of the company which are critical for success.

While analyzing the call center agent job for your organization, you should concentrate on compiling a group of "success factors" that can be used to create a "success profile." This profile will be your starting point for understanding the competencies required for an agent to be successful in your center.

Officially, this process is known as conducting a job analysis. It's defined by the Department of Labor as: "A detailed statement of work behaviors and other information relevant to the job." Conducting a job analysis allows you to identify your call center's success profile, as

well as provides you with the legal documentation you need to support your hiring practices.

### Types of Success Factors

Typically, there are four types of success factors for the call center environment. These fall into one of the following categories:

1. Cognitive ability
2. Planning and organizing
3. Interpersonal
4. Attitudes, interests and motivations

The major difference between these categories is "can do" vs. "will do" (see box). Cognitive ability, planning and organizing, and interpersonal categories are "can do's." In other words, can a candidate do what you need him or her to do? Attitudes, interests and motivations are the elusive "will do's." The attitudes, interests and motivations category looks at: "Will the candidate do what is required of him or her?" This is one of the most challenging and critical areas to measure.

### Selecting the Right Candidate

Once you have identified the success factors, you must then answer the question: "How am I going to determine if my candidate possesses these factors?" According to the Department of Labor guidelines, a multiple-hurdle hiring approach is most effective in making an accurate hiring decision.

A successful multiple-hurdle hiring approach should allow you to assess all needed success factors using lower cost tools in the beginning of the recruiting process, and saving higher cost methods until after you've narrowed your applicant pool.

Typically, most job interviews focus on skills. For example: "Does the candidate possess the problem-solving skills necessary to do the job?" However, this type of interviewing neglects the "will do" part of the job. By assessing motivations, you can determine whether or not

### Call Center Success Factors

COGNITIVE ABILITY (CAN DO)

*Apply information = productivity*
Examples: problem-solving, learning and applying information.

PLANNING (CAN DO)

*Organizing ability = efficiency*
Examples: planning ability, organizing ability, adherence to policies, following rules, accuracy.

INTERPERSONAL (CAN DO)

*Persuasion = upselling*
Examples: customer service, persuasion, getting along with others, teamwork, coaching ability.

MOTIVATION (WILL DO)

*Attitude toward work = turnover*
Examples: Attitude toward work, attendance, flexibility, going above and beyond, energy.

September 2001 ■ Reprinted with permission from *Call Center Management Review*®, www.icmi.com.

8

the candidate wants to use their problem-solving skills in your center.

Evaluating candidates for motivational fit can be challenging. You can use one of the many assessment tools available in the market to help you gauge whether or not a candidate's motivations pertain to job performance. These tools are generally computer-based, Internet-based or can be administered via pencil and paper. Most can provide you with results that indicate how closely the candidate's "motivational fit" matches your call center's needs.

To follow up the motivational assessment, you may also choose to conduct a structured behavioral interview to pinpoint weak areas of motivation. For instance, if the candidate's results indicated that he or she might not have enough flexibility for your organization, you can ask a question that focuses on flexibility. After you have heard the candidate's response, you can make a more informed hiring decision.

Combining motivational fit assessments with behavioral-based interviews is a thorough way to measure attitudes, interest and motivations for the job. Selecting candidates based on both their skills and motivations will help you to decrease turnover. And an additional benefit: You'll have a staff of agents who enjoy coming to work in your call center. CCMReview

### Michelle Cline

*Michelle Cline is a Vice President for FurstPerson, an organization specializing in finding, hiring and keeping call center employees. She can be reached at 773-353-8150 or michelle@furstperson.com.*

**Section 9**

September 2001 ■ **Reprinted with permission from** *Call Center Management Review®*, www.icmi.com.

9

# The Outsourcing Evolution: Economic Trends Make It a More Viable Option

*by Susan Hash*

**Ecommerce, globalization, CRM and the need for high-level technical skills are influencing a rebirth of outsourcing.**

As call centers struggle with the complex task of integrating e-channels with voice – and quickly – more companies are considering outsourcing partnerships to handle some or all of their e-service functions. In the rush to get ecommerce applications up and running, U.S. companies have increased spending on outsourcing for Internet operations. According to International Data Corp. (IDC), a global market intelligence and research firm, spending on Internet operations outsourcing increased from $350 million to $613 million in one year (1997 to 1998). And by 2002, the U.S. outsourcing market could be worth $3.6 billion.

Besides the obvious need in many organizations to quickly get up to speed with Internet services, increased globalization and the spread of customer relationship management (CRM) also have contributed to outsourcing's growth – and evolution.

In the past, many call center managers looked upon outsourcing with some degree of skepticism. It was considered primarily as a strategy to help manage inbound call volume. Generally, calls were outsourced based on specific peak times, peak seasons, special promotions, specific call types or to be able to offer extended operating hours.

However, many managers were not entirely convinced of an outsourcing agency's ability to service their customers with the same quality, expertise and zeal as inhouse agents.

James Witz, Carrier Corp.'s national account manager, looked into outsourcing options a couple of years ago to help with the continuously increasing volume of calls and email (at the time, Witz managed the customer relations call center).

However, he says, the heating and air conditioning equipment manufacturer ultimately decided that keeping calls inhouse made better sense. "Our concern with outsourcing was the lack of technical expertise," he recalls. Carrier's call center handles calls from distributors, retailers and consumers. "We would have had to find and train employees who, technically, would not have been equal to those we already had inhouse. In our industry, technical capabilities are very important. It's what our customers expect."

However, he adds, the company is still considering outsourcing some Web-related functions, such as frequently asked questions and its distributor/dealer locator.

## A New Face, New Focus

Long-term economic trends are creating an environment in which companies need to "focus on their core competencies and seek outside specialists to access world-class processes in non-core yet strategic functions," says Rebecca Scholl, senior analyst for Gartner Dataquest's IT services worldwide group. While she admits this trend is not new, "until recently, many companies were adopting a wait-and-see attitude." What's changed? New tools, such as Web-based collaborative applications and self-service technologies, are available that can add value to the outsourcing relationship and enable companies to keep control of their processes – even though they are outsourcing them – through regular reporting and Web access to information, Scholl says.

In the past year, outsourcing has undergone a renaissance, agrees Peter Bendor-Samuel, founder and CEO of Outsourcing Center (www.outsourcing-center.com), an online community and information center, and author of *Turning Lead into Gold: The Demystification of Outsourcing.*

"The growth of the dot-coms caused a lot of the new-economy companies to turn to outsourcing, particularly for their call center operations," he says. "Interestingly, at the same time, the whole CRM evolution was happening. Call centers were being asked to do more than just pick up the phone, answer questions and take orders. So now you have the administration of the loyalty component potentially being offered as a service."

## The Move Offshore

Another fast-growing outsourcing trend is the movement to take call centers offshore. IDC predicts U.S.-based companies will dramatically increase their spending on offshore outsourcing services in the next few years. A new report indicates the amount will more than triple, from under $5.5 billion in 2000 to more than $17.6 billion in 2005.

Although, historically, cost-savings have been the main driver for using offshore outsourcers, accessing IT talent is quickly becoming the primary motivator. "American companies unable to find, hire and retain skilled IT workers at home are finding a vast pool of highly educated technology-savvy, English-speaking workers available overseas. Companies are sending IT projects offshore to compensate for the limited pool of talent available in the United States," says Cynthia Doyle, research manager for IDC's IT and Offshore Outsourcing Strategies program. "In the past, offshore IT service firms were primarily utilized for their programming, coding and software development work, but they have expanded their

April 2001 ■ Reprinted with permission from *Call Center Management Review*®, www.icmi.com.

10

Section 9

skill sets and expertise and can now deliver enhanced e-business solutions."

Many technical support call centers are finding it cost-effective to send their first- or second-level support calls offshore, while keeping an inhouse operation for third-level support, says Kathy Sisk, president of Kathy Sisk Enterprises, a call center training, consulting and servicing firm. "Paying a tech support agent in the U.S. may cost upward of $50,000 in annual salary, whereas, overseas, they can acquire an individual with the same or higher level of education for probably less than $30,000 or $20,000 a year."

India is best-positioned to capture a large part of the offshore outsourcing opportunity, according to IDC. However, other regions have potential to develop as major sources of offshore outsourcing, including Canada, Mexico, the Caribbean, South Africa, Israel, Ireland and Eastern Europe.

"To be a successful provider of outsourcing services, a region must demonstrate fluency in English, a vast pool of IT talent, a solid infrastructure and experience doing business with Western companies. So far, only India meets all these requirements," Doyle says.

## When is Outsourcing Viable?

When should you consider an outsourcing partnership? In cases where you have technical limitations in your call center, says Pamela Barron Leach, director of Diebold Direct, a provider of integrated delivery systems and services. "Another reason for outsourcing would be in an overload situation where you're not able to keep up with customer demand within a necessary timeframe," she says. It's also common for companies to turn to an outsourcer when there's a lack of language capabilities. For example, in a situation where you need a center to handle calls in a primarily Hispanic or Chinese-speaking community.

Many companies outsource e-service functions to handle the initial overflow or to determine whether or not it's profitable to have an inhouse operation, adds Sisk.

## Tips to Build a Successful Outsourcing Partnership

If you're looking into an outsourcing partnership for your call center, consider the following tips from Kathy Sisk of Kathy Sisk Enterprises (Web sites: www.kathysiskenterprises.com or www.outsourcingintl.com).

- Allow enough time to plan. While the timeline will ultimately depend on the type of project you're outsourcing and its complexity, make sure you allow your partner enough lead time for effective planning. In most cases, a 30- to 60-day lead time is sufficient, Sisk says.
- Assign project leaders who can head a team, who have initiative and who have background experience in the project that's being outsourced.
- Allow a decent budget for adequate setup. Currently, offshore firms are not charging setup fees but, eventually, they will, Sisk says. "In the U.S. and Canada, there is usually a hefty setup fee because there's a lot of prework taking place prior to rollout; for instance, custom work or training to tailor to the client's specific needs."
- Check to make sure the outsourcing agency you're considering has low turnover. Ask to see their HR reports.
- Hand-select the people who you want to be assigned to your account.
- Make sure the outsourcer has a proven background. Don't just rely on their referrals. Speak with a few of their current and/or past clients. Also be sure to interview the management staff who will be assigned to your account.
- Never give your outsourcer full control. Make sure the outsourcer has a method to allow you to assess the operation onsite and/or remotely
- Be sure to stay on top of the project on a daily basis. Often, "once a project is up and running successfully, the client will get comfortable and laid back, and then the outsourcer does, as well," she says. "Then you start to see productivity decline. Make sure everyone is held accountable for results and improvements, and conduct periodic spot-check assessments."
- Include a "way-out" clause in your agreement. First, make sure your expectations are reasonable. But, also ensure that you have a way out if the agency does not meet your expectations for performance.
- Don't focus on the cost to outsource as your No. 1 objective. Consider all other quality assurance factors – experience, history, results – that make the cost factors more profitable.
- Don't have high expectations at the start. Don't expect consistency up front – allow two weeks to 30 days for the outsourcer to ramp up.

In addition, she says, call centers that have consistently high turnover might want to consider outsourcing.

"High turnover is usually caused from a hiring mistake or lack of management support and training. There are three reasons: 1) a recruiting mistake – you hired out of desperation because you couldn't find anybody else and you hired the wrong person; 2) lack of training and management support; and 3) low unemployment – agents can go somewhere else and get paid a little more."

## Relationship Management Is Crucial

An outsourcing partnership can be effective and successful – it all depends on relationship management.

"The key is to develop a flexible contract," says Bendor-Samuel. "Build in very tight accountability and solid metrics. Be very clear in specifying how meetings will occur, how metrics will be communicated and the consequences for not meeting those or if something goes wrong."

April 2001 ■ **Reprinted with permission from** *Call Center Management Review*®, www.icmi.com.

11

Look for a service agency that is in the same industry or business that you're in, says Bob Cote, manager of Consumer Technical Support, Compaq Consumer. Cote manages six call centers in North America, four of which are outsourced.

Also, he says, select the agency that wants to be a partner. "I could have a lot of vendor relationships, but I really need a true partnership – someone who's going to put some skin in the game because they want to support Compaq and its customers."

Cote recommends visiting a potential service agency's call centers to evaluate the type of operation it runs. "Meet with the call center management teams to understand what the pluses and minuses have been for them in the relationship," he says. "Also, sit down with some of the agents on the phones to get an understanding of what types of tools they're using and what kinds of training they receive."

Finally, says Cote, make sure you have a solid quality process in place to ensure the service provider is meeting your expectations. While most outsourcing firms have processes or tools in place, he suggests being proactive in monitoring calls to see how your customers are being handled, and following up with evaluations and improvement processes.

On the flip side, Cote says, "for us to be successful, we have to make our partner successful, as well. You have to provide them with the right tools, training and technology to be able to deliver the support that you want them to deliver. You have to manage it on both sides of the house. If you get the mix right, it works very well." CCMReview

April 2001 ■ Reprinted with permission from *Call Center Management Review*®, www.icmi.com.

12

# Is 'Staff-Sharing' a Viable Option for Handling Seasonal Call Volume?

*by Greg Levin*

Finding skilled agents when you need them – and when all the other call centers in your area are dipping into the same local labor pool – is an art in itself. The staffing hurdles are even higher for centers whose year is divided into explosive peak seasons and extended "slower" periods. These centers must continually play a game of "hire and fire" to avoid the irreparable service damage caused by understaffing during busy months, and the wasteful costs of overstaffing during down times.

While "hire and fire" helps many centers maintain adequate service levels year-round without breaking the bank, it does take its toll – on both call center managers and agents. Managers have to continually endure the stress of finding qualified seasonal people – in a tight labor market – with whom to staff up the center during peak periods. And the seasonal staff have to accept the inevitable fact that, after a couple of months of work in the call center, they'll be out of a job again. This knowledge can have a negative impact on the seasonal agents' motivation, commitment and performance.

But what if instead of laying off your seasonal agents at the end of each peak period, you sent them to further hone their skills at another company's call center whose busy season is just beginning (and which pays agents a similar wage)? And what if that center agreed to send the agents – perhaps along with a few of its own – back to your center in time for your next peak period?

This "staff-sharing" approach can be particularly beneficial to companies located in over-saturated call center regions where hundreds of centers are battling for the same human resources. Many of these areas have extremely low unemployment rates, further complicating the traditional search for seasonal staff. Staff-sharing introduces an interesting "if you can't beat 'em, join 'em" option that could help many centers alleviate their recruiting pains. But does this unique approach have a future in the call center industry?

## Too Many Logistical Thorns?

Despite the allure of its potential advantages, staff-sharing has never been taken seriously by the mainstream call center community. It occasionally captures the attention of managers in search of creative staffing ideas, but it is usually dismissed as having too many logistical thorns to be effectively implemented. The mere thought of the perceived security concerns, cultural differences and training/supervisory challenges scare most managers away before they even begin the search for a compatible call center with which to form a staffing alliance.

## Staff-Sharing Benefits

It may sound like a strange arrangement, but consider the following potential benefits that a "staff-sharing" partnership can provide:

- It enables both centers to cost-effectively manage their seasonal peaks and valleys by reducing the high costs of continuous recruiting and training.

- It allows the centers to collectively offer year-round (or nearly year-round) employment to previously seasonal agents.

- It decreases burnout and enhances employee retention as agents are likely to enjoy the diversity that staff sharing offers, making them less apt to seek employment elsewhere.

- It facilitates cooperation and communication between the two centers, which can lead to other mutually beneficial ventures.

Other call center professionals feel that staff-sharing isn't feasible because of the changing face of customer care.

"The landscape of customer contact has changed such that the companies concerned about customer satisfaction and loyalty don't have the luxury [to share staff]," says Dr. Kathryn Jackson of call center consulting firm Response Design Corporation. "The complexities of customer relationship management along with the product/service mix and industry uniqueness make it nearly impossible to share resources."

## Sharing and Succeeding

Companies like Pleasant Co. and John Deere Credit (JDC) would beg to differ. In 1999, Pleasant Company – creators of American Girl books, dolls and accessories – formed a staffing alliance with lawn-mowing giant JDC as a way to provide seasonal employees with full-time positions and to reduce the number of seasonal people the call center needed to hire each season. According to Julie Parks, public relations manager with Pleasant Co., the alliance is still going strong.

"The partnership is a great way for us to offer more benefit-eligible positions, provide more consistent service throughout the year and keep our employees challenged with a new learning opportunity."

She adds that JDC was a perfect match for Pleasant Company because "JDC's peak season is opposite ours, they are located near our facility, and they have a similar corporate culture and service philosophy."

Carrie Rogers, call center supervisor at JDC, is equally satisfied with the alliance. "We have been very pleased with the relationship over the past two years," she says. "Our cultures and dedication to customer service make it a great pairing."

More than 50 agents from Pleasant

October 2000 ■ Reprinted with permission from *Call Center Management Review*®, www.icmi.com.

13

# Is Staff-Sharing Better as a Short-Term Solution?

While the alliance between Pleasant Co. and John Deere Credit has proven successful to date, recent history has shown that such ventures may not be a long-term solution. In 1996, WearGuard Corp. (manufacturer of work clothes/uniforms) and Cross Country Motor Club captured industrywide attention by creating the first formal call center staff-sharing alliance. The program involved 35 agents from each center and was deemed a success by both companies early on, but ended 18 months later when Cross Country outgrew the alliance and opened a second call center in Tuscon, Ariz.

"The arrangement with WearGuard helped us keep up with call volume when we didn't have the room [for additional staff] in our existing center," said Dotty Leavitt, director of call center operations for Cross Country, soon after the alliance ended. "But when we opened the new site, it didn't make sense for us to continue using WearGuard reps."

Although the alliance turned out to be only a short-term solution, Leavitt still considered it as a very successful venture. "It was like having a remote call center around when we needed it."

Another call center staffing alliance that starting off strongly ended recently in Ontario, Canada. The venture involved an outdoor supply company, whose peak season is March-August, and a retail manufacturer, whose peak season is September-January (both companies requested anonymity). The outdoor supply company originally decided to form the alliance to keep from losing some of its top agents.

"Our call volume dropped off mid-season, and we had too many agents," recalls the call center manager. "At the same time, [the other company's call center] was looking for staff, and one of our best agents went to apply. We realized that we were in danger of losing many of our top employees, so we gave their Human Resources department a call."

Soon thereafter, the staffing alliance was in place, with 10 agents from the outdoor supply company handling calls at the retail call center during its peak season. The agents returned to the outdoor supply company call center in March, when its call volume picked up.

Both call centers were pleased with the project until complications set in about a year later. "Unfortunately, it had to end because the other call center had changes in management as well as challenges with payroll issues," explains the manager of the outdoor supply company.

Today, his center uses temp agencies to meet its seasonal staffing needs. However, the manager says he would be open to forming another staffing alliance if the right company came along. And he recommends that other call center managers seriously consider staff-sharing if the opportunity arises. "I would strongly suggest it; it cuts down on layoffs, losing good agents and the cost of continually training new agents. It also improves staff morale at both companies because agents can see your effort in keeping them employed year-round."

---

Co.'s Middleton, Wis., call center currently participate in the staff-sharing venture. The majority of them handle calls at JDC's call center in nearby Madison from February until June (cleverly called "Deere Season"), with a few agents working through October. A Pleasant Co. supervisor is also on site to manage the shared agents and ensure that they adhere to JDC's performance standards. Then, when things start to slow down at JDC and speed up back at Pleasant Co.'s call center, the shared agents resume their original positions at Pleasant Co.

Because of the difference in call types between the two centers, Pleasant Co.'s agents receive specific training prior to working at JDC. The amount of training depends on the exact call type the agent will be handling and on whether or not he or she has previously participated in the staffing alliance.

To ensure that the shared agents aren't left out of the loop back at their original call center, Pleasant Co. regularly sends them updates and other company announcements via e-mail.

"One of the challenges during the first year [of the alliance] was keeping the job-share employees informed about Pleasant Co. news and information," says Parks. "We've alleviated this problem using e-mail updates."

When working at the JDC center, the shared agents are still considered Pleasant Co. employees; Pleasant Co. continues to provide the agents with their usual wages and benefits, then sends an invoice to JDC for reimbursement. As Parks explains, "These agents are strictly Pleasant Co. employees who split their time between two different call centers."

### Tips for Takers

Managers interested in staff-sharing should keep in mind that it is a unique practice with a short history. As such, there are no consulting companies, seminars or books that can explain exactly how to go about it. However, the handful of call centers that have shared agents can serve as helpful guides. Following are some key suggestions based on their experiences.

■ **Find a good match.** This is the biggest challenge in implementing a staff-sharing alliance, as so many variables need to fall into place. It isn't easy finding a local call center whose peak season is opposite yours, whose products and services don't compete with yours, and whose management is open to the idea of sharing staff. To do so, it's important to network with as many call center colleagues in your area as you can: attend local seminars and association meetings; look up call centers from your city at national conferences and chat with the managers; or simply call all of the local centers you know of. Ask them if they have predictable peak seasons, and how they manage them. If you find a potential "fit," introduce the subject of staff-sharing, and be sure to highlight the benefits to capture their interest.

If the manager is intrigued, schedule a visit to his or her center to further discuss the idea and to see how the center operates. Is the company a good match culturally as well as managerially? Are there performance

October 2000 ■ Reprinted with permission from *Call Center Management Review®*, www.icmi.com.

14

standards similar to those at your center? How much training do they provide agents? Is their technology outdated? Do they micro-manage?

"Make sure there's a good fit," advises Cross Country's Leavitt. "You may not sell the same products or services, but you have to share the same philosophy."

■ **Get executive buy-in.** After you've found a suitable staffing partner, it's time to get approval for the venture from senior management. First focus their attention on your current seasonal staffing challenges and the associated recruiting and training costs. Then describe the financial advantages of the proposed alliance and ask for approval to try it out. Let them know that other companies have successfully shared staff in the past, and that the project could at least serve as an effective short-term solution.

■ **Build a solid foundation.** Once you receive the green light from upper management, create a project team composed of call center managers and supervisors, human resources managers and trainers from each company. The team should meet regularly to discuss the key issues and to draw up a formal agreement documenting how the alliance will work. Make sure you answer the following questions: Will agents from one center or both centers be shared? How many total agents will be involved? Which agents will participate? How will compensation and benefits be handled? How much training is needed, when will it take place and who will provide it?

■ **Develop agent selection criteria.** Your alliance partner may not be able to use all of your seasonal agents, so you need to have objective selection criteria in place to determine which agents will be able to participate in the alliance. Centers typically select staff based on seniority and experience. However, seniority should not be the sole indicator – less-experienced temps who are top performers and enthusiastic can be successful, as well. Also keep in mind the types of calls your agents

will be handling at your partner's center. Perhaps sales skills are needed more than softer skills, or perhaps the position calls for e-mail response skills. Make sure you choose seasonal staff who have the best chance of succeeding at the new center.

■ **Work out a fair compensation and benefits package.** For staff-sharing to work well, agent pay and benefits should be comparable at both centers. To avoid complications and excessive payroll paperwork at each company, most centers keep their own agents on their respective payrolls, then bill the partner for the compensation and benefits costs at the end of each season. Be sure that you and your partner fully understand who will pay for what prior to implementing the alliance, as well as any differences in wages and benefits that may cause problems later on. Don't forget to explain to participating agents exactly how compensation will be handled during the alliance.

■ **Plan on initial and refresher training.** Formal training is an essential aspect of effective staffing alliances. Just because you are using agents who already work in a call center environment doesn't mean that they know how to handle your specific call types. Most centers that share staff spend at least a week training their partners' agents prior to putting them on the phones. And when your agents return from a staff-sharing stint, don't forget to provide then with a day or two of refresher training since some of your procedures and/or technology may have changed since they last handled calls at your center.

■ **Maintain contact to effectively manage the alliance.** The agreement's been signed. The initial training's been completed. Your alliance is set to begin. The key to success from this point on is open communication. Maintain regular contact with your partner center to check the status of the project and to make sure that your agents are happy and performing up to par. Consider having one of your own supervisors on staff at the part-

ner center during its peak season. This will not only help to enhance your communication with your partner throughout the venture, it may also help your agents feel more comfortable in their new environment.

Similarly, when it's your turn to use your partner's agents, do everything you can to make them feel like a part of your company: include them in teams, contests and other incentives. Also, be sure that they fully understand your center's performance objectives and that they are evaluated based on the same standards as your core staff. Unequal treatment of shared agents will only lead to problems on your front lines, problems that can wreak havoc on customer service.

### No Quick Executions While the Jury's Out

Does staff-sharing have a future in the call center industry? The jury is still out. But just because this unique approach to peak-season staffing has yet to make big waves in the industry doesn't mean that, with the right partner and careful planning, it couldn't work well at your call center.

Today's exponential call center growth calls for creative alternatives to traditional staffing techniques. While sharing staff may not make strategic and/or financial sense for your operation, don't write it off before taking a closer look at the approach. After all, just consider what you spent the last few years on hiring and training to prepare for your peak season. *CCMReview*

Greg Levin

*Greg Levin is the former editor of* Call Center Management Review. *Greg is a regular contributor to the publication, and also writes the "In Your Ear" call center humor column. He is currently a freelance writer based in Spain.*

**Section 9**

October 2000 ■ **Reprinted with permission from** Call Center Management Review®, www.icmi.com.

15

# The Role of Corporate Culture in Agent Commitment

*by Jean Bave-Kerwin*

Developing a career development process won't help you retain agents if your culture is not committed to continual learning.

It's no coincidence that the Digital Products Customer Support call center at Eastman Kodak Co.'s Americas Call Center Operations in Chili, NY, can claim a zero turnover rate for the past two years.

Call Center Manager Nancy Sweet's approach to creating satisfied customer service representatives begins with her understanding of what causes agent burnout, dissatisfaction and internal pressure to leave for a better job.

There's been increasing evidence that a "better" job to employees isn't necessarily a higher-paying one. Instead, workers are looking for satisfaction in the type of work performed, respectful treatment by the company, coaching and feedback, and the opportunity to learn new skills – all of which are aspects of company culture.

Well-known customer loyalty expert Frederick Reichheld recently commented in *CIO Enterprise Magazine* that the key to an effective corporate culture is to systematically implement programs which improve "specific aspects of the working environment," rather than to mistakenly assume that better benefits equals a better culture. And the "telltale sign of an effective corporate culture is loyalty – the percentage of employees and customers who stay with the company."

Then, apparently, Kodak is doing something right. In fact, the company has a set of values that are explicit, widely held and clearly understood by all employees. They are:

■ Respect for individual dignity
■ Uncompromising integrity
■ Trust
■ Credibility
■ Continuous improvement
■ Recognition

Naturally, in an organization that lives and works by such principles, managers have a jump-start on the kind of supporting culture which is

---

## Employee Commitment Facts

• *Training Magazine* points to two studies listing the keys to employee retention and loyalty. More pay is not included in the top-ranking factors.

• According to research by The Hay Group, a human resources consulting firm, the most important contributors to employee satisfaction are:

| | |
|---|---|
| The type of work | 89% |
| Respectful treatment | 69% |
| Coaching and feedback | 64% |
| Learning new skills | 61% |

• Aon Consulting of Chicago reported these top five reasons for employee satisfaction:
1. Employer's recognition of personal and family time.
2. The organization's vision and direction.
3. Personal growth opportunities.
4. The ability to challenge the way things are done.
5. Everyday work satisfaction.

---

widely acknowledged to produce employee satisfaction and its logical result, employee retention.

Sweet feels that the journey to achieving agent satisfaction depends heavily on reps knowing what is expected of them, participating in the decisions around those expectations and the certainty that the organization's leadership will support them in achieving individual and company goals.

## The Road to Agent Satisfaction

The journey on the road to agent satisfaction begins with managers and supervisors having a thorough understanding of the business unit which they support. This understanding drives consistency in the process of providing customer support.

---

## A Checklist for Positive Agent Development

• Set up a planned program of skills acquisition for CSRs as a regular part of on-the-job training. Reward them for each level of achievement.
• Hold lunch break seminars on any topic of interest. Ask in-house experts to share info on work-related and nonwork-related subjects. Get agents involved with planning and running the seminars.
• Provide Web-based training or computer-based training to improve customer service skills and/or knowledge sets.
• Provide tuition reimbursement for any outside course, whether or not it's related to work.
• Meet regularly with agents to share information on work-related issues, or to research and solve a problem that's been bugging you.
• Provide continuing education unit credit instruction in enterprise-related fields.
• Use your company's Web page or intranet to link to sites that relate to your business. Encourage agents to explore what's going on in your industry.
• Create a list of subject matter experts in your organization – encourage agents to qualify to be on the list.
• Incent agents to share learning.

---

**Section 9**

Agent Development and Retention Special Issue 2000 ■ Reprinted with permission from *Call Center Management Review*®, www.icmi.com.

16

Frequent communications and feedback loops ensure that agents know what's happening in the business unit and when, so they can be prepared for call volume spikes and new product information. In the Digital Products call center process, there is the opportunity for give-and-take on issues that affect the center's ability to handle the customer traffic.

In addition, call center leadership must work with agents to establish goals, which should be clearly communicated to the entire call center.

Individual performance plans can then be developed for each agent, again, with their input. At Kodak, agents are measures on performance factors like call quality, training adherence and demonstration of company values in their customer interactions.

## Address Agent Development in a Positive Way

The company makes a strong commitment to supporting employee realization of individual goals. Fifty percent of every training dollar spent on employees goes toward fostering success on their current job, and the other half is spent on helping them to be successful in a future position.

Agents receive at least one hour of training every day before the call center opens. Individual coaching is also available. Sweet feels that this incredible level of commitment to continual learning contributes heavily to the high customer satisfaction ratings (97 percent), as well as to the low turnover rate.

Each team has a "sponsor" for every metric. That person is responsible for assuring that the metric is understood, measurements are taken and communicated and that additional coaching is available if needed.

Sweet feels that, to have a high-performance work culture, companies are obligated to position their people so that they can be successful. Her goal is to teach her agents to think, make decisions and act. **CCMReview**

**Jean Bave-Kerwin**

*Jean Bave-Kerwin is president of JBK Consulting, a firm specializing in call center and customer service solutions for the public and not-for-profit sectors, and is founding president of the Call Center Management Association of New York. She has managed six call centers for a large government agency, an entrepreneurial government marketing organization and served as an internal consultant to a number of agencies on call center issues. Jean has experience in organizational development, leadership, process improvement consulting, project management and human resources. She can be reached at jbavekerwin@goer.state.ny.us.*

Agent Development and Retention Special Issue 2000  ■  **Reprinted with permission from *Call Center Management Review*®, www.icmi.com.**

17

Section 9

# Key Aspects of Successful Agent Retention Processes

*by Greg Levin*

Section 9

Call centers are hemorrhaging staff as never before. Typical call center attrition rates fall between the 30 percent to 50 percent range, with rates over 100 percent not at all unheard of.

In recent years, many companies have claimed a renewed focus on and respect of phone staff, but the mass agent-exodus – and the exorbitant costs associated with it – continues. Why?

"I really don't think that the majority of call center managers focus on what needs to be done to improve agent retention," says Laura Sikorski, managing partner of consulting firm Sikorski-Tuerpe & Associates. "They go through the motions of conducting 'exit interviews' with all the agents who decide to leave, but they don't do anything with the information they gather. They seem to have bought into the myth that high turnover is inevitable in the call center environment."

And that's a costly myth to buy into – especially today, with added pressures on call centers and agents to effectively handle an ever-increasing and more demanding customer base using a wide range of contact channels.

*CCMReview* recently scanned the entire industry to pinpoint the key factors associated with high staff retention. Let's take a look at some of those, with examples of call centers that are doing innovative things in specific areas.

## Fair and Creative Compensation

Like anybody in the job market, agents want to be paid not just a competitive wage, but one that reflects the value of their skill, effort and impact on their specific organization.

"We're asking agents to know more, to compile and manage more customer data, to be generalist and specialists, and to upsell and cross-sell, yet the industry has depressed agents' wages because it still insists on viewing the job as entry level," says Mary Beth Ingram, president of call center training firm Phone Pro.

Many of the best-managed call centers not only pay agents a decent starting wage, they've also implemented skills-based pay programs that enable agents to earn additional pay as they attain more advanced skills and knowledge. For example, one U.S. pet supply company starts its customer service agents off at an ample $24,000 a year and gives them the opportunity to earn up to $35,000 if they complete all 20 modules of the center's "skills ladder." One of the center's supervisors says that the starting salary and skills-based pay opportunities play a big part in maintaining the call center's 92 percent agent retention rate.

"People here don't look at the call center as merely a place to begin a career, but as a place to have a career," says the supervisor. She adds that the center's compensation approach not only helps to retain quality staff, it helps to attract a diverse group of quality applicants when the center is hiring; 19 different college degrees are represented among the center's 35 agents.

## Incentives and Recognition

While money can be a strong motivator, agents need additional enticements and encouragement to perform in what can be a very challenging environment, as well as recognition whenever they do perform well.

Strong incentive programs and recognition practices needn't require a significant financial investment. True, cash bonuses and large gift certificates make nice rewards for contest winners, but so do paid time off, recognition in company newsletters, trophies/plaques and time off the phones to work on special projects.

Call centers with the most successful incentive programs offer a mix of monetary and non-monetary awards that are based on both quality and productivity measurements. And they recognize both individual and team or center-wide achievement. (See "Incentives that Rev Up and Retain Agents," *CCMReview*, Feb. 2000.)

Call centers focused on staff retention involve agents in the development and maintenance of the incentive programs, either by asking them for feedback on what type of rewards they prefer or, as in the case of Air Canada, by letting agents run the show. Air Canada's Vancouver call center implemented an agent-led incentive program in 1996 to empower staff and enhance motivation and retention. Leading the program is a six-agent Incentive Committee that creates and promotes each contest and decides on the prizes awarded, such as gift certificates to hotels, restaurants, movie theaters and retail stores. "Agents have their fingers on the pulse of our center, so they are the natural people to create incentives for everyone," says manager Butch Gregoire.

Other call centers encourage agents to recognize each other's accomplishments. For example, mail order cataloger JD Williams in Manchester, England, sponsors a monthly "Flair Award," in which agents nominate peers who demonstrate outstanding performance.

May 2000 ∎ Reprinted with permission from *Call Center Management Review*®, www.icmi.com.

18

## Project Involvement and Decision-Making

One of the best – and easiest – ways to enhance the overall image of the agent position and improve retention is to actively involve agents in variety of important projects, processes and decisions in the call center. Smart call centers are tapping the talent and energy of their agents to enhance such crucial areas as hiring, training, monitoring and, as mentioned earlier in the Air Canada example, incentives/recognition.

Mentoring programs – where veteran agents pair up with new-hires to help guide them through initial training and/or their first days handling calls – have become increasingly popular. For example, trainees at Today's Merchandising's call center in Peoria, Ill., are partnered with experienced agents for nearly a month before going solo on the phones. Since introducing its "New Employee Partners" program in 1996, the call center has seen a significant reduction in turnover – for both new-hires and experienced agents – and an increase in overall performance and morale.

Peer monitoring programs – where agents evaluate each other's calls and provide constructive feedback – are also starting to take off in call centers. Not only does peer monitoring empower agents to enhance quality in the call center and learn valuable coaching skills, it helps to reduce agents' fear of and resistance to having their calls evaluated only by supervisors/managers. Most call centers with effective peer monitoring programs, such as Lands' End in Cross Plains, Wis., use the program to supplement the center's supervisor-led call monitoring methods.

Nobody knows the agent job – and what it takes to succeed in that job – like a call center's existing agents. That's why more and more centers are involving agents in the

hiring process. The benefits of such an approach can be twofold: Turnover among existing agents drops because they see that the company respects their opinion and job knowledge; and turnover among new-hires drops because experienced agents help to enhance the selection process.

A recent study by call center consulting firm Response Design Corp. indicated that when centers include existing agents in the hiring process, new-hires are better matched with the company culture, begin the job with a clear understanding of their roles and responsibilities, and more quickly form bonds with co-workers.

### Transition Training

Much of the turnover that rattles call centers occurs among new-hires. Even centers that offer weeks of training often lose agents early on because the agents are ill-prepared for the challenging and fast-paced world that awaits them on the phones.

Many call centers have stemmed early turnover by implementing some form of a "transition training" program, where new-hires – who've completed or nearly completed adequate initial training – begin handling basic customer calls bator" while under close (see "Ensuring New-Hire 'Transition Training,'" C

---

## Study Identifies Factors Impacting Call Center Culture

Call Center culture has a direct impact on agent retention, as well as productivity, service delivery and financial success, according to *Call Center Culture: The Hidden Success Factor in Achieving Service Excellence*, a study by The Radclyffe Group. The study surveyed nearly 1,500 CSRs and managers in more than a dozen industries to identify the issues that make working in a call center so challenging.

### FOUR FACTORS IMPACT CULTURE

The study found that there are four common factors within call centers that impact the culture or the way agents feel about their jobs:
1. The rules are perceived as stringent and inflexible.
2. The work is stressful by nature.
3. Call centers tend to assess overall performance using quantitative measures.
4. Schedules and phone time are managed in the moment.

### KEY DIFFERENTIATORS OF POSITIVE CULTURE

The study found that, in those call centers in which a negative culture exists, 70 percent of respondents say that the key differentiators to positive culture are missing. Those are: effective communication, professional development, employee job satisfaction and trust.
- **Effective communication.** In centers that ranked high for positive culture, just under 70 percent reported that the the flow of communication within the organization is open and direct, compared with 46 percent in the middle responding companies and only 30 percent reported by the bottom five companies.
- **Professional development.** Only 19 percent of employees in call centers with negative cultures agree that they receive timely feedback for improving their performance.
- **Employee satisfaction.** Nearly 80 percent of respondents say their call center does not encourage them to do their best.
- **Trust.** Only 14 percent of respondents agree that people trust each other in their call centers.

The study also identified specific success factors that were found to contribute to positive call center culture. Those included: reps being proud to work in the organization; having a strong sense of identity within the company; and receiving the direction, training and feedback necessary to do their jobs well and to be successful.

*Source: The Radclyffe Group, 973-276-0522; Web site www.radclyffegroup.com*

May 2000 ■ Reprinted with permission from *Call Center Management Review®*, www.icmi.com.

19

Sept. 1999). In such a nurturing environment, new agents develop the confidence and skills they need to succeed on the regular phone floor, and thus are less likely to end their call center career early due to fear and frustration.

Toyota Financial Service's customer service center – which boasts a mere 10 percent agent attrition rate – credits its in-depth transition training with helping to significantly bolster retention. Following a two-week initial training program, new-hires at the call center in Cedar Rapids, Iowa, participate in the two-week transition program, where they handle basic call types (i.e., billing questions) in a separate "transition bay." A trainer and several coaches support, monitor and provide feedback to trainees, who then head back to the classroom for three more weeks of training. Once that is completed, trainees return to the transition bay to practice handling more complex call types until they are ready to work on the main phone floor.

While such extensive training programs require some capital investment, the pay-off can be extraordinary. "Yes, there are costs associated with lengthening the overall training process," says Dan Lowe, a consultant who has worked closely with Toyota and other call centers that have implemented transition programs. "But consider the costs of not implementing a transition program, [particularly] the costs of rehiring and retraining due to high agent turnover."

## Agent Development and Advancement

Most call centers spend too much time obsessing over Customer Relationship Management and not enough time on Agent Relationship Management. While nurturing customers and maximizing their value is important, it mustn't overshadow the importance of developing powerful and lucrative relationships with frontline staff members.

Arrowhead Water's call center in Brea, Calif., has implemented a formal "Leadership Program" to enhance agent career opportunities and retention. The two-year program is open to any agent who has worked in the center and performed well for at least a year. Agents who are selected for the program learn the details of each call center job and work on a variety of projects that test agents' initiative, time management skills and creativity. As they progress through the program, agents spend less time on the phones and more time working on projects, receiving occasional pay increases as they advance.

After completing the program, agents become eligible for frontline supervisory and other positions in the call center. "We're showing people that they don't have to go elsewhere to grow," says Jim Maguire, manager of the center.

Some call centers – particularly smaller ones – may not have the luxury of implementing a formal career path for agents. In such centers, agent "certification" and skills-based pay programs enable agents to "move up" in the call center while remaining on the phones to handle valuable customers.

Pitney Bowes' Mailing Systems Division has a skill-based pay program in place at its call centers that features 50 skill blocks divided into three categories: 1. core, 2. advanced, and 3. expert. Once an agent completes the training module for a particular skill block, he or she takes a written certification test on that skill block. Those who pass the test are deemed "certified" in that skill, and a specific dollar amount is added to their base salary.

"We have more control over our future now," says Joney Ashley, an agent at Pitney Bowes' call center in Spokane, Wash. "If you know the plan up front and you know there are opportunities, you're more inclined to stay at the company."

### Pre-Employment Testing Can Reveal High-Risk Agents

What's the main reason agents quit their jobs? It's not low pay or a lack of skills to do the work, rather it's simply because they don't like what they do, according to long-term research conducted by human resource consulting firm The DeGarmo Group.

The DeGarmo Group also recently conducted a six-month study to determine the effectiveness of its Call Center Fix Index (CCFI) for identifying candidates who have a high risk, marginal risk or low risk of turnover. The CCFI is a pre-employment test to assess job tolerance and personality characteristics by which candidates can be classified.

The study tracked 72 applicants for entry-level CSR positions at a mid-sized call center. Of the 72 applicants, 25 were rated high risk, 24 as marginal risk and 23 as low risk. At the end of the six-month period, only 12 of the high-risk agents were still employed, while 18 of the low-risk agents remained employed. The marginal risk category was split fairly evenly with 13 still employed. Of the 28 employees who quit, 22 did so within 54 days. Of those 22, only three were categorized as low-risk.

"Depending on how rigorous an organization wants to be with respect to the selection criteria they use, turnover reduction can vary," says Anthony Adorno, vice president, The DeGarmo Group. "In this particular environment, if they hired only low-risk and marginal candidates, turnover could be reduced by 28 percent; if they hire only low-risk applicants, they could be able to cut turnover by 48 percent." He adds that eliminating high- and marginal-risk candidates in the screening process can also help call centers save recruiting, testing and training costs.

*Contact: The DeGarmo Group, 309-820-1435; Web site www.degarmogroup.com*

May 2000 ■ Reprinted with permission from *Call Center Management Review®*, www.icmi.com.

20

## Fair and Attainable Performance Objectives

The simple act of determining your center's service level goals – and how you go about measuring agents' success in meeting those goals – has a huge influence on how long staff will stay in the call center. Too many call centers – often with pressure from upper management to cut operating costs – set unattainable performance objectives that set agents up for frustration and failure, and set the call center up for poor retention and customer loyalty.

One call center, Rodale Books in Emmaus, Pa., has created what it calls a "relationship-based" environment, where call center statistics are practically ignored. Instead, agent and center-wide performance are measured using a formal quality program that incorporated monitoring scores and customer survey results.

"We don't count things like number of calls answered per hour," says Jeanne Dorney, manager of customer service for Rodale and winner of the 1998 U.S. Call Center Manager of the Year award. "We look at how well agents do their job and how the customers perceive the service."

Dorney made the move from a mere transaction-based environment to a more relationship-based one after agents told her that they felt micromanaged. Once she found out how her staff felt, Dorney created a unique "declaration of independence," which lists specific goals that agents strive for independently and a pledge from management to focus less on the daily

## Healthy Agents Work Better, Stay Longer

It's difficult to achieve healthy service levels and customer loyalty without healthy agents. Commitment to effective call center design/ergonomics and stress-reduction practices can have a tremendous impact on staff performance, morale and retention.

That's exactly what Wisconsin Power and Light (a division of Alliant Utilities) was thinking when it introduced its "Keep Well" program at its Janesville, Wis., call center several years ago. In addition to providing all agents with ample 7x7 foot cubicles equipped with ergonomically advanced chairs, footrests/armrests and electric workstation tabletops (so that each workstation can be adjusted to the proper height), the center brings in an occupational therapist to work with each new training class. The therapist shows each new-hire how to adjust their equipment and position their bodies to avoid Cumulative Trauma Disorder (CTS).

The company contracts with a massage therapist to work on tense agents during the peak season (April-October), and the call center also has "quiet rooms" – equipped with comfortable couches/recliners, books and CD players – where agents can retreat when things get hectic. One room even has three exercise machines for agents who want to pedal or jog away their tensions.

The company's investment has paid off; as management says that, since introducing the "Keep Well" program, agent absenteeism and turnover have dropped while productivity has risen.

task sheet that agents complete each day.

## Create Agent Careers

The call center has evolved rapidly in recent years and has the potential to become a powerful entity within the enterprise. But this will not happen until the call center's own agents develop the desire to launch the center to that level.

To create ambition and dedication among staff, companies must show them that they are key players and reward them accordingly. Agents are much less likely to leave if they perceive that they have a career, not a job.

"For many people, the agent profession could be a such wonderful, long-term career opportunity full of pride and satisfaction," says Phone

Pro's Ingram, "But corporations haven't done enough to put the call center or the agent position in that light. It's a matter of equitable compensation, providing fulfilling opportunities and valuing people. It's so damn simple!" CCMReview

### Greg Levin

*Greg Levin is the former editor of* Call Center Management Review. *Greg is a regular contributor to the publication, and also writes the In Your Ear call center humor column. He is currently a freelance writer and teacher based in Spain.*

**Section 9**

May 2000 ■ Reprinted with permission from *Call Center Management Review®*, www.icmi.com.

21

# Understanding the Costly Threat of Agent Turnover

*By Seymour Burchman and Debra Schmitt*

In this burgeoning economy of extraordinary growth, there remains a serious issue that is devastating to profits, especially in call center services companies. The problem is the high cost of employee turnover. In all U.S. industries last year, the median turnover rate was 15 percent. Yet in the call center services sector, it was more than twice that rate, according to research by Sibson & Company, a global management consulting firm, an operating unit of Nextera Enterprises.

Some call centers routinely experience turnover rates well in excess of 100 percent. It's easy to see why turnover is rated by most call center managers as one of the top three managerial challenges. The large cost, compared to both earning and transaction revenues, justifies this concern.

Sibson recently completed a study that focused on frontline employees – those who directly affect a company's customers because they can have a significant impact on revenue generation and growth potential. Let's take a look at the three key areas examined in the study: staff turnover costs, causes and cures.

## Understand the True Cost of Agent Turnover

With the jobless rate at a 30-year low, the tight labor market exacerbates the problem of replacing agents who leave. Recruiting new people in this strong economy is more difficult and takes more time. High employee turnover requires companies to spend resources to replace existing employees rather than hiring for growth. Consequently, many companies are forced to operate under-capacity, limiting sales and market share growth in a strong economic environment.

Replacing an agent is expensive because of:

1. **Direct costs** such as recruiting costs, training costs and paying temporary agency fees and overtime.

2. **Opportunity costs**, which include lost customers due to poor service and quality, decreased productivity and having to operate under-capacity.

3. **Indirect costs**, such as reduced morale, loss of organizational knowledge, hampered growth rates and inefficient use of corporate staff time.

By solving the employee turnover problem, companies have a great opportunity to improve profitability and stock prices. Yet many companies approach the issue with methods destined for defeat. Other organizations accept turnover as a cost of doing business, without calculating the actual expense.

Understanding the true cost of employee turnover builds the business

## Calculating Return on Investment

**Step 1: Identify direct replacement and opportunity costs:**

A. Direct Replacement Costs: $1.3 million
- Overtime cost of peers to cover open positions
- Temporary agency fees to cover for open positions
- Extra overtime by new employees to move up the learning curve
- Percent of time spent by first-line supervisors addressing turnover
- Recruiting costs associated with turnover
- Training costs associated with turnover
- Separation processing costs

B. Opportunity Costs: $4.4 million
- Productivity costs
- Revenue from lost accounts
- Cost of operating under-capacity

**Step 2: Estimate ROI of Reducing Turnover**

A. Determine Potential Cost Savings
(Direct + Opportunity Costs) x (Feasible Turnover Reduction Estimate)
$5.7 million x 50% = $2.8 million

B. Estimate Turnover Reduction Investments
Training and Recruiting Costs: $440,000
Recruiting Fees: $20,000
Reengineering Costs: $200,000
Total Investment: $660,000

C. Calculate ROI
ROI = (Potential Cost Savings) / Turnover Reduction Investments x 100%
$2.8 million/$660,000 = 424%

**Step 3: Estimate Impact on Net Income and Market Capitalization**

A. Determine Potential Improvement to Net Income
(Cost Savings - Investments) x (Effective Tax Rate)
($2.8 million - $660,000) x (1-40%) = $1.3 million

B. Determine Potential Gain in Market Capitalization
(Turnover Reduction Improvement on Net Income) x (Price/Earnings Ratio)
$1.3 million x 10 = $13 million (47% improvement over initial value of $28 million)

November 2000 ■ Reprinted with permission from *Call Center Management Review*®, www.icmi.com.

22

case for change (see box, left). The first step is to identify the employee segments that represent the largest turnover costs. In the Sibson study, the focus was on telemarketing service representatives (TSRs) because of their significant impact on revenue generation and growth potential – a company's top line.

In call centers, there are 2.5 million employees in this category and Sibson estimates that the annual direct cost of turnover in corporate and stand-alone call center services companies is $5.4 billion, or 43 percent of industry earnings. When taken to the level of an individual company, this savings not only has a profound effect on earnings, but also on stock price. Assuming a constant price-to-earnings ratio, a 43 percent reduction in earnings translates into a 43 percent reduction in stock price. These calculations represent only direct replacement costs. They do not take into account the opportunity or indirect costs.

## Research the Root Causes

Although some companies recognize the high cost of employee turnover and have taken steps to reduce it, many managers find that their efforts reap little value because they implement traditional solutions without truly understanding the root causes of the problem. Actions such as increasing salaries across the enterprise may not produce the expected results because the reasons for employee departures vary from group to group. Without a robust qualitative and quantitative fact base, managers cannot determine root causes or estimate the expected return on turnover reduction efforts.

A recommended methodology for determining the multifaceted causes of employee turnover and creating cost-effective strategies for solving the problem, involves three key steps. Managers can develop a solid fact base by:

**Self-Perpetuating Turnover Cycle**

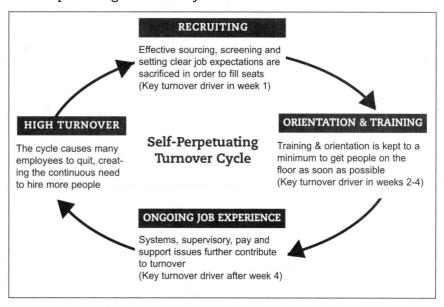

- examining turnover and operational data by agent population,

- conducting agent focus groups and using Web-based employee surveys, and

- analyzing what is causing agents to start looking elsewhere.

This qualitative and quantitative analysis results in the discovery of specific employee populations with the highest costs of turnover and the causes of this turnover.

Once employee populations are identified, it is often necessary to segment the population even further to clearly identify the costs and root causes of turnover. For instance, in one call center, the employees were segmented into categories of part-time and full-time and then divided again into shifts. The overall turnover rate was 386 percent and the rate for part-time employees was 714 percent. Also, turnover among night-shift people was higher than for day-shift agents. This analysis highlighted for management the employee population where turnover was the greatest.

The next analysis focused on attrition rates. Within one week, more than 20 percent of new-hires had resigned. By the end of the first month, more than 40 percent had left. And by the end of six months, the company had lost nearly 75 percent of its new-hires.

The high attrition rate within the first week points to problems in sourcing and recruiting people suited for this type of work. Research revealed that part of the problem was the screening process. During interviews, candidates were not given a clear picture of the job responsibilities, critical skills were not screened for and recruiters were overselling the job. As a result, people who were hired had unrealistic job expectations and inadequate skill sets – setting the stage for high turnover.

The high attrition rate within the first six months – nearly 75 percent – pointed to another problem. Interviews with employees showed dissatisfaction with training and orientation. Initial classroom training was minimal and only covered basic policies and procedures. Moreover, "on-the-job" training was insufficient because of resource constraints and supervisors were ill-prepared to train and coach their employees.

After six months, the research revealed that turnover continued

November 2000 ■ Reprinted with permission from *Call Center Management Review*®, www.icmi.com.

23

because employees were dissatisfied with their on-going job experience and the company's employee value proposition (see box, above). TSRs had trouble understanding the pay and time-tracking system, as well as the bonus program. They also complained about inconsistent management practices, especially in the area of attendance. All of these problems, taken together, created a high turnover cycle, which was self-perpetuating.

## Base the Cure on the Root Causes

After delineating the root causes of turnover in this group of agents, the next step was to develop creative recommendations that used both traditional and nontraditional measures to solve the root problems. For the call center, analyses showed that investment in several areas would improve the situation.

■ The recruiting process was reengineered, including:

a. Defining the desired knowledge, skills and behaviors of a TSR and using this information as the foundation for screening and interviewing candidates.

b. Adding additional recruiters with improved skills.

c. Empowering recruiters to offer higher salaries to more qualified candidates.

d. Scripting interviews so that a realistic picture of the job was provided.

e. Bringing supervisors into the recruiting process. To make it easier for the supervisors to be involved in interviews a "group interview" was implemented, which provided a social setting in which the candidates could interact with several supervisors and peers.

■ A simple database was developed to provide management with up-to-date information on the recruiting, interviewing and hiring decisions. Also, the database tracks the effectiveness of the sourcing mediums and venues (radio, Internet, employee referrals, job fairs, etc.) by calculating the return on the investment.

■ With the right talent sitting in the orientation and training sessions, the overall learning curve was reduced by rethinking the approach to training, including:

a. Restructure the training content to be consistent with the critical TSR knowledge, skills and behaviors identified for the recruiting process.

b. Enhance the overall training experience, moving away from the theoretical to a more practical learning environment by incorporating role-play, simulation and workshops with feedback sessions.

c. Foster a learning environment, making training readily available, e.g. videos, subject-matter-experts, reading material, Web-based training programs, etc.

d. Create a mentoring and coaching program that identifies development opportunities and a personal training plan for each agent.

■ The management and supervisory staff were evaluated, based on key competencies for the job. Those who required skill development were given additional training, while others were replaced. Promotion and performance appraisal criteria were also adjusted to reflect the newly developed competencies. Pay programs were also adjusted to reflect the emphasis on people skills.

■ The pay programs for TSRs were revised and new communication programs were introduced to help explain them. Non-cash recognition programs were retooled and expanded.

## Measure Results by Savings, Morale and Call Center Image

After implementing the changes, the call center reported significant savings, not only to the bottomline, but to the top line, as well.

The final task, of course, is to ensure the process is ongoing – and to follow up on the agent retention program to measure actual savings and the impact on the company's earnings and stock price. The overall effect of an employee retention program is not only measured in monetary terms, but also in improved agent morale, increased business opportunities and enhanced image of the company in the marketplace. **CCMReview**

S. Burchman    Debra Schmitt

*Seymour Burchman is a principal at Sibson & Co. He works with companies to more effectively use human capital to support the business strategies and increase shareholder value. Mr. Burchman can be reached at Sibson's Princeton, NJ, office at 609-520-2700 or burchman@sibson.com.*

*Debra Schmitt is a Senior Consultant at Sibson & Co. Ms. Schmitt develops and implements effective people strategies and practices that improve an organization's return on human capital. She can be reached in the Los Angeles office at 310-231-1781 or schmitt@sibson.com*

November 2000  ■  Reprinted with permission from *Call Center Management Review*®, www.icmi.com.

24

## In The Center with Beverly Kaye and Sharon Jordan-Evans ▬

# Low-Cost (and No Cost) Strategies for Retaining Agents

**Strategies for keeping talented agents that won't strain the call center budget.**

One of the toughest challenges contact centers face is agent turnover. Whether the cause is burnout, dissatisfaction with opportunities, the boss or the pay, well-trained people are leaving contact centers faster than they can be replaced.

Despite the recent softening of the job market, good contact center agents are still hard to get and harder to retain. And as the economy improves and employment opportunities increase in other fields, contact centers can be expected to face even greater retention challenges.

Consider the cost of this talent loss. There is no doubt that losing a well-trained contact center agent is expensive. Industry studies indicate that it costs an average $15,000 to replace a contact center agent. That figure doesn't include the loss of productivity and other costs that are incurred following a talented person's departure and last throughout the orientation and training of his or her replacement.

### Inexpensive New-Hire Retention Strategies

Given the expensive price tag of unwanted turnover, most managers want to do what they can to keep their best people for as long as they possibly can. The good news is, there are many no-cost or low-cost strategies managers can use to engage and retain talent. These approaches have consistently worked in contact centers across industries – and

sometimes despite difficult jobs (with challenging customers) and less than ideal compensation packages. Of course, we're not saying pay doesn't matter. In fact, it is important that you pay agents competitive and fair salaries.

But our research tells us that, beyond pay, there are many other reasons people stay with an organization. Focus on the following strategies and you'll increase the odds of keeping your best agents and supervisors.

■ **Managers (from the top down) must be retention-focused.** A key staff engagement and retention driver often involves developing a new managerial mindset (for some managers and executives). Company leaders must believe that their people are their most critical assets, and that they, as leaders, have more power and influence than anyone else in the retention equation. One company lived this concept particularly well by making employee retention "part of the company DNA." The organization held to that belief by making managers at all levels accountable for engaging and retaining talent.

■ **Make sure hiring processes are designed to identify the right agents.** If you hire the right person for the job in the first place, you'll increase your chances of keeping him or her. This means identifying the critical factors that spell success for the job, such as skills, motivations, attitudes, even work style. Many managers interview their top-performing veteran agents to create a baseline. You can then develop interview questions that will reveal whether a candidate does or does not possess those attributes.

During the interview, it's important to ensure that the questions are posed by several people who represent varying management levels and responsibilities. This will ensure that you get different perspectives and input on each candi-

date.

Regardless of the tough employment market, it's critical to have the courage to reject applicants who, by all indications, won't make it in the long run (even if they're desperately needed in the short run).

■ **Develop an effective orientation and welcome process.** The risk for losing call center talent is highest during the first six months of employment. Recognizing that, once they're hired, you'll want to do what you can to "extend the handshake."

An effective method is to develop a solid orientation process with the call center manager in charge of the proceedings – it's not HR's job. The focus must be more involved than simply informing employees where the supplies and break rooms are located. Instead, this is the time for managers to begin developing a meaningful relationship with each new agent.

During orientation, managers should highlight potential career paths (within the contact center and companywide), as well as all learning and enrichment possibilities that are available. The goal is to help each carefully selected new team member to quickly get connected and to visualize his or her future in the organization.

### Retaining and Engaging Veteran Agents

What about the agents who are already on the job? How do you retain and engage them? Over the past three years, our two organizations have surveyed more than 14,000 employees from a cross-section of industries about what keeps them on the job. Following are a few instructive findings from our "What Keeps You?" survey.

■ **Retention drivers are under the manager's control.** The top five reasons employees stayed with an organization are (in descending order of frequency):

August 2002 ■ Reprinted with permission from *Call Center Management Review*®, www.icmi.com.

25

- Exciting and challenging work
- Career growth and development
- Working with great people
- Fair pay
- Good bosses

Yes, pay is on the list. Although many managers believe it is the most important "stay factor" of all, research (ours and many other industry studies) reveals that money consistently falls below other retention drivers. In fact, for decades, researchers have described money as a "hygiene" factor when it comes to employee retention – and it's a dissatisfier when viewed as insufficient, non-competitive or unfair.

But competitive pay will not retain skilled agents if they're bored, see no career path, dislike their colleagues or dislike their bosses. Significantly, four of the top five "stay" factors just mentioned can be influenced by the manager. In fact, most retention drivers are under the manager's control. One survey found that 50 percent of job satisfaction depends on the employee's relationship with the manager. It is because of this incredible influence that organizations are increasingly holding managers accountable for hiring, developing, engaging and, yes, retaining talent – even tying managerial compensation and bonuses to retention success.

■ **Make the job more interesting.** When the thrill is gone, so are your skilled agents. Job enrichment – making the work more interesting, fulfilling and/or challenging – is a critical retention strategy. It can help you to retain agents, not just physically, but mentally and emotionally, as well. Even if they're physically at their workstations, when agents get bored with the job, they can leave mentally, or "disengage." This surfaces through counterproductive activities, such as high absenteeism and mediocre performance.

Managers, however, can offer various job enrichment opportunities that can

*Managers who can create a team that works well together and vigorously supports each other are well on the way to building a retention culture.*

help to prevent physical departure and/or disengagement.

Enrichment strategies often take the form of tasks and responsibilities agents can take on in ways that promote personal autonomy and creativity. Or managers might consider offering veteran agents extended training or cross-training opportunities, or a rotation of work assignments to increase job variety. Other possibilities include agent participation in project management, brainstorming sessions to focus on how jobs can be enriched, or agent input on team and/or individual rewards and recognition.

■ **Give agents career growth and development opportunities.** Many contact centers are developing career paths for their people, and are getting creative in considering multiple career options (sometimes "upward" positions are in short supply). It's critical for the manager to be involved in this process – agents want their managers to partner with them in discovering and pursuing opportunities at work.

Managers, in turn, need to consider questions like: What's available and what do people want? Would a lateral move be useful or interesting? How can the agent's career goals and the organizational goals and plans mesh? And how can an employee's career goals be accomplished within the context of the contact center structure?

■ **People don't leave companies, they leave managers.** Therefore, it's important to show interest and become adept at holding "career conversations" on a regular basis with each agent you hope to keep. These conversations are critical to your agents' development as well as to their sense of belonging and importance to their manager and organization. Regularly touching base with your agents this way will keep them from looking around for greener pastures – and for a boss who cares.

■ **Develop a sense of camaraderie among staff.** The third key reason for staying in a job from our "What Keeps You?" survey is the ability to work with great people. Coworker relationships are critical to job satisfaction – and managers who can create a team that works well together and vigorously supports each other are well on the way to building a retention culture.

But doing so requires your time and effort. Successful managers take the time to listen carefully to the needs of each individual, and do what they can to help that person feel fulfilled and satisfied in the job. They also create an atmosphere in which people's needs, opinions, values, work-styles and accomplishments are respected, valued and rewarded. The contact center environment presents some special issues when it comes to work/life balance and the importance of schedule adherence. Savvy managers will recognize their employees' needs and creatively partner with them to find solutions that work. That kind of caring will engender loyalty in a era when many think loyalty is dead.

## The Rewards Are Worth the Effort

The tremendous need for more contact centers, coupled with a tight employee market, means that managers need to hire skillfully, and then help their talented agents to grow, develop, and flourish within the contact center environment.

It's a tall order. But it's one that retention-focused contact center managers can efficiently and cost-effectively fill to perfection. CCMReview

**Beverly Kaye and Sharon Jordan-Evans**

*Beverly Kaye and Sharon Jordan-Evans are co-authors of* Love 'em or Lose 'em: Getting Good People to Stay *(Berrett-Koehler, 2002). Beverly is president of Career Systems International (www.careersystemsintl.com), based in Scranton, Pa.. She can be reached at 800-577-6916. Sharon, president of The JordanEvans Group (www.jeg.org) in Cambria, Calif., can be reached at 805-927-1432.*

**Section 9**

# Ensuring New-Hire Success via "Transition Training"

*by Dan Lowe*

One of the biggest challenges facing call center managers is quickly turning new-hires into effective agents. All too often new hires go through an initial training session and are then thrown on the phones where they receive little or no direct support while handling calls. This is the equivalent of showing a new swimmer how to swim, handing them instructional manuals, then sending them to their first race. It's no surprise that call centers that take such an approach often suffer high turnover right after training, as agents find they can't stay afloat on the phone floor.

To avoid the "sink or swim" problem and help battle early attrition, many call centers have successfully implemented a "transition training" program as a part of the new-hire training process. Transition training enables new-hires to "do the job" while still in a nurturing learning environment. It involves having trainees — who've completed or nearly completed the classroom training — handle live calls from customers in a separate area in the call center under close supervision. The transition process can take anywhere from a few hours to several weeks, depending on the complexity of the agent's role in the call center.

This article will discuss how to determine if a transition training program is right for your call center, describe how to implement a successful program, and provide examples of actual call centers that have already done so.

## Time for a Transition?

Answering the following questions can help you determine whether your call center could benefit from a transition training program:

- Are many new-hires who have successfully completed training struggling on the phones?
- Is early agent attrition excessive in the call center?
- Are frontline supervisors spending most of their time working with new agents?
- Are trainees fired up and ready coming out of training, only to quickly become frustrated and stressed out after a few days on the phones?

If you answered "yes" to any of these questions, a well-implemented transition training program could be just what your center needs.

Effective transition training programs provide numerous benefits:

- ♠ Trainers can better assess individual knowledge and phone skills before placing new-hires on the phone floor. Trainees who aren't "cut out" for the agent job are quickly identified and can be reassigned if necessary.
- ♠ Trainees develop a more thorough understanding of processes, information systems, products and services, as well as the confidence needed to succeed on the phones.
- ♠ New agents see the extra support the center gives them and thus feel valued, which results in increased motivation, higher morale, lower turnover and better service/customer satisfaction.
- ♠ Supervisors on the phone floor receive better-qualified trainees who require less supervision and coaching, freeing up supervisors to focus on other key tasks.
- ♠ The program can be used to develop senior agents into effective supervisors by involving them in supervisory roles in the controlled call environ-

ment, where mistakes aren't so costly.

## Implementing a Positive Program

Once you've decided that transition training is appropriate for your center, follow these steps to ensure a successful program:

1) Set and communicate clear objectives. Ensure that everyone involved — trainers, trainees, supervisors, and even existing agents — understand the primary objectives of the transition training program. Explain how it is intended to provide trainees with an opportunity to integrate the skills and knowledge they've acquired from the classroom training in a supportive environment, where they can ask questions, make mistakes and begin to see how everything they've learned fits together.

2) Determine types of calls handled, skill-sets required and training time frames. Decide exactly what kinds of calls will be routed to trainees "in transition"; what skills, product and systems knowledge trainees need to have prior to handling those calls; and finally, how long transition training will last.

Some call centers divide transition training into segments, where the trainee practices handling certain call types/skills in the controlled environment, heads back to the classroom for additional instruction, then goes back on the phones to practice handling the new call types/skills.

Note: In many cases, the addition of a transition process to the new-hire training program enables call centers to reduce the classroom time by 10-30 percent. The reason for this is that agents often learn key "classroom" concepts while on the phones during transition training.

3) Create a "transition bay." The

September 1999 ■ Reprinted with permission from *Call Center Management Review*®, www.icmi.com.

27

transition bay — or "nesting area" as some call centers call it — is where trainees handle calls prior to jumping out onto the official phone floor. The primary requirement for the transition bay is that it provides trainees access to the same telecommunications and informational systems that the existing call center agents have. The transition bay need not take space on the phone floor; it can be set up in virtually any room. Focus on replicating the "true calling environment" as closely as possible.

4) Select trainers/supervisors to oversee the transition bay. This is one of the most critical aspects of implementing a successful transition training program. It's essential to carefully choose the right people with the right skills to coach and nurture new hires on the phones for the first time. Select transition bay supervisors from your pool of trainers, floor supervisors and senior agents. Look for candidates who are patient, have strong knowledge of all call types and a proven ability to provide positive feedback.

The agent-to-supervisors ratio should be lower than it is on the official phone floor. While a 15:1 agent-to-supervisor ratio may suffice for experienced agents in the call center, a 5:1 or 7:1 ratio may be necessary in the transition bay to provide the immediate support that trainees need to develop the skills and confidence to succeed in the center.

## What Is the Cost?

Yes, there are costs associated with implementing an effective transition-training program. These costs are associated with lengthening the overall training process, with using supervisory staff in the process, with using floor space as a transition bay, etc.

But consider the costs of not implementing a transition program: The cost of re-hiring and re-training due to high agent turnover; the costs associated with constant errors and rework caused by unprepared agents; the costs of missed sales opportunities; and the costs of poor service and lost customers.

## Sample Programs

Here are two examples of actual call centers that have successfully implemented a transition training program:

### Company A

*1) Classroom training (two weeks)*

*2) Transition training (two weeks)*

- A trainer and coaches support, monitor and give feedback to trainees in separate transition bay.

- Features a 3:1 trainee-to-supervisor ratio.

- Calls are segmented for the application (s) on which agents have been trained (i.e., billing calls)

- Trainees are occasionally brought back into the classroom to complete relevant modules.

*3) Additional classroom training (three weeks)*

*4) Additional transition training (three weeks, or as needed)*

- Trainees take a variety of general calls under close supervision.

- Training time is based on individual goal attainment and proficiency.

- Transition support staff report trainee's strengths and weaknesses to floor supervisor upon completion of training.

### Company B

*1) Classroom training (two weeks)*

*2) Transition training (two to four weeks)*

- Training takes place within assigned "production" team.

- A supervisor, senior agent and other team members provide general support.

- Each trainee is assigned a mentor.

- Trainees practice approximately 20 percent of the total agent responsibilities.

*3) Additional classroom training (two weeks)*

*4) Additional transition training (flexible — based on needs of trainees)*

- Trainees return to assigned team.

- Receive daily feedback from support staff/mentor.

- Trainees practice a higher percentage of total agent tasks.

- Goals and objectives are geared to needs of individual trainees.

**CCMReview**

Dan Lowe is a trainer and consultant specializing in call center improvement. He has 20 years of training and management experience, the last 11 in the call center industry. He specializes in hiring and training processes, as well as assessments of supervisor effectiveness. Dan is based in Cedar Rapids, Iowa, and can be reached at 319-364-7463 or at GroupLCG@aol.com.

September 1999 ■ Reprinted with permission from *Call Center Management Review®*, www.icmi.com.

28

# Develop A Coherent Training Process For Multiple Sites

*by Susan Hash*

**Break down time and distance barriers with consistent agent training processes.**

Consistency is key in customer service. Customers want to know that, no matter who, when or where they call, they'll get the same level of service, knowledge and expertise.

How can you ensure that type of steady performance if your organization has more than one call center?

Technology is a key solution, to be sure. But by developing a uniform training process that's used across multiple sites, you can ensure your agents are offering the same quality performance in every call center.

Achieving consistency is not a simple task, given the fast-paced changes most call centers are experiencing, not to mention the constant barrage of new information, products, services, features systems, tools, etc.

"It seems like every six months we're introducing a new change," says Dawn Armbrust, managing director of Customer Service Training, Quality and Service Area Administration for Federal Express. FedEx has 17 call centers in the United States, with approximately 2,800 employees.

"The project planning that goes into each change is pretty complex. We want to develop the training fast, but in a format that's easy to deploy. Plus, there's the challenge of trying to schedule a few thousand people in various locations with a static number of trainers and facilities — without impacting the service levels of the operations," she says.

## Create Consistent Tools

Ensuring that all sites use a consistent training approach and curriculum is also a challenge, says Nancee Kates,

learning and quality manager, Customer Relationship Management, AT&T. The organization has 11 U.S. call centers.

"You want to be very clear about the flow of the curriculum and make sure that your instructors have a definite image of what that training should consist of," she says.

Kates oversees a team of about 15 trainers with different areas of expertise. Generally, trainers are not located at a particular site; they travel to various call centers depending on the training need.

She has found that a "train the trainer" program can be particularly helpful to ensure that trainers have the knowledge and the skill sets to administer and guide call center learning. At AT&T, trainers attend learning sessions that cover the entire curriculum they'll be teaching. In addition to training content, they also have a chance to hone their presentation skills. "We make sure we have a role-model instructor so the trainers can clearly see classroom management techniques and styles being demonstrated, as well as subject matter expertise being delivered," Kates says.

When new instructors are launched, they have the opportunity to "team-teach" their first courses to certify their readiness for the classroom, she adds.

Although FedEx also uses a core curriculum for agent training, its instructors are located within the centers, so they can customize the manner in which they present the material for their particular centers.

"We try to know our audiences," says Armbrust. "We conduct front-end analysis — and not in just one call center. We go out and talk with everybody so we know what's going on in all our locations."

## Develop a Solid New-Hire Training Structure

A well-developed new-hire training structure is the foundation for creating uniformity within centers. It gets all agents, in all locations, on the same page from the start.

"Consistency is the key — not only with regard to training materials, but also the structure and the modules," says Jody Leary, service director for Aetna. Both Aetna call centers — locat-

---

## Training for Cultural Differences

Organizations with multiple call center sites will likely also be dealing with a diverse customer base — even within the United States. Take SunTrust Online, for example. It has six call centers located in Nashville, Tenn.; Miami; Orlando, Fla.; Atlanta; Norfolk, Va.; and Richmond, Va.

"Being in the call center business, we felt we had to be very aware of the customers who were calling and where they were calling from," says Mary Beth Brannon, vice president and SunTrust Online training manager. "We have very different cultures across all of our sites."

SunTrust Online's new-hire training program includes a module called "local market training." In it, reps learn the geographic dynamics, such as demographics and culture, of the customers with whom they may be dealing.

"A customer who is calling from Tennessee is different from a customer who's calling from Miami or Washington, D.C.," she explains. "We feel we have great products to fit customers' needs, but we have to be aware of the diversity of both our customers and our employees, and support and respect those differences. Much of the training is geared toward understanding the different locales and servicing those customers in a respectful manner. Also, we want to focus on ensuring that we make each customer feel like we're right there in their neighborhood, and not a big, impersonal call center."

May 2001 ■ Reprinted with permission from *Call Center Management Review*®, www.icmi.com.

29

ed in Hartford, Conn., and Phoenix — follow the same process.

Newly hired customer service associates are grouped into apprentice teams for a six-week training program. "The team starts on the same date — they stay together, work together and get mentored together so that there's continuity of education and a sense of camaraderie," she says.

Service managers at each site work with product specialists and an education and training team to fine-tune the training — before and after each class.

"We know well in advance when we're going to bring on a new class," says Leary. "In the prior quarter, we review the training modules with our education and training team to determine if anything needs to be updated or changed. Then, after each new-hire class, we assess how well they did and their views of the training to decide if there's anything we need to tweak."

New-hire training at SunTrust Online is also set up in modules, says Mary Beth Brannon, vice president, SunTrust Online training manager. SunTrust Online, a line of business of SunTrust Bank, has six call centers that include both phone and Internet channels.

The initial three weeks consists of classroom training. During the second week, reps also spend two hours a day taking phone calls. "We find it's very motivational to do this fairly early in the program. It really peaks their interest in learning and gets them excited about their work," Brannon says. "We only send basic inquiries to our trainees. And our coaches and trainers are in the room to answer any questions that come up."

In the fourth week of training, new-hires graduate from the classroom into a "training bay," which is an on-the-job training environment. Trainees spend their days taking calls under the supervision of coaches and trainers who review call-handling techniques and any issues that arose at the end of each day. New-hires have specific goals to strive for during their time in training bay, such as average handle time, quality lev-

## Tips for Multiple (Or Single) Site Training Success

Whether you run one call center or a dozen, the following advice from the managers of successful multisite operations will help you to develop a productive training process.

- Make sure your field trainers are accountable for using the materials/curriculum provided. Develop a feedback loop to fix any issues that arise.

- Don't try to do it on your own. Partner with your training team and business process owners for a collaborative approach.

- Make sure the training process and delivery is consistent.

- Back up your new-hires with online reference tools and resources that reinforce what they've learned.

- Don't expect your training program to be a cure-all. Training alone will not ensure top-quality customer service after agents leave the classroom.

- Visit every call center site. Talk to the managers at every center and show them that you value their input. Give site managers feedback, on a step-by-step basis, on your plans for deploying a training process. Include in your feedback recognition of their suggestions/best practices that you're implementing.

- Use scorecards for ongoing development. Include basic measures as well as targets for additional skills.

- During new-hire training, run participants through mock scenarios every five to seven days to ensure they can display a minimum level of proficiency in the concepts they've learned.

- Make training fun. Use different themes, conduct team competitions and give out prizes.

els, knowledge checks, and sales referral percentages.

The on-the-job training period is generally a week long after which new-hires become certified and can move out onto the floor. If a rep did not reach a goal, that particular training need is identified for the call center manager or team supervisor to focus on with the rep. The certification results are also included in a quarterly ROI report on the training programs, which goes to SunTrust Online management and the training team.

### Ensure One-to-One Support

After SunTrust Online's new-hires hit the call center floor, they have a lot of internal support. In fact, management has developed a grid that identifies the amount of support per rep.

"We have one coach for every 20 employees, one team manager (or supervisor) for every 20 employees, and we have 'first aid' representatives, who are part of a sort of internal helpdesk," says Brannon. In addition, various specialty

groups can assist newer reps with questions on specific products or services.

However, she notes, the organization's coach population is the critical success factor for ongoing training.

"Our coaches are very involved," she says. "Our goal is for the coaches to spend 50 percent of their time in side-by-sides with the rep — in addition to monitoring calls and conducting formal monthly coaching sessions with each rep on their team."

### Communication is Key

Constant communication is vital to developing a cohesive training approach — within the training team, as well as with frontline agents.

FedEx is currently transitioning from using paper-based publications, such as manuals, standard operating procedures and other training materials, to a knowledge management system that will offer a central repository of information.

Similarly, SunTrust Online makes training modules, leaders' guides, check-

May 2001 ■ Reprinted with permission from *Call Center Management Review®*, www.icmi.com.

30

lists and systems guides available on its intranet site. In addition to trainers' materials, there's an online reference guide for frontline agents called "SunTrust Online Help." It allows agents, no matter where they're located, to instantly access information on products, customers, processes and procedures.

Face-to-face communication takes place in the centers, as well, says Brannon. "We take the opportunity to appropriately communicate to small groups on a weekly basis. I might hold six meetings with five people in each meeting over a Monday and Tuesday. But those 20-minute meetings cover a lot and help to get everybody up to date. We're very careful about how we schedule those meetings. We use workforce management to make sure that it doesn't impair the service levels that we have at our centers."

## Marry Learning and Quality

"A robust, consistent training experience and on-boarding process for agents is extremely important," says AT&T's Nancee Kates. "But you also need to take a holistic approach to managing training. It's not an isolated event."

She believes there are four components that impact call center performance:

- Training — the knowledge (what to do and why you need to do it).

- Practice — developing the skills (how to accomplish it).

- Environment — in some cases, it's not a training or skills issue, rather the environment may be getting in the way of agents being successful.

- Motivation — do agents want to do what you're asking them to do?

"I don't think we can look at training as a standalone answer to the customer experience," she says. "Consider whether or not you have good performance management models in place so that you're giving regular feedback and developing action plans — and follow through on those plans."

At AT&T's Customer Relationship Management directorate, the learning and quality components were recently brought under one umbrella. "It was a natural marriage because we put a lot of emphasis on our quality processes," Kates says.

A team of 20 full-time quality analyzers observes calls and provides biweekly feedback to the call centers on various quality components, including soft skills and technical information.

"Our QAs go further than simple call monitoring," Kates says. "We're not just interested in how we handle a call verbally; we want to make sure that repeat calls are not necessary from a customer's perspective."

The quality team inspects call outputs to see whether or not work that was agreed upon with the customer actually took place and that it was accurate. The group also identifies service gaps and trends, and then puts together programs that call center coaches share in team meetings.

"Those are designed as mini-training courses, and the coach is the facilitator of the learning," she says.

The training/quality alignment is a good basic structure, agrees FedEx's Armbrust. The training organization at FedEx, likewise, has a quality assurance arm. "We are one organization under one direction — we manage the communication, the operating procedure definition and the documentation process," she explains. "In some companies, that can be dispersed — not just geographically, but organizationally. With the pace of change that most companies are dealing with these days, I find that having it in one house — even if it's not physically all in one place — makes all the difference in terms of effectiveness, communicating and being able to work together." **CCMReview**

May 2001 ■ Reprinted with permission from *Call Center Management Review*®, www.icmi.com.

31

Section 9

# Training and Support for Frontline Supervisors

*by Dan Lowe*

Training programs for frontline call center agents have evolved over time to include many of the important elements to help new employees succeed in this diverse role. Many challenges in the call center environment – including high CSR attrition rates and ever-increasing customer satisfaction expectations – have given call center managers the incentive to develop comprehensive and thorough CSR training processes.

However, few call centers focus adequate attention on high-quality training and development processes for their frontline supervisors. And yet, most managers would agree that in today's business environment of low unemployment, low job loyalty and high competition for qualified CSRs, it is critical that the frontline supervisors be strong leaders with the knowledge and skills to create positive circumstances in which agents can thrive.

How can you ensure that your supervisors have the tools they need to be effective leaders? Let's explore a proven supervisor development process.

### Examine Your Agent Training Processes

You can begin by looking at agent training "best practices" as used by leading call centers. Figure 1 gives a clear description of the most common phases of a typical training and support plan for frontline agents. It also includes the purpose for

*Supervisors who go through a comprehensive training and support process will be far more self-sufficient and, therefore, require less time of the call center manager or human resources in the long run.*

each phase of the training process.

New supervisors need a similar kind of developmental process in order to succeed and to help their teams to succeed. Too many companies make the mistake of assuming that a competent frontline agent can quickly (and magically) evolve into a successful supervisor. While the fundamental skills sets provide a good foundation, supervisors require additional management skills that are generally not accounted for in a formal training program. The box on page 10 lists a few of the key training areas required for both frontline staff and supervisors.

With this in mind, where does the newly promoted call center supervisor get the additional skills and knowledge needed to handle the normal daily flow of issues and situations? In most cases, the answer is "on-the-job training" or "learn as you go." New supervisors may be able to pick up bits of knowledge from more experienced managers (many of whom also learned through a hit-or-miss, inconsistent manner). But there is a better way!

### Four Key Steps to a Supervisor Training and Support Process

You can use the frontline agent training process as a model to build a comprehensive supervisor training program. There are four steps recommended to ensure the success of the

FIGURE 1

## Agent Training Phases and Purposes

| Phase | Description | Purpose |
|-------|-------------|---------|
| 1 | Company orientation | Provide information about company, benefits, job expectations, measurements, etc. |
| 2 | CSR training | Provide general and then detailed information on specific tasks to be completed in position. Provide introduction and practice with tools, automated systems, etc. |
| 3 | Nesting | Provide time in production area with experienced CSRs as models. Provide closely supervised "on-the-job" training. Provide the opportunity to fail in a safe environment. |
| 4 | Monitoring/coaching | Observe CSR performance to provide feedback on specific performance-related behaviors. Identify negative behaviors that could turn into bad habits. Identify and praise positive and appropriate behaviors. |
| 5 | Performance appraisal process | Provide regular feedback using company performance management or appraisal format. Provides feedback in all major and important job performance areas. |

August 2000 ■ Reprinted with permission from *Call Center Management Review*®, www.icmi.com.

32

new supervisor:

■ **Orientation.** New supervisors should be given some kind of introduction to the position. This can be formatted in different ways, but the main objective is to clearly identify the roles and responsibilities of the frontline supervisor. Human resources personnel and upper management can help to offer the right perspective for orientation.

■ **Training.** The actual training process for supervisors should be conducted using a variety of methods (i.e., classroom, seminars, self-paced, mentors, etc.). The focus of the training should be to identify knowledge and skill areas that are outside of the frontline agents' knowledge and skill set. Many of the skills and knowledge areas listed in the box (right) should be included. Training in these areas is usually done by human resource professionals, training staff members, call center managers or other experienced supervisors. The best supervisor training programs also include situational role playing. This gives the trainee a chance to use new knowledge and skills in a realistic, but simulated environment.

■ **Nesting/Shadowing.** Many call centers find that providing new supervisors with a "nesting" opportunity by having the person shadow or "co-manage" a team for a period of time can help to ensure the individual's success as a leader. Nesting gives new supervisors a chance to observe an experienced supervisor's work flow. They have the opportunity to review organizational and time-management practices, employee interaction skills and team meetings. The supervisors selected to be "shadowed" should be effective role models for the new supervisor.

■ **Coaching and/or Mentoring.** Every new supervisor should be

## Agent and Supervisor Skill Sets

### AGENT SKILLS

- Customer interaction
- Systems manipulation
- Basic problem-solving
- Teaming
- Company process knowledge

### SUPERVISOR SKILLS

- Customer interaction
- Employee interaction
- Communication
- Systems manipulation
- High-level problem-solving
- Team leadership
- Company process knowledge
- Company HR policies and procedures knowledge
- Decision-making
- Conflict management
- Reports and data analysis
- Monitoring
- Coaching
- Performance management process knowledge
- Employee motivation and recognition

assigned a mentor. This may be his or her immediate manager, but does not need to be. The role of the mentor is to meet with new supervisors on a regular basis for the first several months in the position, as well as making themselves available on an as-needed basis. Mentors provide experienced insights on any challenges faced by new supervisors, as well as counseling and career direction. It is best to have a formal process in place to ensure all necessary ground is covered. In addition, supervisors should also be paired with a representative from human resources for staff issues. This is especially important for new supervisors who are learning policies and procedures connected

with interviewing, hiring, performance management, disciplinary actions and termination.

## Time Investment Will Pay Off for Managers

Developing a formal supervisor training and support process will require a time commitment from your company. But the benefits to this kind of comprehensive approach are significant. The new supervisor will be able to gain the necessary knowledge and skills to be successful and help his or her team succeed.

It's important to keep in mind that this development period is an investment that will be paid back over time. Supervisors who go through a formal development process will be far more self-sufficient and therefore require less time from call center managers or human resources in the long run. Think of it as a "pay me now or pay me later" proposition.

Overall, providing your supervisors with adequate training processes is as important as frontline agent development programs. Just as well-trained agents produce higher quality customer interactions, well-developed supervisors impact both internal and external satisfaction. *CCMReview*

**Dan Lowe**

*Dan Lowe, president of Lowe Consulting Group, is a consultant and trainer specializing in call center development. LCG provides call center process assessments, including hiring, training, transition process and supervisor effectiveness. Dan developed a comprehensive supervisor training program for Kirkwood Community College in Cedar Rapids, Iowa. He can be reached at 319-364-7463 or at GroupLCG@aol.com.*

**Section 9**

August 2000 ■ Reprinted with permission from *Call Center Management Review*®, www.icmi.com.

33

# Tap the Potential of Technology-based Call Center Training

*by Leslie Hansen Harps and Laurie Solomon*

Section 9

Early CD-ROM training programs were generally viewed more as a novelty than a viable method of training. That's not the case today. Technological advances and increased agent familiarity with computers, multimedia and the Web have made technology-based training (TBT) a powerful addition to traditional classroom training.

Technology-based training is on the rise in companies across the United States. In fact, 54% of companies use CD-ROM programs to deliver in-house training, according to *Training* magazine's 1999 industry report.

While CD-ROM use is steadily climbing, training delivered via the Internet or World Wide Web is the fastest-growing method – 36% of respondents said they offered training via the Internet in 1999, up from 31% the year before. Likewise, training offered over company intranets rose from 21% in 1998 to 24% last year.

A wide range of TBT programs are available today, including several developed specifically for customer service and the call center, as well as computer/technical skills and professional skills, such as communications, problem-solving, project management, team-building, time management and writing.

## Call Centers Integrating TBT into the Training Mix

The growing interest in TBT among call centers can be linked to industry trends affecting the training environment, such as: 1) offering pieces or components of training rather than full courses; 2) a focus on performance support ("just in time" and "just enough" rather than "just in case"); 3) widely distributed workgroups (by time and location); and 4) rapidly changing information.

*CCMReview* recently spoke with two call centers that have effectively integrated TBT into their overall training programs.

WebVan, a new online megastore based in the San Francisco Bay Area, uses a CD-ROM program for new-hires and as a coaching tool for ongoing training (1-800-For-Service™ from Ulysses Training Corporation). The training program presents a series of call center plots, walking agents through four different companies.

"They interact with the CD-ROM through a list of scenarios that gives them a chance to build what they're going to say to the customer," explains training development specialist Darren Gant.

"Putting the CSR in the actual environment in which they're going to be working is great for natural learning," he says. However, WebVan trainees aren't expected to use the CD-ROM in a vacuum. "I go through one of the scenarios with them as a group, then set them off," he says.

WebVan recently hired a project manager to investigate the various kinds of TBT available. One of the project manager's priorities will be to explore modules on how to write effective e-mail. Gant is open to the possibilities offered by all sorts of TBT and envisions growing the company intranet into a rich resource for training. Agents could access the intranet and "grab a world of information about the company, procedures, policies, con-

---

## Technology Based Training Benefits and Limitations

CD-ROM and Web-based training are the two fastest-growing types of technology-based training. Consider the following benefits and limitations of each when selecting the technology that will best meet your overall training needs:

| | Benefits | Drawbacks/Issues |
|---|---|---|
| CD-ROM | • High-density storage<br>• Rich multimedia for animation, audio, graphics and video<br>• Inexpensive to duplicate<br>• Self-paced, available 24 hours<br>• Can be purchased off-the-shelf or customized | • Firm limit on storage<br>• Static – difficult to update<br>• Technology is varied (computers)<br>• Little or no interaction with others<br>• Feedback and user-tracking is difficult |
| Web-based | • Can be used across multiple platforms, browsers<br>• Easy to update (just-in-time development)<br>• Easy to manage courses (testing, tracking, feedback)<br>• Offers interaction with other participants/instructor<br>• Can be off-the-shelf or customized | • Bandwidth required<br>• Access issues (i.e., desktop hardware, resolution, processor speed, firewalls, browsers, etc.)<br>• Technical skill of developers and users required<br>• Time and money to develop<br>• Project team requirements |

---

March 2000 ■ Reprinted with permission from *Call Center Management Review*®, www.icmi.com.

34

tent... It would make the training binder obsolete," he says.

Like WebVan, Total Solutions – a credit card/banking service bureau in Columbus, Ga. – combines formal, instructor-led training with TBT modules for ongoing training. Each of the 700-plus agents in the call center participates in a weekly, hour-long session held in the company's training room, which is then supplemented with training that is pushed out to the agent's computer.

To produce the TBT, Total Solutions uses a software product that enables its trainers to write their own modules (KnowDev from Knowlagent). "It's like doing a Power Point presentation," explains Willie White, vice president of training. The trainer keys in the content, adds color and illustrations, and the software then delivers it to the agent's desktop. During phase two of the program, the trainer will be able to add audio and video to the training module.

Agents complete exams or quizzes produced on the software to demonstrate their understanding of what is being presented. The exams are then scored by the program. "The exams are a management tool for me," White says. "They tell me whether or not we need to provide additional training in a particular area, or if an individual agent needs more training or special attention."

In addition, after a formal training session, White can produce exams that can be used to measure the effectiveness of a particular instructor or training module.

Total Solutions has been working with the software product since last summer. "We love it; it's easy to use," White says. The company is also evaluating various CD-ROM training programs, and exploring whether or not to develop its own TBT in house.

## Best Training Approach is a Mix

Despite its benefits, technology-based training (TBT) is not a magic bullet, states Fay Wilkinson, senior partner at Questeq Learning Programs. The Orangeville, Ontario-based company specializes in consulting and customized training for help desks and call centers.

"It's not a replacement for other types of training." For effective learning on the service side, she says, "you need the interaction of people with people," such as the personal interaction agents have with the instructor and others in the training group.

To get the best results from training programs, managers should consider the four phases of learning (assess, acquire, practice and feedback), and try to work technology-based training into parts of each, suggests Todd Beck, product manager for AchieveGlobal, Tampa, Fla., which offers customer service CBT programs.

For example, an agent might acquire skills and knowledge through a blend of classroom training, one-on-one coaching and the use of TBT; get some practice both in the classroom and using TBT; and receive feedback from an instructor via e-mail as well as through a computer-based assessment.

For the best results, the material covered via TBT should be reinforced later by the call center manager. For example, during a pre-shift meeting, managers can refer to recent training, explaining the importance of the skills being learned and discussing how to use them in to the specific call center environment.

While White is very satisfied with the benefits that TBT has provided and plans to add more tools in the future, he has guarded his training staff against the danger of becoming TBT junkies. "[TBT] will never replace the instructor. It's best to use it to enhance what you're doing, not to replace your one-on-one or student-instructor interface. Without such interaction between agents and instructors, you can't really tell if your [agents] understand the information you sent them."

In addition to training, TBT programs can also be effective in testing and screening agent applicants for call center jobs. For example, Olsten Staffing Services, Melville, NY, uses "Selection Advantage" from Kaplan Learning Centers to supplement its own proprietary applicant testing tools, according to Linda Gherardi, director of teleservices product development for Olsen.

The interactive CD-ROM program tests candidates for abilities such as customer service skills, influence, investigative skills and

## Types of Training Methods in Use

Here are the top training methods companies are using, according to *Training* magazine's 1999 industry report on training trends:

| | 1998 | 1999 |
|---|---|---|
| Live classroom programs | 88% | 90% |
| CD-ROM | 50% | 54% |
| Internet/WWW | 31% | 36% |
| Intranet | 21% | 24% |

Section 9

March 2000 ■ Reprinted with permission from *Call Center Management Review*®, www.icmi.com.

35

problem-solving skills. Candidates listen to a series of 25 calls, then choose the best response from four or five possibilities.

## Using TBT: Take a Look at the Call Center Environment

When considering the use of TBT in the call center, managers and trainers should keep in mind its limitations and the realities of the call center environment. For example:

**1. The call center can be distracting.** While agents are used to working in the call center environment, training requires concentration. This can be hard to do at the workstation.

**2. Agents may benefit more from a break rather than training.** Some companies like TBT because it enables them to integrate training into a call center agent's workday, fitting training in between phone calls. That may be a mixed blessing, says Todd Beck of AchieveGlobal. Agents who have been taking call after call all day with just a few minutes in between may not be able to quickly shift their mindsets when training is routed to them.

In addition, training may be the last thing an agent wants to do with extra time, Beck says. While the training program provides a change of pace, it takes place at the same workstation, using the same screen the agent has looked at all day. In some cases, the agent might be more refreshed and re-energized by standing and stretching, or a quick change of scenery.

## Selected Sources of Call Center TBT

www.achieveglobal.com

www.ikp.net

www.itclearning.com

www.ulyssestraining.com

**3. Off-line practice is important.** Don't have agents complete a Web-based seminar or a CD-ROM program, then immediately try their new skills and knowledge out on the phone, Beck advises. "Do you really want their first practice to be with a live customer?" It's more effective to build in opportunities for agents to practice their new skills and knowledge, perhaps during team or shift briefings or by bringing in a facilitator for role-play or practice.

On the plus side, an effective and balanced TBT approach can break up the monotony of static classroom training. The more diverse, individualized and interactive your training program is, the more motivated agents will be to learn – and the better they'll retain information.

*Leslie Hansen Harps is a freelance business writer specializing in customer service and call centers. Formerly president of the Customer Service Institute, she is author of several books, including Motivating Customer Service Employees, published by The Customer Service Group. Leslie can be reached at 202-363-5822.*

*Laurie Solomon is president of LKS Training Services Inc., an independent call center training and consulting firm. She is also a Certified Associate of ICMI. Laurie can be reached at Laurie_Solomon@msn.com or 630-665-6007.*

CCMReview

March 2000 ■ Reprinted with permission from *Call Center Management Review®*, www.icmi.com.

36

# Measuring the Effectiveness of Customer Service Training in Call Centers

*by David Freemantle*

A recent report in the British journal *Customer Service Management* stated that one in three call centers fail to meet expectations. Not only are 20 percent of callers abandoning, but call center staff are failing to seize the opportunity to develop customer relationships and loyalty.

Three other independent pieces of research show that the main reasons customer defect from a company is not because of the quality of product or the price, but because they perceive the supplier as being indifferent to their needs. Too many call center staff come across as not being interested in who's calling them, causing customers to feel like just another item on the production line.

While most call center managers agree that training plays a vital role in eliminating such problems, very few measure the effectiveness of the training their companies invest in.

The measures that can be developed should relate to the call center training matrix shown on this page.

Let's discuss each item in the matrix in turn:

**Skill.** It is relatively easy to measure the application of most agent skills, such as keyboard speed and accuracy, screen handling capability, and order process-ing. The effectiveness of skills training can therefore be measured readily by assessing the skill levels of trainees before and after training.

**Knowledge.** The same applies to knowledge. Call center staff need to have a large store of knowledge about the company's products, services, policies and procedures. This can be assessed easily via testing/role playing before and after training.

**Attitude and emotional energy.** These two are the most difficult to measure and are essential for forming effective relationships with customers. The best way to measure these is to obtain a customer rating on individual call center staff before and after training. Senior managers at one company I've worked with call customers who have just spoken to an agent who is about to attend customer service training. Customers are asked to rate how the agent handled the call. Once training is provided, a second telephone survey is conducted on the agent to establish whether any improvement has occurred.

**Routine interactions.** Most of the interactions that agents have are routine in nature. Consequently, it is relatively easy to establish a set of standards that assess an individual's capability before and after training. For example, when handling calls from customers who inquire about the status of their accounts, agents follow a simple routine to obtain the required information. With such routines, speed of response (skill), understanding the account (knowledge) and warmth of communications with customers (attitude) are relatively easy to assess.

**Non-routine interactions.** Much more difficult to assess are non-routine interactions. Some of the more progressive companies I work with are developing advanced training programs to help agents develop an approach to handling "difficult" customers, or those who have complex/unusual requests or problems. Assessing the effectiveness of such training relies on a high degree of subjectivity on the part of the trainer, the call center manager and, ultimately, the customer.

## A Closer Look at Measurement Methods

Research has shown that companies that invest heavily in training and that measure its effectiveness tend to be more successful in business as a whole. Companies like British Airways and Federal Express – reputed to be among the best in their industry when it comes to service – invest heavily in these areas.

For example, FedEx's call center in the UK at Coventry measures the effectiveness of call-handling after intensive training provided to all staff. They use a simple "scattergram" like the one on page 8 to determine average response times over a month for each agent.

Whenever an agent deviates widely from the norm, counselling takes place to establish why the average call length is so short or so long. These sessions often uncover valid reasons for the deviations. For example, an experienced

| TRAINING MATRIX | Routine interaction with customer | Non-routine interaction with customer |
|---|---|---|
| **Application to:** ↗<br>**of:** ↑<br>**Skill** | | |
| **Knowledge** | | |
| **Attitude and emotional energy** | | |
| **End result** → | **Customer rates you highly** | |

agent might be assigned more complicated calls and therefore will have a higher average response time than most other agents.

Many call centers I have worked with place greater emphasis on assessing the emotional value that agents add to customer relationships. These centers have initiated training programs to develop such key emotional connections, and assess the emotional intensity provided. Such companies conduct an "emotional audit" of customers to determine how they feel about the service provided by the call center.

Some companies examine the "emotional management" of each call and assess the effectiveness in relation to the training provided. For example at the Yellow Pages call center at Reading in the U.K., a computer randomly selects and records calls made to agents. The agents are then invited to listen to the dialogue and determine how well they feel they have "emotionally managed" the call.

### Influential Factors

One of the reasons it is so difficult to establish a direct correlation between the effectiveness of customer service training and levels of customer satisfaction is that there are so many factors which actually influence such satisfaction. Quality customer service does not automatically result from effective training. Managers must develop a strong, customer-oriented culture, reward and help motivate agents, as well as provide them with excellent performance management, systems capability, and information.

However, such complexity is no excuse for not trying to develop ways to measure training effectiveness. The most progressive companies I work with have some measurement process in place and boast of its effectiveness in helping to improve service.

### Four Steps to Success

When measuring the effectiveness of customer service training in your call center, remember to focus on these four steps:

#### 1) Evaluation of trainees immediately before and after training

Evaluate the customer service skills,

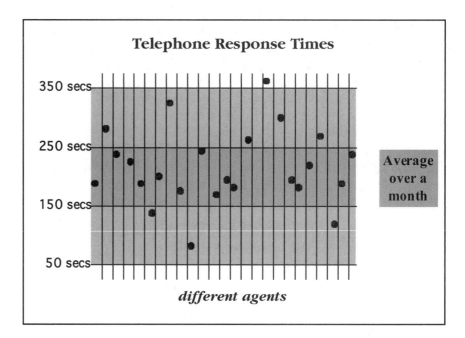

**Telephone Response Times**

*different agents*

Average over a month

attitudes and knowledge of the trainees prior to the commencement of the training and immediately after the training. The evaluation process will need to be carefully developed and based on objective criteria.

#### 2) Agent evaluation of training

Ask trainees to evaluate the effectiveness of the training immediately after they have received it. Normally this is done using a simple survey based on various rating criteria.

#### 3) On-the-job competency evaluation

One-to-three months after the customer service training is provided, reassess agents using the previously determined criteria to measure the degree of "tailing off" that invariably occurs once the short-lived "positive training effect" has worn off. Once severe tailing off is identified, action can be taken to further develop the required skills by undertaking a reinforcement or refresher training program.

#### 4) Customer evaluation of end result

The ultimate test of the effectiveness of customer service training must be based on the customer's assessment of the service provided. However, as previously mentioned, it is often difficult to establish a direct correlation as there are many other variables besides training that have an impact on customer satisfaction.

### Paramount Principle

The "science" of measuring the effectiveness of customer service training is not well-developed in most call centers, but the underlying principle is of paramount importance. Common sense dictates that no center should invest in customer service training without direct evidence that such training results in substantial added value.

**CCMReview**

*David Freemantle*, *based in Windsor, U.K., is the author of nine best-selling business books and a leading expert on customer service. He has helped hundreds of companies around the world improve customer service in their call centers via his writing and stimulating seminar presentations. David has recently completed a lecture tour of the Far East and Africa and is currently working with a number of international financial service companies. For more information on David or to contact him, please visit his Web-site at: www.superboss.co.uk or e-mail him at: team@superboss.co.uk.*

January 1999 ■ Reprinted with permission from *Call Center Management Review*®, www.icmi.com.

# Service Level Notes with Brad Cleveland
## Measuring Individual Agent Performance

Editor's Note: Due to the numerous requests from readers for information about how to fairly and effectively measure individual agent performance, we're running this popular article that was originally published in April 1996.

Want to start a lively discussion among call center managers? Float the issue of performance measurements for agents by them. Since performance measurements are usually tied to expectations and standards, that will raise issues about fairness, what agents can and can't control, why people have different capabilities and drives, and the processes that they are working within. Few subjects elicit such strong and varied opinion.

Consequently, there are about as many different sets of performance measurements and standards as there are call centers. Here, we will look at three types of performance measurements — calls per hour, adherence and qualitative measurements — commonly used in assessing individual performance. We'll also discuss why calls per hour is fading, while the other two types of measurements continue to gain acceptance.

### Calls Per Hour

Traditionally, calls per hour has been an almost universal productivity measurement. In fact, many call center managers have viewed calls per hour as virtually synonymous with "productivity." Sure, there have always been concerns about sacrificing quality for quantity. But in practice, calls per hour has been the preferred benchmark for establishing productivity standards, comparing performance among agents and groups, and assessing the impact of changes and improvements to the call center.

However, as a measure of performance, calls per hour is, and

> ### As a measure of performance, calls per hour is, and always has been, problematic.

always has been, problematic. Many of the variables that impact calls per hour are out of agents' control: call arrival rate, type of calls, knowledge of callers, communication ability of callers, accuracy of the forecast and schedule, adherence to schedule (of others in the group), and absenteeism.

There are also mathematical realities at work that are not within the control of an individual agent.

For example, smaller groups are less efficient (have lower occupancy) than larger groups, at a given service level (see Table 1). Since the number of calls changes throughout the day, so does average calls per hour for a group or an individual in the group.

And, as is often pointed out, if calls per hour is over-emphasized, quality can suffer. Agents may even "trick" the system to increase their call count and achieve a set standard. (Many call center managers get a sheepish smile when this point comes up in discussion. One could surmise that more than a few, once upon a time, have "accidentally" clicked off or erroneously transferred a call or two.)

Some call center managers convert raw calls per hour into an adjusted measurement that is more fair and meaningful. For example, occupancy, which is not within the control of an individual, can be "neutralized" by dividing calls handled by percent occupancy. Using the numbers in Table 1, 5.6 average calls per agent divided by 65 percent is 8.6 "normalized" calls, as is 6.7 calls divided by 78 percent, 7.7 calls divided by 90 percent and 8.1 calls divided by

### Table 1

| Calls In 1/2 Hour | Level: | Reps Required: | Occupancy: | Avg. Calls Per Rep: |
|---|---|---|---|---|
| 50 | 80/20 | 9 | 65% | 5.6 |
| 100 | 80/20 | 15 | 78% | 6.7 |
| 500 | 80/20 | 65 | 90% | 7.7 |
| 1000 | 80/20 | 124 | 94% | 8.1 |

*Assumptoions: Calls last 3.5 minutes. Calculations based on Erlang C for 1/2 hour's calls.*

**Section 9**

June 1999 ■ Reprinted with permission from *Call Center Management Review®*, www.icmi.com.

39

94 percent. Others go a step further and develop statistical control charts to determine whether the process is in control, what it's producing, and which agents, if any, are outside of "statistical control."

But even with further analysis, calls per hour begins to lose meaning as technologies such as CTI, skills-based routing and Web integration, which enable increasingly sophisticated and varied call- han-

> *Calls per hour begins to lose meaning as technologies such as CTI, skills-based routing and Web integration, which enable increasingly sophisticated and varied call-handling routines, proliferate.*

dling routines, proliferate. For many who have depended on calls per hour, this has left a vacuum: How can we measure productivity in an increasingly varied and complex environment? Enter adherence and qualitative measurements, which are gaining increasing acceptance.

## Adherence Measurements

Adherence factor, or signed-on time, is a measurement of how much time an individual is available to handle calls versus the time he or she was scheduled to handle calls. If adherence factor is 85 percent, an agent would be expected to be in adherence .85 x 60 minutes, or 51 minutes on average per hour. Adherence consists of all plugged-in time including talk time, after-call

work (wrap-up) time, time spent waiting for the next call and making necessary outgoing calls. Lunch, breaks, training, etc., are not counted as time assigned to handle calls. Adherence factor should be established at a level that is reasonable and that reflects the many things that legitimately keep agents from the phones. It should also be flexible (adjustable downward) when call volumes are low.

Some have developed adherence factor into a more refined measurement that also incorporates timing — when was a person available to take calls, in addition to how much time they were available. The idea here is to ensure that people are plugged in mid-morning when calls are barreling in, and are saving special projects for Thursday and Friday afternoon when calls slow down. ACD and forecasting/scheduling software has improved adherence reporting significantly in recent years.

The advantage of adherence factor is that it is reasonably objective. Agents cannot control variables such as the number of staff scheduled to answer calls, the number of calls coming in, the distribution of long and short calls or the distribution of easy and difficult calls. But they can generally control how available they are to take calls.

## Qualitative Measurements

In most call centers, qualitative criteria, which focus on knowledge of products and services, customer service and call-handling skills, and the policies of the organization, continue to become more refined and specific. Most use some form of monitoring (i.e., remote, side-by-side, or record and review) to evaluate individual performance and identify training and coaching needs.

An important and developing aspect of quality is that agents take the necessary time to do the job right — no more, no less. This means not rushing calls, but also not spending excess time on calls over

and above what is necessary to satisfy callers and handle them completely and correctly. If qualitative measurements are refined enough to ensure that agents are spending the appropriate amount of time handling calls, then adherence and qualitative measurements make a powerful pair. In fact, measuring calls per hour becomes unnecessary.

This is easier said than done in environments where qualitative measurements are vague and indeterminate. And many managers still

> *Well-defined qualitative measurements are beginning to erode reliance on measurements that are after-the-fact outputs.*

believe that tracking production outputs, such as calls per hour or average handling time, is necessary. But the trend is clear: well-defined qualitative measurements are beginning to erode reliance on measurements that are after-the-fact outputs.

## Cultivating Success

Calls per hour, which used to be an almost ubiquitous productivity measurement, is fading. It is increasingly being replaced by focused and specific qualitative and adherence measurements. Agents can concentrate on being available and on handling each transaction according to its individual needs. If implemented well, qualitative and adherence measurements can cultivate a better working environment, better quality — and higher productivity.

CCMReview

July 1999 ■ Reprinted with permission from *Call Center Management Review®*, www.icmi.com.

40

## In the Center
# Maximizing the Value of Your Call Monitoring Program

*by Dr. Miriam Tracy Nelson*

Call monitoring is:

- a quality metric used to evaluate agents

- a means for developing agents' skills

- a management tool to drive customer satisfaction, loyalty and profitability.

Call monitoring is arguably the best quality metric for evaluating the level of service that agents provide to customers. Beyond that, monitoring can provide information that can also improve critical business practices in your call center and throughout your organization. How powerful is your monitoring program?

The ultimate goal of monitoring is to provide management with a tool to drive customer satisfaction, customer loyalty, revenue and profitability. The service-profit chain finds that customers who perceive value from the service and products provided by the organization will be satisfied, will spend more, and will be among the customers who are more profitable. Monitoring data must be used to target and increase that perceived value.

This article will help you to enhance your application of monitoring results and the overall effectiveness of your monitoring program.

### Getting the Most for Your Monitoring Dollar

Monitoring data can be used in several ways:

**1) Measuring quality.** Call centers have become astute in capturing average talk time, average handle time, average speed of answer, adherence to schedule statistics, and a glut of other productivity metrics. Because productivity is relatively easy to measure and is objective, productivity unfortunately often becomes the primary driver of agents' behavior. To motivate agents to provide both efficient and effective service, a quality metric is needed. Monitoring is the best measure of quality and should be weighed the same as productivity metrics. Monitoring must be comprehensive so that it evaluates all of the drivers of customer satisfaction and loyalty, including customer treatment behaviors, as well as compliance and accuracy.

**2) Individual coaching and follow-up.** Report monitoring data in such a way that it can support skill development. Feedback must be timely, and focus on specific, changeable agent behaviors, not on broad summary outcomes. For example, telling an agent that he achieved an overall monitoring score of 87 tells him nothing about what or how to change. Feedback should be specific and ongoing, utilizing individual development plans to track behavioral improvements. Make tools available to the agent and supervisor for ongoing training, targeting the specific skills identified as developmental opportunities.

**3) Reward and recognition.** If – and only if – monitoring is conducted objectively, reliably and representatively, the results will provide a quality metric that can be incorporated into the performance evaluation process. This requires immediately recognizing monitored calls where the agent demonstrated outstanding service. Such recognition not only motivates agents to perform, it also helps them to view the monitoring program as a tool for development, rather than as a threat. Implementing both individual- and team-level recognition and incentive programs will quickly drive performance improvement.

**4) Trend analysis.** When you track customer service performance over time, patterns of effectiveness can be identified across call types, teams and centers. Valid monitoring results are a leading indicator of customer satisfaction. Changes in monitoring scores enable an organization to take quick action, rather than wait for changes in customer survey results.

**5) Identifying training needs.** Based on the profile of skills that emerges from monitoring, you can identify training needs for each individual agent and across the entire agent population. With this data, training can be targeted to individuals with particular developmental needs.

**6) Refining the employee selection process.** The profile of skills that emerge from monitoring will also identify the strengths and gaps in the employee selection process. For example, if monitoring indicates that agents are generally lacking interpersonal skills or basic communication skills, consider whether more stringent selection standards could screen out individuals with low skills in these areas. Why spend resources training and coaching agents on skills that can be screened for prior to hire?

**7) Identifying business process opportunities.** While monitoring calls, listen also to the customer. Track frequently asked questions, issues that create customer confusion or anger, and cues for offering additional services. Pick up on the ways agents are able to explain policy or procedures so that they are understood and sound customer-focused. The information that you glean will have significant use to your marketing, MIS, sales, and technical units.

**Section 9**

April 1999 ■ Reprinted with permission from *Call Center Management Review*®, www.icmi.com.

41

**8) Communicating the strategic vision.** Monitoring is a key communication medium. Tactically, the standards communicate to agents how calls should be handled. Beyond that, the standards are a direct reflection of how senior management expects customers to be serviced. Monitoring is a key agent of change. If expectations of agents change, so too must the monitoring standards. For example, if you traditionally have had a strictly service culture and are now asking agents to offer additional services, then monitoring must be changed to reflect those new expectations. Set detailed standards to reflect the desired behaviors, i.e., identifying customer cues, transitioning smoothly, offering tailored solutions, asking for the sale, etc. Monitoring firmly establishes the organization's strategic vision by putting it into behavioral terms.

## Resource Commitment Required for Exceptional Results

Effective monitoring – whether done remotely, side-by-side or via call taping – requires a commitment of resources. The real question is how to invest those resources to maximize the return on investment. Most call centers struggle in this area. Considering the increased management responsibility in call centers today, more and more call centers are beginning to hire in-house quality assurance specialists to focus on monitoring functions. This frees up managers and supervisors to focus on other key management areas such as forecasting/scheduling, training and motivation. Other call centers are outsourcing their monitoring functions to third-party quality assurance specialists who formally monitor agent calls remotely using criteria provided by the call center. The use of either internal or external monitoring experts provides managers/supervisors with valid and objective skill profiles for each agent.

Costs can be easily justified if monitoring results provide clear utility. Think within your call center and beyond. Consider how your different functional areas, such as Marketing, IS, Human Resources and the business leaders profit from the wealth of information that can be gathered via effective monitoring. Your company will profit by reaching across any functional silos and focusing on outstanding customer service as the organizational goal.

*Miriam Tracy Nelson, Ph.D., is vice president of Assessment Solutions Incorporated (ASI), a New York-based firm that partners with organizations to select, train and develop outstanding employees. She received her doctorate in Industrial/Organizational Psychology from Stevens Institute of Technology. Miriam can be reached at 212-319-8400 or at nelson@asisolutions.com.*

## Monitoring Practices Recommended by Incoming Calls Management Institute and *CCMReview*

1. If monitoring takes place, inform job candidates.

2. Inform agents of precisely when they are being monitored in accordance with each agent's preference or by appropriate law.

3. Tell agents which lines can be monitored and where to find unmonitored lines for personal calls.

4. Monitoring equipment should monitor what is said on the line, not what is said by agents between calls at their workstation.

5. Permit only qualified personnel to monitor for quality or to evaluate the results of monitoring.

6. Clearly inform agents about the purpose of monitoring, how it is conducted and how the results are used. Post written monitoring policies for all employees to see.

7. Do not publicly post monitoring results by name or other data that could identify an individual agent.

8. Do not single out agents for unsatisfactory performance that is common to a group of agents; more than likely the poor performance is the result of a management/training problem – not an individual performance problem.

9. Use standardized and consistently applied evaluation forms and monitoring techniques.

10. Use objective criteria in evaluation forms and monitoring techniques.

11. Monitor all agents periodically to determine where the performance level of the group is centered. New-hires and agents in need of additional coaching/training should be monitored more frequently.

12. Permit only personnel with a legitimate business need to monitor calls for orientation purposes (i.e., new call center personnel who will be involved with call handling, consultants working on call center improvements, etc.)

April 1999 ■ Reprinted with permission from *Call Center Management Review*®, www.icmi.com.

42

# Creating a Successful Peer Monitoring Program for Your Call Center

*by Leslie Hansen Harps*

An increasing number of call centers are relying on peer monitoring programs to enhance their quality assurance efforts while empowering agents. Having your call center agents monitor their peers' calls and provide feedback on their performance has many benefits:

✓ It involves agents directly in the quality process, helping to strengthen their commitment to delivering quality service, and making them an integral part of the quality assurance team.

✓ It can reduce agent resistance to monitoring by supervisors and managers. Some agents will feel less defensive when working with a colleague thus may be more open to frank, constructive feedback.

✓ It enables agents to learn from each other, reinforcing the lessons they've learned from supervisory and management staff.

✓ It provides a different perspective on customer contact, allowing the agents conducting the monitoring to observe how certain responses and phrases — which they themselves might use — actually sound to the listener. This in turn may motivate them to improve their own performance.

✓ Peer monitoring can be a form of job enrichment, providing task variety while recognizing the agents' professionalism and contribution.

✓ While peer monitoring may not replace monitoring by management, it can reduce the amount of time managers and supervisors spend on monitoring, thus freeing them up to work on other important tasks.

✓ Providing feedback through a peer monitoring process enhances agents' communication skills, as they learn to listen more carefully and to give and receive focused, constructive feedback.

## Steps to a Powerful Peer Program

But peer monitoring, like any other type of monitoring, won't happen by itself. Preparing your call center agents to monitor each other requires thoughtful planning and preparation on your part as well as training and coaching of the peer monitors. Here's how to do it:

**1) Plan early, and often.** Think through how the peer monitoring program would work. What are you trying to accomplish? Will peer monitoring replace monitoring by lead agents, supervisors or managers — or will it supplement it? How will you schedule the monitoring sessions? How will you make sure they take place as scheduled? Who will monitor whom? How will you ensure that the monitoring program is fair and consistent? Do you want to test peer monitoring through a pilot program in which senior agents monitor junior agents — say, those who have been in the call center for less than six months?

**2) Strive for a win-win environment for quality improvement.** Developing a feeling of trust is crucial to the success of any peer monitoring program. Agents need to know that the peer monitoring will take place in a safe and constructive environment, and will not embarrass them. For peer monitoring to be successful, don't incorporate the peer evaluations as part of your formal evaluation process, where an agent's future may be affected by a peer's comments.

Introduce peer monitoring in a limited way and phase into it as agents begin to feel comfortable in both giving and receiving feedback.

**3) Solicit agent input.** For best results, present the concept of peer monitoring to your staff as a positive learning tool. Explain that peer monitoring gives agents an opportunity to share their experience and knowledge with each other, and is a method of training and evaluation that has been found to be very successful in other call centers.

Ask agents to identify the benefits of having monitoring performed by peers instead of supervisors or managers. Then ask them to identify potential problems that might occur and, as a group, to identify ways to overcome these obstacles. For example, agents may say they worry about giving or receiving feedback. This is particularly true in multi-generational environments where younger workers may hesitate to provide frank feedback to an older co-worker. Similarly, a more experienced agent may be less receptive to feedback from a younger or less experienced agent. It's far better to air any potential problems up front than to have the peer monitoring program sabotaged by reluctant agents.

Point out to agents that your peer monitoring program will begin with training on how to give and receive feedback. Emphasize the service quality aspects of all monitoring and reinforce the benefits of peer monitoring. Ask agents to help you develop some ground rules for peer monitoring and turn these into a monitoring process. For example, require that service observers use a monitoring checklist (see step 5), and restrict their comments to the elements that are on the checklist. In addition, specify

**Section 9**

Monitoring and Coaching Special Issue 1999 ■ **Reprinted with permission from** *Call Center Management Review*®, www.icmi.com.

43

## Try Self-Monitoring, Too

Allowing call center agents to monitor their own personal performance on the telephone can also be a very effective method of quality assurance and empowerment. Have agents listen to a taped sampling of their phone conversations with customers. Ask them to rate their own performance, indicating what they did well, what they might have done differently and how they think the call might have been improved. Also have them set goals for improvement and track their own performance over time.

that each feedback session begin and end with a positive comment.

Some people may be reluctant to bring up concerns during a staff meeting, so be sure to give agents the option of responding to you via e-mail or a one-on-one consultation.

**4) Decide exactly what agents will monitor.** Do you want agents to replace supervisors and managers in the monitoring process, listening for and providing feedback on all of the elements of the phone call? If so, that will require significantly more training before peer monitoring can take place.

An alternative is to introduce the peer monitoring process by having agents focus initially on certain easily measured elements, such as use of the proper greeting and closing, and using the customer's name.

**5) Develop observation forms and guidelines.** Once you decide what agents will observe, develop a checklist for agents to use while monitoring phone calls. Clearly define each of the elements to be observed to avoid different interpretations of what is being monitored. Describe specific, observable behaviors that make up each component. For example, "establishing rapport with the caller" may include using the person's name, matching the caller's communication style (rate of speech, tone of voice) and demonstrating empathy through phrases such as "I know what you mean."

Develop a ranking system that is well understood by all agents, and train them in its use. Your goal is to develop a ranking system that

has a consistent meaning to everybody. For example, agents may differ widely in their use of a 10-point scale, while they might be more consistent in their use of evaluating whether a co-worker "always," "frequently," "seldom" or "never" used the customer's name during a phone call.

Once you've developed the checklist and ranking system and had it reviewed for clarity, test it on your agents. First, have them review the form and question anything that isn't clear. Then, ask for volunteers who would be willing to have their phone calls monitored by a manager or supervisor using the form, and test it to iron out any bugs. Finally, have agents use the revised form to evaluate several of their own calls and report any potential problems that may still exist. Finalize the form and have agents review it one last time. Having agents participate actively in the development of the observation checklist and rating structure will go a long way toward building their trust.

**6) Train agents to participate in a constructive feedback process.** Use of an agreed-upon observation checklist and a well-understood ranking system will help remove some of the defensiveness that some agents may feel when first receiving feedback from a co-worker. Training agents on how to both give and receive such feedback is another important step in implementing an effective peer monitoring process.

In addition to showing any of a number of videos available on giving constructive feedback, develop and use role-play scenarios so that agents can practice giving and receiving feedback. Suggestion: have two lead agents or supervisors do the first several role plays so that they can model the type of behavior you want.

**7) Supervise and coach.** Have a manager, supervisor or lead agent observe the initial peer monitoring sessions. Coach both the receiver and the provider of feedback. Talk about what was helpful about the feedback process and what needed to be improved. Ask how each felt when giving/receiving feedback. Ask each agent to think about how they can improve their peer monitoring performance.

Continue observing the peer monitors in action until you're confident that they can do the job on their own. Then observe on a sample basis, and continue to review completed observation checklists. Be alert to potential problems and modify the peer monitoring program accordingly. The results will be well worth the effort.

**CCMReview**

*Leslie Hansen Harps is a business writer specializing in customer service and call center topics. Formerly a customer service trainer and editor of* Customer Service Newsletter, *she was a charter member of the International Customer Service Association (ICSA). Leslie can be reached at 202-363-5822.*

Monitoring and Coaching Special Issue 1999 ■ **Reprinted with permission from** *Call Center Management Review*®, www.icmi.com.

44

# Monitoring Quality in the Multi-Channel Interaction Center

*by Matthew Page*

The Internet has opened new avenues of communication for customers to communicate with your company. Call centers are evolving to interaction or contact centers, handling multiple types of inquiries through multiple channels. E-mail, Web chat, collaborative browsing, and Web call-back are the new media your call center may have or perhaps are considering implementing.

While these new communication technologies provide a competitive advantage that your customer can benefit from, they present new challenges to your interaction center management team. The issues are:

- How do we effectively manage and monitor all media types for quality?
- How do we know that our representatives are consistently delivering the brand promise in written and phone interactions?

In this article, we'll examine the new recording and monitoring tools and technology available to call centers. By effectively deploying these tools, you can look forward to creating a contact center in which interaction quality across all channels of contact meets or exceeds your company's standards, and your reps consistently deliver the brand promise to your customers.

## Process and Systems

Deploying a recording solution requires a clear monitoring and quality strategy, combined with the tactical processes to effectively implement and leverage the benefits that the tool offers.

We have found that many companies have installed the latest recording solution only to discover that they are under-utilizing the tool's capabilities, and drowning in recorded interactions that they can't possibly monitor! Supervisors and managers in these interaction centers complain that they do not have the time to listen to the recorded calls. In most cases, the problem arises from a lack of processes or guidelines to effectively sample, analyze, score and, most importantly, provide feedback to each representative. These companies need to begin by defining their brand and how it's applied during customer interactions for their representatives. Next, they need to ensure that the brand and quality service are provided through implementation of a concise and manageable monitoring and coaching process that leverages the technology tool.

## Value of the Interaction

Companies have begun to realize the value of each individual customer/prospect interaction. The interaction center is a goldmine of information – who's buying, future product opportunities, brand definition or dilution (and brand valuation), and how responsive a company is to its customers.

In the past, access to this information has been driven primarily through exhaustive database analysis. But customer data represents only a small piece of the overall picture. Imagine marketing and senior executives learning about their customers through hearing and reading selected customer interactions. Is the company delivering on or diluting its brand promise? Are the millions of dollars spent promoting and advertising the brand being leveraged through phone and online interactions? Does your product or service provide real value to your customers? What improvements can be made to your products and services that will drive additional value to your customers? The best resource for remaining competitive is often the information gathered when a customer engages your interaction center.

## Help is On the Way?

There are two ways to monitor the quality of an interaction – real-time (live monitoring) or by reviewing the interaction through voice and data recording. The traditional recording vendors have solutions that simultaneously record the voice and the representatives' use of the customer management tool. This way, managers get a complete picture of each customer interaction when monitoring representatives, for instance:

- Does the new customer management system speed up or slow down each customer interaction?
- Is data verified for accuracy?
- Does the system usage help the call flow?
- Was training effective? Can the representative put all the pieces in place for each call?

## Beyond the Screen Scrape

Initially, data recording was just a series of captured screen graphics, commonly referred to as "screen scrape." Recently, vendors rolled out solutions that provide a screen scrape, as well as event and application integrated solutions. Imagine interaction center managers and supervisors having access to the voice and data recording of all orders or hot leads. These interactions can be saved in a file (in an AVI file format) for distribution for training purposes or for system improvements.

---

### Monitoring Systems Vendors

Comverse Info Systems Inc.
516-677-7400
www.cominfosys.com

Dictaphone (recently acquired by Lernout & Hauspie)
800-447-7749
www.lhsl.com

Envision Telephony
(206) 621-9384
www.envisiontelephony.com

Eyretel, Inc.
(800) 895-0803
www.eyretel.com

Nice Systems LTD
888-577-6423
www.nice.com

Witness Systems Inc.
888-3-Witness
www.witness.com

---

Call Center Technology Update 2001 ■ Reprinted with permission from *Call Center Management Review*®, www.icmi.com.

45

## The New Media

The next step to providing full media coverage is recording online interactions: Web chat, e-mail and collaborative browsing. The quality of these text-based interactions is proving increasingly crucial to most call centers. Customers frequently save the written records from e-mail interactions and Web chat sessions (if transcripts are provided at the completion of chat sessions). The quality, accuracy and tone of these interactions is critical because they are documented and provide irrefutable proof of interaction quality, delivering (or not) of brand promise, and overall service quality.

Companies that have deployed interaction management software, such as Kana, eGain or Servisoft, have embedded tools to review e-mail and text-chat content for accuracy. Each online representatives' interaction logs can be accessed for content review, coaching and training purposes. Live interactions such as Web chat sessions can be monitored in real-time in addition to after-the-fact access to session archives. Call centers need to carefully evaluate and define the most effective method for monitoring and reviewing e-mail and chat content. Some examples, include:

■ All recording vendors have products that integrate with the leading ACD manufacturers including: Avaya (formally Lucent), Nortel, Aspect, Rockwell and Siemens. Additionally, Comverse, Witness and Nice have taken steps to integrate with the leading CRM and interaction management solutions. Thus, marketing, sales, R&D or product development – as well as the senior executive team – can learn first-hand from their customers. For instance: An interaction center manager wants to analyze the quality of calls for those customers waiting in queue for more than two minutes. Most recording applications will provide the tools (CTI bridge) to listen to recordings based on ACD metrics. In this case, the call center manager can listen to how representatives handle calls with long hold times. These recordings can be used for training new and existing representatives by pulling the best calls for later replay.

■ Companies using Nice's Call System Analysis can go beyond the traditional CTI based recording analysis. Call-routing data can be used to provide call recordings. For example, a report can be run on all calls that were transferred more than two times. Management can drill down in the report to learn more about the reasons for multiple transfers. Once the reasons are understood, these issues can be addressed and resolved proactively – through training, call flow and/or IVR design, service level agreements or other appropriate measures.

■ CRM integration – Comverse's recording solution allows companies using Siebel to access the call history data as entered by a representative and listen to the call directly through the Siebel application. Comverse offers an add-on product that can analyze the recording "stress level" (in other words, the tone of the call, the voice quality of the representative) and forward applicable recordings to a manager based on a set of pre-defined business rules.

## Interaction Center Performance Evaluation System

Look for tools that can automate your current system. Your monitoring forms should be easily re-created using the recording and monitoring tool, and your scoring system should be readily supported. A fully integrated system will allow forms to be shared with the representatives, with the digitized voice recording allowing reps to listen to their calls and view their scoring and feedback forms concurrently.

## Brand Reality

Innovations in the recording industry are driving closer examination of policies and procedures implemented in the interaction center. Interaction recordings can and should be shared with various groups outside of the interaction center, including senior executives. What better way to demonstrate the marked differences between the organization's vision, the brand and the operational realities that drive overall execution? Key customer interactions can provide eye-opening opportunities for your executive team and set the stage for strategic and operational changes that will enable your interaction center to more effectively deliver your brand promise to your customers. CCMReview

---

## Making the Right Decision: Tips for Vendor Selection

Clearly the functionality and depth of recording solutions has increased significantly in the last year. With the pressure to quickly develop and release product, some vendors have announced functionality that has yet to be fully implemented.

Advanced functionality such as event-driven recording, integration with CRM and Interaction Manager solutions are still in development or, in a few cases, have reached beta-testing stage. Most vendors will begin shipping these advanced solutions in 2001. However, according to Comverse spokesperson Linda Dunlea, the company began installing Siebel integrated solutions at the beginning of 2000.

Making the right selection decision and understanding clearly what functionality is currently available is best achieved through a formal Request For Proposal (RFP) process in which your interaction center's recording and monitoring needs and functionality requirements are clearly defined. A key component to the RFP process is to schedule site visits to centers using the solution you choose. Make sure that the site visits reflect a similar deployment of the tool to how it will be deployed in your contact center. After all, nothing replaces real-world experience when it comes to installing and setting up new technology!

### Matthew Page

*Matthew Page is a Senior Consultant with Initiatives Three Inc., a leading call center consulting company committed to the significance of delivering your brand at the point of interaction. He can be reached at 207-761-2400; Web site: www.initiatives3.com.*

Call Center Technology Update 2001 ■ Reprinted with permission from *Call Center Management Review*®, www.icmi.com.

46

## Service Level Notes with Brad Cleveland

# Principles of Effective Motivation (Part 1)

**There is no specific recipe for creating motivation. But the principles that drive it are timeless and proven.**

There are countless books, articles and seminars on the subject of motivation. It is among the most popular topics on the professional speaking circuit. Thousands of successful leaders — across dozens of centuries and from virtually every known civilization — have recorded their theories on motivation. And yet, some of the most common questions we receive from call center managers include: How can we keep our people motivated; and what are others doing to motivate their employees?

I initially hesitated to write this series. There obviously has been plenty already written and said about the subject. I certainly don't propose to have all the answers. Also — I say this in all sincerity — by looking at the names, titles and companies in our database, we have reason to believe that *CCMReview* subscribers are among the best and brightest leaders in the industry. You haven't built the types of organizations you are part of without being clued in to principles of leadership and motivation.

But the reality remains — motivation is a topic that continues to resonate with call center managers. Can we ever know enough about this topic? And given the ever-changing economy and sense of uncertainty so many employees feel, it is as important as ever.

Consequently, we are enthused about running this series. This first installment summarizes key interrelated principles that drive motivation. I believe in these

*Motivation is a topic that continues to resonate with call center managers.*

principles. I have seen them at work in many diverse environments. They are dependable. And they are timeless. They include:

■ **Who you are is more important than the techniques you use.** Many programs in management training offer techniques for motivating people — e.g., provide positive reinforcement, celebrate success, create a "fun" environment, etc. There's nothing wrong with using techniques unless they become manipulative — for instance, used solely for the purpose of getting something from someone else. But in a leadership position, who you are as a person matters much more than the techniques you use. Thomas Jefferson once said, "In matters of principle, stand like a rock; in matters of taste, swim with the tide." The reality is, we trust and perform for leaders who are predictable on matters of principle and who make their positions known. Convictions, sense of fairness, consistency of behavior and stated values, belief in the capabilities of people — these things have much more impact than any motivational approach could.

■ **People respond to a clear, compelling vision.** A prerequisite to creating a motivating environment is to address the whys and whats — why does the group, team, call center and organization exist? What is it trying to achieve? What's in it for customers? What's in it for employees? Quite a few people have been through the process of creating "vision statements" that, for one reason or another, have had little impact. Nonetheless, a clear focus that is cham-

*Who you are as a person matters much more than the techniques you use.*

pioned by the leader is key to pulling people in, aligning objectives and motivating action.

■ **For better or worse, culture is always at work.** Culture — the inveterate principles or values of the organization — guides behavior and can either support and further, or hamper, a motivating environment. Peter Drucker, a noted authority on corporate management and professor at Claremont Graduate School, once said, "So much of what we call management consists of making it difficult for people to work." Creating a motivating environment is often more a matter of what you eliminate than what you put in place — for example, looking for ways to scrap unnecessary hierarchies cumbersome bureaucracies and "stupid rules" can create a culture that supports and rewards action.

■ **Effective communication is essential to trust — and to motivation.** Communication creates meaning and direction for people. Organizations depend on what Warren Bennis, author and professor of Business Administration at the University of Southern California, calls "shared meanings and interpretations of reality," which facilitate coordinated action. When good communication is lacking, the symptoms are predictable: conflicting objectives, unclear values, misunderstandings, lack of coordination, confusion, low morale and people doing the bare minimum required. Effective leaders are predisposed to keeping their people in the know. They actively share both good news... and bad.

■ **Fear inhibits action and hampers motivation.** Creating a high-perform-

January 2002 ■ Reprinted with permission from *Call Center Management Review*®, www.icmi.com.

47

ance culture in which effective communication thrives means driving out fear. This was a theme that renowned management consultant W. Edward Deming spoke of passionately, especially in his later years, and is the subject of one of his famous "14 Points." However, sometimes fear goes unrecognized by managers. For example, agents who are manipulating their statistics and "cheating the system," essentially, may be more afraid of reporting accurate statistics than of "fudging the numbers." That is a symptom of what Deming would have called fear. Of course, there are those things that we should be fearful of, such as the consequences of being dishonest or grossly irresponsible. But it's the wrong kind of fear — such as, the fear of taking reasonable risks or the fear of constructive dissent — that we must work to eliminate.

■ **Listening encourages buy-in and support.** There is a common myth that great leaders create compelling visions from gifted perspectives or inner creativity that others don't possess. But those who have studied leadership point out that, in fact, the visions of some of history's greatest leaders often came from others. Further, when people have a stake in an idea, they tend to work much harder to bring about its success. Being a superb listener — in big and small ways — pays.

■ **People tend to live up to expectations.** It has been proven time and again that people tend to live up to the expectations others have of them. Expect the best and you'll likely get the best. Expect disappointing performance and that's what will likely happen. Think of the people who have had the most positive influence on your life and, chances are, they expected a lot. Those coaches or teachers who believed in us typically weren't ones who were the easiest on us. And they often weren't the kind to win popularity contests. But they believed in us — and we reached a little deeper to live up to those expectations.

■ **Sincere recognition goes a long way.** In a study by Dr. Gerald H. Graham of

Wichita State University, participants said that the most powerful motivator was personalized, instant recognition from their managers. In other words, begin recognized for a job well done. (Other top motivators in the study included managers writing personal notes, organizations using performance as basis for promotion and managers publicly recognizing employees.)

■ **Most people have yet-to-be discovered talents.** Writer and editor Elbert Hubbard once said, "There is something that is much more scarce, something far finer, something rarer than ability. It is the ability to recognize ability." This represents a huge opportunity for organizations and for individuals. After all, call centers require more diverse skills than perhaps any other part of the organization. Customer behavior, information systems technologies, queuing theory, forecasting, statistics, human resources management, training, written and verbal communication skills, reporting, real-time management and strategy are all an inherent part of the environment. That call centers lose capable people to environments that are allegedly more interesting is quite an irony. Developing attractive career and skill paths remains a vast frontier of opportunity for many call centers.

■ **Conflict will happen; how it is channeled and addressed makes the difference.** In any organization, conflict is inevitable. People need to feel free to express themselves, to vent, to "air things out." Teaching basic conflict management principles can go a long way toward keeping things on track and building a motivating environment.

■ **Accurate resource planning is essential.** What does accurate resource planning have to do with motivation? In call centers — a lot! While everyone in the

*It has been proven time and again that people tend to live up to the expectations others have of them.*

*That call centers lose capable people to environments that are allegedly more interesting is quite an irony.*

organization may be genuinely "busy," those of us in the call center can't come in early to get a head start on the day's work — nor stay late to handle calls that stacked up in the afternoon. We've got to be there when the work arrives. If we're not, bad things happen: queues build, callers get unhappy, occupancy goes through the roof. It's stressful and, if chronic, it zaps motivation and encourages people to reconsider what they are doing for a living.

■ **Actions speak louder than words.** There are countless organizations that post their values but then encourage an entirely different set of behaviors by their policies and actions. For example, building customer relationships may be the stated objective, but lack of staffing resources or standards that stress volume-oriented production may represent perceived — or very real — conflict in the messages being sent. When it comes to influence, actions always win out over words.

## Motivation Principles Are Unchanging

Like leadership itself, effective motivation cannot be bought or mandated. It defies a specific recipe for those who want to create it, and attempts to formulize it often backfire. But the principles behind motivation are reliable, necessary and unchanging. Next month, we'll explore the application of these principles — and how to address specific thorny issues that can threaten the morale in your environment. Until then, please feel free to forward specific questions, input or challenges on the topic to me: bradc@icmi.com.

Happy New Year! CCMReview

**Brad Cleveland**

*Brad Cleveland is president of Incoming Calls Management Institute (ICMI) and publisher of* Call Center Management Review. *He can be reached at 410-267-0700 (ext. 958), or bradc@icmi.com.*

## Service Level Notes with Brad Cleveland

# Principles of Effective Motivation (Part 2)

*Editor's note: This article is the second in a series on effective motivation principles.*

Like leadership itself, effective motivation defies a specific recipe for those who want to create it, and attempts to formulize it often backfire. Even so, there are dependable, interrelated principles that significantly impact motivation:

- Who you are is more important than the techniques you use
- People respond to a clear, compelling vision
- For better or worse, culture is always at work
- Effective communication is essential to trust – and to motivation
- Fear inhibits action and hampers motivation
- Listening encourages buy-in and support
- People tend to live up to expectations
- Sincere recognition goes a long way
- Most people have yet-to-be-discovered talents
- Conflict will happen; how it is channeled and addressed makes the difference
- Accurate resource planning is essential
- Actions speak louder than words

These principles were summarized in Part 1 of this series. They are universal in application. They are timeless. They are at work in every call center – indeed, in every organization of any type. They must be understood and practiced by anyone in a position of supporting, enabling and leading other individuals (i.e., directors, managers, supervisors, team leaders).

However, the real challenge is in application. This month, we'll examine five common challenges/scenarios at the organizational level. In Part 3, the final installment in this series, we'll look at scenarios that occur at the individual level.

## 1. Motivation Begins Outside the Call Center

Our seminars and consulting projects give us the chance to look inside call centers of all types and sizes. Cultures vary widely. Leadership styles run the gamut. And the backgrounds and personalities of individuals working in call centers are wonderfully diverse. Assuming the basics are in place – e.g., a clear mission and direction, reasonable pay and career opportunities, leadership that brings out the best in people – the single most important factor to overall motivation is the call center's value contribution and how that contribution is perceived throughout the rest of the organization.

People are perceptive. When the call center is viewed simply as the department that handles problems, inquiries, or sales – or, especially, when it is seen as a "cost center" – there is an insidious, low-level drain on morale that will defy all other attempts to improve motivation. In other words, the greatest impact call center leadership can have on motivation is often by doing the things that heighten the call center's standing with people throughout the rest of the organization. This goes to the heart of vision, culture and communication. When others see the call center's strategic contribution for what it is, then call center employees will know that what they do really makes a difference. And that will make all the difference in their level of motivation!

## 2. Even the 'Small Things' Can Undermine Trust

Another major factor in overall motivation is the level of honesty, consistency and trust inherent in the organization. If you're thinking, "Yes of course that's true... but it's certainly not a problem here," don't be so sure.

The vast majority of call center managers I've worked with have unquestionable integrity as individuals, and would be deeply troubled by the notion that anything less than honest was happening in their centers. And yet, seemingly incidental decisions and policies can undermine an environment that is otherwise trustworthy and dependable.

For example, there are plenty of ways agents can "trick the system" to make reports come out in their favor. And they often learn from the best – many managers are producing executive level reports that interpret call center results in such a way as to put the call center in better light than one might find by investigating the details. I know, because I've often been on the other side of the fence, tasked with interpreting these reports to uncover underlying problems and improvement opportunities.

There's rarely an outright intent at either level to "cook the books." But it's important for leaders to be aware of gray areas and minimize the chance that interpretations will vary. Otherwise, a lot of second-guessing will undermine collective confidence – and motivation.

## 3. Fundamental Question: Is There a Future Here?

ICMI's *Agent Staffing & Retention Study Final Report* noted a host of reasons for agent turnover. The top four included better opportunities outside the organization, compensation issues, better opportunities inside the organization and lack of career opportunities – all of which underscore the importance of developing legitimate career and skill paths.

There are two basic approaches to employee advancement: career paths and skill paths – either can significantly and positively impact motivation. A typical career path model requires the development of job families, which are comprised

Section 9

February 2002 ■ Reprinted with permission from *Call Center Management Review*®, www.icmi.com.

49

of a number of jobs arranged in a hierarchy by grade, pay and responsibility (e.g., agent, team leader, supervisor, manager, senior manager, director). Because the historical corporate-ladder approach to staff development can be limited for call centers (due to the finite amount of supervisory and management positions available), a more effective approach may be the skill-path model. Skill paths focus on an individual's acquisition of skill sets. Every call center – even small environments with seemingly limited career path opportunities – can build attractive development and advancement opportunities for employees.

And pay? Many managers are quick to point out that pay is just one factor in motivation, and often not the most important one. But there's a point at which this argument gets carried too far. Pay matters. It does impact motivation and it must be in balance with prevailing opportunities for the skills and knowledge your center requires.

It's quite simple. Advancement opportunities foster motivation. Dead-end jobs erode motivation.

## 4. Conflicting Objectives are Counterproductive

While few call centers have performance objectives that are diametrically opposed, many do have expectations and standards that are at least partially in conflict, either with each other or with call center realities. For example, the nature of the calls, the processes you have in place, tools available, the skills and knowledge of your agents and other variables determine how long calls should be. If qualitative measurements are refined enough to ensure agents are spending the appropriate amount of time handling calls, then average handling time standards are potentially counterproductive.

Similarly, many of the variables that impact contacts handled per agent are outside of their control (e.g., call arrival rate, call types, callers' knowledge, callers' communication abilities, forecast accuracy and scheduling, coworkers' adherence to schedule). Counting contacts handled per agent as a measure of productivity can also be counterproductive… and demoralizing. Abandonment rate, occupancy and various work-mode quotas are also problematic.

But the other side of this coin is a different world: Objectives that are understood, consistent, fair and that further the creation of strategic value are powerful motivators. Objectives and standards vary widely from one call center to the next. This area represents a significant, ongoing opportunity to further vision, build a supportive culture and establish compelling expectations (see "Establishing and Meeting Call Center Performance Objectives: Parts 1-3," *CCMReview*, October-December 2001.)

## 5. Workload Planning is a Significant Motivation Factor

Call center staff can't come in early to get a head start on the day's work, nor stay late to handle calls that stacked up in the afternoon. We've got to be there when the work arrives. We exist in a queuing environment, and being even slightly understaffed during some intervals of the day creates low service levels, high agent occupancy (the percent of time agents are handling vs. waiting for calls), and long queues for customers (see figure below).

Understanding and managing the precarious balance between staffing resources and workload is especially important to motivation. The single greatest contribution that some organizations can make toward improving motivation and morale is to improve resource planning and do a better job of matching staff with workload. For example, many tech support reps love working with customers and helping them solve problems. But both become infinitely more difficult when dealing with customers who are frustrated by a long wait to get through. "Those are the days when I can literally feel the tension in my back and shoulders when I go home," one person told me. Such workforce management imbalances motivate agents to find work that preserves their well-being, as well as their backs and shoulders.

## There's No Single Solution

I'm often asked for best practices when it comes to "motivating employees." The reality is that motivation is largely the result of a systemic, interrelated system of causes that spans everything from resource planning, to objectives, to career opportunities and recognition. There's obviously a lot more to it than pizza feeds or charismatic leaders with a knack at firing up the troops.

In the final article in this series, we'll examine scenarios at the individual level. Again, please feel free to forward specific questions, experiences or feedback to me at bradc@icmi.com. We always appreciate and value your input!

*CCMReview*

**Brad Cleveland**

*Brad Cleveland is president of Incoming Calls Management Institute (ICMI) and publisher of* Call Center Management Review. *He can be reached at 410-267-0700 (ext. 958), or bradc@icmi.com.*

## Sample Base Staff Calculations

**Talk Time: 240 sec; After Call Work: 30 sec; Calls: 150 1/2 hr.**

| Agents | SL % in 15 sec. | ASA (in sec.) | Agent Occupancy | Avg. Calls Per Agent |
|---|---|---|---|---|
| 23 | 14% | 476 | 98% | 6.5 |
| 24 | 38% | 121 | 94% | 6.3 |
| 25 | 56% | 55 | 90% | 6.0 |
| 26 | 69% | 29 | 87% | 5.8 |
| 27 | 79% | 16 | 83% | 5.6 |
| 28 | 86% | 10 | 80% | 5.4 |
| 29 | 91% | 6 | 78% | 5.2 |
| 30 | 94% | 3 | 75% | 5.0 |
| 31 | 96% | 2 | 73% | 4.8 |
| 32 | 98% | 1 | 70% | 4.7 |
| 33 | 99% | 1 | 68% | 4.5 |

Section 9

February 2002 ■ Reprinted with permission from *Call Center Management Review*®, www.icmi.com.

50

# Principles of Effective Motivation (Part 3)

*Editor's note: This article is the third and final in a series on effective motivation principles.*

The subject of motivation represents an interesting paradox. On one hand, it is a topic that has been addressed by thousands of successful leaders across centuries. The principles of effective motivation – create a clear vision, establish effective communication, believe in the capabilities of people, lead by example and others – are simple and universal in application. And yet, motivation remains a hot topic among leaders of all types. It seems we can never quite know enough about it, especially in times of change and uncertainty.

Part 1 of this series identified universal principles of motivation, which must be understood and practiced by anyone in a position of supporting, enabling and leading other individuals (e.g., directors, managers, supervisors, team leaders). In Part 2, we looked at common challenges/scenarios at the organizational level. In this final installment, we'll focus on issues that impact the individual.

## 15 Fundamental Needs

While I am convinced that effective motivation defies specific recipes or formulas, there are definable prerequisites to motivation at the individual level. As individuals, we must:

- Know that our contributions matter – that we make a difference
- Believe in the value of the organization's mission
- Trust the integrity, intentions and competence of those in leadership positions
- Feel equipped and ready to do the work to which we are assigned
- Get constructive feedback on how we are doing
- Believe that our skills, abilities and interests are reasonably well-matched with the job
- Have enough variety in our jobs to keep things interesting
- Know the rules and expectations
- Have clear and accessible channels of communication with executive management
- Believe that we are compensated fairly for our contributions
- Have a reasonable fit (balance) between our work life and personal life
- Work in an environment that is safe and comfortable
- Enjoy a reasonable degree of autonomy in our work
- Have challenging yet attainable standards of performance
- Get the chance to demonstrate and apply our creative abilities

From the leader's perspective, understanding these 15 needs is essential to creating an environment in which motivation flourishes. Together, they should serve as a backdrop to decisions related to employee involvement, performance standards, individual development and other initiatives within the call center.

## Employee Involvement

Without exception, call centers that produce the most strategic value for their organizations have a well-defined mission and involve employees in key operational activities that support it. A major precept of the modern quality movement is that those closest to the work know and understand it best. Agents are in an ideal position to help define what constitutes a quality contact, and how processes, training and systems can be improved. Agent involvement also promotes ownership and empowerment, both key components of quality improvement and job satisfaction.

Involvement at all levels encourages innovation. As the story goes, James Watt started the industrial revolution by observing the power of steam escaping from a teakettle. This principle still holds true:

The most astounding innovations often come from fresh observation of mundane activities right under our nose. I know of an insurance company that redesigned its screen layout based on the ideas of a new agent; the improvements, which no one else had previously thought of, boosted productivity throughout the center.

There are few things as motivating for individuals as seeing their ideas make a positive difference in an organization. Opening channels of communications, encouraging input and following up with communication on those ideas that do or do not get implemented (and why) contributes to a motivating, innovative and rewarding culture.

## Performance Objectives

The way in which performance standards are established and enforced has a big impact on motivation – or the lack thereof. For example, using average performance or relative rankings as benchmarks is a potential mine field. It's easy to forget a mathematical principle – about half of any group will perform above average and half below – regardless of the actual proficiency with which the group as a whole is performing. As those below average improve, the average shifts – relegating much of the group to perpetual below-average status. Not exactly a recipe for peak motivation. The same thing is true for relative rankings – one out of every 10 is in the top ten percent, while one is in the bottom 10 percent, regardless of how the group performs.

You can avoid the potential problems that come from using averages or relative rankings by determining acceptable (minimum) performance standards or establishing a sensible range of performance. Either way, getting past relative comparisons will help to avoid a world of potential trouble.

How objectives are enforced also makes a big difference in morale. For example, adherence to schedule is an important performance measurement. But misapplication of real-time monitor-

March 2002 ■ **Reprinted with permission from** *Call Center Management Review*®, www.icmi.com.

51

Section 9

ing systems, which can measure adherence to the second, can quickly backfire. Today's environment is characterized by empowered agents and participative management styles; yes, schedule adherence is important, but a top-down approach is usually counterproductive. The best approach generally involves educating individuals and teams on the implications of the call center's time-sensitive environment and providing them with the tools and means to track adherence and coordinate adjustments. In other words, monitoring and "enforcement" are moved to teams and individuals as much as possible.

## Raising the Bar

Many managers advocate a process sometimes referred to as "shifting performance curves," which aims to turn average performers into top performers. This approach involves identifying competencies (knowledge, skills, abilities, behaviors) of top performers and moderate performers, assessing the gap, and then establishing training needs, performance expectations and relevant objectives to close the gap. The process is designed to actively raise the bar and encourage better performance.

However, this approach must be pursued in the right context. In any group of people, there will be a distribution of talents and skills. Constantly pushing average performers can disenfranchise those who, for whatever reasons, are in the middle of the pack. Further, an age-old complaint workers have against management is that all they receive for good performance is a new set of performance expectations – "No good deed shall go unpunished," as the old saying goes. It can leave people wondering what the rules and expectations really are.

There's a fine line that divides this negative perspective from the positive energy coming from reaching a new goal that you have a part in setting. Leaders who are cognizant of how raising the bar can backfire, typically make an extra effort to involve employees in setting standards. They discourage relative rankings and individual incentives that can undermine the team, and have a good sense of when to migrate performance standards or expectations to a new level. With a participative approach, individuals and teams often push expectations higher than those that would feasibly be established by a top-down approach.

## Individual Development

Grooming promotable agents for analyst, supervisory or management positions while they are still agents brings many benefits to those individuals and to the organization. Their interest in the call center environment often increases. They understand the context of their current positions better. They are less likely to look for positions elsewhere. They are better equipped to contribute to operational improvements and innovations. They tend to inspire their peers to think like managers (e.g., cause and effect, customer retention, bottom-line impact, etc.)

It takes a reasonably structured plan to effectively develop individuals. The plan may include internal and external seminars, participation in crossfunctional planning activities or involvement in special projects. It takes time, commitment and money to develop individuals. But the returns become clear when their unique (and often untapped) talents and abilities begin to blossom – and their enthusiasm for the opportunities that the call center presents becomes evident.

## Applying the Principles

Call centers are made up of a myriad of personalities, goals, skills, needs, etc. – which is why off-the-shelf motivational prescriptions or formulas often eventually fail. For leaders, the challenge is less a matter of "motivating people" and more one of creating an environment in which the motivation already resident in each person can flourish.

As this series on motivation comes to a close, I'd like to suggest some action items:

■ Reread the first two articles in the series. You may want to assemble a small, representative team from various roles in the call center and discuss these issues. Identify the areas that need attention.

■ Discuss each of the 15 fundamental needs and the degree to which your environment supports these needs.

■ Discuss the call center's current major policies and initiatives (e.g., performance standards, skill or career paths, efforts to encourage involvement and others) within the context of the 15 fundamental needs.

■ Identify the potential steps that can address these needs while furthering the mission of the call center. Assess the cost, time and effort associated with proposed steps and develop a plan.

■ Identify two or three low- or no-cost actions you can take immediately to further conditions that foster motivation. Put them into practice.

■ Let me know how things are going (bradc@icmi.com).

There has never been a time when call centers have faced more change – nor a time when we have as much opportunity to positively impact the lives of our employees, customers and organizations. That reality, in and of itself, is motivating! **CCMReview**

**Brad Cleveland**

*Brad Cleveland is president of Incoming Calls Management Institute (ICMI) and publisher of* Call Center Management Review. *He can be reached at 410-267-0700 (ext. 958), or bradc@icmi.com.*

March 2002 ■ Reprinted with permission from *Call Center Management Review®,* www.icmi.com.

52

Section 9

# In the Center
## with Laura Sikorski

### Keeping Absenteeism to a Minimum in the Call Center

*Laura Sikorski, managing partner of Sikorski-Tuerpe and Associates in Centerport, N.Y. (516.261.3066), has over 28 years of experience in the telecommunications and call center industry. She is a member and past-president (1993-1995) of the Society of Telecommunications Consultants and an Honorary Certified Member of the National Bureau of Professional Management Consultants.*

What does it really mean to be "absent?" According to Webster's Dictionary: 1: not present or attending : missing  2: not existing : lacking  3: inattentive, preoccupied.

You can keep absenteeism to a minimum in the workplace only if you have taken precautions to control it. The key areas within your control that can help reduce absenteeism in your call center include:

- office environment/ergonomics
- hiring practices
- training programs/performance criteria
- motivational techniques
- compensation/benefits

### Stop "Sick Building Syndrome" in its Tracks

Whenever an agent is sick, you probably think there is nothing you can do about it. I disagree. Having remodeled many call center office environments in the past 28 years, I have found that many centers suffer from "Sick Building Syndrome (SBS)." Germs will be germs, and they stay wherever they are welcome.

When was the last time the ceiling air vents were cleaned at your call center? If the HVAC (Heating, Ventilation, Air-conditioning) system is turned off at night and/or on weekends, bacteria will be in the office every day pounding down on you and your staff when the system is turned on. If fresh air is coming from the bottom of an air-shaft as opposed to the roof, or if there is less than 15 percent fresh air in the HVAC systems, you are just recycling bacteria. I strongly recommend a meeting with your landlord or

> *As every call center manager knows, mental/emotional absenteeism causes the most nightmares. We have the "buns in seats," yet reps "just aren't there."*

facility manager to set-up a regular maintenance program and review/modify air intake/outtake from your office space.

How about general janitorial services? Do the restrooms in your call center contain anti-bacterial soap dispensers? Do you have "during the day" services to clean and pick-up refuse from the restrooms and lounge area?

### Eyeing other Environmental Issues

Does your staff complain about headaches? This problem, all too

*Laura Sikorski*

common in a call center, can be caused by glare on the monitor screens. To reduce glare, change the lens cover in your light fixture from solid plastic to parabolical (1-inch grid). Install pink fluorescent bulbs in the fixtures. Install alternate light controls for the ceiling fixtures. This will allow you to turn on two bulbs at a time instead of all four. Install glare screens on the monitors.

Incorrect eyeglass prescriptions can also cause headaches. Remind your agents to tell their eye doctors that their daily work involves using a PC monitor. The prescription needed to read a book is quite different than the prescription they need to read a screen.

Does staff complain about stiff necks or wrists that hurt?  Buy footstools. Buy wrist pads for the keyboard. Take a few days to walk the floor and watch your staff in their workspace. Maybe you have too many gadgets that are causing the staff to get backaches due to awkward reaching or repetitive movements. Or what you thought was writing space is not being used at all because it is too far away due to the keyboard or mouse extension tray. If

**Section 9**

April 1998  ■  Reprinted with permission from *Call Center Management Review*®, www.icmi.com.

53

your agents have file cabinets, are they restricting chair movement due to being to close to their knees?

Do you have policies regarding sending staff home if they have a cold, fever etc.? You should. If you don't, you'll pay a high price. One person comes in sick and it seems the rest of the office suddenly gets sick. If you do have such a policy, don't stray from it. It MUST apply to everyone — including management staff.

## Healthy Hiring and Training

Now that we know we can control absenteeism caused by illness/injury, let's explore what you can do to deal with Webster's 2nd and 3rd definitions. As every call center manager knows, mental/emotional absenteeism causes the most nightmares. We have the "buns in seats," yet reps "just aren't there."

First and foremost, analyze your hiring practices. Look at the personality traits and telephone voices of agent applicants. Also look for candidates that will be successful long-term. Are they creative, decisive, persuasive, analytical, able to make decisions? Do they have good oral and written communications skills? Develop tests and ask questions that will help to reveal who the ideal candidates are.

Does your training program really teach, develop and empower new hires and existing staff? Does your program provide techniques for controlling the caller, up-selling, handling irate/abusive callers, stress management? Do your performance evaluation policies have standards that are clearly measurable? You would be surprised at the interpretation of what "good" "fair" and "poor" mean to different people.

## Agent Involvement, Innovative Incentives Foster Enthusiasm

Are you controlling burnout among agents? Answering phone calls day-in and day-out is, to say

the least, tedious and boring. Are you providing time-off the telephone for special projects, career enrichment with CBT (computer-based training), outside seminars, in-house seminars by outside professionals? Do you change ACD gate assignments? When was the last time you sat at your desk for two hours and couldn't go anywhere unless you asked someone? You have the flexibility to get up when you want to, your reps don't.

Have you used the task-force approach for selecting "complaining agents" to solve an issue? For example, if an agent doesn't like the current monitoring process, ask him to find better ways to evaluate calls. Or create a general task force in charge of creating ways to make agents' jobs easier and more fun. If you give agents the opportunity to change the system, you will be amazed at how motivated and committed they will become.

Contrary to popular call center belief, mere cash incentives are not enough to motivate agents and maintain high morale over long periods. Cash is cash, and when it is spent it is forgotten. One alternative is to award agents with points for jobs well done and allow them to redeem their points for gifts, hours or days off, gas vouchers, metro/subway vouchers, theater tickets, etc.

Are you compensating staff based on what skills they need to have? Keep in mind that you get what you pay for. When was the last time your Human Resources Department did a salary survey? If your pay is less than the average within your industry, staff generally "walks" for more money. The average cost to train a new hire is approximately $2,500. Just think of how much money you could be investing in existing staff if your call center did not suffer from "happy feet" — the term I use to describe the above "walking-syndrome."

Have you recently reviewed your

benefits package? Why not add a vacation day, personal day, day-off for perfect one-year attendance, day-off for a birthday?

Is a staff member pre-occupied due to a pending family event, like a wedding. Why not adjust his or her hours for a couple of weeks? How about making it easier for reps to swap hours with other reps without getting "Board of Director" approval?

Have you ever considered making a rep a "supervisor" for the day/week? Let them experience your issues first hand.

## The Human Side of the Call Center

If you really want to reduce agent absenteeism, put yourself in your agents' shoes. What would keep you coming in to the call center and doing the best possible job day after day? If you are a manager/supervisor who started out as an agent, it's easy to forget what bothered you when you were on the phones.

My strongest advice to be successful at keeping absenteeism to a minimum is to remember the human side of your call center. Your agents are mothers, fathers, sisters, brother, husbands, wives, boyfriends, girlfriends, uncles, aunts, etc. Although some of you would like to think agents are just the means to achieve service level and numbers, remember that your staff has the same emotions and problems as you do. Reps must feel they are important to the company. For they are, in fact, your most important asset. Don't minimize their value. If you do, you will never minimize absenteeism. Your staff will be calling in sick while going out on job interviews, and you will always be behind the eight-ball.

**SLN**

April 1998 ■ Reprinted with permission from *Call Center Management Review*®, www.icmi.com.

54

# Use Incentive Programs to Link Desired Behaviors with Rewards

*by Leslie Hansen Harps*

**Regularly reinforce agents who perform well. The more often you reward behavior, the more you'll get it.**

Incentive programs "are intended to link the behavior of individual employees to the types of performance that you need in the organization," observes Gerry Ledford, practice manager of employee performance and rewards for Nextera's Sibson Consulting Group in Los Angeles. Incentive programs in some call centers achieve only lukewarm results or, worse yet, backfire and reinforce the wrong kind of behavior, while others exceed expectations.

"Incentive programs that are aligned with customer satisfaction, have clearly identified performance standards and are consistent" can work very well in the call center, says Anne Nickerson, principal of Call Center Coach, Ellington, Conn. She cites a successful call center incentive program in a highly complex financial industry in which the goal was to improve the accuracy of information given to customers. When the incentive program was implemented, all the necessary tools were put into place, including clear standards and expectations, a system that provided accurate information, training and "mini-trainings" for the call center agents, and a monitoring and coaching process. Reps who performed well became peer coaches and all coaches were trained and calibrated to ensure consistency in their evaluation.

Unfortunately, many call center incentive programs "tend not to be very well-implemented and often are not very well-designed," Ledford says. Probably the single most common problem of design, he says, is failure to use a broad enough measurement base. "You need a balance of measures to reflect the differ-

ent kinds of performance you want from people. Otherwise, you'll suboptimize."

Design an incentive program that rewards productivity, such as handling more calls in an hour, and your service quality may suffer. But if you incent only quality, Ledford says, "you almost certainly will see productivity decline."

A well-designed, well-implemented incentive program may have as many as three to five variables or even more, he says. Finding the right mix and balance is one of the keys to a successful program.

## Broadening Measures

Boston Coach, an executive sedan service, revamped its incentive program to increase the number of measures, reports Nancy Leeser, vice president of international reservations and customer service for the Boston-based company. "When we first introduced the incentive program," she says, "it was based purely on quality," measuring number of errors per transaction. CSRs who met their goal received an incentive of 5 percent of their salary. The program was deemed to be too subjective, and "we weren't sure we were getting our money's worth," Leeser says.

A supervisor in the call center worked with CSRs to develop a revised incentive program through which reps can earn up to 5 percent of their salary. "It's a multi-faceted program," Leeser says. To determine the categories, "we selected the things that were important to us in running the business." Reps earn points in the following categories:

■ Individual attendance and punctuality.

■ Schedule adherence.

■ Number of transactions.

■ Level reached in the company's career pathing program (with number of points awarded increasing as the level increases).

■ Improvements in number of service failures for the center as a whole.

Depending upon overall point total, a CSR can earn a 100 percent payout, a 50 percent payout – or no payout at all.

"We are getting what we hoped for" from the program, Leeser says. Implemented last year, the program was fine-tuned this year, combining attendance and punctuality into one category and moving to a quality measure that rewards group, rather than individual, performance.

## Rewarding with Recognition

In addition to its corporatewide recognition programs, the service area of Independence Blue Cross (IBC) also uses a multi-faceted recognition program called "Blue Diamond."

"It's a monthly program that recognizes our service reps," explains Hank Kearney, senior director of member service for the Philadelphia-based company. The program keys in on four areas:

■ Attendance and punctuality.

■ Accuracy and professionalism, as determined through monitoring (reps must receive a rating of 99.5 percent or more).

■ Performing "at expectations-plus" in categories such as staff time, after-call work and follow-up work.

■ Going above and beyond the call of duty.

Contributions in the last category are noted by a rep's supervisor, says Roe Tabasco, manager of quality assurance and training for IBC. For example, a rep may have helped train others within the unit, handled special projects with timeliness and accuracy, worked overtime, received complimentary letters from members, made suggestions for improving work operations or simply may have been an enthusiastic, motivated coworker.

April 2001 ■ Reprinted with permission from *Call Center Management Review*®, www.icmi.com.

55

Blue Diamond awards are given out on the last Friday of each month on "Blue Diamond Day." Reps who have earned a Blue Diamond receive a certificate, a blue diamond to put on the certificate and a gift voucher for the company cafeteria. The number of individuals who receive Blue Diamonds varies, with perhaps 10 to 20 of the 225 service reps at the call center recognized each month.

Once a year, a recognition breakfast is held for the top Blue Diamond winners. Awardees receive a certificate, an American Express gift certificate and a gold coin (part of the company's corporatewide recognition program).

The program has been in place for more than five years and is very successful, Kearney says, especially with reps who are making the call center their career.

### Balance Service and Productivity

When developing an incentive program, suggests Gerry Ledford, first define what role the call center plays, then identify key measures that support that role. That way, you can tie rewards for the individual to the type of performance you want from the call center. For example, "if you don't see the call center as a sales channel to reach customers and expand the business, then rewarding cross-selling is a waste of time," he says.

Use a balanced mix of metrics, Ledford advises. For example, a productivity measure, such as number of calls per hour could be balanced with a metric from customer satisfaction surveys or measures of individual quality. It's crucial not to reward productivity at the expense of service quality, and vice versa.

"Productivity is a lot easier to measure than quality," according to Nancy Leeser. "You have to put your money where your mouth is on the quality piece, going out of your way to reward quality." Boston Coach does not include number of phone calls in its incentive program, she says. "We reward things which lead to that – if you're in your seat, adhering to your schedule, you will take more phone calls. But we've never given a target number of calls reps need to take in a day."

---

### A Different Look at Incentive Programs

"To me, delivering a certain level of quality and efficiency with productivity is how you keep your job," notes Donna K. Richmond, president of the Richmond Group, a customer service consulting firm located in Wheaton, Ill. "I think that an incentive should be for above and beyond the call of duty."

Richmond has strong feelings about incentive programs in the call center. "The goals have to be a real stretch, but they also have to be reachable." She cites the case of one call center paying a base salary of $20,000, with a potential incentive payout of as much as $10,000. "But the incentive was nearly impossible to get," Richmond says. "Once the agents realized it wasn't doable, they either quit or stopped trying."

She also suggests that managers examine whether they can achieve the results they desire without an incentive program. "Can you get the same or better results by paying people more money, and getting more talented, more experienced people?"

Finally, she advises, don't treat the incentive program in a vacuum. "If you're monitoring people for the program, take advantage of the an opportunity to look at the whole picture." Examine the process and root out barriers that may get in the way of agents doing their jobs.

---

Independence Blue Cross intentionally does not include a productivity category in its recognition program. "We want to send the message that we'd rather have it done right the first time, so we do not emphasize the reps having to take a certain number of calls, or having a certain average talk time," says Hank Kearney. "I'd rather have a rep with a higher talk time who delivers quality service – one who's leaving customers wowed – than a rep who moves customers in and out quickly."

### A Learning Opportunity

For an incentive program to change behavior, it's important to combine it with coaching – particularly when it comes to service quality, says Anne Nickerson. She describes an ideal incentive program as one that has "clear, consistent rewards tied to improvement in behavior, with opportunities for everyone to understand and learn what that behavior is and looks like."

This would include giving call center agents feedback immediately after a call and letting them know what they can do to improve their score, as well as their management of the customer. "Deliver the feedback in a way that's very specific," Nickerson advises. "Give examples, models and approaches that the person can use" to improve their performance

An incentive program combined with coaching will get better results, agrees Gerry Ledford. "People tend to act as if you can announce an incentive plan, turn on the switch and it will work. That's not the case. You have to do all the hard management labor of communicating, training, reinforcing, monitoring and coaching" to get the results you want.

"It's quite possible to get unintended results, to unintentionally reinforce behaviors you don't want," he says, so it's critical to monitor the incentive program to make sure you're getting the results you expected.

### What Type of Reward?

"All things being equal, dollars are going to be more effective than praise" as a reward, according to Ledford. "While different things have different reward value for individuals, almost anybody is going to find money motivating." The question is, how much money does it take to drive a change in behavior?

"The available evidence suggests that an incentive becomes powerful when it represents 5 to 10 percent of base pay," Ledford says

"Money is one incentive, but there are many more," observes Anne Nickerson. "I also see incentives that are fun, that help improve morale." At one call center, for example, agents who earned a certain number of points could put leaves on the

April 2001 ■ Reprinted with permission from *Call Center Management Review*®, www.icmi.com.

56

branch of a tree. Each completed branch was worth so many points, which could be turned in for rewards such as massages, manicures and pedicures, free pizza and certificates at the local mall. Agents loved the program and the prizes.

At a health care and financial services call center, Nickerson says, when agents met and maintained a specified quality goal, managers would make and serve breakfast or serve reps an afternoon treat from a fully equipped snack cart. In another call center, an entire team that cleaned up a database earned a trip to Las Vegas by "beating the clock."

Whatever reward you decide to use in your incentive program, remember that "the more often you reward behavior, the more often you'll get it," Ledford says. Monthly or quarterly incentive programs are the most common. If the time horizon is longer than that, the program is less likely to reinforce the behavior you're seeking. So make sure there's lots of communication and publicity to keep interest high.

## Are They Worth It?

Incentive programs that are designed and implemented well can pay off handsomely. Gerry Ledford cites a study conducted for the American Compensation Association. The study, which looked at 660-plus incentive plans across a range of industries, identified the net return on payout as 134 percent. "That's for an average payout of three percent," Ledford says. "Typically, the higher potential for gain, the higher the success rate." Companies in the most successful quartile in this study had a whopping net return of 378 percent.

While there have been some whopping failures, on the whole, incentive programs are quite successful, Ledford says. "And they're one of the most successful types of intervention you can come up with." CCMReview

Leslie Harps

*Leslie Hansen Harps is a freelance business writer specializing in customer service and call centers. She is the former president of the Customer Service Institute, and author of several books. Leslie can be reached at 202-363-5822.*

**Section 9**

# Agent Compensation Evolving as Industry Growth Continues

*by Susan Hash*

**Industry growth and an increase in customer access channels have paved the way for better pay and career opportunities.**

As call centers continue to expand — both in the number of centers, as well as roles and responsibilities within the organization — staff positions and compensation are beginning to reflect the industry's increased visibility.

Market analysis firm Datamonitor estimated the number of call centers in the United States to be 69,500 in 1999, and predicted that number to increase to 78,000 in 2003.

"Companies across all industries are launching call center operations, most frequently, to handle some aspect of customer service or sales, or to outsource certain job functions," says Kim Witt, the leading call center compensation analyst with William M. Mercer Inc.

William M. Mercer's most recent research reveals two fast-growing call center management positions, which reflect the evolving nature of the industry: 1) managers of multiple call center sites; and 2) executive positions with overall call center responsibilities.

"Five years ago, it was unusual for a company to have multiple call center sites or to assign oversight responsibility to a senior executive," Witt says. "Today, call centers are central to the business strategy as a way to deliver products or services. As a result, they're getting more attention from management."

Larry Reissman, head of the Hay Group's New England Rewards Practice, based in Boston, agrees. "The changes in pay reflect the changing role of the call center," he says. "It has become more of a strategic role because of the multiple [customer access] channel issues."

## Additional Access Channels Are Impacting HR Strategies

The addition of electronic customer-access channels, such as email and text-chat, are presenting another challenge for human resource strategies, as well as compensation issues.

"The complexion of customer service is changing dramatically in support of e-business," according to Connie Caroli,

---

## Pay Variations by Call Center Type

| TYPE OF CALL CENTER | AVERAGE TOTAL CASH COMPENSATION* |
|---|---|
| **JOB: TEAM/GROUP SUPERVISOR** | |
| Inbound with selling | $45,600 |
| Credit/collections | $42,400 |
| Inbound order entry | $41,500 |
| Customer service | $40,900 |
| Outbound with selling | $36,700 |
| **JOB: ENTRY-LEVEL PHONE REPRESENTATIVE (HOURLY)** | |
| Customer service | $10.80 |
| Inbound with selling | $10.57 |
| Credit/collections | $10.48 |
| Inbound order entry | $10.20 |
| Outbound with selling | $9.80 |

\* Total cash compensation equals base pay plus short-term incentive pay.

*Source: 2000 Call Center Compensation Survey, William M. Mercer Inc., www.wmercer.com*

---

## CSR Regional Salary Trends

As would be expected, pay scales differ depending on an organization's geographical location, according to the *2000 Customer Service Industry Survey* by the International Customer Service Association (ICSA). The majority of respondents (83 percent) reported that their customer service departments manage inbound call centers.

Following is the breakdown of average CSR salaries according to U.S. region:

| | STARTING | AVERAGE | TOP |
|---|---|---|---|
| All companies | $23,993 | $28,876 | $33,614 |
| East North Central | $27,001 | $27,854 | $32,557 |
| West North Central | $23,139 | $28,207 | $34,818 |
| Mid-Atlantic | $25,285 | $27,898 | $34,187 |
| West South Central | $20,881 | $24,184 | $29,296 |
| South Atlantic | $26,784 | $30,902 | $36,433 |
| East South Central | $22,800 | $26,670 | $29,450 |
| New England | $28,607 | $32,802 | $39,379 |
| West | $23,143 | $27,816 | $32,938 |
| Mountain | $20,124 | $22,082 | $30,084 |

Most respondents (67 percent) to the ICSA survey indicated that their compensation system was job-based rather than skills-based.

---

July 2001 ■ Reprinted with permission from *Call Center Management Review*®, www.icmi.com.

58

Section 9

president of TeleManagement Search, which produces the annual *Call Center, TeleSales & Customer Service National Salary Guide.*

"In addition to live-operator customer service, there is an increasing demand for email customer service," she says. "This presents the next big challenge in customer service — hiring and training agents who can not only speak articulately, but who can write grammatically or, at least, intelligibly."

According to Witt: "The use of the Internet as a communication channel is substantially changing job roles at many call centers, requiring employers to change their recruitment, training and overall reward approaches. Written communication may be a new component to an existing job or an entirely new job at the call center, she notes.

## Starting Salaries in Multichannel Centers (Hourly)

| POSITION | LOW | MEDIAN | HIGH |
|---|---|---|---|
| Phone-only agents | $6.10 | $12 | $60 |
| E-contact agents | $6.75 | $12 | $75 |
| (handling only e-mail and text chat) | | | |
| Multichannel agents | $6.75 | $13 | $75 |
| (handling all channels) | | | |

Source: *CCMReview's Multichannel Call Center Study Final Report*

## Support Salaries on the Rise

The *2000 Technical Support Salary Survey* by the Association of Support Professionals and *Softletter* reveals a median pay increase of 3.1% to 12.5% for various categories of support staff. Following are year-to-year comparisons for support employees in major job categories.

| POSITION | 1999 | 2000 | CHANGE |
|---|---|---|---|
| Senior support executive | $90,000 | $97,000 | +7.8% |
| Department manager | $56,350 | $60,000 | +6.5% |
| Analyst/project manager | $52,500 | $54,380 | +3.6% |
| Senior support technician | $43,000 | $45,000 | +4.7% |
| Field support technician | $40,000 | $45,000 | +12.5% |
| Support technician | $33,950 | $35,000 | +3.1% |
| Customer service rep | $27,000 | $29,000 | +7.4% |

## Sources for Compensation Data

- *2000 Call Center Compensation Survey*, William M. Mercer Inc.; $650 for survey participants, $1,500 for non-participants; phone: 502-561-45000; Web site: www.wmercer.com. (Note: William M. Mercer's *2001 Call Center Compensation Survey* will be released in August.)

- *2000 Customer Service Industry Survey*, ICSA; $70 for member, $120 for non-members; phone: 312-321-6800; Web site: www.icsa.com.

- *2000 SOCAP Salary & Job Description Study*, SOCAP; $75 for members, $150 for non-members; phone: 703-519-3700; Web site: www.socap.org.

- *Agent Staffing & Retention Study Final Report*, Call Center Management Review, $79.95; phone: 800-672-6177; Web site: www.icmi.com.

- *2000 Technical Support Salary Survey*, ASP; free to members, $60 for non-members; phone: 617-924-3944; Web site: www.asponline.com.

- *2000 Call Center, Telemarketing & Customer Service National Salary Guide*; Telemanagement Search; $35, send a business card to Telemanagement Search, 114 East 32nd St., Suite 927, New York, NY 10016.

Seventy-four percent of respondents to the *2000 SOCAP (Society of Consumer Affairs Professionals in Business) Salary & Job Description Study*, reported an increase in the number of email contacts last year. Thirty-six percent reported an email volume increase of between 1 and 25 percent, while 24% said their email volume rose between 26 and 50 percent.

The SOCAP study respondents also reported the most advantageous skills anticipated for the future to be verbal and written communication skills (27%, up from 23% in 1998), while the three areas of computer (19%), technology/systems (19%) and Internet/Web/email skills (18%) totaled 56%, up from 43% in the last study.

As the call center agent's job becomes more complex, career and pay opportunities also are greater, says the Hay Group's Larry Reissman. "Career paths are being reconsidered. It's not just about being able to handle more — the complexity of the job allows companies to create career paths around different capa-

bilities and the variety of skills needed in the center. There's more interest in skills-based pay and progression. It's providing agents with the opportunity to move from what was once perceived to be a dead-end job into a career."

### Base Pay Plateaus, Incentives On the Rise

Call center starting salaries, which had been rising substantially over the past few years, have leveled off this year, says Caroli. Although, she adds, "we've already begun to see a rebound in the last month or so. Since the stock market rebounded somewhat since the first quarter of this year, there has been a rebound in companies who have been taking hiring freezes off. I think a full rebound is going to happen in the fourth quarter of this year."

While pay levels have plateaued, according to Mercer's research, the use of incentive pay remains high.

"We didn't see a significant change in base pay from last year's survey," says

July 2001 ■ Reprinted with permission from *Call Center Management Review*®, www.icmi.com.

Section 9

Witt. "However, it has become common to use incentive pay as part of the overall compensation package for call center employees." Almost two-thirds of the respondents to the Mercer study (64%) use individual, team and/or overall call center incentives to reward employees.

The survey also shows that pay can vary depending on the specific task performed by a call center. For instance, a team/group supervisor would receive an average total cash compensation (base pay plus short-term incentive) of $45,600 in a center that handles inbound sales calls, compared to $36,700 in a center that makes outbound sales calls (see box, page 3).

The Hay Group's research finds that, although the labor market is driving up salaries, "it's fragmented to certain pockets," explains Reissman. "We're not see-ing broad-based, large-scale salary changes. But we are seeing increased interest in incentive compensation and bonuses."

He adds that performance measures for incentive and bonus pay have evolved, as well. Call centers are moving away from traditional productivity and/or quality measures to revenue-gen-eration measures — either through direct sales or referrals.

## Keeping Up With Growth

While the anticipated annual growth rates for agent positions in the United States vary from 6.5 percent to as high as 20 percent, analysts agree that the growth will continue. To keep pace, call centers will need to focus on retaining skilled agents.

"Attraction and retention are at the top of the list in terms of employer 'pain,'" says Witt. "High turnover in the frontline phone rep position creates a tremendous cost for the employer in terms of recruiting, training and lost pro-ductivity."

In fact, respondents to *CCMReview's Agent Staffing & Retention Study Final Report* identified the top reasons for call center attrition to be "better opportuni-ties outside the organization" (28% responded "very frequent," while 42% said "sometimes"), which was closely fol-lowed by compensation issues (29%, very frequent; 30%, sometimes).

The solution, Witt says, is managing call center employees holistically, looking at a total package that includes compen-sation, benefits, work environment, reward/recognition mechanisms and managerial/leadership skills. CCMReview

July. 2001 ■ Reprinted with permission from *Call Center Management Review®*, www.icmi.com.

60

# Effective Career Progression Programs Balance Both Staff and Business Needs

*by Susan Hash*

The competition for skilled agents shows no signs of relenting. The increase in call center openings, available contact channels and types of agent skills required make it a job-seeker's market – and the outlook is pretty grim for call centers that don't have some type of agent development and retention process in place.

The historical corporate ladder approach to staff development has never been a viable option for call centers. After all, there are a finite amount of supervisory and management positions available.

Instead, a more effective staff-development approach is to prepare agents for the future of your business by taking into consideration individual staff needs and company goals. You'll also find that it's easier to get executive-level support and funding for call center career programs if they're aligned with overall business needs.

Depending on the type of advancement opportunities available in your organization and call center requirements, most centers follow one of two basic approaches to agent development. One focuses on an individualized acquisition of skill sets, while the other involves more structured tracks or levels through which agents can progress.

## Identify the Skills Your Company Finds Desirable

AT&T's Consumer Services call centers (which include some 30 various-sized call centers nationwide) has created a career development program for its Customer Care Reps called the Associate-to-Management Advancement Program (AMAP). It addresses two specific business needs that surfaced a few years ago:

■ Local call centers recognized the need for a more disciplined approach to career progression (specifically, from the nonmanagement account rep positions into management and supervisory positions), which would be perceived as objective by account reps.

■ AT&T wanted its management, organizationwide, to have consistent leadership skills. It developed a management-leadership framework, which consists of 10 competencies identified as the core leadership skills required for AT&T managers.

The call centers' AMAP process was designed with this framework mind. "We wanted the people who were being promoted or hired into our call center management positions to have demonstrated the relevant competencies in this new management leadership framework," says Jerard Kehoe, sourcing and selection director for AT&T.

## Skills-Based Development Relies on Individual Assessment

AT&T's AMAP essentially works as a skills-acquisition process, in which agents can learn new skills at their own pace. At the same time, all of AMAP's phases are based on the management-leadership framework, and target several of the skills outlined in it, such as planning and organizing, implementing with excellence and continuous learning.

In fact, as an individual moves up the AT&T management ladder, his or her performance continues to be appraised on that same framework, says Kehoe. "We've integrated AMAP with the other HR levers and strategies that represent the way AT&T wants to develop its managers – that's one of the program's strengths."

Candidates for the program are identified by the local supervisors, who have the responsibility of coaching agents, not only for on-the-job performance, but also with an eye toward developing skills for eventual promotion.

The first stage of AMAP is called "Readiness Assessment." Supervisors assess agents' readiness to enter into the AMAP process based on their own judgment and the agent's past work behavior. The supervisor's evaluation also needs to be confirmed by the call center's local human resources manager.

After an agent is identified as being ready, he or she can participate in the next cycle of skills-assessment procedures, which are scheduled at each center two or three times a year.

## Skill Paths Should Be Flexible to Meet Changing Caller Needs

Another company that has taken the skills-development approach to agent growth is Earthlink. The organization recently completed a merger with MindSpring Enterprises to create the second-largest Internet service provider in the United States with seven technical support call centers, which range from 150 to 500 agents.

Director of Technical Support Mark Hinkle describes Earthlink's skills-development process as similar to getting a college degree. Agents can take various classes; once they pass, they move on to the next course. While there is a slight hierarchy in the order of skills, the path is pretty varied depending on the agent's personal goals and customer need.

An important component of Earthlink's agent development program is the flexibility to react to changing customer demands, says Hinkle.

For instance, recently, the technical support organization expanded its agents' skills to focus on the Macintosh platform. "When the Apple iMac came out, the demand for Macintosh technical support just went through the ceiling," says Hinkle. "We've expanded the ability of our reps to take those calls. If we'd stayed with any kind of rigid hierar-

Agent Development and Retention Special Issue 2000 ■ Reprinted with permission from *Call Center Management Review*®, www.icmi.com.

61

chy, we would be doing a disservice to our customers."

### Group Skill Sets to Create a More Structured Career Path

A more structured approach to agent development calls for outlining specific levels or scales of progression and identifying the specific skill sets contained in each level.

While that seems like an overwhelming task "if you dig deep, you can find them," says Kim Weakley, assistant vice president, national call center manager, World Savings and Loan, San Antonio, Texas.

"But for the call centers that use skills-based routing, it becomes even easier. That's a very clear-cut way to build a career-progression model that will allow agents to grow," Weakley says.

In her call center, there are nine progression levels in the scale – three overall position levels and three sublevels within each. For instance, Basic I, II and III Reps; Advanced I, II and III Reps; and Expert I, II and III.

All new-hires are considered Basic I Reps. They're given an initial, eight-week training program in products, systems, customer service skills, as well as an overview of call center statistics "to understand the information we're going to be feeding back to them," she says.

After the first 90 days, new agents' skill levels are evaluated. At that point, most have reached the Basic III Rep level and they can sign up for the skills-assessment testing, which is conducted once a month.

Agents are individually coached by supervisors on the specific skills they need to attain to progress to the next level. The call center also has an inhouse team of trainers who work with agents on technical skills.

Unum Provident Insurance has developed a similar career path for its centers. "We've created a trainee position for entry-level reps, plus a Rep I, Rep II and Specialists jobs," explains Call Center Director Anne O'Neil.

Within each Rep job there are three tracks, each of which contains

different skill sets based on various products. And the Specialist position contains three separate career paths agents can select:

■ Super reps are customer-focused agents who truly enjoy working in the call center on the phone dealing with customers. They generally want to acquire more product and systems knowledge, but aren't really interested in managing others. This path allows them to become subject-matter experts, crosstrain on products and act as mentors for newer agents

■ Training/quality/technology experts are trained to offer immediate internal support for the call center. "Even though we have support areas within I/T, it's beneficial to have people on staff with the ability to respond to technology issues quickly," says O'Neil. "They can often look at a situation with a system and get our people back on track within minutes vs. having to call something in and wait."

■ A leadership path is available for management-oriented agents. "We give them opportunities to participate in reviews, act as backup for management, attend meetings in place of managers and conduct call observations," she says.

### Develop an Objective Assessment Process

One of the most critical aspects of an agent development program is an assessment process that's viewed as fair and unbiased by participants.

Kehoe feels that AT&T's AMAP assessment procedures make it distinct in that area. "It has formalized steps to objectively assess the skill levels the account reps have developed," he says. That process includes three events:

1. a written test that measures problem-solving and information-processing skills;

2. an "in-basket exercise" in which agents simulate being a manager by handling problem situations in a virtual in-basket; and

3. a discussion with a panel of trained

## Differentiate Between Service and Management Skills

When developing a career-progression model, it's important to consider a path for agents who are not management- or career-oriented. "The reality is that there are some agents who are not interested in promotion, or who might not be viewed as potential candidates for promotion," says Jerard Kehoe, AT&T sourcing and selection director. "Success as a Customer Care Rep does not necessarily predict success as a supervisor. The decision about how to develop reps into supervisors and which ones to select for promotion should be based on the skills that are relevant to supervision."

At Unum Provident Insurance, for instance, managers found that clear differentiators existed between being a senior-level rep and a specialist, says Anne O'Neil, call center director. For instance, some specific abilities identified were:

• Change management
• Problem identification and resolution
• Interaction with peer
• Conflict resolution.
• Group leadership abilities

To develop agents displaying management-type skills, the Unum Provident call centers created Mentor and Leadership Certification tracks in its career-progression model, with "distinct definitions of the behavior we're looking for and the competencies," O'Neil says. Agent progression in these areas is measured through 360-degree feedback and management observation.

Agent Development and Retention Special Issue 2000 ■ Reprinted with permission from *Call Center Management Review*®, www.icmi.com.

62

interviewers who score agents based on a set of criteria.

While testing procedures need to be consistently applied to avoid any appearance of favoritism, it's also important to know your agents, says World Savings' Weakley.

At her call center, agents go to a "test region" off the call center floor to process five to 10 customer requests, which can range from customer address changes to more complicated, sensitive issues like fixing checks that have been encoded incorrectly.

An unanticipated discovery with this process, however, was that some agents have "test phobia," she says. "They may be extremely proficient at performing certain types of tasks or calls on the floor, but when they know they're doing their monthly skills assessment, they freak out."

Weakley has worked around certain agents' test anxiety by using "sneak attacks. We may give them something that needs to be done, and we don't tell them it's a skills assessment." The only potential hazard was that agents would be handling test issues live on the system, she points out, but adds that "we make sure we check it the same day, so we can delete those transactions and not impact the customer," she says.

### Extend Growth Possibilities Beyond the Call Center

If your agent development program is limited to your call center, at some point, you may find that you have a staff of highly trained experts – with no place else to go.

While the AT&T AMAP process is specifically focused on the progression from Customer Care Rep to the entry-level call center supervisory position, agents who become qualified for entry-level management positions via the AMAP process can go into any number of positions that involve entry-level management within AT&T, says Kehoe.

In fact, the organization has an internal post-and-bid staffing process that allows Customer Care Reps to scan a staffing system for vacancies outside the call center in which they might be interested.

Earthlink's company culture also follows a promote-from-within philosophy, says Hinkle. In fact, he adds, "the majority of our company is staffed out of our call center. There are a lot of folks in executive-level positions who started out on the phones, including myself."

Typically, he says, agents move into areas like network operations, engineering, telecommunications and the MIS department.

Call center managers at Earthlink make a point of helping individual agents to progress and take into consideration any skills or interests agents have – even those not used in the call center. For instance, if an agent has an interest in Web design, their supervisor may give them a nonphone project to help showcase their skills for the company's Web Design Group.

Related company areas offer another avenue to boost agent growth. World Savings' call center extends agent learning through cross-training with its tax and insurance call center groups.

It's a win-win for both areas, says Weakley. Her center trains reps from the tax and insurance groups to take calls when the volume gets heavy. At the same time, her agents crosstrain on tax and insurance functions for those times when the tax group gets backed up. "Once we complete this, we're going to roll out a new skill level called a Universal Agent," she says.

### Compensate Agents for Growth

Naturally, you can't expect agents to be motivated to learn and grow if there is no compensation for their efforts. Unless, of course, they're planning to take those skills elsewhere, which undermines your program's fundamental goal.

## Aligning Agent Programs Across Cultures and Centers

Mergers and acquisitions have a definite impact on agent-development programs in terms of growth potential, skills involved, job descriptions, promotional opportunities and the consistency of assessment. Trying to integrate two (or more) distinct points of view on staff development can be trying for managers when different cultures, customers and procedures are involved.

Last year, after Unum and Provident merged to create Unum Provident Insurance, managers were tasked with creating one agent-development program for the company's three call centers, located in Chattanooga, Tenn., Columbia, S.C., and Portland, Maine, each of which served different types of customers.

At an initial planning meeting, which included representatives from each site, each manager detailed the programs currently in place at their centers. "We were trying to determine what would make sense [for all three centers]," she says. "It really came together based on what we heard from the agents in terms of their needs, and also what we, as the management team, felt we could manage. Each site had something that was a little different which we could leverage – and we took the best practices of each site."

The model was tested at the Portland call center to make sure it would work effectively and to give managers a chance to make adjustments. Next, O'Neil presented the model to an internal "roles group," which acts as a sounding board for programs developed around call center jobs, for more feedback and to identify any gaps in skills or job families. And the final test was a review by the Human Resources department.

Eventually, O'Neil says, the goal is to bring other related areas under the same umbrella, such as a customer claims call center, employment call center, sales support center and a broker commissions group.

Agent Development and Retention Special Issue 2000 ■ Reprinted with permission from *Call Center Management Review*®, www.icmi.com.

63

Agents at Unum Provident Insurance are assessed and certified for learning the skills included in their job-level tracks. After they've successfully demonstrated those skills on the job for six months, they receive a pay increase.

Because the program was just recently implemented, it's currently being self-funded with call center budget dollars. But, O'Neil says, since agent salaries were "not that far from where they needed to be, it's not a huge hit." However, she adds, based on the progression tracks that have been set up and the potential for retaining more experienced staff over the long term, her company's HR and finance managers have indicated that the future increases in compensation for agents are not unreasonable.

At World Savings, there are team and individual bonus opportunities associated with skills development.

Pay-for-performance bonuses are paid quarterly to teams that reach pre-set expectations. Some goals are center-wide, such as service level objectives, while others focus on team projects and the skill level of team members. So, for instance, to get the team bonus, all members must be able to test at a certain skill level, such as Advanced I Rep.

Bonus opportunities for individual agents increase with each level, as well as for working less-desired shifts.

Here's how it works: An Advanced I Rep can receive a bonus of up to 2.1 percent of his or her salary; an Expert 3 can receive almost 5 percent. "There's quite a jump in compensation and it's incrementally staged going up the scale," says Weakley.

Also, in each of the categories, there is an A, B and C designation for shifts. For example, A is the 8 a.m. to 5 p.m. shift (highly desirable); B is 9 a.m. to 6 p.m.; and C is 10 a.m. to 7 p.m. (the least preferred shift). "We pay higher bonuses for C shifts," she says.

"We try to cover all angles so that we can keep people on the less pre-ferred shifts, and there's an incentive

to learn more on their own, be able to handle more tasks and create a greater repertoire of skills," she explains. "But we also wanted them to cover for each other – so if you have somebody who's a little bit slower at developing skills on your team, you're not going to bash them, you're going to help them. And it really has worked out well."

## Do Agent Development Programs Impact Retention?

Absolutely, says Weakley. In 1998, her call center's turnover rate was between 55 to 60 percent. "We had a churning," she says. "We'd get them in and train them. They'd stay for six months and then they'd leave. We've dropped that rate to 17 percent."

AT&T is in the process of developing a plan to evaluate the effectiveness of the AMAP process, which has been in place for about two years.

However, Kehoe points out that, based on employee satisfaction surveys, agents feel more positive about their progression opportunities.

In addition, he says, "the early indications are that the people who are promoted via AMAP are demonstrating success in those management positions." Currently, about 670 Customer Care Reps have started the testing portion of the program. And of those, about 56% have successfully completed testing and have became qualified for promotion.

The effort of setting up a program is well worth it, says O'Neil. "Don't be afraid of negative thinking in the beginning or anything in your current environment that tells you it won't work," she says. "Just open up your thinking and be willing to explore all possibilities." *CCMReview*

## CSR Regional Salary Trends

The greatest challenge for managers over the next two years will be hiring and retaining frontline employees who are qualified to handle technology associated with Web-based service, Customer Relationship Management and e-commerce, according to the *2000 Customer Service Industry Survey* released this month by the International Customer Service Association (ICSA). The majority of respondents (83 percent) reported that their customer service departments manage inbound call centers.

While the technological skills required will likely impact CSR salaries, to date, the association's 1999 Customer Service Compensation Study shows that the average percentage increase for CSRs (across industries) was 4 percent last year.

As would be expected, pay scales differ depending on an organization's geographical location. Following is the breakdown of average CSR salaries according to region:

|  | STARTING | AVERAGE | TOP |
|---|---|---|---|
| All companies | $23,993 | $28,876 | $33,614 |
| East North Central | 27,001 | 27,854 | 32,557 |
| West North Central | 23,139 | 28,207 | 34,818 |
| Mid-Atlantic | 25,285 | 27,898 | 34,187 |
| West South Central | 20,881 | 24,184 | 29,296 |
| South Atlantic | 26,784 | 30,902 | 36,433 |
| East South Central | 22,800 | 26,670 | 29,450 |
| New England | 28,607 | 32,802 | 39,379 |
| West | 23,143 | 27,816 | 32,938 |
| Mountain | 20,124 | 22,082 | 30,084 |
| Canada | 23,407 | 26,300 | 35,998 |

Most respondents (67 percent) to the ICSA survey indicated that their compensation system was job-based rather than skills-based.

*Source: ICSA, 312-321-6800; Web site: www.icsa.com*

Agent Development and Retention Special Issue 2000 ■ **Reprinted with permission from** *Call Center Management Review®*, www.icmi.com.

64

# Understand the Employee-Customer Satisfaction Link for Positive Impact

*by Leslie Hansen Harps*

"Treat your employees well, and they'll treat your customers well," call center managers have long been told. While they may know intuitively that this makes sense, call center managers want hard numbers they can use to cost-justify to senior management various investments in their employees' well-being and professional development.

A magic bullet has yet to be discovered, but research has established that there is a definite link between employee satisfaction and customer satisfaction. For example:

■ A large bank in Canada found that the branches that had the highest level of customer satisfaction also had the highest level of employee satisfaction, according to Michael Hepworth, CEO of Hepworth & Company, Toronto.

■ A national service organization discovered that customer satisfaction was driven by employee training, innovation and recognition for service.

■ A major retailer found that improving employee satisfaction paid off in hard dollars. In this case, a six-point improvement on the retailer's employee satisfaction scale was linked with improvement of one percentage point on the customer-related issues that mattered the most for profit. This, in turn, was related to a one-half percentage point improvement in sales – or $4 million in additional revenue.

These last two examples come from Gantz Wiley Research Consulting Group Inc., a Minneapolis-based consulting firm that conducts linkage research. The research identifies elements of the work environment, as described by employees, that link to critically important organizational outcomes such as customer satisfaction.

Understanding the link between employee and customer satisfaction as well as long-term business performance can help you make investment decisions that yield the greatest positive impact on customer satisfaction.

## A Question of Climate

According to Scott M. Brooks, Ph.D., a consultant and manager of research and development for Gantz Wiley, employee perceptions of the workplace can be divided into two broad categories:

■ Climate for employee well-being. This category includes employee relations factors, such as job satisfaction, loyalty and commitment – how the employee feels about working at his or her place of employment.

■ Climate for service. Factors in this category include how conducive the workplace is to serving the customer, to adding value and getting work done.

Linkage research done by Gantz Wiley indicates that there is a definite link between employee satisfaction and customer satisfaction. On the other hand, "there's a lot going on with employees being happy or satisfied or loyal" that doesn't have to do with customer satisfaction, Brooks says.

Employees may be satisfied because they have the skills and knowledge they need to do their work, their work environment is well-equipped with the resources agents need to do their jobs, and top management fully recognizes the call center's value. On the other hand, some employees may be satisfied when they don't have to work hard, or are in a job relatively free of frustration because they don't have to push the envelope.

So it's no surprise that Gantz Wiley's research has found that, while employee satisfaction is important for customer satisfaction, there's an even stronger link between customer satisfaction and the service climate in an organization. Armed with that information, you can make better decisions regarding where to invest your resources.

Take compensation, for example. "I wouldn't immediately jump to pay as the main factor for improving employee satisfaction and rely on it to improve customer satisfaction," Brooks says. "Pay is not always the primary driver of employee satisfaction."

Instead, he says, "I would put my first dollars into providing the right customer service infrastructure." This includes making sure that employees are well-trained, have the knowledge and information they need to do their jobs, work with customer-friendly processes and procedures, have clear standards of performance and work in an environment where exceptional service is recognized.

Think of service climate as an automobile engine, and the climate for employee well-being as a turbo, the consultant suggests. "A turbo without an engine doesn't go anywhere – it doesn't translate into motion or value. But an engine by itself is all you need in a lot of cars." Add the turbo to the engine – combine high levels of employee well-being with a climate of service – and you can really soup up performance via an aligned and satisfied workforce that contributes to improved customer satisfaction.

## Findings Can Guide Managers

Linkage research hasn't been around long enough to have yielded a master formula – such as "an X percent increase in employee satisfaction will yield a Y percent increase in customer satisfaction, which leads to a Z percent increase in revenue," Brooks says. However, "it is possible for a company to determine its own" by conducting linkage research, which involves surveying customers and employees.

Even without conducting company-specific analysis, the consultant says, the research indicates certain findings that can help call center managers focus their performance improvement efforts.

"When certain leadership practices are present in the environment, we

July 2000 ■ Reprinted with permission from *Call Center Management Review*®, www.icmi.com.

65

see the results of having employees who know what to do, are aligned within their teams and who experience fewer frustrations and more success," Brooks notes. The leadership practices include:

■ service orientation,

■ quality emphasis,

■ employee training, and

■ employee involvement and empowerment.

"The more these leadership practices are present in the work environment, the more energized and productive the workforce is," Brooks says. "The more energized and productive, the more customers are satisfied. Having customers who are satisfied and loyal leads to better business growth over the long haul."

## Focus on Employees First

When tackling customer dissatisfaction, "the focus should first be on fixing the relationship with the employee, and then on looking at the customer," Michael Hepworth says. "If you completely focus on the customer, you may be intervening at the wrong place, and won't optimize your results." It's better to tackle the barriers that prevent employees from serving and satisfying customers.

Employee perceptions of service – especially from direct customer contact employees who have been around for a year – "are often strongly related to customer satisfaction," Brooks says. That's why he suggests treating your employees as effective observers of the values and practices that define your workplace.

One approach is to conduct focus groups to learn more about employee perceptions of their work environment. Be sure to ask questions, such as:

■ What do you like best about working here? What do you like least?

■ What helps you to be the most effective here? What gets in the way of being most effective?

■ How do you feel about the level of emphasis we place on service here?

■ How do you feel about the training you have received to do your job?

■ Do you have the information and

### FIGURE 1

## The Agent's Hierarchy of Needs

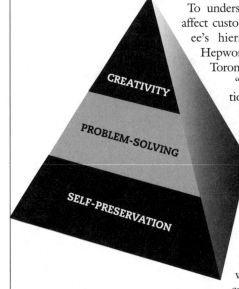

CREATIVITY

PROBLEM-SOLVING

SELF-PRESERVATION

To understand how employee satisfaction can affect customer satisfaction, consider an employee's hierarchy of needs, suggests Michael Hepworth, CEO, Hepworth & Associates, Toronto, Canada.

"The most basic need is self-preservation. If employees are focused all the time on protecting themselves – on looking out for No. 1 – they have no time for problem-solving or creativity," he says. "If they don't constantly feel they or their jobs are at risk, they can focus on problem-solving, on fixing what needs to be fixed. When that's under control, they can then focus on creativity and going the extra mile. That leads to delighting the customer," which is where customer satisfaction comes from.

knowledge you need to do your job?

Your agents know very well what leads to customer dissatisfaction. So ask them to help diagnose and resolve issues that affect customers. For example, one of the key survey items used by Gantz Wiley to gauge customer satisfaction is "customer problems get resolved quickly." Ask your agents to identify the problems that customers experience, discuss how quickly they are corrected and identify reasons why they aren't corrected more quickly.

## Calculating Benefits

"If you understand the link between employee and customer satisfaction at your organization," Hepworth observes, "you can use that information to cost-justify investments in improving employee satisfaction."

He suggests identifying service problems that customers might experience, then determining what effect these problems may have on customers' behavior – and the impact this may have on revenue. (According to research Hepworth's company has conducted, the average company has 11 percent revenue at risk.)

Calculating how much business a particular service problem puts at risk

enables you to understand the potential damage that problem may cause. Say, for example, that customer research indicates that rude and rushed agents may be putting $2 million in revenue at risk each year. You confer with call center agents, and learn that their apparent rudeness stems from pressure to handle a high volume of calls, with no time to complete after-call work.

Your next step is to calculate the investment required for various options – such as hiring new agents – determine those with the best payback and then cost-justify the expense to senior management. CCMReview

Leslie Harps

*Leslie Hansen Harps is a freelance business writer specializing in customer service and call centers. Formerly president of the Customer Service Institute, she is author of several books, including* Motivating Customer Service Employees, *published by The Customer Service Group. Leslie can be reached at 202-363-5822.*

July 2000 ■ Reprinted with permission from *Call Center Management Review*®, www.icmi.com.

66

# Empower Agents with the Resources and Authority to Satisfy Customers

*by Susan Hash*

What call center manager wouldn't want to have a staff of agents who proactively take personal responsibility for the customer's experience? Wishes aside, today it's a necessary element for business success.

Empowering frontline agents by providing them with the knowledge, skills and decision-making authority to take care of callers quickly and efficiently will enable them to represent your company as world class, says JJ Lauderbaugh, president of Lauderbaugh & Associates Inc., a customer relations training and consulting firm in Los Gatos, Calif.

Empowered agents are more committed to the organization's success, she says. "They recognize that they're not just a part of customer service or support, but also involved in marketing and sales."

The nature of the multiple-channel call center environment demands an empowered workforce. The addition of a customer service Web site at HomeSide Lending Inc., a mortgage company headquartered in Jacksonville, Fla., demonstrated that necessity, according to HomeSide Lending's Director of Customer Service Tom Reilly.

Although many of the simpler e-mail responses to customers can be automated, there are also more complex messages that include several inquiries. "Our e-mail customer service agents have to be very skilled and empowered," Reilly says. "They have to have good discernment skills to ensure they're answering all of the customer's questions correctly in the first response."

## Initial Obstacles to Overcome

Creating an empowered environment in which agents are focused on customer retention and call center productivity is a journey – and not without a few roadblocks at the start.

A focus group study of South Florida business leaders by Northwood University revealed that nearly all of the participants said they encountered obstacles in launching empowerment processes. For instance, initially, both managers and staff resisted the effort. Many managers admitted they were reluctant to share decision-making activities with the front line, while others feared losing staff who develop new skills and capacities.

On the frontline side, the study found that staff who seldom had been given a voice in decision making often view the empowerment process with suspicion and distrust. The results further revealed that, at the beginning, organizations suffer a sharp drop in morale and productivity and an increase in turnover among managers and the front line.

## Agent Buy-in Is Critical

"Frontline people who have never been given a high degree of responsibility are often afraid of it," says Lauderbaugh. "Or sometimes there's the view that empowerment just means having to do more work."

Probably one of the biggest fears for newly empowered frontline agents is that they will be reprimanded (or worse) for making mistakes.

To get agents to accept decision-making power, Lauderbaugh says it's important to clearly communicate the specific advantages to the agents of learning new skills and taking on more responsibility.

The ability to advance in their careers is a particularly attractive benefit. At electric appliance manufacturer Braun Inc., the empowerment process offers consumer service reps a visible career growth opportunity. Reps can advance through three tiers to become product specialists, says Consumer Service Manager Ann-Marie O'Keefe. In fact, two of the department's current supervisors were promoted from within, which "is very encouraging for new reps," she says.

Of course, not all agents are the same when it comes to decision-making abilities. "You must know them well enough to understand who is trained and capable of taking responsibility," Lauderbaugh says. Often that has to do with whether or not an individual is goal-oriented. She suggests screening for goal-oriented agents during the recruiting process by asking each candidate what he or she has won in the past. "If someone can't come up with anything that he or she has ever won, they're probably not goal-oriented," she explains.

---

## Empowerment Barriers

A study of employee empowerment in small businesses, conducted by Sam Houston State University, found five common barriers to empowerment:

- A lack of managerial commitment to the concept.
- An unwillingness to change on the part of the employee and/or manager.
- A reluctance on the part of employees to take on responsibility of making decisions.
- Poor communication between employees and managers.
- The failure to realize that, in the short run, performance may dip as empowerment is implemented.

---

**Section 9**

February 2001 ■ Reprinted with permission from *Call Center Management Review®*, www.icmi.com.

67

"They haven't given up something to win something."

## Different Types of Empowerment

To build an empowered culture, agents need clear decision-making guidelines for dealing with customers. For instance, what's the dollar limit for returns? Can they give away free products? What options can they offer to customers?

Braun consumer service reps have specific policies and procedures for handling different types of product calls. "Our reps are empowered to make decisions, such as whether or not to extend a warranty, provide a repair or a replacement," says O'Keefe. "We don't want callers to have to go to a supervisor for that – it's within the reps' realm of responsibility."

Besides service support, Braun's empowerment process involves product knowledge. The company's 22 consumer service reps are encouraged to learn as much as they can about the various products. (Braun has eight product lines, which include hundreds of appliances and products.) Agents can borrow products to take home and get familiar with them, or they can buy them at a discount.

Through the career progression process, reps can train to become product specialists, then becoming responsible for training the rest of the department on their specific products and handling any out-of-the-ordinary calls involving that product.

At HomeSide Lending, agents at its Jacksonville call center also increase their level of responsibility as they advance within the center, says Jeanne Babbitt, Jacksonville call center manager. Senior and lead agents are empowered to make more risky decisions than the typical frontline agents. "They provide a support function to the supervisor as well as the phone reps," she says.

Another position in the center is a mentor, which is "a very empowered rep who can make supervisory-type decisions and support reps with more complex issues," she says.

## Training and Feedback Are Key

A study conducted by Sam Houston State University found training to be an inherent element of empowerment. A well-defined training process ensures "the development of employee skills, as well as the exchange of information about job requirements, organizational performance and customer satisfaction," the study reports.

"Our training and empowerment process starts the minute the rep walks in the door," says HomeSide Lending's Babbitt.

Call center supervisors sit in on new-hire training (which is conducted by corporate training staff) to ensure that it's on target for the call center. "They audit the training content (as well as the response from the class) to make sure it's going to meet our needs once those reps hit the floor in the call center," she explains. Managers meet with the training staff on a monthly basis to give them feedback on new-hires' progress. "We also provide our training staff with a list of primary call drivers to incorporate into the training to help reps meet customers' needs," she says.

The company's ongoing training process, about 35 hours a year, includes team training, event-driven training (i.e., government regulatory changes, year-end mortgage process changes, etc.) and updates on soft skills.

## Continuously Identify Empowerment Opportunities

HomeSide's empowerment process includes a 360-degree review of rep training. Customer service mentors, who support frontline reps, log any calls they receive from reps. The logs are checked regularly to find out how many calls mentors received,

from whom and why. Managers can then identify which reps may need additional training, says Tom Reilly. In addition, mentor calls are further dissected to determine any overall training gaps.

The reps themselves can identify empowerment opportunities in focus group sessions that meet on a regular basis or are pulled together for a specific function. "We have focus groups targeted to customer service functions that we handle, such as taxes or insurance. The reps have a very vocal voice in identifying what the empowerment issues are," says Reilly.

In another program, called "Voice of the Customer," reps are encouraged to electronically share caller comments – good or bad – that may be improvement opportunities or simply customer kudos.

## Encourage Agent Involvement

Getting agents engaged with other departments helps to foster a

February 2001 ■ Reprinted with permission from *Call Center Management Review*®, www.icmi.com.

68

Section 9

sense of commitment to the company. Braun's product specialists act as a liaison between consumer services and marketing. They attend marketing meetings, as well as regularly communicating via e-mail or phone, says O'Keefe.

Product specialists regularly review call data to pinpoint common product issues and offer suggestions to the marketing, quality or technical services departments.

Reps also are encouraged to offer their suggestions for improving processes, such as order turnaround, shipping issues, etc. "The reps are better able to recognize issues quickly because they're the front line," says O'Keefe. "We encourage them not to wait until it shows up on our reports but to constantly share their feedback. Over time, agents become very knowledgeable at all levels.

Knowledge is power, and it gives them the ability to handle any issue that comes their way."

## Managers Have Responsibilities, Too

Empowerment is not simply a matter of delegating tasks. For call center managers, the leadership responsibilities evolve.

"Managers need to be role models to the agents in the call center," says Lauderbaugh.

"They need to focus on growing, mentoring, coaching and counseling their people. As agents witness the empathy supervisors feel for them, as well as concern for their individual growth, they will have a tendency to treat the customers the same way. All call center managers should treat their agents the same as they want their agents to treat callers," she says.

"You have to listen to your employees and your customers," adds Jeanne Babbitt. "Sometimes managers are afraid to give up control but, in the long run, it increases employee satisfaction and customer satisfaction."

Reilly agrees. "That customer satisfaction translates into bottomline savings. One stop calls are definitely the way to go, and if you empower reps so that they can answer the call and provide a solution that does not result in more calls, then we are dollars and dollars ahead of where we need to be.

"With rep empowerment, you never quite get to the destination because you're always finding new opportunities because of the changing nature of the business that we're in. I encourage my staff not to be satisfied – there's always something more that you can do." CCMReview

February 2001 ■ Reprinted with permission from *Call Center Management Review*®, www.icmi.com.

69

Section 9

# Answers to Exercises

# Answers to Exercises

**Organizational Structure and Strategy:**

1. True

2. a, b, c

3. a, a, b, c, b

4. False

5. s, g, s, g, s, g, s, g, g

6. b, c

7. 1, 6, 5, 3, 4, 2

8. False


**Hiring and Retention**

1. a. Structured interviews diminish bias and increase consistency

   b. Telephone and/or text chat interviews are recommended in call centers since they simulate the job's performance requirements.

   c. Behavior-based questions explore how individuals behave in certain job-related situations by asking the applicant to describe events in his or her work history.

2. Screen applicants; Interview applicants; Expose applicants to the work environment; Evaluate candidates; Make the hiring decision; Extend the offer

3. i, i, i, a, i, i, a, a

4. (12 ÷ 87) x (12 ÷ 7) = (0.14) x (1.71) = 0.24 or 24%

5. Separation; Recruiting and hiring; Training and orientation; Indirect

6. Careful selection (or effective hiring processes)


**Training and Development**

1. d, c, b, a

2. Knowledge; individual

3. False, false

4. c, b

Section 10

5. False, true

6. It establishes what present practices are; It projects what the desired results should be; It provides the basis for cost justification

7. Those due to the individual; Those due to management; Those due to the organization.

8. n, a, n, a, a, a

9. Analysis; Design; Development; Implementation; Evaluation

10. b, a

11. Reaction; Learning evaluation; Application to job; Evaluating the impact and ROI

**Measuring and Improving Performance**

1. False, true, false, true, true, false, true, true

2. b

3. c

4. Goals/objectives; Requirements; Standards; Scoring system; Calibration; Coaching; Employees

5. b, b, a

6. Numerical scoring; Should not; Should not; Recorded

7. Electronic Communications Privacy Act; Federal Communications Commission

8. Summarize; Ask for input; Formulate plan; Express gratitude

9. Employee development; Financial

10. Motivational; Informational

11. m, m, h, h, h, h, m, m, m, h

12. 4, 1, 2, 5, 3

13.

|  | Will | Won't |
|---|---|---|
| Can | No problem | Collaboratively explore ways to motivate the employee |
| Can't | Train, give feedback and provide opportunities for practice | Determine if the employee is appropriate for the job and, if not, search for other jobs that may be a better fit |

14. Verbal warning; Written warning; Suspension; Termination

**Maximizing Human Resources**

1. Assessment phase; Direction phase; Development phase

2. a, a

3.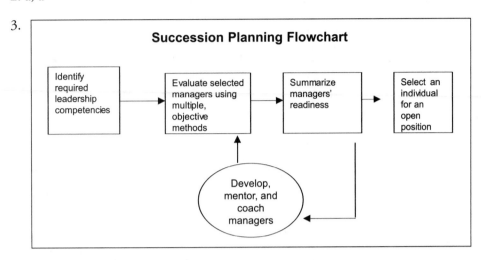

4. True, false

5. Base pay; Incentives; Benefits

6. b

7. a.  It is generally better to begin with those items that can be implemented quickly.

   b.  Qualitative questions do a better job of capturing the themes and ideas of employees.

8. False, true

9. Topical; Personal; Relational

10. b, e, d, a, c

11. a.  Assets, liabilities

    b.  Organization, individuals

12. b, d

13. Form, Storm, Norm, Perform

14. f, c, d, b, e, a

15. c, c, c, b, a

16. True, true, true

# CIAC Certification Overview

**People Management**

**The Call Center Industry Advisory Council (CIAC)** is the global standards and certifying board for the contact/support center profession. It was established in response to the need for an industry-governed, non-partisan body to provide an industry-sanctioned, standardized process for assessing the competence of people who work in contact and support centers. CIAC is a 501(c)(3) non-profit organization; it is not a professional association or membership organization, nor does it provide training.

The mission of CIAC is to elevate the performance of contact/support centers by advancing the theory, practice, and professional growth of the people who lead, manage and work in these centers through competency-based industry certification that instills commitment to:

- High Performance
- Integrity
- Professionalism
- Continuous Improvement

CIAC Objectives:

- Elevate the performance of contact/support center professionals and organizations worldwide
- Establish industry-sanctioned competency standards representative of high-performance for the job role requirements
- Certify contact/support center professionals based on demonstrated mastery of industry competency standards for the job role
- Define a career path for the contact/support center profession
- Provide a framework that enables training providers to effectively prepare contact/support center professionals to master the requirements of their job role
- Heighten awareness of the strategic and economic value of contact/support centers

**INTRODUCTION TO CIAC CERTIFICATION -** CIAC Certification is based on the premise that the key to a center's success is its people and their ability to perform at a high level of competence on the job. It establishes a vendor-neutral standard of performance excellence applicable to contact and support center professionals worldwide, in all types and sizes of centers across all industries. CIAC Certification is achieved through a professional development framework consisting of:

- Highly-focused learning based on industry best-practice competency standards. The standards are specific to the job requirements and drive results-based performance.

- Testing that validates competence and the ability to perform on the job in accordance with industry standards. The validity of CIAC Certification has been established through comprehensive psychometric analyses that assure testing is applicable worldwide, free of bias, and non-discriminatory.

- Re-certification to encourage a commitment to lifelong learning and continual improvement.

**Section 11**

The knowledge, skills, and abilities required for certification can be acquired through any means such as training, on-the-job experience, formal education, or a mixture of. Although CIAC does not provide training, a variety of educational and training programs are available to certification candidates through the CIAC Certification Training Consortium. The Consortium is an independent group of select, high-caliber training providers that provide quality learning programs to prepare candidates for successful CIAC Certification testing.

CIAC Certification empowers contact and support center professionals through an industry-recognized credential. The 'CIAC-Certified' distinction indicates: 1) mastery-level comprehension of the job requirements; 2) ability to apply expert knowledge and skills on the job; 3) industry leadership and role model; and 4) commitment to continuous improvement and professional development.

**Industry Certification for Center Managers and Executives** - Research of industry leading organizations worldwide indicates that leadership is the single most important factor to a center's success. **CIAC Management Certification** validates and formally recognizes the leadership and managerial competence of contact/support center managers and executives. CIAC Certification promotes the cultivation of a generation of role model managers and executives who create world-class centers and mentor others in their organization and the industry at large who desire a career in contact/support center management.

CIAC Certification is based on "job roles" because titles are often narrowly defined and differ across organizations. Testing that is 'role-based' more accurately captures the responsibilities of a position and allows certification in the designation that best defines the candidate's actual job tasks/activities and scope of authority and influence; it also allows for overlap of job responsibilities.

CIAC Management Certification Designations:

**CIAC-Certified Strategic Leader (CCSL)** – The CCSL designation is for senior executives who are responsible for the strategic management and leadership of a center. This role typically has bottom line responsibility for the center and is responsible for aligning center objectives with corporate business goals. Typical job titles are vice president, director, senior-manager, etc. In some organizations the title 'manager' has both operational and strategic responsibilities.

**CIAC-Certified Operations Manager (CCOM)** – The CCOM designation is for managers who are responsible for day-to-day operations of the center. This role has tactical responsibility for the center operation including administering the budget and managing staff. The typical title for this role is manager; however, in some organizations supervisors have responsibilities that include operational management.

**CIAC-Certified Management Apprentice (CCMA)** – The CCMA designation is for individuals who are pursuing a career in center management – i.e., entry-level.

**CIAC-Certified Management Consultant (CCMC)** – The CCMC designation is for professionals who provide contact/support center management consulting and/or training. The CIAC-Certified Management Consultant designation indicates specific expertise in the operational and strategic management of contact/support centers.

*Industry certification for agent/support specialist, team leader, and supervisor job roles will be available in the near future. Contact CIAC or a CIAC Partner for additional information.*

CIAC is committed to building a strong relationship between on-the-job performance and industry certification. Accordingly, CIAC Certification assesses contact/support center professionals against industry standards that link their knowledge, skills, and behaviors with the performance requirements of their job role.

Testing for the CIAC Management Certification designations is based on competency standards established by a globally representative body of senior contact and support center practitioners and validated through industry surveys, focus groups, secondary research, and panel review. The standards address the full scope of knowledge, skills, and abilities necessary for high-caliber management and leadership of a contact/support center.

The CIAC Management Certification Competency Standards cover four key functional areas (domains) of center leadership and management:

- People Management
- Operations Management
- Customer Relationship Management
- Leadership and Business Management

Within each competency domain, there are knowledge, skill, and behavioral components indicative of mastery-level comprehension. The standards are designed to cultivate an expert command of the job role responsibilities.

CIAC Management Certification testing is directly linked to competency standards for the job role. Thorough comprehension of the standards is required for successful testing. CIAC does not dictate the method by which comprehension of the required subject matter is acquired. For a copy of the 'Contact Center Management Standards', contact CIAC at info@ciac-cert.org.

CIAC Management Certification testing is Internet-based and administered online. All testing must be completed within two years from the date the first assessment is taken to achieve certification.

The first stage of testing consists of four knowledge assessments that are administered in a proctored environment. Knowledge testing is conducted on-site (employer site) and at select public testing centers. The Certified Strategic Leader and Certified Operations Manager designations are also assessed on the *application* of knowledge and skills with a Work Product Assignment; these designations also complete a 360° Review that assesses behavioral traits.

The CIAC Management Certification knowledge assessments each consist of 80-100 multiple-choice, scenario-based questions. The four knowledge assessments are typically taken one at a time (i.e., train then test per competency domain); however, candidates have the option to complete the assessments in any number and sequence desired. The test questions are thought provoking and require conceptual comprehension of the subject matter in addition to hands-on job experience; the questions also cover a wide range of reasoning to assure testing of both high-end and low-end comprehension.  The knowledge assessments are computer-scored and structured to have one correct answer.

The Work Product Assignment is issued to CIAC-Certified Strategic Leader and Operations Manager candidates upon successful completion of the knowledge assessments.  The Work Product Assignment assesses application of knowledge and skill on the job. Six-weeks or thirty-workdays are allowed to complete the Work Product Assignment.  Upon completion, the Work Product Assignment is reviewed and approved by the candidate's manager, then submitted to CIAC for evaluation and scoring.

The Work Product Assignment is an evaluation of the center's operating environment and procedures which results in a detailed action plan to improve operational performance of the center based on outcomes of the evaluation.  It is a valuable component of CIAC Management Certification because it helps organizations discover how to increase productivity and reduce operating expense without incurring additional costs.

The certification process for Strategic Leader and Operations Manager designations also includes completion of a 360° Review to assess leadership and managerial behavioral characteristics. The 360° Review is completed by the candidate, his/her manager, selected peers, and direct reports; three weeks or fifteen (15) workdays are allowed for its completion. The 360° Reviews are computer-scored, providing totals and mean values for each competency area. Candidates receive a detailed report of the 360° Review evaluation results for professional development purposes.  The 360° Review can be completed at any time during the CIAC Certification process.  CIAC often encourages that it be completed first because of the insightful information provided as an outcome and the usefulness of this information when a group or team of management professionals is completing the certification process together.

Testing and Scoring Requirements for CIAC Management Certification:

- **CIAC-Certified Strategic Leader** – CIAC Certification in this designation requires a minimum of one year job experience in a strategic management role in a contact/support center. A minimum score of 75 percent is required on each of four knowledge assessments. For the 360° Review a mean score of 3.0 (on a scale of 0 – 5) is required for each competency category and an overall score of 3.5. Candidates must pass all knowledge assessments to receive the Work Product Assignment.

- **CIAC-Certified Operations Manager** – CIAC Certification in this designation requires a minimum of one year job experience in a operational management role in a customer care and/or support center.  A minimum score of 75 percent is required on each of four knowledge assessments.  For the 360° Review a mean score of 3.0 (on a scale of 0 – 5) is required for each competency area and an overall score 3.5.  Candidates must pass all knowledge assessments to receive the Work Product Assignment.

- **CIAC-Certified Management Consultant** – CIAC Certification in this designation requires a minimum score of 75 percent on each of four knowledge assessments.  This designation does not complete a Work Product Assignment or 360° Review.

Section 11

- **CIAC-Certified Management Apprentice** – CIAC Certification in this designation requires a minimum score of 70 percent on each of four knowledge assessments. This designation does not complete a Work Product Assignment or 360° Review.

All management designations are required to re-certify every three years (from the initial date of credentialing) to maintain an active CIAC Industry Certification credential. Re-certification testing consists of (one) Master Knowledge Assessment. To avoid a lapse in certification, the re-certification process should be completed prior to expiration of the candidate's current CIAC Certification. Re-certification can be attained only in the current CIAC-Certified designation (e.g., CIAC-Certified Operations Manager re-certifies as same). CIAC strongly encourages that certified professionals actively participate in industry/profession-specific professional development activities such as attending conferences; speaking; authoring articles and white papers; membership in industry associations; etc.

A team of CIAC-Certified Management Professionals assures a world-class center that consistently and efficiently delivers superior service and high value customer satisfaction. Additional information on CIAC Management Certification can be found at, www.ciac-cert.org or by contacting CIAC or a CIAC Industry Partner.

**Section 11**

**CIAC Certification Process**
Management Track

Refer to the CIAC Certification Handbook for additional information on each step of the certification process. Go to www.ciac-cert.org to view and/or download the Handbook.

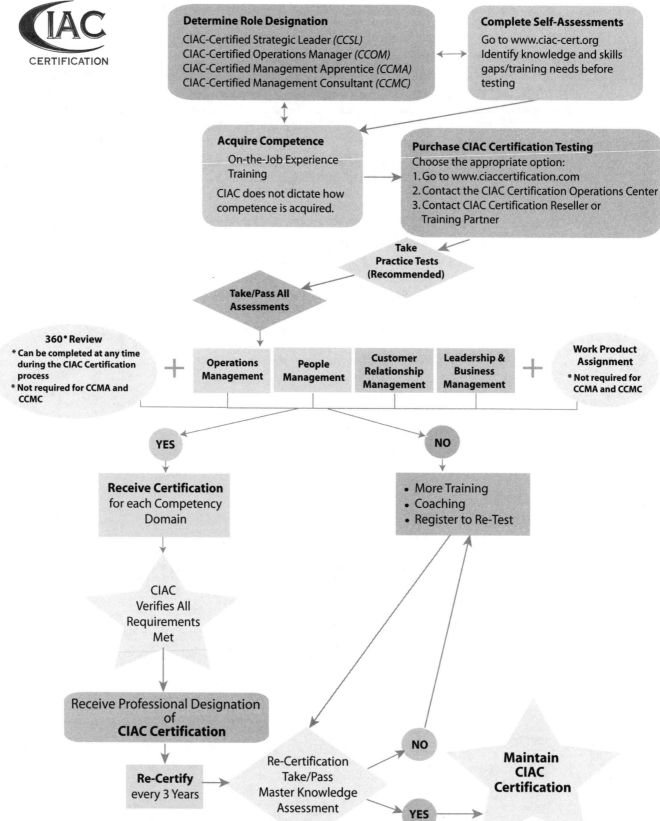

**Determine Role Designation**

CIAC-Certified Strategic Leader *(CCSL)*
CIAC-Certified Operations Manager *(CCOM)*
CIAC-Certified Management Apprentice *(CCMA)*
CIAC-Certified Management Consultant *(CCMC)*

**Complete Self-Assessments**

Go to www.ciac-cert.org
Identify knowledge and skills gaps/training needs before testing

**Acquire Competence**

On-the-Job Experience
Training

CIAC does not dictate how competence is acquired.

**Purchase CIAC Certification Testing**

Choose the appropriate option:
1. Go to www.ciaccertification.com
2. Contact the CIAC Certification Operations Center
3. Contact CIAC Certification Reseller or Training Partner

**Take Practice Tests (Recommended)**

**Take/Pass All Assessments**

**360° Review**
* Can be completed at any time during the CIAC Certification process
* Not required for CCMA and CCMC

**Operations Management** · **People Management** · **Customer Relationship Management** · **Leadership & Business Management**

**Work Product Assignment**
* Not required for CCMA and CCMC

**YES**

**NO**

**Receive Certification** for each Competency Domain

- More Training
- Coaching
- Register to Re-Test

CIAC Verifies All Requirements Met

Receive Professional Designation of **CIAC Certification**

**Re-Certify** every 3 Years

Re-Certification Take/Pass Master Knowledge Assessment

**NO**

**YES**

**Maintain CIAC Certification**

Section 11

# About ICMI

## About Incoming Calls Management Institute

ICMI Inc. is a global leader in call center consulting, training, publications and membership services. ICMI's mission is to help call centers (contact centers, help desks, customer care, support centers) achieve operational excellence and superior business results. Through the dedication and experience of its team, uncompromised objectivity and results-oriented vision, ICMI has earned a reputation as the industry's most trusted resource for:

• Consulting
• Seminars
• Publications
• Management Tools
• Conferences and Networking Events
• Professional Membership

Based in Annapolis, MD, ICMI was established in 1985 and was first to develop and deliver management training customized for call centers. Through constant innovation and research, ICMI's training has become the industry's gold standard, and is recommended by 99.3% of those managers who have experienced its value first-hand. Over the years, ICMI has become the industry's leading provider of membership services with an impressive line-up of call center management resources, including instant access to prominent research, expert advice and career development tools, and a networking forum that spans more than 40 countries worldwide. ICMI is not associated with, owned or subsidized by any industry supplier—its only source of funding is from those who use its services. For more information about ICMI, visit www.icmi.com, or call 800-672-6177 (410-267-0700).

Incoming Calls Management Institute
Post Office Box 6177
Annapolis, Maryland 21401
410-267-0700 • 800-672-6177
icmi@icmi.com
www.icmi.com

**Section 12**

## Bring This Content to Life in Your Own Organization!

Want to instill the most important principles from this series into the culture and operational dynamics of your organization? What would it be worth to have your entire management team truly working in sync to create services that generate loyalty and create exceptional value?

ICMI's powerful educational seminars provide you with real-world solutions to help you improve performance and achieve better business results. Benefits of bringing one of ICMI's seminars into your organization include:

• Content is based on the experiences and practices of the world's leading call centers.

• Programs are delivered by the industry's top facilitators.

• Content is tailored to your specific environment.

• Courses build a common understanding throughout your organization.

• ICMI's first-hand knowledge of the call center environment eliminates misconceptions and fads from the seminar content.

• You are guaranteed an objective, educational experience, since ICMI is independent and is not associated with, owned or subsidized by any industry supplier.

• Learning occurs in a stimulating atmosphere that is both productive and fun!

Visit www.icmi.com for a current listing of Web-based, public and in-house seminars. Or contact ICMI at 410-267-0700, or icmi@icmi.com

## ICMI's Mission

Incoming Calls Management Institute (ICMI) exists solely to advance the call center profession by promoting managerial excellence. We are dedicated to fostering the development of a new breed of call center management professionals – individuals with the vision, expertise, and commitment necessary to enable their respective organizations to thrive in an era of fast-changing, networked economies, global competition and heightened customer expectations.

**Section 12**

## Order Form

| QTY. | Item | Member Price | Price | Total |
|------|------|:---:|:---:|:---:|
| | Driving Peak Sales Performance in Call Centers** | **$33.96** | $39.95 | |
| | Call Center Management On Fast Forward: Succeeding In Today's Dynamic Inbound Environment** | **$23.76** | $34.95 | |
| | Call Center Technology Demystified: The No-Nonsense Guide to Bridging Customer Contact Technology, Operations and Strategy** | **$33.96** | $39.95 | |
| | ICMI's Call Center Management Dictionary: The Essential Reference for Contact Center, Help Desk and Customer Care Professionals** | **$21.21** | $24.95 | |
| | ICMI's Pocket Guide to Call Center Management Terms* | **$5.12** | $5.95 | |
| | **ICMI Handbook and Study Guide Series**<br>Module 1: People Management***<br>Module 2: Operations Management***<br>Module 3: Customer Relationship Management***<br>Module 4: Leadership and Business Management*** | **$169.15 ea.** | $199.00 ea. | |
| | **Topical Books:**<br>**The Best of** *Call Center Management Review*<br>Call Center Recruiting and New Hire Training*<br>Call Center Forecasting and Scheduling*<br>Call Center Agent Motivation and Compensation*<br>Call Center Agent Retention and Turnover* | **$14.41 ea.** | $16.95 ea. | |
| | **Forms Books**<br>Call Center Sample Monitoring Forms**<br>Call Center Sample Customer Satisfaction Forms Book** | **$42.46 ea.** | $49.95 ea. | |
| | **Software**<br>QueueView: A Staffing Calculator—CD ROM*<br>Easy Start™ Call Center Scheduler Software—CD-ROM* | **$41.65**<br>**$254.15** | $49.95<br>$299.00 | |
| | Call Center Humor:<br>The Best of *Call Center Management Review* Volume 3* | **$8.45** | $9.95 | |
| | The Call Centertainment Book* | **$7.61** | $8.95 | |
| | Shipping & Handling @ $5.00 per US shipment, plus .50¢ per* item, $1.00 per** item and $2.00 per*** item. Additional charges apply to shipments outside the US. | | | |
| | Tax (5% MD residents, 7% GST Canadian residents) | | | |
| | TOTAL (US dollars) | | | |

Please contact us for quantity discounts

For more information on our products, please visit **www.icmi.com**

## Order Form

❏ Please send me a free issue of *Call Center Management Review* (ICMI's journal for members) and information on ICMI's publications, services and membership.

Please ship my order and/or information to:

Name _____

Title _____

Industry _____

Company _____

Address _____

City _____ State _____ Postal Code _____

Telephone (     ) _____

Fax (     ) _____

Email _____

Method of Payment (if applicable)

❏ Check enclosed (Make payable to ICMI Inc.; U.S. Dollars only)

❏ Charge to:   ❏ American Express   ❏ MasterCard   ❏ Visa

Account No. _____

Expiration Date _____

Name on Card _____

Fax order to:   410-267-0962
call us at:   800-672-6177
            410-267-0700
order online at:   www.icmi.com
or mail order to:   ICMI Inc.
                  P.O. Box 6177, Annapolis, MD 21401

**Section 12**

## About the Authors

**Brad Cleveland** is President and CEO of Annapolis, Maryland based Incoming Calls Management Institute. Recognized for his pioneering work in call center management, he has advised organizations ranging from small start-ups to national governments and multinational corporations, and has delivered keynotes and seminars in over 25 countries. Brad has appeared in a wide range of media, including *The Washington Post, Wall Street Journal,* and on PBS, CNBC and Knowledge TV. His critically-acclaimed book, *Call Center Management on Fast Forward: Succeeding in Today's Dynamic Inbound Environment,* co-authored with journalist Julia Mayben, is used by call center managers around the world.

**Debbie Harne** is Director of Educational Services for ICMI, and spearheaded the launch of ICMI Membership, a network of management professionals from over 40 countries. With a background in training and education, Debbie has been instrumental in developing ICMI's technology-based educational services, and has responsibilities for the quality and direction of ICMI's instructor-led and Web-based management seminars. She is proficient in instructional design and ensuring the transfer of training to the job, and has customized ICMI educational services for innovative, in-house study programs in a variety of companies.

### How to Contact the Authors

Do you have suggestions for future editions? Comments? Feedback? Please contact us!

Incoming Calls Management Institute
Post Office Box 6177
Annapolis, Maryland 21401
410-267-0700 • 800-672-6177
icmi@icmi.com
www.icmi.com
Brad Cleveland, direct: bradc@icmi.com
Debbie Harne, direct: debbieh@icmi.com

Section 12